MW00932594

A.G.I.L.E. L.E.A.D.E.R.S.H.I.P. with a G.R.I.P.

A TWENTY-FIRST CENTURY JOURNEY:
From Street hustler to Strategic hustler™

Dr. Frank Lee Harper Jr., PMP®
James Smith Jr., Chief Editor

ISBN-10: 1479207187
ISBN-13: 9781479207183

Library of Congress Control Number: 2012916156
CreateSpace Independent Publishing Platform
North Charleston, South Carolina

A.G.I.L.E. L.E.A.D.E.R.S.H.I.P. with a G.R.I.P.

There are hundreds of books about "leadership" often written by CEOs. Many debate the "nature versus nurture" aspects of relative contributions of genetic inheritance and environmental factors to a leader's development. If any of these books had the undisputable answer then organizations would likely be much better performers. What is enjoyable about Dr. Harper's book is he explores the issues with personal examples and logic that makes sense to a reader. His book has inspiration that is not common in books on leadership, and one can apply it to one's personal life as well as professional career.

—Gary Cokins, MBA Founder and CEO,
Analytics –Based Performance Management, LLC
Noted Author, and International Performance Management Thought Leader

Students of leadership used to reading about traditional styles of leadership will find enlightenment in Dr. Harper's book. This book is not in the traditional form of leadership books like James McGregor Burns, Michael Fullan or Barbara Kellerman who seldom venture into practical realities of everyday leadership. Harper's critical lens was framed on personal experiences combined with concrete business savvy and real life experiences which allows the author to present a unique perspective.

—Dr. Clayton Alford, M.Ed., Ed.D.
Visiting Assistant Professor of Education and Mentor at Warnborough College, UK
Supervisor and Online Professor of Special Education, Walden University

The book uses the letters in **"A.G.I.L.E. L.E.A.D.E.R.S.H.I.P. with a G.R.I.P."** to provide logical knowledge as an attraction for a professional wanting to learn self-improvement and sharpen leadership skills to achieve excellence in performance. The logical order inspires a professional to become glued to the book in an encounter and search for details to evaluate their shortcomings in leading and managing with the end goal of uncovering their mistakes and learning why expected results weren't achieved. This is the exact affect the book had on me!

—Muhammad (M.) Aslam Mirza, CEngr, MBA, PMP®, LMG
- President/Principal Consultant,
Integrated Management Services, Pakistan
Past-President Project Management Institute (PMI)-Karachi Pakistan Chapter
Graduate PMI-Leadership Institute Masters Class

The excerpts from the book are Excellent. Dr. Harper's use of acronyms pulls the busy reader in and keeps them interested to see how he will unveil the words and meanings behind the acronyms. Great strategy! He also TELLS HIS STORY! For example, "From hell to Yale," is a wonderful way of allowing the reader to not only embrace his principles of leadership - but to also connect with Dr. Harper on a personal level.

—Rev. Dr. DE Paulk, BS, DDiv (Honorary)
- Co-Founder and Senior Pastor, Spirit and Truth Sanctuary
Board Member, Southern Christian Leadership Council
Author, The Holy Bible of Inclusion

Even though my business is small, I definitely can use, and will use your techniques. What a BLESSING!

—T. Kiana Austin
Owner/Screenwriter, Voices of the People, LLC

It is a great work; key points of Agile Leadership very well-articulated; with persuasive content, format, and presentation. I can see myself applying Dr. Harper's G.R.I.P. method immediately. The book will be of immense use to any one serious about leading and managing in modern times.

—Dr. Mohan K. Bavirisetty, MS, MBA, Ph.D.
Chief Innovation Officer, Modern Renaissance
Founder and Executive Chair at Innovation and Entrepreneurship Society

Dr. Harper's very unique approach and style to highlighting behaviors for leading and managing will inspire both young and experienced leaders. I found it valuable personally and professionally.

—Dr. Shyam Sundaram, MS, Ph.D.
Senior Technology Leader, NTT Data
Mumbai, India

I liken your book to somewhat of a leadership bible for anyone that really wants to embrace leadership and get ahead of the success game! Personal Mastery and Energizing People is what I'm bathing in right now. Awesome work Dr. Frank!!

—Dave Wess, Sr., BS, M.Ed.
- Pastor and Senior Technology Executive
Author, Don't Stay Stuck, Unlock the Success Within!

Dr Harper's book is not prescriptive. The challenges that face leaders vary by group, organization, culture and situation (sometimes even by the hour). It is also not a gimmicky read (memorize AGILE and you'll have it figured out). Each reader will come away with a different contextualization. Notwithstanding, at the most basic level, each reader will likely experience a shift in awareness.

—Cecilia Wandiga, LSSBB, ISO 9000 QSA, MS, DBA *(candidate)*
CEO & Founder, Global Ectropy

This book shares the life experiences of ordinary people who have hustled their way to accomplish extraordinary things. I liked that the book challenges the reader to aspire to greatness but in the same breathe offers a roadmap to getting there. Thanks Dr. Frank Harper Jr. for sharing your knowledge with readers to become great leaders.

—Shetonjela Barber, MBA
Caretaker to Cancer Survivor
Supervisor, Government Affairs, Equifax

My dreams have become reality, but what qualities allowed me to transition from Street hustler to Strategic hustler ™*?*

*We are what we repeatedly do. Excellence, therefore, is not an act, but a habit (process). – **Aristotle***

*Forgetting those things which are behind, and reaching forth unto those things which are before, I press toward the mark for the prize of the high calling of God in Christ Jesus.–**Philippians 3:13-14***

Your beliefs become your values. Your values become your thoughts. Your thoughts become your words. Your words become your actions. Your actions become your habits. Your habits become your destiny.
—Mahatma Mohandras Gandhi

Leader of one; leader of many
If you can't lead one; you can't lead any.
*–**Unknown***

Keep on reading and learning.

Table of Contents

A Letter from the Author

As an advocate of leadership and life skills coaching, I have always been impressed by one's ability to be innovative and an entrepreneur. The phrase *"innopreneurship"* best describes these two inseparable qualities igniting my journey to becoming a *Strategic hustler*™. At the age of thirteen, out of necessity, I learned to be a *Street hustler*. Thanks to college, and college internships, I began to learn the value of being a *Strategic hustler*™. A key lesson learned from both roles was to *brand* myself as "a business." Tenaciously working as a *Street hustler* or *Strategic hustler*™, (*"hustler"* being a term that is *controversial* but *revealing* as you will learn), required having an *"innopreneur state of mind"* learning specific leadership and management behaviors that allowed me to turn my dreams into realities. My journey, growing into a scholar practitioner, was fueled by a quest to uncover behaviors of the innopreneur state of mind mentality essential for innovation and serial entrepreneurship in the twenty-first century. For years, I have speculated and researched key behaviors necessary to become a twenty-first century *Strategic hustler*™. Confidently, I have reached a point where lifelong lessons provide me the experiences to remove any speculations. This book is written to educate, inspire, and provide valuable information to springboard your dreams into your reality. Allow me to digress.

At the height of the dot-com era, traditional notions of leadership, many of which favored a strictly hierarchical command structure, came under attack from writers who prophesied the emergence of a business culture defined by lateral, fluid, and loosely affinitive relationships. The problem with this management ethos is that it was not based on carefully researched principles or a deep appreciation of the fundamentals of human behavior. Instead, the pundits of the day seemed to take the prevailing view of corporate identity—which privileged mobile, volatile, reactive organizations like Enron—and transpose it onto the workplace, creating a philosophy of leadership that was merely a mirror image of their theory of market dynamics. Hence, the enormous interest in leadership books that sprung up as the economy faltered, sending once-promising business ideologies into oblivion. Of all the books that have attempted to address the post–new-economy question of corporate culture, those that offer insights both grounded in science and reinforced by research are the most helpful.

Because the problems of management are universal, many authors, academics, and practitioners have filled many pages with advice on how to lead, organize, control, develop, and otherwise manage people. Some of what has been written is even useful, but it is rare to find material that is not too academic and sterile at one extreme, or too restricted to one person's experience at the other.

There are many challenges of leading any initiative—i.e., organization, movement, cause, etc. Their common denominator is the fundamentals of effective leadership that include behavioral science concepts and theories and simple-to-use behavioral science techniques.

Some concepts in the behavioral sciences give good ideas to think about, but they do not always provide a how or when to apply those ideas in situations requiring leadership or management or both. The result is people do not achieve their reality. This book is an account of my personal journey from being an at-risk youth [statistic] living in heavily-crime ridden areas shining shoes, or *Street hustler*, to becoming a global scholar-practitioner, or *Strategic hustler*™, using the letters in the book's title [**A.G.I.L.E. L.E.A.D.E.R.S.H.I.P. with a G.R.I.P.**] along with other acronyms to articulate the world-class leadership behaviors and management practices learned along the way. ***Said another way,*** it is my roadmap from a TROUBLED-BODY to a SOMEBODY who is reaching out to help ANYBODY. I am especially excited to share enlightening stories of roles models, colleagues and friends from all walks of life whom share how they turned their dreams into their reality.

Whether you are a student, parent, entrepreneur, businessperson, educator, athlete, manager, or executive, this book provides gold nuggets to leading and managing in the twenty-first century. It teaches how effective leaders minimize the knowing (leading) and doing (managing) gap in turning dreams into reality.

There is no specific order in which to read this book. You determine the order just as *you* determine *your* reality. Each letter of the book's title represents a chapter in this book. You will find your journey through *every* chapter filled with actionable information to help springboard your dreams into your reality.

Putting on my coaching hat, to get the most out of this book:

1) Read the material.
2) Meditate on the material.
3) Keep it in your heart and mind by "Putting it in your tool box."
4) Live it when you have the opportunity. This is first of many lessons you will learn.

Now it is time to "Get Your Hustle On" and do what successful people do—*read* and *lead*!

I hope you enjoy reading and learning from this book as much as I did writing it.

Enjoy the journey!

Dr. Frank L. Harper, Jr., PMP®

Acknowledgments

First, I thank God, from whom all blessings flow. There are many acknowledgments due when a book represents forty years of life lessons from the street room to the schoolroom to the boardroom. I would like to start, however, with a special thanks to the person who helped me find my voice and worked so hard to bring my ideas alive on the written page, James (JS) Smith, Jr. JS debated me into clarity on a number of issues and then wrote what I meant instead of what I said. His partnership has been invaluable to me. Thanks, JS! Special thanks to Mr. James Smith Sr. for unknowingly inspiring me and giving the world such a valuable resource in JS—rest in peace "Mr. Boss Man!"

Because this book represents a lifetime of work, it is impossible to name and adequately express my appreciation to all the individuals who have shaped my ideas, my values and who have energized me over the years. Therefore, I want simply to express my gratitude to the thousands of young people and professionals whose thoughtful questions and eagerness to learn have kept me excited about learning and teaching. My professional thanks to my peers and corporate executives with whom I have had the joy of sharing the journeys of mutual enlightenment in such companies as Keane, BBVA Compass Bank, Sikorsky Aircraft, Wachovia, JP Morgan Chase, Citibank, Comerica, Fifth-Third Bank, Merial Pharmaceutical, ChoicePoint, Freightliner, Walmart, Warner Brothers, Centers for Disease Control and Prevention, Sterling Software, McDonald's, the Coca-Cola Company, General Electric, Procter and Gamble, United Technologies, City of Atlanta, State of Georgia, Internal Revenue Service, Central Bank of Nigeria, South African Reserve Bank, Banque SCS Alliance and Federal Reserve Bank of Atlanta, to name a few. These experiences contributed to fulfilling my entrepreneurial dreams.

My academic debts are large. I am forever grateful to: my mentor Tesfaye Ketsela, Ph.D., dean of the School of Administration and Management, Columbia Commonwealth University (CCU), who opened my heart and mind to transformational leadership in mind, body, spirit, and community; Dr. Michael McCrimmon for overseeing my defense of my doctorate; Dr. Russell Archibald, PMI Fellow, and Dr. J.P. Debourse for acknowledging my work on the ""Project Managers as Senior Executives" research project sponsored by The Project Management Institute (PMI) and the Fonds Régional de Garantie Nord-Pas-de Calais (France).

To the leadership research teams of CIO magazine and PMI for supporting my doctorial research, thank you. Special thanks to my many colleagues from Africa, Antarctica, Asia, Australia, Europe, North America, and South America who, in their own unique way, unknowingly contributed to my leadership development.

A village raised this anointed child of God that consisted of a cadre of people who provided inspiration for me to aspire for excellence. Clyde Powers, a Vietnam War hero and cousin, stirred my creative juices. The late former Grammy Award nominee the Reverend Dr. Donald Vails, another cousin, told me and then showed me that *"greatness comes from within."* Ralph Avard and Julius "J-Rock" Stone introduced me to organized sports, which saved and changed my life. Van Spruill, my Park-Rec football coach/mentor, taught me the importance of leadership and teamwork. Mr. George Clarke, Mr. and Mrs. Boomer, and Lloyd Parchmen planted the seeds to having an innopreneur state of mind. The Reverend Dr. Curtis M. Cofield, who was the first educated black man I knew with a doctorate degree, was my spiritual father, who, like my dad, encouraged me to always put God first.

I am forever grateful for my high school coaches, administrators, and alumni who, at a critical moment in my life, refused to let, "one of the most decorated scholar-athletes in New Haven high school history fall by the wayside." Edward Joyner, a then high school teacher always stressed the importance of a college education. Mr. Joyner is now Dr. Joyner, a world-renowned college professor. Dr. Edward George, my electrical engineering professor at University of New Haven, drew a sketch of a football player kicking a successful field goal when I got an "A" on an electrical engineering test after receiving a "D" on the previous one. Special thanks to my college coaches Tom Bell (football) and William Farrow (basketball) who saw beyond my athletic ability and provided the additional inspiration I needed to become the person I am who continually strives to make a difference.

And to all my surrogate parents: John & Helen Jones, Louise Gaither, Edna Fletcher, and Charles Neal Sr. who took time out of their busy schedules to love me as if I were their own. To all of you – this book is written in your memory.

To Loretta Camp, my "Nana", who at 100 years young continued to show me the strength to love and forgive—I love you grandma rest in peace.

And to David White, who kept me from being a victim of my own success. Thanks "Soul Daddy Number One!"

Thank you James Jahim Jones (3J); for giving me my first lesson in energizing people with ever-greater challenges. I'll never forget how you "tricked" me into teaching after I vehemently said I never wanted to teach.

Osie and Carsandra Carraway thank you for helping me to overcome my family circumstances. You helped turn my dreams into reality. Osie I finally got it right, ***"It's the same soup but a different bowl!"*** I am ready to share it with the world.

I am a first-generation high school and college graduate. This accomplishment comes with many responsibilities. Because of the aforementioned people, I was prepared to handle these enormous responsibilities. Most importantly, I thank my family and especially my daddy, Frank L. Harper, Sr., for unknowingly reinforcing the idea that **L.E.A.D.E.R.S.H.I.P.** must be **A.G.I.L.E.** and applied with a **G.R.I.P.** to be effective and successful.

Special thanks to my other spiritual leaders (Archbishop Earl Paulk, Pastor/Teacher Stanley G. Wise, and Pastor/Teacher DE Paulk) for their guidance and teachings which have allowed me to continue my covenant with my Lord and Savior Jesus Christ—the only way I could finish this book and continue to do God's will.

I conclude as started, by giving God all the glory, honor, and praise for blessing me with the knowledge, wisdom, and understanding to continue to work for the ultimate proclamation— "Well done my good and faithful servant!"

About the Author

Dr. Frank L. Harper, Jr., PMP®, *Strategic hustler*™, associate professor, senior process and technology leader for Intelligent Systems Services LLC and innopreneur. His technology savvy, leadership, teaching, mentoring, solutions-focused thinking and execution has contributed to strategic programs/projects with combined budgets of over $4 Billion supporting business units to identify, develop, and implement business solutions that maximize throughput, operational efficiency, customer service, and competitiveness. The effectiveness of these efforts generated combined revenues and savings of over $10 Billion for global companies and governments.

A thirty-plus-year career has seen a professional progression with fifteen in international operations spanning five continents. Dr. Harper has performed in strategic, tactical, and operational roles. He has been featured in various media for his trailblazing successes delivering value through innovative solutions. Project Management Institute (PMI®), the global leader in project management, applauded his leadership in assuring the quality of PMI's Organizational Project Management Maturity Model® (OPM3®)-a globally-recognized standard that helps organizations translate strategy into successful outcomes consistently and predictably. He was also acknowledged for his research during the seminal project, *Project Managers as Senior Executives*, sponsored by PMI® and Ecole Supérieure de Commerce de Lille (ESC Lille School of Management), the largest PMI®-accredited business school in France.

As a recognized community leader, Dr. Harper developed outstanding community-based proactive educational programs. His thoughts on education have been recognized by local, city and state government leaders, in addition to President Bill Clinton. He has served as a State Advisor to the United States Congressional Advisory Board, a board member to the Georgia School Age Care Association and Vice Chairperson to the School Council of Towers High School located in Decatur, Georgia. Additionally, he has delivered inspirational speeches to global audiences and "Career Day" programs at various elementary and high schools in Georgia.

A product of public housing, Dr. Harper, an adjunct associate professor of business administration at Cambridge Corporate University in Switzerland, is a lifetime member of Omega Psi Phi Fraternity, Inc. was a two-sport letterman in high school and college—along with brief stints professionally. He served as a mentor/coach and Sunday school teacher to students' ages ranging from 4 to 70. He earned a PhD, with distinction, from Columbia Commonwealth University in administration and management, an MBA in marketing, MSc in industrial engineering, and BS (cum laude) in computer technology all from the University of New Haven. A Kepnor-Tregoe, Rummler-Brache, and Prosci practitioner, Dr. Harper holds many professional certifications, the most current being: Project Management Professional (PMP®), IT Service Management (ITIL), Certified Six Sigma Green Belt (CSSGB), Certified Process Improvement Facilitator (PIF) and Certified in Governance of Enterprise Information and related Technology (CGEIT). A member of the International Biographe Centre of Cambridge England "World Who's Who Hall of Fame", his biography appears in numerous *Who's Who* publications (high school, college, professional, and executive).

Dr. Harper a proud grandfather, uncle-daddy, legal guardian and godfather; is devoted to the "Christ-like" mindset and enjoys spiritual truth seeking. A mentor, teacher and coach to thousands his favorite motto is "Every Child Deserves a Chance!"

CHAPTER 1

Leaders Are Born to Be Made

Introduction

It is Sunday evening. I am sitting in my study doing one of the things I do best, thinking. Earlier, I attended the Sunday morning service at the Cathedral of the Holy Spirit and was blessed by Pastor D. E. Paulk's sermon, entitled "Living Stones." I make it a point that whomever I am blessed to hear speak, regardless of the topic, I grab at least one point to remember. James Smith, a former Wall Street bank executive, taught me this early in my professional career. He also gave me my first job on Wall Street.

Pastor D. E., like his uncle, the late Archbishop Earl Paulk, provides "Points of Power." The point(s) worth mentioning include: (1) God has and always will sustain us! (2) Money has never been our motivation, our source, or our God. (3) Be not weary in well doing! and (4) The Book has already been written! My meditation on these points allows me to personalize them. Restating them: (1) God has and always will sustain *me*! (2) Money has never been *my* motivation, *my* source, or *my* God. (3) Be not weary in well doing! Which translates to, God's promises to *me* can only be seen if I refuse to *give up*! and (4) *My* storied life has already been written; it is now up to me to share it to encourage others.

This becomes more pronounced as I look around my study at the many mementos of a storied career helping people, young and mature, develop leadership skills through community, athletic, and professional endeavors. It proves that *"Leaders are born to me made!"*

Growing up in New Haven, Connecticut, I lived in a public housing facility called Ethan Gardens. Ethan Gardens was on a block categorized as part of a red zone because it was one of the most crime-ridden areas in New Haven. The block consisted of Orchard Street, where I lived, Chapel Street, Kensington Street, and Edgewood Avenue. I witnessed a police raid on the New Haven

1

headquarters of the Black Panther Party, in addition to prostitution/drug rings, organized crime and neighborhood gangs. There were murders, drug usage, and gay/lesbian activity as a normal course of living in the area. Friends, associates, and siblings were shot, stabbed, raped, or beaten, suffered from drug and alcohol abuse, and unfortunately a few died of drug overdoses and AIDS. I had my moments: run-ins with the police, overcoming bullies, playing with my dad's loaded guns (thank God he had the trigger locked!), using force to chastise unwanted solicitors into the neighborhood, dealing with a mother battling depression and an alcoholic suicidal baby sister, protecting myself from a child molester, fighting with an older jealous and abusive stepbrother, neighbors, or people who tried to get me to do things that were not in my best interest. As designated protector of my younger brothers and sister, there came a time that I had to stand face to face with the barrel of a shotgun. These experiences contributed to what I will refer to throughout this book as *"street smarts."* At the same time, a ten-minute walk from my neighborhood would bring me to the campus of one of the most prestigious universities in the world, Yale University. As I reflect on where I came from and what God has allowed me to accomplish, I am embellished with the words of Pastor D. E.'s past teaching, *"What God produces, God parents and purifies, because I am predestined."*

Coming from hell to Get to Yale

I was blessed with a father, who stood six foot three, weighed 305 pounds, and was a strict disciplinarian. The latter made him a "daddy"! He was the youngest of fifteen children raised in Royston, Georgia, who moved north because he wasn't going to work in cotton fields. Since I was his firstborn, man did I get some lessons on being different. Prior to living in Ethan Gardens, I lived in another public housing facility that was in a demilitarized zone (DMZ). This was "my hood." Or, to be more succinct, it was "my hell." I had to grow up fast recalling my first lesson in street smarts having to intervene at the age of eight to prevent my dad from committing murder. My dad had a drinking problem that could sometimes get the best of him. But it didn't, and he used that experience to teach me why having God in my life was so important. He pushed me to be a better person, control my temper, and to "never be afraid to be *great!*" In the fifth grade, as a straight-A student, I was nominated and selected to participate in the Ulysses S. Grant Foundation Summer Program sponsored by and held at Yale University. Thanks to this program, my aim was to become a college graduate. Let me give you a little background on this program.

The Ulysses S. Grant Foundation (U. S. Grant) was an academic summer program for talented and motivated middle school students from New Haven, Connecticut. Since 1953, U. S. Grant has drawn on the experience and enthusiasm of Yale undergraduates to challenge students so they can acquire the academic preparation and skills needed to enter and succeed in college and excel in their current school environment. The program is designed for bright students who might have limited opportunities and resources to participate in academic enrichment activities.

U. S. Grant offered a six-week summer program on the Yale University campus. Each morning, in small, single-grade classes of eight to fifteen students, Yale undergraduates taught classes of their own design to challenge and excite their students. In humanities classes, students studied history and wrote speeches, read and discussed poetry, and did creative writing of their own. In investigations classes, students developed their problem-solving skills through fun, hands-on projects in the natural and social sciences. In the afternoon, students participated in electives and clubs that offered them the opportunity to learn in a more relaxed environment with students from other grades. Typical afternoon activities included sports and games, creative classes in music and the performing arts, debates and mock trials, and a book club. In addition, students enjoyed a variety of local and regional field trips.

U. S. Grant also offered a six-week winter program on the Yale University campus. The academics were similar to the classes offered during the summer, but there were meetings twice a week in the evenings and no field trips were offered.

The kids who attended U. S. Grant were of various races, genders, and socioeconomic backgrounds. My classroom performance during the summer session earned me an invitation to attend the winter session. In fact, I attended the summer and winter sessions at Yale University from the sixth grade to the eleventh grade. I chose not to attend my senior year to work at a local supermarket located on Dixwell Avenue. During my six years in the program, I received a heavy dosage of math, science, English, and other liberal arts/humanities topics. In addition to the academic rigor, I was exposed to the facilities of Yale University. We ate in the Yale Commons Dining Hall. The field trips we attended were awesome. I recall a weekend excursion in the Green Mountains of Vermont! Can you imagine a kid from the ghetto in the mountains? Wow, I was learning to be different.

U. S. Grant students had access to Yale's famed Payne-Whitney Gym. I met such Yale football greats as Calvin Hill, Don Martin, and Dick Jauron, all of whom went on to play in the National Football League (NFL). Don would eventually become my workout partner during the summer when I was preparing to attend college. I learned to compete in many sports winning many awards in the process. In fact, I did not like to lose. As a Yale University college preparatory student, my innate leadership treasures were being mined.

At the age of thirteen, we moved to Ethan Gardens. This was a fresh new start in a clean neighborhood where I made new, lifelong friends. I started playing organized sports. Whether it was a team sponsored by Dwight Community

Center, YMCA, or park recreation organizations like St. Luke's basketball, Walter "Pop" Smith Little League Baseball (WPSLLB) and Albie Booth Midget Football League (ABMFL), my experience with U. S. Grant sparked my interest to try them all. Ralph Avard, who is white, was my first coach. He taught me how to play baseball, especially the art of pitching. Ralph bought me a glove and pulled some strings allowing me to play for his team, the Elm Adults of WPSLLB. I was good enough to make the all-star team. My biggest moment came when I pitched a seventeen-strikeout one-hitter against the perennial league champions, the Knickerbockers. My history with Ralph laid the groundwork for my laser like focus—a key trait to being a leader. He graduated from Valparaiso College in Indiana and I never saw him again, but he planted a "*leadership*" seed.

At the same time I met Ralph, God brought Julius "J-Rock" Stone (nicknamed for his Elvis Presley impersonations) into my life. He was two years older, and knowing his family (Mr. John, Ma Helen, Valarie, and David) proved invaluable as each had a key role in developing me and keeping me out of trouble. Father God was ensuring the *leadership* seed planted by Ralph was continually watered by "J-Rock" and this loving family. I admired J-Rock because he filled the void of not having a big brother who wanted the best for me. To digress, he introduced me to ABMFL; helped me to rise above my family issues; encouraged me throughout little league, high school, and college; and the reason I never became a smoker is because when I took a puff of a cigarette around him, he slapped me upside my head. Well, when J-Rock was disappointed; he had this bulging eye stare that said, *"You're better than that!"* Trust me it was effective. His lifelong friendship is cemented through his two grown sons, my godsons, who call me "Uncle Frank." J-Rock reinforced what Ralph started—don't follow the crowd. Currently, J-Rock *walks the talk* with an MSc in Social Work (MSW) and being a Licensed Certified Social Worker (LCSW) leading the Forensic Unit at a Connecticut-based mental health facility. His life surely personifies the title and subtitle of this book.

My Epiphany

Every successful person has an "aha" moment, an epiphany which jump-starts them to greatness. Mine occurred during my second season playing for Van Spruill, head coach of the Bears in the Albie Booth Midget Football League (ABMFL). Van, a former semiprofessional football linebacker, was an excellent teacher and secondary father figure. After my first year of playing organized football, my goal was to try out for my high school team. Van thought I needed another year under his watchful eye before trying out for the high school team. He convinced me to forego freshman tryouts to play another year with the Bears. He told me his goal was to win the ABMFL championship and he knew I would be a "key player" to help the team dethrone the six-time ABMFL Champion Lions. Winning First Team All-Star honors and not winning the championship left a sour taste in my mouth—provided additional incentive to stay. Well, Van was right! He along with assistant coaches "Tank" Richardson and Barney Waters architected a midget football league program that enabled me to complete my second year of playing organized football as a champion. During the season my team the Bears, defeated the Lions twice on our way to winning the ABMFL title. In leading my team to the championship, I had a banner year, receiving trophies and awards for being a champion and all-star. Furthermore, I received two awards that would change my life. The coaches and team gave the first award to me. It was an "Outstanding Leadership" trophy. Reverend Dr. Curtis Cofield, my pastor from Immanuel Baptist Church, gave the second award to me. It was a "Valuable Player" plaque.

As with most awards, there is a brief storytelling on why the award is being given to an individual. I remember hearing words: desire, discipline, and determination. Van skilfully gave examples that I could recall as he spoke each word. You see, Van never said he would teach me to be a leader. He just told me I would be a key player in helping him achieve his "strategic" goal. Unbeknownst to me, this experience from a Little League football program helped create the moral compass of my being today in reflecting and realizing the "moment" where **A.G.I.L.E. L.E.A.D.E.R.S.H.I.P. with a G.R.I.P.** began. The leadership seeds planted from a community-based program were continually being watered throughout my life as you will learn. At an early age I was experiencing the phrases describing the unique behaviors associated with each letter.

A Leader is Unleashed

As a freshman attending James Hillhouse High School located in New Haven, Connecticut, I became a legend in midget football while also participating on the school's varsity track team. My reputation as an athlete preceded me, and because of this, a lot was expected from me. Van and my dad helped me keep a level head and there were always upperclassmen—Rudy Howell, Larry Waters, J-Rock, Teddy Hines, Albert Brice, Gerald Smith, Terry Law, Andy Tisdale, and Danny Lathrop—who edified but never discouraged me. Danny, a senior who was a captain of the football team and a top football player in the state of Connecticut, had the biggest influence on me because he was such a great student, athlete, and person. He was a first-class guy. A six-foot-three, 220-pound, muscular specimen, nobody messed with Danny. I was a little star stuck because he was always in the paper for football, basketball, track, academics—all of which he excelled at, but he was a down-to-earth guy. Danny led by example, and his piercing hazel eyes told you he meant what he said. However J-Rock was the catalyst as he led the charge the others followed inspiring me to focus on, in street vernacular; books, ball, and babes—in that order. To be more specific they meant go to class and study; go to practice every day; and then be nice to the young ladies. Despite their efforts I was hard headed getting caught up in the hype of being a sophomore playing varsity football and running on the varsity track team. I started sowing my royal oats, if you know what I mean. I wanted to hang with the upperclassmen. This almost led to my demise. During my sophomore year, while joy riding with upperclassmen instead of going to class as my dad and J-Rock had told me, we were involved in a serious car accident. We were in route to a housing project called Brookside when one of the tires exploded. The next thing I knew the car was flipping. The driver of the car, who happened to be the captain of the football team, grabbed the passenger seated in the front seat, who was on his way out the window. I was in the back seat with a close friend, thinking, "When is this car going to stop flipping?" Glass shattered all around us. I attribute my survival to having my seat belt on, curling up in a fetal position, and my praying parents and grandma. When the car finally came to a stop it was almost a complete pancake. We crawl out of the car and, in a state of shock; I decide to look for my favorite ink pen. Can you image that? Well, the person in the back seat with me brought me to my senses, grabbing my arm so we could make our way back to school. Man that was the longest trip I had taken anywhere! I was thinking, "My daddy and J-Rock told me to go to class, I am in trouble!" News of the accident travelled very fast. When I got back to school J-Rock was anxiously waiting. His you're better than that eye stare was replaced with a "worried now I'm relieved" look. You see he had double concern because the close friend who pulled me to my senses was his younger brother David. He gave us a big hug jokingly scolding us as he and David made fun of me with "Big Head" jokes. Before noon, everyone knew about the accident. My parents were called. When I got home, they didn't scold me; they just grabbed me, hugged me, and wouldn't let me go! I could feel both them shaking. My dad then spoke these unforgettable words: "I bet you'll take you're a- - to class the next time." From that point on I swore to myself that I would never let anyone convince me to do anything I didn't want to do. Especially if I knew it would hurt my parents. Thank God, because of those prayers I survived a car accident with a bruised shoulder, glass in my afro, and a shattered ego. It has been over thirty years since that accident, but I am inclined to think of it as the news is filled with teenagers killed in car accidents. That was my "think *before* you leap" wake-up call. That experience caused me to become immune to peer pressure. I refocused to excel my junior and senior years, becoming a straight-A student. This renewed attitude adjustment allowed me to graduate from James Hillhouse High School with an honors diploma, National Honor Society Award, National Football Foundation and Hall of Fame Scholar-Athlete Finalist recognition, and Athlete of the Year Award, along with a host of other sports, academic, and community service awards.

Not only did I excel in the classroom, but I was able to sharpen my leadership and business skills performing after-school activities. My after-school activities included shining shoes, working as a stock boy at a neighborhood retail store, and working with the Special Olympics. My favorite uncle, Eugene Camp, added to my street smarts by teaching me how to "get my hustle on" in the streets by shining shoes. He gave me a green shoeshine box! It was all about business as I would squeeze a couple of days a week between classes to canvass downtown New Haven, "getting my hustle on." I lived around the campus of Yale University either shining shoes or going to class. Mr. and Mrs. Boomer, Lloyd Parchmen, and Mr. George Clark, all of whom operated small businesses, exposed me to the retail business. They were my *Strategic hustler*™ role models.

I learned my humility as a volunteer for the Special Olympics. Watching the special children of God compete despite their shortcomings made a lifelong impact on my life. Never would I complain about anything! My involvement helped a record number of students win a record number of gold, silver, and bronze medals in addition to a can do attitude.

Upon graduating from Hillhouse, I narrowed my college choices to Purdue University and Virginia State College. I selected Virginia State and attended for three semesters. I will talk later about this experience. As my dad would say, "It's not how you start, it is how you finish." Attending this historically black college contributed to my growth as a leader. Circumstances required transferring to the University of New Haven (UNH).

As a cum laude undergraduate from UNH, I was the first African American in its history to graduate from its nationally accredited engineering school with a degree in computer technology. I also was very involved in extracurricular activities such as football, basketball, and the school newspaper in addition to the lead student operator at the computer center. God allowed me to accomplish some great things in each of these capacities, which will be discussed later in this book. Being nominated and selected to W*ho's Who among Students in American Universities and Colleges* was the pinnacle of my college career. In completing UNH's dual masters program, I was the first UNH computer technology undergraduate to accomplish this feat, resulting in my earning an MBA in marketing and MS in industrial engineering. My numerous professional and philanthropic accomplishments have earned me a Lifetime Achievement Award nomination from the International Biographical Centre of Cambridge, England.

From a *Street hustler* to a *Strategic hustler*™, I learned to adapt, set goals, and be intelligent through innovation, insight and initiative, and influence; to be interpersonal with integrity; to embrace learning; and to strive for excellence by being effective. Thus, I learned to be **A.G.I.L.E**. Watching a football game, the most agile players are the ones who avoid injury and are the most successful. With this agility I developed the ability and willingness to look to challenge the status quo, energize myself and others with ever-greater challenges, acknowledge a burning platform, deliver results by delegation, learn to make the tough hard decisions by maintaining an edge, respect diversity, realize success is adding value and sustaining excellence, have a *teachable* point of view, encourage ideas through uplifting values, and realize perseverance is the most important behavior trait to **L.E.A.D.E.R.S.H.I.P.**. This brings us to the **G.R.I.P.**, which focuses on operations excellence management. Before discussing **G.R.I.P.**, allow me to share a quote from Warren Bennis, PhD, a highly regarded leadership scholar, which differentiated the extremes of management and leadership in a number of provocative ways:

"Leaders conquer the context—the volatile, turbulent, ambiguous surroundings that sometimes seem to conspire against us and will surely suffocate us if we let them—while managers surrender to it." *Surviving the perils of an inner-city red zone made me a leader.* As Dr. Bennis continues, he fuels **A.G.I.L.E. L.E.A.D.E.R.S.H.I.P.** with a **G.R.I.P**. He continues, "Leaders innovate; the manager administrates. The manager is a copy; the leader is an original. The manager maintains, and the leader develops. The manager focuses on systems and structure; the leader focuses on people. The manager relies on control; the leader inspires trust.

The manager has a short-range view; the leader has a long-range perspective. The manager asks how and when, the leader asks what and why. The manager has an eye on the bottom line; the leader has his eye on the horizon. The manager imitates; the leader originates. The manager accepts the status quo; the leader challenges it. Managers do things right; leaders do the right things."

G.R.I.P. is an acronym specifying management of **G**oals, **R**esources, **I**nterfaces and **P**erformance. Using the most appropriate and best practices by ensuring **Goals** are understood and agreed to; **Resources** required and their roles are clearly defined; effective and efficient communication occurs across all **Interfaces**; and optimum **Performance** is supported by an effective human performance system.

This book shares the life experiences of ordinary people who, like me, have "*hustled*" their way to accomplish extraordinary things. How did they do it? You are about to embarked on a journey uncovering the mysteries of behaviors comprising of **A.G.I.L.E. L.E.A.D.E.R.S.H.I.P. with a G.R.I.P.** Leadership and management are lifelong skills. Remembering the speech Van gave when explaining why I received the "Outstanding Leadership" award; he mentioned the word "desire." To emphasize this word, I am going to use the phrase "You gotta wanna or you ain't a gonna!" taken from a book that was required reading for a project management class delivered by a nationally recognized corporate trainer to a world-renowned company—no, not me! You will learn more about both later. My success was predestined by Father God, but faith without work is dead. **Said another way**, the only place "success" comes before "work" is the dictionary. My work was driven by "desire" teamed with dedication and determination, blessing me with the realities shared with you in this book. The aim is to hopefully inspire you to reach for your reality. Putting on my coaching cap, I challenge you to dare to be *great!*" Let's start the journey with Ⓐ, the first behavior of Ⓐ.G.I.L.E. L.E.A.D.E.R.S.H.I.P.— Ⓐdaptable behavior.

CHAPTER 2

Adaptable Behavior

Introduction

When interviewed by a representative of the notable *Who's Who* publication, I was asked the question, "What do you attribute your success to?" Three points came to mind:

1. My ability and willingness to deliver results that exceed expectations
2. My ability and willingness to reinvent myself
3. My ability and willingness to assimilate into the social culture of the organization

Notice that I've used the words "ability" and "willingness" in each phrase. Allow me to explain. I am blessed being one of over 14 million managers across the globe who have been trained using the Situational Leadership® Model developed by Dr. Paul Hersey—internationally recognized as a leading authority on training and development in leadership and management. This leadership approach is based on interplay among:

1. The amount of guidance and direction a leader gives
2. The amount of socioemotional support a leader provides
3. The readiness level that followers exhibit in performing a specific task

This concept was developed to help people attempting leadership, regardless of their roles, to be more effective in their daily interactions with others. It provides leaders with some understanding of the relationship between effective style of leadership and the level of readiness of their followers. The key word "readiness" is the state or quality of being ready; preparation; promptness; aptitude; willingness. I remember the late Archbishop Earl Paulk saying, "You are only a leader if you have followers." The next few pages will apply real-world scenarios in explaining some behavioral science theory.

Readiness means different things to different people. It has nothing to do with the person's beliefs, traits, age, etc. Specifically, we are referring to how prepared mentally, physically, and emotionally a person is to perform a specific task. This concept of readiness has to do with specific situations—not with any total sense of readiness. People tend to be more or less ready in relation to a specific task, function, or objective that a leader is attempting to accomplish. Thus, a salesperson may be very responsible in securing new sales, but very casual about completing the paperwork necessary to close on the sale. As a result, it is appropriate for the manager to leave the salesperson alone in terms of closing on sales, but only supervise closely in terms of paperwork until the sales person can start to do well in that area, too.

In addition to assessing the level of readiness of individuals within a group, a leader may have to assess the readiness level of the group as a group, particularly if the group interacts frequently in the same work area, as happens with students in the classroom. Thus, a teacher may find that a class, as a group, may be at one level of readiness in a particular area, but a student within that group may be at a different level. When the teacher is one-to-one with that student, the teacher may have to behave differently than when working with the class as a group. In reality, the teacher may find a number of students at various readiness levels. For example, when I taught computer literacy, my students' ages ranged from seven to seventy. During the course, I would find one student not doing the assigned work regularly, and when the work was turned in, it was poorly organized and not very well done. I initiated a structure and supervised that student closely. Another student, however, would be doing good work but may be insecure and shy. With that student, I may not have to engage in much task behavior in terms of coursework, but needed to be supportive to engage in a two-way conversation, and to help facilitate the student's interaction with the class. Still another student may be competent and confident in performing the assigned work and thus can be given minimum assistance. I could share with you thousands of these types of stories from my roles as a corporate trainer, parent, corporate executive, and football coach.

Situational Leadership® consists of two major components of readiness: ability and willingness.

Ability is having the physical, mental, financial, or legal power to accomplish something. Recall the saying, "Knowledge is power," well in the realm of ability knowledge is familiarity with someone or something, which can include facts, information, descriptions, or skills acquired through experience or education. To use the vernacular of my teen-age kids, to have ability means that *"you got skills."*

In my various leadership roles, one of the keys to being an effective leader involved considering the ability level of others to perform a specific task. When serving as an assistant football coach, the head coach would always admonish us to know our player's abilities. This would allow us to use a player who had the most appropriate skills for a specific game situation—i.e. on a obvious third down passing situation a running back who had problems blocking an opposing team player, running pass patterns or catching the ball would be of little help in allowing the team to pick up a crucial first down. This truism also applies to business. A person with PhD in Chemistry may be of little help in the design of a new helicopter.

To have skills is not enough. You need *willingness* to do the job. Willingness is a cheerful readiness to do something. How do you know if someone, or a group, is willing to perform a task? Good question. I have learned to assess their confidence, commitment, and motivation to perform a task. An athlete may be confident in their abilities; but may not be committed to the team's goals because he or she cannot see how they help attain personal goals; this will affect their motivation. This loss of commitment and motivation makes the person *unwilling*. It might imply that they are regressing. The concepts of ability and willingness are siblings. We all know siblings are different, but they interact to influence one another. Remember that ability and willingness have a direct affect on each other. Recall the phrase, "you gotta wanna or you ain't a gonna," think of this as describing one's willingness. **Said another way,** a willing person or team has a "will do" attitude. This "will do" attitude enables growth in ability allowing the leader and team to soar to amazing heights. When challenged with leading a person or team with a poor attitude an effective leader will use adaptive behavior to win their minds and minds because that is the only way to produce acceptable results. An in-depth discussion on the various readiness levels comprising the different combinations of ability and willingness that people bring to a task is beyond the scope of this book. However, it is important to know the continuum of follower readiness is divided into four levels. These levels are labeled: Readiness Level 1 (**R1**), Readiness Level 2 (**R2**), Readiness Level 3 (**R3**), and Readiness Level 4 (**R4**). They identify behavior patterns of followers for the different combinations of ability and willingness brought to a task. People can grow from being incompetent to competent to incompetent as they transition from R1 to R4. Keep on reading and learning to find out more about my experiences with this phenomenon.

Remember "Leaders Are Born To Be Made," therefore any abilities can be learned which leads to the building of the behaviors that comprise willingness—confidence, commitment, and motivation.

Table 2.1 Readiness Levels provides a definition along with examples of behaviors I've witnessed for each level.

Table 2.1 – Readiness Levels

Readiness Level 1 (**R1**)	The follower lacks ability, commitment, motivation and/or confidence ✓ Not meeting performance standards ✓ Absence of intelligent behavior (See chapter 4) ✓ Continuously asking questions about the task ✓ Shows no initiative
Readiness Level 2 (**R2**)	The follower lacks ability but is trying and needs guidance ✓ Listens effectively ✓ Shows potential ability ✓ Has a "gotta wanna" attitude ✓ Demonstrates a stick-to-it work habit
Readiness Level 3 (**R3**)	The follower has the ability but is not willing or is insecure about doing it alone ✓ Has proven ability ✓ Appears hesitate to take initiative ✓ Needs guidance ✓ Solicits frequent and timely feedback
Readiness Level 4 (**R4**)	The follower has the ability, is committed, motivated, and confident about doing the task ✓ Demonstrates intelligent behavior (See chapter 4) ✓ Is solutions oriented ✓ Practices G.R.I.P. management (See chapters 17 – 20) ✓ Finishes tasks strong ✓ Performs to high standards – wants the "Last Ten Percent"

The R1 to R2 to R3 Experience

I have witnessed people going from being insecure (R1) to confident (R2) and then becoming insecure again (R3). The reason being is when learning you are being directed by a leader. Think of the periods when you were being instructed by a teacher, parent, boss, or coach. These decisions are *leader directed.* As the transition is made to the higher levels (R3, R4), the leader is now empowering the follower(s) to make decisions. For example, the amount of play calling responsibility given to a quarterback increases as they demonstrate the ability to understand the playbook and execute on the field [call the 'right" play; minimize mistakes; show resiliency; etc.]. These decisions are *follower directed* or *self-directed.*

The Situational Leadership® Model is based on the concept of leadership style and the individual or group readiness level, or maturity. The four leadership styles include:

- **Telling (S1)** - involves one-way communication in which the leader defines the roles of the individual or group and provides the what, how, why, when and where to do the task
- **Selling/Coaching (S2)** - while the leader is still providing the direction, he or she is now using two-way communication and providing the socio-emotional support that will allow the individual or group being influenced to buy into the process
- **Participating (S3)** - involves shared decision-making about aspects of how the task is accomplished and the leader is providing less task behaviors while maintaining high relationship behavior
- **Delegating (S4)** - the leader is still involved in decisions; however, the process and responsibility has been passed to the individual or group. The leader stays involved to monitor progress

Each of these leadership styles is appropriate for the previously mentioned readiness levels. Let take a brief look at each.

The Telling (**S1**) leadership behavior is appropriate for a follower who lacks competence (ability) and commitment (willingness). This equates to Readiness Level 1 (**R1**).

The Selling/Coaching (**S2**) leadership behavior is appropriate for a follower who lacks competence (ability) but has some commitment (willingness). This equates to Readiness Level 2 (**R2**).

The Participating (**S3**) leadership behavior is appropriate for a follower who has competence (ability) but is not committed (willingness) to performing alone. This equates to Readiness Level 3 (**R3**).

The Delegating (**S4**) leadership behavior is appropriate for follower who is both competent (ability) and committed (willingness)—Readiness Level 4 (**R4**).

So what does this mean? Keep on reading and learning. Table 2.2 Leadership Behaviors provides scenarios that further explain when each leadership behavior is appropriate.

Table 2.2 Leadership Behaviors

Telling (S1)	When followers have high commitment (willingness) but not a high competence (ability). See Readiness Level 1 (R1) - When the task is challenging and the followers performing it are inexperienced it is necessary to give instructions as to how the job should be done. The instruction style implies a high focus toward the task, and low focus toward the person
Selling/ Coaching (S2)	When followers have some competence (ability) but low commitment (willingness). See Readiness Level 2 (R2) - When the task is challenging, but the follower has some skill they need direction and supervision because of their inexperience. They also need an occasional "way to go" to build their confidence and involvement to restore their commitment which may have declined because of frustration/storming of the team. We will talk more this later we cover *Adaptability and Team Dynamics*
Participating (S3)	When followers have high commitment (willingness) and variable competence (ability). See Readiness Level 3 (R3) - During this period the follower's skill has increased but support is still necessary to sustain motivation and bolster their confidence. The leader may take a back seat giving acknowledgment and praise when necessary
Delegating (S4)	When followers have both competent (ability) and commitment (willingness). See Readiness Level 4 (R4) - They are able and willing to work on a project by themselves with little supervision or support. Occasional monitoring allows the leader to stay informed and ensure the followers have the necessary resources

For a more detailed discussion on the Situational Leadership® Model, visit www.situational.com. Let me provide some additional examples on how to successfully apply this behavioral science theory.

As a leader of a team at Sterling Software, my focus was convincing customers worldwide how they could use Sterling's technology to transform their organizations to make them consistent winners in their chosen market space. These transformations included adoption of new technologies, major strategic shifts, process reengineering, mergers and acquisitions, restructurings in different sorts of business units, attempts to significantly improve innovations, and cultural change. The common thread of these transformations was each had a burning platform. Keep on reading to learn more about a burning platform. The reality was that in some of these companies, the existence of a burning platform was more obvious than others. In either scenario, a leader who could apply adaptable behavior was required to lead change in an environment when everything is perceived to be all right, when actually they are to the contrary. Let me share a personal experience that illustrates four points to leading change when everything is all right. I am going to call this company NEWTECH.

When Dr. Margaret J. Foresight became vice president (VP) of advanced technologies for a leading gaming technology and services NEWTECH in 2002, the company was in clover. The high-tech firm had captured 70 percent of its market, its stock price had skyrocketed, and it had a loyal customer base.

But Foresight knew trouble could lie ahead. She stated, "Our systems are old, inflexible, and highly proprietary. Unless the company overhauls its technology platform, we won't be able to innovate quickly or affordably enough to meet customers' needs." While Foresight had the firm's executive team's enthusiastic support, she encountered stiff resistance from the people who would have to carry out the change. Because the company was doing so well, they did not see a reason for such a dramatic transformation. As John Kotter argues in his book *Leading Change* (Harvard Business School Press, 1996), successful change starts with a sense of urgency. When business is good, how do you create that urgency? Here is what has to happen.

1. Communicate and educate constantly

Make the business case for your initiative in irrefutable terms and communicate it repeatedly. Foresight bluntly expressed the peril facing NEWTECH: "We won't be able to serve our customers in the future."

She and other managers traveled to NEWTECH'S international offices to visit the roughly one thousand product developers who would be most affected by the change effort. Foresight also sent repeated messages about the need for change through every communication and educational channel available. She invited outside experts to come in for brown-bag lunches and talks about the new technologies. She had programmers from Sun Microsystems, IBM, and other firms visit NEWTECH to speak "peer to peer" with employees. E-mails, articles, and streaming video on the company's intranet and regular staff meetings further turned up the volume.

2. Set boundary conditions

Dictate the business requirements that need to be met, but let employees decide how they'll fulfill those requirements. Let them come to a conclusion about how well they could meet those requirements without making changes. For example, Foresight gave NEWTECH programmers a list of the capabilities the new systems would need, such as the ability to integrate third-party software. Then she invited them to assess how well their current system met those requirements. When they said, "Our old technology doesn't do that," Foresight said, "How do you plan to meet the defined conditions?" When you tell people what they need to do but let them figure out how it's going to get done, you get much better buy-in.

3. Acknowledge difficulties and admit your mistakes

Probe for difficulties employees may encounter in making the transition. Acknowledge your own errors and be willing to make midcourse corrections. Foresight had extensive expertise with the web-based technologies he was proposing for NEWTECH, but he was new to gaming software. When an employee proved to her that the third-party software Foresight had insisted on installing presented integration difficulties, Foresight agreed to jettison the product—even though NEWTECH already had paid $1 million for the license to use it.

4. Adjust your leadership style

Applying Situational Leadership® theory will help when it's time to dictate and when it's time to use a more collaborative approach to leading change. A key point to remember is having adaptable behavior allows adjusting your leadership style to lead effectively. We will talk more about being effective later. You can't implement a major change through command and control. You can't make people learn something they don't want to learn. To persuade rather than force resistant employees to embrace change, Foresight told employees, "If we don't make this change, we will not only have problems satisfying our customers, we will also find it harder to comply with government procurement requirements," which can make or break a provider's chances of winning a contract. Once employees were led to see the consequences of being inflexible, they got behind the change. Think about how differently you would approach changing a situation when business is bad. How would you create a sense of urgency?

To Adapt or NOT To Adapt – That is the Question

Up to this point we've talked about ability and willingness in relating leadership behaviors to readiness levels. Dr. Foresight demonstrated her ability and willingness to be adaptable in winning the hearts and minds of her staff to lead the change. We will talk more about **C.H.A.N.G.E.** later—the acronym may be confusing but keep on reading and learning. But for now, know that during my career in business, athletics, or community leadership situations, I've witnessed many never get past the "po in potential" because they could not get out of their own way. Later, we will dig into this deeper when discussing character in chapter 4, "Ⓘntelligent Behavior." But for now know their inability to adapt played a major role in them not reaching their full potential.

When a leader lacks adaptable behavior they miss opportunities to effectively lead a group through the series of stages of development all groups go through before performing in its most effective and mature state. We will cover this later during our discussion on *Adaptable Behavior and Team Dynamics.* However deciding "*NOT To Adapt*" creates a breeding ground for the following negative team communication traps:

- Inarticulate – has a hard time communicating their thoughts
- Tangent – goes off on tangents, tends to ramble
- Constant commenter – comments too frequently
- Sarcasm – always responds with a sarcastic comment or put down
- Mute – does not share their opinions
- Inflexible – refuses to support a group decision
- Poor listener – tunes out or distracted easily
- Interrupter – cuts others off
- Challenger – challenges all ideas
- Late arriver – arrives late and disrupts the flow of the meeting
- Early leaver – breaks the meeting momentum and drains the team of energy

Strong team facilitation skills are critical to overcoming these negative communication team traps. Later were going to discuss the importance of being able to "get in where you fit in." But for now let us move to the next topic on adaptable behavior and **C.H.A.N.G.E.** As you read this information and the rest of this book, continue to think how you can use this information to help turn your dreams into your reality.

Adaptable Behavior and C.H.A.N.G.E.

Having adaptable behavior requires **C.H.A.N.G.E.** Think of **C.H.A.N.G.E.** as **C**reating a **H**ealthy **A**nd **N**ew **G**rowth to **E**xcellence. Any change not focused on improvement toward excellence is a waste of time. I challenge you to change for the best. You don't have to be as well educated as Dr. Foresight; all you need is a desire to be different, to be *great*! I wasn't always Dr. Frank L. Harper, Jr., but there was a burning desire to *not* be an at-risk statistic.

Said another way, you gotta wanna or you ain't a gonna! Yes, I have a PhD, and these words may not be appropriate. However, this is a leadership and management book for the ages, and everyone from youth to mature adults can relate to these words. I am going to switch gears now and call a person with adaptable behavior an adaptable leader.

An adaptable leader initiates and manages **C.H.A.N.G.E**. An adaptable leader is a mover, doer, and improver. **C.H.A.N.G.E**. is challenging, hard, and can be fun. Change requires making a transition. During my youth, events occurred that required me to make an individual change to prevent being an at-risk statistic. As a professional, this experience taught me how important individual change management was in leading organizational change and I sought to learn from world-renowned change management experts. This knowledge is being shared with you. Within an organization, effective change management requires multidisciplinary, structured, and integrated processes and the best practice in the areas of:

- Leadership—defining and communicating "why," "where," and "when"
- Organization design and operations reengineering—defining "what"
- People change management (PCM)— expediting the "who"
- Program/project design and management—managing the "how"

People Change Management within Organization Change:

- Is structured processes, tools, and techniques (T-N-T)
- Increases and expedites user adoption, proficiency, and ultimate utilization, thereby optimizing business and results
- Includes sponsor support, stakeholder management, change readiness, business impact, communication, training, and change metrics, as well as contingency planning and interventions as required
- Reduces people-related risks (e.g., resistance and misunderstandings) that affect costly delays, rework, error/waste, and turnover
- Engages users in the change, shares information, improves solutions, and expedites the transition to the "new state"

My street smarts prepared me to lead and contribute to organization change management efforts to bring about **C.H.A.N.G.E**. in corporate America. Growing up in an inner-city red zone, there were organizations like the Dwight

Community Center or Ethan Gardens Apartment committee that staged "Stop the Violence" campaigns. They were accomplished through various activities, mostly sports oriented. The Black Panther Party tried to be effective, but people like my dad didn't like their cause or movement, thus the organization's efforts proved fruitless in the community. Nonetheless, the community activities were only as effective as the people involved. *Said another way*, a person's heart and mind must embrace the benefits of any organization's movement or cause before they will make a committed effort to support it. These experiences support my argument that organizational change management will not be effective until there is people change management—starting with the individual. Here's why.

- Successful organization change results only when individuals are successful at change.

  ➢ How valuable is a new process that no one adopts? How valuable is a new web-based tool that no one uses? How valuable is an ERP if no one uses it correctly? The answer to these questions is the essence of the fact that organizational change is only successful *when each impacted individual* makes his or her own successful transition. In fact, a poorly managed change can actually have severe adverse impacts. I remember hearing a story about a man working in a warehouse who was being told by the system that he could not ship a product, despite the fact that it was sitting in front of him on the shelf. A customer was being deprived of a product because someone upstream had not used the new ERP system correctly. Any organizational initiative that impacts how people do their jobs *is only as successful as each employee* at making the personal change. *Note:* An enterprise resource planning (ERP) system integrates internal and external management information across an entire organization, embracing finance/accounting, manufacturing, sales and service, customer relationship management, etc. ERP systems automate this activity with an integrated software application. Their purpose is to facilitate the flow of information between all business functions inside the boundaries of the organization and manage the connections to outside stakeholder. ERP systems can run on a variety of hardware and network configurations, typically employing a database as a repository for information.

- While we are all different, as human beings we respond to change fairly predictably.

  ➢ At first glance, your reaction might be "oh, no, everybody is unique"— and you are correct. However, the way we as human beings respond to change is actually very similar. For instance, it is basic human nature to be curious about why a change is happening and what has resulted in the need for change.

According to Prosci, the world leader in change management research, in times of change—whether at home, in the community or at work—individuals need the following to successfully make a change:

- **A**wareness of the need to change
- **D**esire to participate and support the change
- **K**nowledge on how to change
- **A**bility to implement acquired skills and behaviors
- **R**einforcement to sustain the change

Recall my story in the section "Coming from hell to Get to Yale," where I talked about my rise from the streets to attend Yale University at the age of thirteen. I had to make a change. Using key events discussed, let me apply the globally-recognized Prosci® ADKAR® Model for individual change to my situation.

(A)wareness of the need to change:

I lived in another public housing facility, which was my demilitarized zone (DMZ). This was "my hood," or, to be more succinct, "my hell." I had to grow up fast, recalling having to intervene at the age of eight to prevent my dad from committing murder. My mother suffered from a seventeen-year bout with depression. There came a time when I had to intervene and have my mother committed to a mental institution for rehabilitation. In my reality, I watched my sibling and friends succumb to perils of the street.

After each traumatic experience, I didn't have to be a rocket scientist to know that change was needed.

(D)esire to participate and support the change:

My dad pushed me to be a better person, control my temper, and "never be afraid to be *great!*" He created the desire for me to participate in something that would put me in a different environment. Additionally, my experiences with the U.S. Grant program created a desire to continue learning, growing, and striving for a better education and future.

(K)nowledge on how to change

The knowledge gained from the U.S. Grant program combined with "my hood" lessons taught me the skills needed to make a life change. The knowledge earned from the U.S. Grant program ignited my desire to learn new information and discover things I was passionate about. I learned effective study habits to pass college-level math, science, English, and other liberal arts/humanities topics. In addition to the academic rigor, the extra-curricular activities—sports, field trips, social functions—all jumpstarted my desire to; continue to excel in elementary, middle, and high schools; play sports; attend and graduate from college; travel the world and meet new people; and help my family and fellow man. *Said another way*, I learned there was another way to "get my hustle on."

(A)bility to implement acquired skills and behaviors

Throughout high school, college, and my professional career, I applied the knowledge on how to change to achieve my dreams. The study, athletic, and social skills learned at U.S. Grant allowed me to achieve scholastic, athletic, and community excellence. Recall earlier I spoke of being able to meditate on what you've read; hide it in your heart; and live it when you have the opportunity. Integrating the mind, body, spirit, and community, learning requires the ability and willingness to read, understand, and do. This wisdom allowed me to experience tremendous learning opportunities. Later when discussing *"trilogy of success"* and "Reap What You Sow" you will learn more about these opportunities. For now, know success is attributed to the ability to implement acquired skills and behaviors.

(R)einforcement to sustain the change

The elements that kept me from becoming "another-at-risk-statistic" were people; conveying the message "don't follow the crowd"; opportunities; good performance was rewarded in the classroom and extra-curricular activities; and determination; my desire to be successful. The latter being the most important. Remember, you gotta wanna or you ain't a gonna! This drive motivates my quest to be a lifelong learner focused on staying ahead of the curve that constantly changes. Testimonies to this are the following professional recommendations:

Colleague #1:

"I hired Dr. Harper to lead an RFP proposal project for the Department of Energy (DOE). Though he was not familiar with our proprietary technology, he did a good job of collaborating with our team of PhDs and chemical engineers to allow us to deliver our proposal to the DOE. His performance led to me hiring Frank as our director of IT and then expanding his role to cover commerce. He has performed admirably in both capacities and has strategically provided technical and commercial solutions to support our growth in a cost-effective manner. I would recommend him as a competent IT director who has performed in any environment under any circumstance."

Colleague #2:

Dr. Harper and I met in 1984, when I worked for Manufacturers Hanover Trust Co.(MHT)a once major bank in New York City Wall Street Area. At the time, Frank was a partner of CATT, Inc. As a consultant, system engineer, and programmer, I hired him to customize a software product he and his partner built to assist me in my job as an officer of DP, Human Resources.

"In 2000, our paths crossed once again. From 2000 till 2006, Dr. Harper trained PDS clients as a subcontractor. He developed and modified proprietary training materials for clients' target delivery. Dr. Harper is unique; he is well educated and informed on the latest technical developments, an excellent instructor, in addition to being a consultant with a unique and personal way of endearing students to him, making them take an active role in class participation.

"Many clients request Dr. Harper time and again to service them. He makes learning fun."

For those of you who wish to learn more about the Prosci® ADKAR® Model table 2.3 provides additional insight into the factors that influence success. An in-depth discussion is beyond the scope of this book but I suggest visiting www. prosci.com for additional information.

Table 2.3 ADKAR Factors Influencing Success

ADKAR® Elements	Factors Influencing Success
Awareness of the need for change	• A person's view of the current state • How a person perceives problems • Credibility of the sender of awareness messages • Circulation of misinformation or rumors • Contestability of the reasons for change
Desire to support and participate in the change	• The nature of the change (what change is and how it will impact each person) • The organizational or environmental context for the change (his or her perception of the organization or environment that is subject for change) • Each individual person's situation • What motivates a person (those intrinsic motivators that are unique to an individual)
Knowledge of how to change	• The current knowledge base of an individual • The capability of this person to gain additional knowledge • Resources available for education and training • Access to or existence of the required knowledge
Ability to implement required skills and behaviors	• Psychological blocks • Physical capabilities • Intellectual capability • The time available to develop the needed skills • The availability of resources to support the development of new abilities
Reinforcement™ to sustain the change	• The degree to which reinforcement is meaningful and specific to the person impacted by the change • The association of the reinforcement with actual demonstrated progress or accomplishment • The absence of negative consequences • An accountability system that creates an ongoing mechanism to reinforce the change

Adaptable Behavior and Team Dynamics

The criteria that bring a team together can actually pull it apart. Initiative, expertise, decisiveness, years of experience, a strong point of view and a laser-like focus on results… The employees and leaders on whom you most depend exhibit these qualities. Yet when these talented individuals join forces on a leadership team or a high-profile project team, their personal strengths don't always mesh effectively to deliver on mission-critical goals. Too often, bad teams happen to high performers. So how do you deal with them? Let's talk about Dr. Bruce Tuckman's **Forming – Storming – Norming – Performing** model. This model addresses the dynamics of group development maintaining these phases are all necessary and inevitable in order for the team to grow, to face up to challenges, to tackle problems, to find solutions, to plan work, and to deliver results. Like the other leadership/management behavior theories its emphasis is on being adaptable. Table 2.4 Team Dynamics illustrates the phases of the model, behavior characteristics during the phase, and tips for leading teams through each phase.

Later during a discussion on integrity, we'll cover connection, communication, coordination, and collaboration. For now, know that poor and ineffective communication can hinder team effectiveness. Good communication practices for all team members include:

- Honest, and candid team feedback
- Balance positive and negative feedback
- Support ideas with examples, information, data, or pictures
- Listen actively and effectively
- Be adaptable, or flexible

Forming	Storming	Norming	Performing
• Excitement, anticipation, optimism • Fear, anxiety about task at hand • Hesitancy to participate	• Resistance to work methods unaccustomed to • Competition for roles, team conflict • Decrease team productivity • Change in attitudes	• Team cohesion • Members confide in each other • Establishment of roles and boundaries • Constructive communication	• Understanding and respect for others • High morale and confidence • Conflict is eliminated or worked through • Constructive self-change undertaken
• Build trust and confidence • Help members to get acquainted with each other • Provide clear direction and purpose	• Develop agreements on how decision will be made • Empower team members • Resolve issues of power and authority	• Encourage collaboration (See Chapter 4) • Energize with team challenges (See Chapter 8) • Respect Diversity (See Chapter 12)	• Inspect what you expect and celebrate success • Advocate for the team throughout the organization • Document lessons learned

Summary

So there it is. "It is not the strongest of the species that survives, nor the most intelligent, but the one the most responsive to change" (Darwin, 1990). Different situations, different pulls, requires a different self. Thus as a leader you are going to have to behave differently. The leadership behavior demonstrated when dealing one on one with a team member should be different when dealing with a group as a whole. Stated differently, leaders must adapt to the situation to achieve the desired goals. As Stephen Covey states, "Begin with the end in mind." As Dr. Harper adds, "Be adaptable in getting there."

Former General Electric (GE) CEO Jack Welch, PhD, states "Before you can be a leader success is all about *growing yourself.* When you become a leader success is all about *growing others.*"

The next chapter uncovers goals to achieving both aims. Let's examine Ⓖ, the second behavior trait of **A.Ⓖ.I.L.E. L.E.A.D.E.R. S.H.I.P.**—Ⓖoal-Oriented Behavior.

CHAPTER 3

Goal-Oriented Behavior

Introduction

My dad gave me my first lesson in having ideas and setting goals—which are essential to goal-oriented behavior. I will deal with goals in this chapter and ideas (dreams) in a later. But make no mistake: you cannot have far-reaching goals without first generating awe-inspiring ideas. It is a process with the first step to turning dreams into reality is writing them down as goals. Back to my dad, his permission was required for me to go anywhere. He would ask me, "Why are you going?; What are you going to do when you get there?" Man! talkin' 'bout being all up in my business; with him I had none. If my answer was, "I don't know," or seemed unsure he would say, "No." Eventually maturity gave me the courage to ask him why he would say no. He explained, "God has a purpose for you, so you must have a purpose for you. That purpose is your goal for going anywhere or doing anything." After that speech he would always say, "*Shoot for the universe, because if you ever miss you will be among the stars. You serve a big God and that is his purpose for you!*" Reflecting on these words, my dad was telling me to have those awe-inspiring ideas mentioned earlier, and we will discuss in more detail later. Imagine a teenager hearing those words. My dad was a Southern gentleman with a third-grade education, but he instilled in me to set goals to be a man of integrity, honesty, character, and spirit. These are the most important goals any human being can set for himself and others. In fact, without these life goals, business goal setting becomes a futile exercise.

Business Goal Setting

One of my favorite readings is a book titled *Glorious Accidents—How Everyday Americans Create Thriving Companies*. Michael J. Glauser, PhD, is the author, whom I had the pleasure meeting at an International Who's Who Congress in Orlando, Florida. As he states, accidents happen, and "glorious accidents" are created! I love the book because it shows how everyday Americans used their ideas to create organizations that have succeeded beyond their wildest imaginations. In every instance I saw street hustling qualities transformed into strategic hustling ones. The process is not always well planned, but it isn't random either. After interviewing dozens of business founders from New York to California, Dr. Glauser identifies ten keys successful entrepreneurs use to build thriving companies. The leadership/management practices of these successful entrepreneurs are examples of **A.G.I.L.E. L.E.A.D.E.R.S.H.I.P. with a G.R.I.P.**. These keys are going to be rephrased as "*Strategic hustler*™ Goals to Success" in this chapter. Recalling Dr. Welch's statement on growing. The first six (6) goals: know the terrain, seize the opportunity, find a mentor, radiate zeal, work with tenacity, and give mind-boggling service, focus on growing yourself. The final four (4) goals: build a powerful team, get more from less, notch it upward and onward, and passionately give back to your community focus on growing others. The more these goals are present in a business and life, the greater the probability of success. Let's look at these goals in more detail.

Goal 1: Know the terrain

A *hustler* is an enterprising person determined to succeed. Thus you have to: 1) have a passion for making money; 2) accept the consequences of your actions; 3) act today and think tomorrow (*Strategic hustler*™ *behaviors*); and 4) know where the opportunity and danger lie, as well as the terrain. There were various avenues to make money in my neighborhood; recall I lived in a red zone, but I choose to shine shoes and work in a grocery store. If I wanted repeat customers, the shine had to be great in their eyes, so I worked on my technique. I knew the streets. I found a market, downtown New Haven and the Yale University campus, with customers who would pay for a shoeshine. It was a cinch—and it was *safe*! My dad was a gun inspector and barber. In fact, I was getting fades at the age of five, so he taught me this skill. It served me well in college, allowing me to be the personal barber for the entire basketball team, coaching staff, and various students on campus. As a college graduate, I hustled making money modeling men's lingerie; selling Amway; and managing multi-dwelling housing properties.

My leadership roles for major software companies and major consultancies required turning an idea into a profitable business through intelligent risk taking and innovation. For example, as the principal consultant/engagement manager for Sterling Software, the eighth largest software company in the world, executive management selected me from a global pool to present at the company's international user conference. They entrusted me to deliver the company's inaugural speech introducing conference attendees, a global audience, to Sterling's new data warehousing product/service offering. My experience working as a data warehousing architect for USAIR, The Coca Cola Company, and McDonald's prepared me to deliver the presentation, *"Introduction to Data warehousing,"* detailing how repurposing proven technology would add value to their bottom line. This contribution helped Sterling exceed revenue projections, almost doubling the number in a shorter period of time! My efforts were rewarded with: nominations for membership to International Who's Who of Professionals and as one of the top five IS project managers in North America; and a promotion to acting global practice director. *Street hustler* trust contributed immensely to the effectiveness of the company's marketing effort. How? You will learn how later when I cover integrity.

When reflecting back on successes in each of these ventures, the entrepreneurs started by knowing and understanding the industry or knowing the terrain. According to Dr. Glauser, the entrepreneurs he interviewed were already heavily involved in the industry or marketplace in which they started their business. Most worked for another company in the same industry; some were serious and frequent consumers of the products or services. Being in the industry not only sharpens future entrepreneurs' abilities and willingness, but also exposes them to the products, services, mentors, customers, networks, opportunities, sources of distribution, major players, strengths and weaknesses of competitors, and so forth. I call this "putting on your armor." The fact is that you can't create a successful enterprise in a vacuum. I have never met an entrepreneur who quit a job, refused to work for someone else, and sat around trying to think up something to do. While it may happen, it doesn't happen very often. To the contrary, many of these entrepreneurs were just like me—extremely successful in their jobs, well-liked by their companies, and highly regarded in the industry. Being in the thick of the action gave them ideas to contemplate and test while still drawing a paycheck. The higher level of knowing revealed the missing pieces that led to the ideas that led to new enterprise.

Goal 2: Seize the opportunity

As a captain of the football and track teams my senior year in high school, I recall a few of the words written on an award nomination form completed by my coach, Dan Casey: "stingy defensive back" and "never reached potential as an offensive halfback" jump out at me. Generally, excuses are unacceptable, but this time there were good reasons—Gerald Smith and Kenny Gaither. They were awesome players and teammates. For two years I was the second option to Gerald, an upperclassman, and Kenny, a classmate. Gerald was voted a starter in the Connecticut high school all-star game, called the Nutmeg Bowl. He was the Player of the Week, First Team All-District, Honorable Mention (HM) All-State, and HM All-American. He received a football scholarship to Syracuse University. This same school produced such greats as Jimmy Brown, Ernie Davis, and Floyd Little. During our senior year Kenny duplicated Gerald's success and received a scholarship to West Point. However, I never lost confidence, seizing every opportunity given to me to perform on the field—*remember, I was taught to be a leader.* Being adaptable, my laser like focus was on becoming the best football player possible. As a junior, my performance earned me HM All-District and HM All-State as a defensive back, along with Most Improved Player for my all-around performance as an offensive, defensive, and special team player. My senior year, despite having a losing season, I received most of the same honors as Kenny in addition to being ranked in the top 4 percent of my senior class. I also excelled as a track hurdler. The most humbling honors were being named HM All-State and HM Prep All-American, crowned with being named my high school's Athlete of the Year.

I was recruited to play Division One level football at Purdue University, Yale, Harvard, Princeton, West Point, and University of Connecticut (UCONN), to name a few. Purdue, West Point, and UCONN offered me scholarships—that were not requiring attending prep school. I initially committed to Purdue but *puppy-love;* if you don't know what this means you better go ask somebody; caused me to attend Virginia State College (VSC)—who never recruited me. VSC was a well-known prestigious historically black college/university (HBCU) that played Division Two level football. The difference between Division One and Division Two college football did not matter to me. My talent was second to none and when given the opportunity my performance would do my talking for me. This self-confidence lit a determined fire in me to become: (1) a scholarship walk-on, (2) a starter, (3) an all-American, and (4) a professional football player in the National Football League (NFL). Lofty goals for a walk-on player, but remembering my dad's shoot for the universe lecture gave me courage. Therefore, I seized the opportunity to shine making plays proving my value to the team. As a red-shirt freshman, my performance during the annual Blue and Orange spring football game earned me Most Improved Player and one of the Outstanding Player recognitions. More importantly, I was awarded a full football scholarship. Because I seized the opportunity, the scholarship goal was achieved! I eventually worked my way into the playing rotation until another opportunity surfaced. *Note: At the time it was a perceived as a big problem; keep on reading and you will see in a few sentences why it is called an opportunity.*

As the oldest dependable son, I was the "guardian angel" of my younger brother and sister. You have probably heard the saying, "Out of sight; out of mind." Well in my absence they seemed to forget everything taught to them about street life and were having problems back in New Haven. The bottom line was they needed my help. After three productive semesters as a Dean's List student, my GPA was 3.49, in the business information systems program;

it was time to transfer from Virginia State College. Where? I did not know but my baby brother and sister were *my kids*; so letting them become victims to the streets was not an option. On the surface, my hard work academically and athletically seemed to be in vain. However, making and surviving this critical life decision would provide a very important lesson that has sustained me throughout my professional career and life. *Every problem is an opportunity for a solution.* A leader recognizes this and seizes it!

This decision allowed me to give my "good, better, best" attempt to save them. And thanks to my daddy; teamwork of high school administrators: football coach, guidance counselor, and principal; my efforts at James Hillhouse High School and Virginia State were *not* in vain. They helped me enroll in the University of New Haven (UNH) without having to sit out a semester. Because of my willingness to save somebody; God saved me! *He* gave me another university to continue to seize the opportunities and to continue to give *him* glory! Allow me to share with you what happens when you constantly focus on seizing the opportunity by putting God first; keeping your eye on the prize; and refusing to give up!

The first adjustment was to adapt to the environment. Virginia State College (now Virginia State University) with its HBCU roots had a predominately black student and teacher population; this differed in that UNH was a private institution with a predominately white student and teacher population from over twenty-five countries! Coming back to "my hood," I got caught up in the minutia and lifestyle adjustments had to be made. It took me three semesters to regain my laser like focus. The determination to succeed was fueled by my desire to be a leader! My new major, computer technology with a minor in industrial engineering, required attending the School of Engineering. When attending Virginia State, a degree in business information systems required attending the School of Business. The coursework at UNH required a paradigm shift. I recall my Asian physics professor scolding me because he did not appreciate my line of questioning during an office visit. My determination to succeed stood out among 110 students in the class when I got the highest grade of 98 on the final exam!

Graduating cum laude from UNH earned me the distinction of being the first African American to earn a degree in computer technology from its nationally accredited engineering program. The fact that it was done with honors can be attributed to my goal to be excellent! As an athlete, I earned varsity letters in football and basketball. As a junior football player, leading the junior varsity and varsity in almost every statistical rushing category, after having my sophomore year end due to a knee injury, brought me Most Improved Player and Outstanding Offensive Back honors. An off-season knee injury going into my senior year required me to go through an aggressive rehabilitation program to be ready for summer camp. Thanks to my head coach and the team trainer, I reported to summer camp ready to compete for the starting running back position. My abilities, determination, and discipline allowed me to outperform bigger and more highly touted running backs to win the starting job. However, my goal to lead my team to its first winning season in the school's history was derailed, as the knee could not handle the rigor of practice and games. With a 4-0 won-lost record, I was forced to become a spectator, unable to participate and enjoy the game that gave me so much. I watched my team complete the first winning season in UNH's history and some of the greatest players and coaches in the world go on to have successful careers in the National Football League (NFL).

As for basketball, I was given the opportunity to be the official NCAA statistician and scorekeeper for the varsity team. I also accepted the challenge of being an assistant to the sports information director to lead a campaign to get UNH's star player, James "Jimmy" Allen, selected as an All-American. I was awarded a varsity letter in basketball for my contributions. In fact, Jimmy not only was named UNH's second basketball All-American, he also became the first and only NBA draft choice in UNH's history when the Boston Celtics selected him in the fifth round.

My crowning achievement at UNH was being named to *Who's Who among Students in American Universities and Colleges*. I was the pride of the school and my community, especially Dan Casey (head football coach), Red Verderame (principal), and Jack Garrity (counselor) — these were the gentleman from my high school who got me into UNH. Because they never gave up on me; I will never give up on myself or anybody else.

My football aspirations focused on an NFL tryout with the New England Patriots. When that failed, later you'll learn what failure really means, I coached at-risk youths in the tough Newhallville community of New Haven. These kids were diamonds in the rough and reminded me of myself at their ages. My baby brother was a star player on the team. A couple of former NFL players and college all-stars asked me to join the coaching staff; I was honored. What started as "something to do" turned into a twenty-two-year passion—starting in Connecticut and ending in Georgia. This passion made me forget about my dreams of playing in the NFL. There was something much more important. A coaching colleague brought this to my attention when a disagreement with the one of the head coaches of the teams I was working with caused me to think about quitting. He said, "You have an awesome gift that these kids respond to; they want to play *hard* for you; you push them to do things they never thought they could do." Wow, talkin' 'bout some epic words! I give God all the glory, for *he* allowed me to use my knowledge, wisdom, and understanding to teach and inspire these kids. Over the years, I have been blessed to witness the successes of these young men who were once labeled "at risk." It pains me to even think about how different our lives—the kids and mine–would be if I had quit on them. Van Spruill's coaching and mentoring gave the world many young people who were coachable—including me. They have all become leaders. To this day, I am truly humbled, like Van, for the leaders I've had an infinitesimal part in grooming! Their growth was bigger than me—"bigger than me"—this is a concept that will be developed later.

My ability to seize the opportunity learned in sports transitioned into my professional career. *Note: During the course of this book, I will refer to this list in bringing to life the points you need to understand. These opportunities included:*

- As vice-president level business process strategist, lead business transformation consultant for BBVA Compass Bank, mentored and contributed to an internal consulting team working collaboratively across the bank to design and implement end-to-end processes improving customer experiences and back office operations projected to reduce the bank's risk exposure by ten if not hundreds of millions of dollars

- As director of commerce and information technology/acting chief information officer (CIO), created from the ground up best-in-class departments for information technology and supply chain management/procurement for well-funded biotech startups Sriya Innovations, Inc., and Sriya Green Materials, the former now called Rematrix, Inc—process and technology improvements resulting in savings in excess of $3 million

- As the deputy chief information officer (DCIO) for the city of Atlanta, leveraging previous successes, effectively turned around a faltering division with a multimillion-dollar operating budget and project budget to deliver key process improvement projects and deliver a process excellence program with projected savings of $50 million to $60 million over a five-year period and increased revenues of over $100 million

- As turnaround specialist, executive program/project management consultant-coach and technology trainer championed business modernization and process improvement projects with combined budgets of over $4.5 billion to deliver combined savings and revenues in excess of $10 billion for foreign/domestic governments and Fortune 50/100/500/1000 companies—recognized as a "great" or "excellent" instructor/mentor/executive consultant by students/protégées/clients

- Led a virtual team of quality assurance professionals based in Hong Kong, Pakistan, South Africa, India, Canada, and the United States of America for the largest project management organization in the world—PMI (Project Management Institute), delivering a standard organizational project management maturity model globally-recognized as the most effective tool to help enhancement of organizational competence

- As founder and program advisor, created a unique computer literacy program for ages seven to seventy, training more than four hundred students and resulting in receiving "CompuKamp™ Day" proclamations from the mayor of Atlanta, the governor of the State of Georgia along with a special letter of recognition from President Bill Clinton
- As founder/CEO/president, started Intelligent Systems Services Corporation and created one of the personal-computer industry's first construction management software systems for small to midsize contractors, selling it for a multimillion-dollar price tag
- As principal consultant/engagement manager for Sterling Software, the eighth largest software company in the world and the leading CASE tool vendor ignited a new division startup to achieve record-breaking revenue performance—lead contributing author on executive briefings in the areas of *Business Modeling* and *Risks in Selecting Third Party Software*, published in the United Kingdom and distributed globally
- As lead data warehouse consultant for the Coca-Cola Company and McDonald's Corporation, led data modeling projects for business intelligence solutions to track performance in sales, franchising, and real estate
- As the youngest member (age 28) from the State of Connecticut serving as a State Advisor to the United States Congressional Advisory Board was recognized by late Congressman and former American Football League star quarterback Jack Kemp for my contributions in the areas of military, education, and social reform
- As programmer/analyst intern for E.I. DuPont, developed critical software solutions for the company's first international transportation management information system
- As long-range planning engineer intern for Southern New England Telephone Company, designed and coded the first computer program to conduct engineering economy analysis determining the loop electronic costs of copper vs. fiber optics
- As VP of research and development for CATT, Inc., a startup company, delivered the first PC-based human resource product demonstration for the Wall Street Training Group, resulting in training and consulting engagements
- As senior project manager/business-to-business (B2B) XML standards evangelist for eXcelon Corporation, selected to deliver inaugural B2B standards presentation at first IBM WebSphere Advisor Developers Conference

- As senior programmer/analyst–engineer for Sikorsky Aircraft Division of United Technologies, design and coded the first interactive mass property system and electronic planning and tooling computer software systems in the helicopter industry
- As programmer/analyst for General Electric, designed and coded the first online sales and marketing reporting software system for the Housewares and Audio Business Division and received nomination for GE's Financial Management Program

These experiences show failures can lead to successes—only when you have the courage to seize opportunities with persistence and perseverance. From a business perspective, *Strategic hustlers*™ lock on to a true business opportunity, and then take action. A legitimate opportunity includes:

1. An idea for meeting or better meeting a need
2. A uniquely credible position in the industry
3. Access to the resources required to implement the concept
4. A handful of customers who are ready to buy the product or service right now

To quote the words of my Harvard PhD marketing professor:

1. Find a need
2. Fulfill the need
3. Provide a service
4. And a guarantee

This is *"Marketing 101."* Naively, many aspiring leaders believe that the idea component (Find a need) is everything, and that once you have it, anyone can do the rest. While this may have been the case in past decades, today's swirling economy requires superb execution—components 2 through 4. Being intimately involved in the industry—*said another way,* "*knowing the terrain*"—dramatically enhances the odds that all four components will align themselves at some point in time. And when they do, the entrepreneur-to-be must have the courage to take the risk and face the challenge—be determined to succeed, get your hustle on! Actually, stepping up to the challenge is much less risky when these four components are present in sufficient strength. When many effective leaders launched their ventures, they were amply equipped with knowledge, skills, experience, resources, contacts, and built-in customers—the key elements of a true business opportunity! However, you will need someone to be your guiding light in the midst of the storm. You will need a mentor.

Goal 3: Find a mentor

Van Spruill was my mentor during my childhood years. He kept me from being a victim of a troubled neighborhood and a troubled household. He reinforced the lessons my dad was trying to instill in me. I had a few role models who looked after me, but Van made their job a lot easier.

Note: I did not know the word "mentor" existed until I graduated from college.

I would not have enjoyed the success in corporate America and as an entrepreneur without a mentor. I have been blessed to have worked with some of the sharpest minds in the business world. As we journey through this book, you will learn how they blessed me. They saw the zeal—remember that word—and energized me with ever-greater challenges.

During the process of formulating an opportunity, I needed support from a significant character—it could have been a parent, spouse, sibling, customer, friend, professor, or boss. In retrospect, that person had to have the credibility to endorse the notion and champion the plunge. To launch my ventures, I needed and received serious encouragement, seed money, a first contract, free consulting, feedback on ideas, introductions to vital contacts, ongoing financial support, and so on. The encouraging mentor was a luminous ray in a murky tunnel of snarl-faced naysayers. You need encouragement because you will face very discouraging times. Spiritually, my faith was grounded in these biblical verses:

- Romans 8:28: "All things work for good to those who love the Lord and are called to his purpose"
- Romans 8:31: "If God be for you, who can be against you"
- Romans 8:37: "Nay, in all these things we are more than conquerors through him that loved us"

The bottom line: seeking an encouraging mentor will prevent you from letting naysayers steal your dreams.

Goal 4: Radiate zeal

Good teachers, when they want to talk about a subject, make sure you have an understanding of the word(s) they emphasize. This is especially true when a word is used in a variety of contexts. This brings the discussion to the word "zeal." The dictionary defines zeal as "eager and ardent out of trouble, barbering, modeling, and selling anything people would buy. The money was interest in the pursuit of something." Its synonyms are *fervor, enthusiasm,* and *passion.* When I meet or watch an effective leader their zeal radiates like a bright sunny day. Zeal is contagious, like the emotional human wave at a football game. One section starts and before you know it, you have hundreds of thousands of people engaged. Zeal draws people to the idea; it attracts members to the team; it entices customers to buy; it enables an average bunch of folks to beat the more talented teams. Zeal is captivating, infectious, and powerful! I have never seen a new venture get off the ground without a hearty dose of zeal.

The key to success is that you must love what you are selling. A love for the product or service is definitely the source of zeal for many leaders. However, the zeal can be for independence, excellence, accomplishment, and success— not the products or services involved. In my case, I never experienced a pounding pulse to go to Nigeria to become one of its most respected contractors and investors, but I did have a longing to create an excellent company that could contribute to the well-being of a third-world country. So zeal definitely needs to be there; when it's not, fledgling entrepreneurs will not have the energy to make it up the steep hills. People who are naturally pessimistic, overly cautious, excessively critical, or unduly obsessed with the numbers can never generate the power necessary to make anything new happen.

Goal 5: Work with tenacity

Another way to express this goal is with the phrase "Get your hustle on." Earlier you learned a *hustler* is an enterprising person determined to succeed. Two kinds of hustlers exist—*Street hustler* and *Strategic hustler*™. The commonality between both types of hustlers is they work with tenacity and are smooth-talking gamblers. Let me explain the difference. *Street hustlers* look for immediate monetary gratification. Their behaviors fuel short-term growth but hinder long-term opportunities. A thin line exists between a *Street hustler*'s ways and means to being perceived socially *acceptable* and being socially *unacceptable.* For example, my socially *acceptable street hustling* consisted of shining shoes, shoveling snow, delivering newspapers, baby-sitting, cutting hair, modeling men's lingerie, etc. Do you get my drift? At the other end of the continuum are the socially *unacceptable* behaviors a street hustler engages in—i.e. pimping, robbery, prostitution, drugs, illegal gambling, scams—etc. These activities if caught may result in mortuary, hospital, or prison. The word "if" appears because people can turn their life around for the good of humankind.

On the other hand, the *Strategic hustler*™ is a bridge builder who plans for both short-term and long-term growth. As for being a smooth-talking gambler, they are the "*calm in the center of storm*" and their gambling is "*intelligent risk taking.*" Immediate gratification doesn't come in the form of money but in terms of progress. Integrity, strategic attitude, strategic aptitude, and strategic altitude are the foundation to establishing a mission, goals, objectives, strategy, tactics based on socially acceptable values. The common denominators of both types of hustlers are they work with tenacity and display varying degrees of the behaviors comprising **A.G.I.L.E. L.E.A.D.E.R.S.H.I.P. with a G.R.I.P.**

My journey from street hustler to Strategic hustler™ required dealing with the ebb and flow of life—building my life muscle. My tenacity drove my laser-like focus on my strategic hustle—continuing my education by climbing the corporate ladder and going through formal education programs with the ultimate goal of running my own firm.

My first job out of college was with General Electric's Housewares and Audio Business Division working as a computer programmer. My manager quickly realized my work ethic and tenacity as tasks given to me were consistently completed ahead of schedule and according to specification. He recommended me for GE's prestigious Financial Management Program, which grooms recent college grads for GE leadership roles. However, my short-term goals pointed me in another direction prompting me to pursue an opportunity as a service consultant with a regional telephone company. As an intern I worked as a long-range planning engineer for them and thought this new role would be challenging. It was, in terms of public speaking, business etiquette, and dressing for success. Being in the right place at the right time, another opportunity was offered to me by Sikorsky Aircraft of United Technologies, the largest helicopter manufacturer in the world. I joined the Computer-Aided Design/Manufacturing (CAD/M) group as a junior programmer analyst-engineer.

Working with tenacity, I seized the opportunity to attend graduate school at the expense of my employers [Sikorsky Aircraft, Keane, and Pitney Bowes], who would pay for graduate tuition when the chosen field of study allowed the employee to bring additional value to the company and when the grade received per course was a B or higher. An opportunist for a challenge, I enrolled in the dual masters program at the UNH while working as a full-time employee with Sikorsky Aircraft. This marked another first in my career; being the only computer technology graduate accepted in this very demanding program. I recall my mentor and former professor with a PhD in industrial engineering from Carnegie Mellon stating if anybody could complete the program, he knew I would. He said, "Just take it one course at a time." This was truly a big deal.

Later we will talk about an integrity character trait of finishing strong. Just know that one of the topics covered will involve converting your task into actionable chunks. Tackling this dual-degree program required taking a *divide and conquer* approach. I use the word *tackling* because when reflecting on the effort required to complete this program it reminds me of the toughness needed for an 185 pound defensive back to tackle a 235 pound running back with sprinter speed—multiple times during a game. You win some battles and lose some battles but in the end you win more than you lose achieving the victory winning the war with excellence. A kid from an inner-city red zone was about to embark on a journey that unbeknownst to me would result in accomplishing one of the greatness things in my life.

Table 3.1 list the courses required to complete this dual-degree masters program.

Table 3.1 Dual-Masters Degree Course Requirements

Business Core Courses	Advanced Business Courses	Industrial Engineering Courses
• Macroeconomics Theory	• Managerial Accounting	• Queuing Theory • Linear Programming
• Microeconomics Theory	• Marketing Management	• Probability Theory • Advanced Statistics
• Finance	• Marketing Workshop	• Industrial Engineering Workshop
• Management	• Organizational Behavior	• Decision Analysis
• Marketing	• Product Management	• Quality Analysis
	• Strategic Management	• Human Engineering I
	• Marketing Research	• Systems Simulation
	• Data Information Systems	• Inventory Analysis
	• Forecasting	• Facilities Planning
	• Industrial Relations	• Work Analysis

My street smarts, book smarts, and athletic competitiveness made me an effective *Strategic hustler*™. They allowed me to maintain a B average in both and a high level of performance on-the-job.

My performance (work tenacity) earned me a promotion to senior programmer/analyst-engineer and global recognition as the CAD/M expert who developed the first systems to support helicopter development and testing in the world. Despite the efforts of a jealous team leader, my stellar performance overshadowed his attempts to hinder my growth and I was eventually promoted to project leader. However, this only happened because I had a mentor. Allow me to explain. My team leader verbally assaulted me publicly, with a profanity-laden outburst, because we disagreed on the approach to solve a very critical problem. This is when I discovered a solutions delivery approach called **P.R.O.G.R.E.S.S.** employed by a major American manufacturing conglomerate involved in aircraft, the space industry, both defense-oriented and commercial electronics, automotive and truck components, printing presses, valves and meters, and industrial automation. I will talk more about **P.R.O.G.R.E.S.S.** later. For now, I saw it as a more efficient way of solving the problem(s) not only technical but also business. Having a mentor proved beneficial as he coached me into controlling my feelings and negotiating a promotion to project leader a highly visible role to further demonstrate my work tenacity. Being a project leader allowed me to deliver software and industrial engineering solutions to increase productivity/revenue, save the company millions in rework costs, and improve customer service. The customer, in this case, was the US armed forces. Sikorsky was a great company, but my goal was to learn business applications of "information management and movement," not to retire with a gold watch for twenty years of service. The entrepreneurial blood was flowing through me. It was time to execute the next step in my career strategy. With the help of my mentor, I decided to acquire experience as an information technology consultant with my new employment alliance, Keane Consulting, a top-flight consulting company.

My tenacity as senior principal consultant for Keane Consulting landed me in leadership roles on mission-critical projects for such companies as GTE, City of Bridgeport, Blue Cross Blue Shield, and C.H. Dexter Corp. Working for John Keane, the founder, was truly a blessing, allowing me to learn the consulting business. Keane's "Six Principles of Productivity Management" is one of the hallmarks to my success. I repeatedly have applied the following principles to delivering projects to meet customer expectations, on time, and within budget:

1. Define the job in detail
2. Get the right people involved
3. Estimate time and costs
4. Deliver tangible deliverables in eighty hours or less (the eighty-hour rule)
5. Define a change procedure
6. Agree upon an acceptance criteria

John Keane provided me with socially acceptable lessons learned from the streets that projects don't fail, people do. So whether you are a *Street hustler* or *Strategic hustler*™, your success is determined on how effectively you *lead* and *manage* people. My career at Keane, though rewarding, was short lived. Traveling 90 percent of the time made it extremely challenging to deal with family issues and emergencies. My accomplishments at General Electric, Sikorsky Aircraft, and Keane served me well as I was recruited and hired away from Keane by Pitney Bowes Global Headquarters.

As lead systems analyst for Pitney Bowes, I led the design of complex software solutions to support corporate objectives. Being the youngest and one of the brightest; senior management assigned me project leadership roles helping to implement business solutions having budgets ranging from $250,000 to $50 million. The first project required leading a team of twenty-five in implementing an interim telemarketing system. This system received a nomination from the client for Pitney Bowes' "One Standard of Excellence" award. The team was pictured along with a front-page story in the company's newsletter. The second project required designing the company's first online sales and marketing reporting system, which happened to be the first system of its type in the world using IBM's database technology called DB2. After another success, senior management put me on a fast track to ascend to a corporate director position. They assigned me to another leadership role on a large technology transformation project that when completed would revolutionize the company's business model. However, during the final semester of graduate school, my zeal to climb the corporate ladder took a back seat to becoming an entrepreneur. I began moonlighting with a computer software startup that was pioneering a very unique product. The days were long, but the work prepared me for my next strategic move. What was it? Keep on reading and learning.

After five challenging years, my graduation day arrived. I became the first computer technology undergraduate to complete this dual masters program. My tenacity allowed me to maintain a combined GPA of 3.25 on a 4.0 scale in earning degrees in master of science (M.S.) in industrial engineering and master of business administration (M.B.A.) in marketing. At the age of twenty-eight, diligent preparation provided me with knowledge and courage to execute my next strategic move. Please understand that tenacity requires "doing something"! It means having the courage to decide and *take action.* My next move was not popular with certain people, but as stated earlier I became immune to peer pressure in high school. My strategic move required leaving Pitney Bowes and a fast-track career to senior executive, to join CATT Inc. (Computer-Assisted Training and Technology). This was the startup where I had been investing my time moonlighting. My performance led to being recruited and hired into the challenging role of chief software architect and project leader.

This role required leading and managing a team of software engineers building **IBIS (Interactive Business Information System)**, an expert system focused on helping executives run their small to medium sized businesses more effectively and efficiently—the first of its kind in the personal software computer industry. An expert system is a computer system that emulates the decision-making ability of a human expert. In today's world, **IBIS** would be called an **Enterprise Resource Planning (ERP)** system—we spoke of this earlier. My passion drove me to work long and exhaustive hours. Later I will talk about visioning and purposing. But for now, the vision of building a *"bleeding edge expert system"* integrating finance/accounting, manufacturing, sales and service, customer relationship management, for small to medium sized businesses was exciting. Having a minimal budget challenged me to do "more with less." The financial fortune that would be realized did not drive me. It was taking on the ever-greater challenge of building the world's first software application of this type. Rather than bailing out when times got tough, I did whatever it took to make the business work! Leveraging my athletic competitiveness, I discovered ways to go over mountains, under hurdles, and around roadblocks—taking *no* for an answer was not an option! Part of it was a passion for the business—the zeal! Another part was a strong belief in controlling my destiny. I survived the perils of the streets because of my courage to take control of my life. A former *Street hustler* turned *Strategic hustler*™. Controlling my destiny required taking full responsibility for my life, my business, and the consequences of my actions. I was a warrior who simply didn't play the blame game. This *"ain't no stoppin' me now"* attitude empowered me to act courageously, change courses, try again, whittle away, start something new, and relentlessly persist. This mindset is essential to being a *Strategic hustler*™ who conquers the rocky road of life and being an entrepreneur. The end result for me was building a world-class product and receiving a promotion to vice president of research and development.

People have a tendency to blame others for things that don't go right. I've witnessed this behavior internationally, in our education system, in corporate America, and in various levels of the United States government. Oh, by the way, I initially learned this behavior from the street. **Said another way, it's the same soup but a different bowl.** You've probably noticed the repeated use of the phrase, "**Said another way.**" Now you are introduced to another phrase, "**it's the same soup but a different bowl.**" They will be used repeatedly throughout the book. Keep on reading to learn more about their origin later when we talk about integrity.

I was, am, and will always be a hands-on person. My character does not allow me to be the all-too-frequent and halfhearted person who hopes of getting something going, letting others do the work, and then making money while lying on a beach. So if your objective in life is to pile up lots of money without doing much, you probably need to inherit it, marry it, or try your luck in Las Vegas. Tenacity is a goal to aim for if you want to produce results. Unbeknownst to me, these experiences where laying the foundation for **A.G.I.L.E. L.E.A.D.E.R.S.H.I.P. with a G.R.I.P.**

Goal 6: Give mind-boggling service

Recall my discussion on adaptable behavior. When asked during an interview, "What do you attribute your success to?" Three points came to mind:

1. My ability and willingness to deliver results that exceed expectations
2. My ability and willingness to reinvent myself
3. My ability and willingness to assimilate into the social culture of the organization

These comprise my "*trilogy of success*." It is a three-pronged attack plan to keep you relevant throughout your career. The first component deals with results. You absolutely have to deliver outstanding results and do it consistently. If you want to be taken seriously and gain credibility, you must deliver *solutions*! If you can't deliver, the conversation ends. The second component deals with improving your competencies and capabilities. That's really just managing your portfolio of skills, making sure you're committed to lifelong learning, and adding things to your skill set. Each year you have to add something to your game that's marketable. I will be giving ideas throughout this book. The third part is what I call behaviors. Organizations are social institutions. How do you interact with your boss? How do you interact with your colleagues? Do you make the workplace a better place to work? Do you add to the organization? I will elaborate more on the "reputation" that is built later when we talk about intelligent behavior and respecting diversity.

For now, having an entrepreneur state of mind embraces the trilogy of success, focusing you on giving mind-boggling service. Don't forget to include a good dosage of Marketing 101.

These tenets have to result in an elated customer. Over my thirty-year career, I've witnessed successful leaders/entrepreneurs realizing this and wanting desperately to stabilize their fragile new ventures. The actors in this drama go way beyond industry standards in serving customers. You'll see them offer stupendous support, astounding speed of delivery, unheard-of prices, money-back guarantees, lots of face-to-face interaction, and real insights into people's needs. These all contribute to seriously overshooting their customer's expectations. Hence, this is the reason for my first point. The customer-is-everything attitude is absolutely critical to the survival of any venture. It wins the accounts, produces important long-term relationships, and renders a splendid competitive advantage. Delivering beyond customers' expectations, creates loyalty, engages word-of-mouth marketing, and generates repeat customers. Winning companies promote loyalty programs to maintain their customer-focus and grow the business.

Goal 7: Build the team

As an athlete, you learn the value of being a great teammate and having great teammates. As a coach, you learn the value of building a team that gets the job done. Having been both, I confidently argue that successful leaders/entrepreneurs thrive on the experience of others. We all lack some of the deftness required to maneuver expanding enterprise, so enlisting cohorts to fill in the voids—and in some cases, straddle the chasm. You must be a super team builder who can quickly put the puzzle pieces in place. This means finding players with compensating talents, enthusiasm for teamwork, and fervor for the startup environment. Bringing in strong team members early, then sharing the credit and rewards is critical to getting new ventures over the inevitable humps of being an entrepreneur. Leaders who hold on to everything and try to do it all themselves usually sputter, and then tumble. Through teamwork a good leader delivers solutions through effective delegation. You will learn more about effective delegation in a later chapter. For now, here are my thoughts regarding teamwork.

As much as any team likes to measure itself by its best people, the truth is that the strength of the team is impacted by its weakest link. No matter how much people try to rationalize it, compensate for it, or hide it, a weak link will eventually come to light. One only needs to look at sporting events as each team tries to exploit the opposing team's weakness. This truism is a fact of life.

A mistake often made early in my career building a team was thinking that my personality and shared vision would inspire people to join the team. There were several reasons that fueled my belief. First, I see the potential for greatness in people—even if they don't see it themselves. My challenge is to inspire them to reach for that greatness. Second, my goal is to uplift as many people as possible. Contributing to another person's success inspires me. Third, because my vision and goals are worthwhile and beneficial. I sometimes naively assume that everyone will want to go along with me.

But just because I wanted to take everyone with me did not mean that it would always work out that way. My experiences in athletics, business, and community have proven that team building and teamwork are inseparable. When it comes to teamwork…

1. Not everyone will take the journey.

Some people don't want to go for personal reasons. For other people the issue is their attitude. They don't want to change, grow, or conquer new territory. They hold fast to the status quo. All you can do with people in this group is kindly thank them for their past contributions and move on.

2. Not everyone should take the journey.

Other people should not join a team because of their personal agenda. Where you're going isn't the right place for them. They have other plans. The best thing that you can do for people in this category is wish them well and, as far as you are able, help them on their way so that they achieve success in their venture.

3. Not everyone can take the journey.

For the third group of people, the issue is ability. They may not be capable of keeping pace with their teammates or helping the group get where it wants to go. How do you recognize people who fall into this category? Well, they are not very hard to identify. Often they:

- Can't keep pace with other team members
- Don't grow in their areas of responsibility
- Don't see the big picture
- Won't work on personal weaknesses
- Won't work with rest of the team
- Can't fulfill expectations for their areas

If you have people who display one or more of these characteristics, you need to acknowledge that they are weak links. If you have people on your team who are weak links, you really have only two choices: train them or trade them. Of course, your first priority should always be to try to train people who are having a hard time keeping up. Help can come in many forms: giving people books to read, sending them to conferences, giving them new challenges, or pairing them up with mentors. I believe that people often rise to your level of expectations. Give them hope and training, and they usually improve.

But what should you do if a team member continually fails to meet expectations, even after receiving training, encouragement, and opportunities to grow? This is usually the case when a person who has great technical skills finds himself, or herself, at a new level, where many or most duties revolve around managing people—not a technical skill. On rare occasions it may happen in reverse order—great people skills but poor technical skills. In either case this person has been promoted to their level of incompetence. This is known as the Peter Principle. Somebody who is a weak link on your team might be a superstar on another team. You need to give that person and opportunity to find his or her own level somewhere else.

If you are a team leader, you cannot avoid dealing with weak links. Team members who do not carry their own weight not only slow down the team, they impact your leadership. Take a look at some of the things that happen when a weak link remains on the team.

1. The stronger members identify the weak one.

A weak link cannot hide (except in a group of weak people). If you have strong people on your team, they always know who isn't performing up to the level of everyone else.

2. The stronger members have to help the weak one.

If your people must work together as a team in order to do their work, then they have only two choices when it comes to a weak teammate: They can ignore the person and allow the team to suffer, or they can help and make the team more successful. If they are team players, they will help.

3. The stronger members come to resent the weak one.

Whether strong team members help or not, the result will always be the same: resentment. No one likes to lose or fall behind because of the same person.

4. The stronger members become less effective.

When you're carrying someone else's load in addition to your own, it compromises your performance. To endure inadequate performance for an extended period will ultimately make the whole team suffer. A weak link always eventually robs the team of momentum and potential.

5. The stronger members question the leader's ability.

Finally, any time the leader allows a weak link to remain a part of the team, the team members forced to compensate for the weak person begin to doubt the leader's courage and discernment. You lose the respect of the best when you don't deal properly with the worst.

If your team has a weak link that can't or won't rise to the level of the team—and you have done everything you can to help the person improve— then you have got to take action. To take the advice of a former *Street hustler* colleague, be clear, be honest, and be brief. Then, once the person is gone, be open about your decision with the rest of the team and maintain full respect for the person who moved on. It is normal to have compassion for others as human beings, and therefore you may have second thoughts before or afterwards. Remember this: as long as a weak link is part of the team, everyone else on the team will suffer.

Goal 8: Get more from less

Effectiveness is achieving your goals; efficiency is doing it with as few resources as possible. When delivering technical training on how to design/architect effective and efficient computer software applications, I would quote Ludwig Mies van der Rohe, a German-American architect. He sought a rational approach that would guide the creative process of architectural design and was known for his use of the aphorism *"less is more."* I learned to be a master of efficiency. Earlier I mentioned establishing the IT department for a well-funded biotech startup. What I purposely did not mention was this was accomplished with a minuscule IT budget. It required me to create something from practically nothing, getting more out of less along the way and keeping costs beneath industry levels. Contrary to popular belief, many of the entrepreneurs I've met are not lavish risk takers—very few of them bet the farm in the beginning.

Instead, they use an abundance of assets other than money to get started: they fiddle with ideas while they're still getting paid, enlist others who are also willing to fiddle, work on old desks in basements, partner up with their first customers and use someone else's plant rather than building one. Consequently, the capital meter doesn't tick very long before revenue is generated, which greatly increases the chance of financial success.

Not only do entrepreneurs keep startup costs down, but they also orchestrate remarkable efficiencies during the stages of business growth—the lessons learned in early bootstrapping apparently carry over. Throughout the stories, these folks defer salary, work extra hours, hire one person when two are needed, stretch cash flow, lease rather than buy, incur new costs only after increasing revenues, and build with cash flow. This keen eye for getting more from less has enormous competitive advantages with the big boys, often fat with corporate and industry tradition. It yields lower costs, better prices, superior products, and finer services that many better-established companies can provided. While we must give our entrepreneurs some credit for this genius, having any money goes a long way toward sharpening this skill. Those who have cash spend it; those who don't, learn to finagle without it. It's difficult to fully comprehend this mind-set of getting more from less without wearing the entrepreneurial moccasins. Those steeped in traditional corporate life may never fathom the multitude of ways to solve problems and generate big-time results with small means.

Goal 9: Notch it upward and onward

The one word that brings home this goal is transformation. In today's bumpy environment, a leader must be able to adjust and move forward. Here's what happens repeatedly. First, small and attainable goals are set. Second, a simple plan is devised for accomplishing the goal. Third, the plan is executed with zeal and tenacity. And fourth, the objective is achieved and the thrill of success is enjoyed. This process provides experience, new contacts, increased confidence, and energy to tackle something a little more challenging. Now the cycle begins again, as the same sound principles are applied at a higher level: objective, plan, work, and success. Effective leaders cycle through an upward spiral of incremental steps, each building upon the last; these propelling events thrust the leader forward following each success and as new opportunities arise.

The forward movement comes in two flavors. First, leaders continue to expand what they are already doing—*notching it upward.* And second, they extend into new products and services outside the business—*notching it onward.* I transformed my company, Intelligent Systems Services, from a software company, to a consulting company, to a training company. In short order, notching it onward means positioning yourself to take advantage of new opportunities. This ability to alter the very nature of the business is critical for long-term survival in today's economy. Personally you must be able to re-invent yourself. We mentioned this earlier but it warrants more discussion in later chapters. But for now it's really the practice of quickly shifting resources to new and more fruitful opportunities over time. Aggressive leaders who constantly monitor their customer's changing needs stay attuned to *notching it upward* and *notching it onward*. Companies and individuals who fail to make this transformation are doomed to failure. Blockbuster and Starbucks are a couple of examples. Blockbuster and Starbucks have rapidly lost market share to Netflix and McDonald's, respectively.

Goal 10: Give something back

I earned my doctorate from Columbia Commonwealth University, whose motto was "Mind, Body, Spirit, and Community." The school's focus was on producing scholar-practitioners who would benefit their communities. My purpose in life is to enjoy every moment of helping to uplift society. This book is one of the byproducts to fulfilling that purpose.

Because someone took time out of his or her busy schedule to invest in my growth, I am obligated to reciprocate and help as many people as humanly possible. Thus, I have to give something back to my community. Later we will look at the psychology of reciprocity when discussing one of the *six I's* of intelligent behavior—influence. But for now know that people like George Frazier, founder and CEO of FraserNet, Van Spruill, Owen Montague director of information technology for Atlanta Business League and others personally benefit because of their spirit of giving. I met George when he was working with Owen, who was then president of the Atlanta Exchange, Inc., to launch his *SuccessGuide* magazine in Atlanta, Georgia. Owen, a Wharton Business School graduate, asked me to pick George up from the airport. While driving from the airport George, a networking guru, engaged me in a friendly conversation. We shared information on our backgrounds, business and life goals then George spoke these epic words: "When it comes to the community, you have to be willing to give and give until it hurts." The "hurt" is not physical but speaks to the sacrifices that one feels obligated to make to uplift their fellow man. It has been over twenty years since hearing those words and they are just as true now as they were then.

I take pride in living my life under the motto "Pay it forward." Earlier I mentioned my high school experience working with kids to prepare them for the Connecticut Special Olympics. A record number of these athletes won a record number of medals. I not only taught these kids valuable lessons but they also taught me a very valuable lesson—*never give up!*

My many years of volunteer work with at-risk youth, Sunday school, computer literacy advisor and teacher, and various not-for- profit institutions are attributed to my never-ending thirst to give something back. Oh yeah, "until it hurts"; I've invested thousands of dollars of my own money along with thousands of hours of my time reaching back to uplift my fellow man.

Let me conclude *"giving something back"* provides a reason to contribute to something bigger than you. One only has to look at the many professional organizations in business and sports whose community outreach programs contribute resources—people, money, facilities, etc.—to benefit others less fortunate.

Summary

These ten goals fuel the goal-oriented behavior essential to having an innopreneur state of mind. For the remainder of this book when you see *Strategic hustler*™, think innopreneur, and these ten goals to success. The first six goals explain how leaders can *grow themselves* to be *the business*. The last four goals shed light on how the leaders grow their businesses over time by *growing others*. You must have a goal(s) to lead. Remember the following:

Leader of one; leader of many
If you can't lead one; you can't lead any.
—Unknown

Your behavior must be adaptable, goal-oriented, but you also need intelligence. The intelligent behavior embraces innovation, insight, initiative, influence, integrity, and interpersonal skills, the "six *Is*" of intelligent. In the next chapter you will learn about the Ⓘ in **A.G.Ⓘ.L.E. L.E.A.D.E.R.S.H.I.P.**

ⓘntelligent Behavior

Introduction

This chapter provides information to becoming a strategic thinker. For years, I have searched for literature to support how to transition from being a *Street hustler* to a *Strategic hustler™*. The information in this chapter was not learned in a classroom. It was learned through the school of hard knocks, a.k.a. life. I was introduced to a book entitled *Blue Ocean Strategy: How to Create Uncontested Market Space and Make the Competition Irrelevant* (W. Chan Kim and Renée Mauborgne, international strategy experts). Master barber extraordinaire/entrepreneur Mr. Wendell White introduced me to the book. For over seven years, Wendell has masterfully semi faded my balding head with the skill of a sharpshooter. Wendell's formal education credentials don't mirror mine; however, his book and street smarts were showcased as we engaged in many enlighten conversations about transitioning from *Street hustler* to *Strategic hustler™*. What impressed me about Wendell was his ability to open up barbershops with innovation, insight, initiative, and influential thinking grounded with integrity. A pioneer, Wendell introduced the marketing concept of "*5 Dollar*" to his reality when he founded the world's first "*Five Dollar Barbershop.*" But most importantly, Wendell is a people person, meaning he has excellent interpersonal skills. Thanks to my many conversations with my friend and barber, I've been able to compose the six *I*s of intelligent behavior. As Wendell was explaining his philosophy to me, he mentioned the book. He is a Blue Ocean strategist, and the book *Blue Ocean Strategy* has since been a valued addition to my library.

Before discussing these behaviors, let me define each in the context of this chapter. I will then proceed to talk about my experiences in each. The chapter will conclude with a challenged to you to "Dare to Be Different" as we discuss becoming a Blue Ocean strategist.

The 6 Is of Intelligent Behavior

Innovation is a change in the thought process for doing something, or the useful application of new inventions or discoveries. It may refer to incremental emergent or radical and revolutionary changes in thinking, products, processes, or organizations.

Insight is the act or result of understanding the inner nature of things or of seeing intuitively. It is an understanding based on identification of relationships and behaviors within a model, context, or scenario. An insight that manifests itself suddenly, such as understanding how to solve a difficult problem, is also known as an epiphany.

Initiative is a personal behavior. Initiative is the ability and tendency to initiate (to start) an action, including coming up with a proposal and giving or helping without first being requested to do so.

Influence is the ability of a person or group to produce effects indirectly by means of power based on wealth, high position, etc.

Interpersonal skills are how well you communicate with someone and how well you behave or carry yourself.

Integrity is more than an adherence to moral principles honesty. It's having the courage to face the demands of reality. I recall my dad always saying, "Your word is your bond. Say what you mean and mean what you say."

I have some wonderful things to share with you regarding each. Let's get started.

Innovation—The First I of Intelligent Behavior

Earlier I mentioned, "Leaders innovate; the manager administrates." Leaders aspire to be different. Let's return to my discussion on Blue Ocean strategy.

Blue Ocean strategy challenges leaders to break out of the red ocean of bloody competition by creating uncontested market space that makes the competition irrelevant. Instead of dividing up existing—and often shrinking—demand and benchmarking competitors, Blue Ocean strategy is about growing demand and breaking away from the competition. There are a set of analytical tools and frameworks enabling you to systematically act on this challenge, in addition, there are principles that dcfine and separate Blue Ocean strategy from competition-based strategic thought. This requires the ability and willingness to think outside of the box. I've witnessed *Strategic hustlers*™ execute this dare-to-be-different attitude for years—with success! Along with Wendell, here is a list of some of my favorites—Bill Gates, Dr. Yamile Jackson, Bernie Marcus, Jay-Z, Tracy Marrow (Ice T), James Todd Smith (LL Cool J), Curtis James Jackson III (Fifty Cent), Dana Elaine Owens (Queen Latifah), O'Shea Jackson (Ice Cube), Will Smith, Jada Pickett Smith, John Dutton, Captain Barrington Irving, Mary J. Blige, Marshall Bruce Mathers III (Eminem)—they all are, in their own unique ways, Blue Ocean strategists.

Many great professionals, or *Strategic hustlers*™, have delivered innovation to their respective areas because they dare to be different. I've been fortunate to work for top-tier IT consultancies during my career. As an MBA graduate, I took great interest in studying the growth of these companies. With an innopreneur state of mind mentality, I provided a service to these companies for a salary and benefits while learning how to grow my business. As mentioned earlier, I was learning the terrain. I have witnessed their growth and creative destruction. Keane was the first IT services firm I worked for as a senior technical consultant during the early 1980s. I then worked for CATT, Inc., as VP of research and development and project manager in the late 1980s. In the 1990s, I was employed by both KnowledgeWare as chief information engineer and Sterling Software as a global practice director. I also worked with Ernst & Young, IBM, and Deloitte Touché. The following pages provide some case studies in innovation from Keane, CATT, and Sterling Software, respectively.

Case Study Number 1: Keane, Inc. Innovation

Keane was founded in 1965 in Boston, Massachusetts. The company's initial focus was in the health care technology sector. The company grew to over one hundred employees within ten years. By the 1990s, Keane had become a publicly traded company and expanded into software engineering, application maintenance, program management, and consulting services.

In 2007, Caritor acquired Keane, Inc. The combined entity retained the name of Keane. The corporate headquarters was relocated to San Francisco, California and then to Boston, Massachusetts. As of this writing, the company has over twelve thousand employees in twelve countries. As I watched Keane grow through innovation, I chronicled some key dates:

Key Dates:

1965: John F. Keane founds his company to provide software services to businesses.

1970: Keane's company goes public.

1971: Keane develops a productivity management process to avoid project overruns.

1975: Keane establishes its Health Care Services Division under the name KeaMed Hospital Systems, to provide software services to hospitals and other health care facilities.

1986: After experiencing its first-ever quarterly loss, the company refocuses on its core business of delivering software services.

1987: Keane forms an educational alliance with Boston University and establishes an accelerated software development program for students there.

1988: Keane develops its Application Management Methodology (AMM), an application maintenance process that evolves into the company's Application Outsourcing solution.

1996: Keane begins offering Y2K solutions.

1997: Keane launches its first Advanced Development Center (ADC) in Halifax, Nova Scotia, to provide near-shore outsourcing.

1998: Company revenue surpasses $1 billion for the first time.

1999: Strategic acquisitions include Jamison/Gold in Los Angeles, Parallax Solutions Ltd. in the United Kingdom, and ANSTEC, Inc., in Washington, D.C.

2000: Keane consolidates its consulting subsidiaries and forms Keane Consulting Group; key acquisitions include Denver Management Group and Care Computer Systems.

2001: Keane acquires Metro Information Services, Inc.

2002: Keane acquires SignalTree Solutions Holding, Inc. and gains two ADCs in India.

2007: Keane is acquired by Caritor, retains Keane name.

Case Study Number 2: CATT's Innovation

Computer Assisted Training and Technology (CATT) was founded by Mr. James Jones and a couple of his ITT colleagues. James, a brilliant man, is a friend and my first mentor. My respect and love for him could fill the place where you are reading this book. I left a promising career at Pitney Bowes to work for CATT as VP of research and development and project manager. We were an innovative bunch of entrepreneurs. James was able to leverage training contracts to support the development and growth of the company. I learned how to develop computer-based training using a product called the Educator. James also introduced me to being a corporate trainer. To this day, I consider him one of the most brilliant men in the world. I've already spoken of his influence in chapter 3, "(G)oal-Oriented Behavior," but he was one of the first *Strategic hustlers*™ who showed me what it meant to be a family man!

While at CATT, in addition to bringing in training revenue, using artificial intelligence (AI) logic, I directed and managed the development of the world's first real-time PC-based business management and accounting expert system called **IBIS** (Interactive Business Information System). The system was targeted to small businesses. James and I were very innovative on how the product was designed and developed. I continued with this innovation in acquiring and developing a project team by working with the local colleges—Yale University,

Quinnipiac College, and the University of New Haven—to hire student interns. Included in this team was a programmer who attended Massachusetts Institute of Technology (MIT) and worked for me while in Switzerland. I also hired a young man, Mr. Robert Vaughn, who attended Winston-Salem State University and who went on to build his own multimillion-dollar consulting business.

Since we were using Microsoft products and stretching them to the limit, I recall talking with Bill Gates and other members of his staff to resolve issues with their Basic and Visual Basic products. IBIS used (AI) to increase the accuracy, productivity, and efficiency of business operations. It performed the same functions as systems costing thousands of dollars more without the complexity. IBIS received glowing reviews from independent auditors and Price Waterhouse. A colleague of James introduced him to the founding investors of Digital Equipment. The goal was to take us public. My sweat equity earned me $1,050,000 in stock.

They flew James to Rodeo Drive in California and met with him to develop a business plan. Once the business plan was complete, they came to New Haven to perform their due diligence. They flew in a British gentleman from Germany whose job was to uncover flaws in the IBIS software's technical design, adherence to Generally Accepted Accounting Principles, and ease of use. This person was a top-level software engineering expert for a company called SAP (System Analysis and Program Development). After two days, he finally let out a yell in his British accent, "By Jove, I think we've got it! This is a *splendid* piece of software!" These same sentiments were shared by independent auditors and Price Waterhouse.

Self-confidence through humility—we will talk more about this later—has been my hallmark in leading and/or managing a team—sports, business, or community related. Constructive feedback is always a good thing! Hearing world-renowned experts give such a glowing stamp of approval was the turning point in my entrepreneurial life! Whether this venture was a success or failure this experience proved invaluable. Keep on reading and learning how no one fails. They just discover ways that don't work!

Case Study Number 3: KnowledgeWare's Innovation

Acquired and absorbed by Sterling Software, Inc., in 1994, KnowledgeWare Inc. built its reputation as a leading developer of computer-aided software engineering, or CASE, tools. Much more complex than word processing programs, CASE systems are used by computer professionals for the development of applications ranging from payroll to financial management. CASE tools can also be used to customize, modify, or speed up existing programs. As a result, they can greatly increase the efficiency of computer systems and the profitability of the companies that use them. KnowledgeWare's Application Development Workbench (ADW) was used by over four thousand companies and became the industry standard. But what goes up will eventually come down. You have to continuously add value and demand excellence. We will talk more about this later. Nonetheless, after making a series of rapid acquisitions in an effort to regain its position, KnowledgeWare was left cash-strapped with sagging revenues, and Sterling Software then swallowed it up. For those of my readers who don't know how mergers and acquisitions (M&A) work, that was your 60-second lesson. Allow me to give you some background information.

James Martin, a software expert, founded KnowledgeWare in 1979. The company teamed with the accounting consultancy Ernst & Young to develop a product called Information Engineering Workbench, or IEW, that enabled programmers to quickly and easily build customized programs to handle a variety of specialized financial management tasks. Gradually the company built up a clientele.

During the 1980s, Minnesota Vikings quarterback Fran Tarkenton was wrapping up his distinguished career in professional football and beginning a new career as a public speaker. The articulate athlete began giving motivational speeches before employees of corporations, and his colorful and surprisingly effective message for building teamwork inspired greater enthusiasm and raised productivity. During his tours of the corporate circuit, Tarkenton discovered that many companies were crippled to a great extent by the inadequate state of their computer systems. This prompted him to hire a team of programming experts in order to market the additional services of management consulting and troubleshooting to companies with unstable or poorly managed computer systems. Tarkenton named his enterprise Tarkenton Software, Inc., and the new company soon began marketing a software development productivity tool.

To grow his company, Tarkenton merged his small enterprise with James Martin's KnowledgeWare, whose software "workbenches" were in great demand. The symbiotic relationship created by this strategic move proved to enhance his company's product because it could now provide the marketplace with a software product that streamlined the development of software applications. As a result, KnowledgeWare quickly established a powerful reputation in the industry. Large companies with thousands of employees and increasingly complex accounting needs found its software essential to maintaining financial order. Furthermore, they appreciated the flexibility of the programs, which could be tailored to the companies' own needs.

In the late 1980s, KnowledgeWare introduced its first desktop-based code generator, called IEW/Construction Workstation. The system enabled customers to analyze business requirements, design new applications, and write new code for mainframes, using only a personal computer.

As KnowledgeWare continued innovation of its product line, it drew hundreds of new clients. The company was the largest and fastest growing CASE company in the market, and IBM—which produced its own CASE programs—was determined to latch on to the company and ally its product line with KnowledgeWare. They made a multimillion-dollar investment in KnowledgeWare, which helped preserve IBM's position in the market.

With such a powerful vote of confidence, KnowledgeWare became popular on Wall Street. The company seized the opportunity by launching a public offering which generated over $15 million.

A month after IBM's investment in KnowledgeWare, the KnowledgeWare programs were incorporated into IBM's AD/Cycle mainframe CASE product. A few months later, KnowledgeWare introduced its Application Development Workbench, or ADW, program which garnered the Analysts Choice award from *PC Week* magazine. At the time, ADW was the only CASE system that was compatible with IBM's popular new OS/2 system. IBM customers who wanted to use ADW first had to upgrade their systems to OS/2, providing IBM with the increased sales it had projected.

In 1990, KnowledgeWare doubled its sales over the previous year with profits rising by 54 percent. On paper, IBM's investment in KnowledgeWare was a smashing success.

I am going to talk more about integrity later, but here is an example of what happens when there is a perception of a businessperson or business entity having no integrity. The company's smashing success came to an abrupt halt when internal conflict at the executive level, a strained partnership with IBM, failure to continue to innovate, and a lawsuit in which a Security Exchange Commission (SEC) ruling exonerated the executives from any wrongdoing proved to be a public relations disaster.

The bottom fell out in July 1994 when the company reported a third quarter loss of $25.8 million. In response, KnowledgeWare laid off 240 people—one quarter of its workforce—in a bid to lower expenses, I was one of them! In August, Sterling Software—a Dallas-based software company that managed data processing center operations and was successful in network management—offered $143 million to acquire KnowledgeWare, which would thereafter conduct business as Sterling. I watched KnowledgeWare's growth through innovation and demise through creative destruction. I've chronicled some key dates.

Key Dates:

1979: James Martin founds Database Design, Inc. (later renamed Knowledge-Ware).

1985: Fran Tarkenton's Tarkenton Software, Inc. merges with KnowledgeWare.

1988: KnowledgeWare introduces its IEW/Construction Workstation.

1989: IBM purchases an 8.7 percent stake in KnowledgeWare; KnowledgeWare launches its Application Development Workbench (ADW) program.

1994: Sterling Software, Inc. acquires KnowledgeWare.

Case Study Number 4: Sterling Software Innovation

Earlier I stated being one of the 240 employees laid off by KnowledgeWare. This was my first experience. Unlike most of my colleagues, who were disillusioned, my entrepreneur state of mind had me focusing on the next opportunity. God blessed me with the skills set, and within a month, my persistence and perseverance landed me a consulting contract with USAir in Crystal City, Virginia. An initial three-month contract turned into a fourteen-month assignment ending with the effective implementation of a Computer Aided Software Engineering (CASE) tool to streamline and improve the quality of developing mission-critical software applications. My tenacity allowed me to succeed where other consultancies failed.

In the meantime, Sterling Software made a strategic move to implement a consulting division to help their clients efficiently and effectively use its products. You see, one of the problems with KnowledgeWare was a communication disconnect between research and development, sales and marketing, and information technology. As a result, KnowledgeWare's internal IT department was not using the products being sold and used by over four thousand clients worldwide! This proved to be an opportunity for me. After a nationwide search, I was hired as KnowledgeWare's first and only chief information engineer to close this gap. I worked for Bill Wise, a Georgia Tech graduate, who was impressed with my ability and willingness to direct and manage the implementation of methodologies and tools in a practical and applicable way. He liked my understanding of managing the development of computer software application programs along with how KnowledgeWare tools could be efficiently used to increase productivity. I hit the ground running and within a short period of time had successfully trained the entire IT department. With the IT department skills level up and the adoption of new tools in use, my job was done and I moved on.

People always come into your **life** for a **reason**, a **season** and a **lifetime** (Ecclesiastes 3:1 to 8). My performance at KnowledgeWare remained in the minds of my colleagues who survived the rift. On a referral from a number of well-respected IT employees, Dr. Michael McCrimmon, the consulting services operations director contacted me. Honestly, being an independent management consultant was appealing to me, so I didn't jump at the opportunity to be rehired as an employee. But Dr. McCrimmon was persistent and the challenge of growing a world-class consultancy and working among the best CASE tool consultants in the world was appealing. I accepted an offer to join Sterling Software as a principal consultant in the Applications Development Group. It turned out to be one of the best strategic moves made during my career.

As principal consultant, I earned the reputation as being the go-to guy for solutions delivery worldwide. My *good-better-best* attitude drove me to be the only principal consultant who delivered services for Sterling Software's Application Development Group, Information Management Group, and Business Intelligence Group. From Canada to South Africa to Europe to Australia to Croatia to major markets in the United States, I was called to be the subject matter expert to turn-around faltering accounts, help develop training material, give insight into product presentations, and assist in writing white papers. I also received private lessons in leadership from Dr. McCrimmon that can be summarized as, "Let me do what I do so that you can do what you do." Dr. McCrimmon is an expert in relationship management whom I've benefited from tremendously in life. With proper mentoring and performance delivery, I earned a promotion to engagement manager and was assigned to Information Management Group reporting to Michael Robinson, another high-potential executive. Michael Robinson energized me with the ever-greater challenge of becoming a world-renowned global expert for Sterling. Mike recognized my entrepreneurial spirit and challenged me to leverage that to grow Sterling's business. It was up to me to find and exploit the opportunity.

Mike inspired me to identify and exploit revenue generating opportunities. I was in the right place at the right time as Sterling was introducing a new product and service offering to help their customers improve how they manage and move information. I convinced Sterling's marketing and consulting executives to allow me to develop and deliver the inaugural marketing presentation to a global audience who would attend Sterling's 1996 International User Conference. Before a standing-room-only audience of customers, vendors, resellers I delivered a well-received presentation laying the foundation for the newly formed Business Intelligence Group. This marketing presentation teamed with aggressive sales/consulting execution allowed the division to achieve record-breaking revenue performance. My efforts and accomplishments earned me: a.) a nomination and selection into International Who's Who of Professionals; b.) nomination and selection as finalist as a top five IS project manager in North America; c.) the distinction of being the only consultant named to Sterling's global top five billable *and* utilization consultants; and d.) the designation as acting global practice director. However, the results and the information provided during my annual performance review convinced me that my talents at Sterling Software could earn better compensation elsewhere.

Dr. McCrimmon and Mr. Robinson would eventually leave Sterling to pursue other opportunities. However, thanks to the mentoring and help of Larry Zoneshine, a Sterling vice president, I would eventually transition out of Sterling Software and sign a multiyear contract with the State of Georgia, serving as information engineer contributing and leading projects totaling over $100 million funded by the federal government. Contracts like this, along with selling of proprietary software, allowed Intelligent Systems Services Corp to attain revenues in excess of $2 million.

Innovation and Creativity

"It's not a single product model, nor a single manager, nor one ad, nor a single celebrity, not even a single innovation that's the key to Nike. It is the people of Nike, and their unique and creative way of working together".

– Phil Knight, chairman of the board, NIKE cofounder

If you work for NIKE, Inc., you will be changed forever. If that excites you, keep reading.

You will be changed because you will grow. You will grow because you will be challenged. You will be challenged because you will work with the best talent, the best athletes, and the best business partners in the industry. We set the bar high. And then we raise it higher. We believe smart, passionate, curious people will rise to the occasion.

The collective culture of NIKE, Inc. is dynamic. Whether you work for Nike, Converse, Hurley, Umbro, the Jordan Brand, Nike Golf, or Cole Haan, wherever you work around the globe, there is no finish line. We are rebels at heart, we are risk-takers, and we celebrate original thinking.

Does this sound like an environment where you would thrive?

I have long been an admirer of Mr. Knight and Nike. While other companies come and go, their staying power is the reason why he and his company are in this book. This quote epitomizes how important innovation and creativity are to the success of any effort. To be innovative you must be creative. Creativity is more about psychology than intellect, and there are no secrets to being creative. Actually, *there is no such thing as "being more creative"; you are already a creative being.* This is a lesson first learned from the streets.

I'm sure we can all relate to moments when we felt stuck trying to tap into our own creativity. Did you know that this block is merely your mind at work? Your mind is creating all sorts of assumptions, self-imposed constraints, and self-limiting inhibitions. I have found that we can remove these assumptions just by being in the moment—start doing and stop thinking. Stop over-thinking and just do it!

Here are seven habits found in highly innovative and creative people that I've organized and summarized from *The Myths of Innovation* (Berkun, 2007).

1. **Persistence**—Innovation involves more than just great ideas. We need faith, hard work, and a laser-sharp focus in order to persevere in the face of roadblocks. We tend to see the end result of a creative idea in awe, but what we don't see are the actions, hard work, and persistence behind the scene to make the vision a reality.

   "Invention is 1 percent inspiration, 99 percent perspiration."

   –Thomas A. Edison

2. **Remove Self-Limiting Inhibitions**—Under the spell of inhibition, we feel limited and stuck. We need to free ourselves from these mind-created constraints by removing assumptions and restrictions. This is what we refer to when we say, "Think outside the box." Encourage ourselves to be open to new ideas and solutions without setting limiting beliefs. Remember, innovation is more about psychology than intellect.

3. **Take Risks, Make Mistakes**—I believe that part of the reason why we create self-imposed inhibition is due to our fear of failure. Expect that some ideas will fail in the process of learning. Build prototypes often, test them out on people, gather feedback, and make incremental changes. Rather than treating the mistakes as failures, think of them as experiments. "Experiment is the expected failure to deliberately learn something" (Berkun, 2007). Instead of punishing yourself for the failures, accept them, then take your newfound knowledge and put it toward finding the best solution. Live up to your goal of producing the best result, but understand you might hit roadblocks along the way.

> *"I have not failed. I've just found ten thousand ways that won't work."*
> –Thomas A. Edison

4. **Escape**—Our environment can and does affect how we feel. The more relaxed and calm we are internally, the more receptive we are to tapping into our flowing creativity. This is why ideas sometimes come to us in the shower or while we're alone. Each of us has different triggers to access our creative energy. I get into the "creative zone" by going to the gym and riding the stationary bike. Many great thinkers go on long walks to help them solve problems. Experiment and find what works for you.

5. **Write Things Down**—there are three types of memory; short term, long term, and paper and pencil—with emphasis on paper and pencil. Many innovators and creative people keep a journal to jot down ideas and thoughts. Some keep a sketchbook, scrapbook, Post-It notes, and loose paper. They all have a method to capture their thoughts, to think on paper, to drop their inhibitions and start the creative process. Bill Gates purchased Leonardo da Vinci's famous notebook for $30.8 million.

6. **Find Patterns and Create Combinations**—Ideas come from other ideas. Did you know that Edison was not the first one who came up with the invention of the lightbulb? He was the first to build a workable carbon filament inside a glass bulb that made lightbulbs last longer. You can increase your exposure to new ideas, look for patterns, and see how you can combine ideas to improve upon existing solutions.

7. **Curiosity**—Many innovators are just curious people who are inquisitive, and like to *solve problems*. Practice *seeing things differently*. For example, when seeing the solution to a problem, ask yourself, "What are some alternative ways to doing this?" Ask a lot of questions and challenge the norms or existing methods.

The following are some techniques you can apply to cultivate creativity:

- **Keep a journal**—Practice writing every thought, idea, and inspiration down. Practice brainstorming and thinking on paper.
- **Solve the opposite problem**—The idea is to invent and brainstorm by solving the opposite problem to the one you are trying to solve. So, for example, if you are trying to create "the best laptop design," then start with ideas to create "the worst laptop design." For each idea you come up with, flip it. If "heavy and clunky" is one idea for "the worst laptop design," then flipping that might give me "light and sleek," which can be used in "the best laptop design." This technique works especially well when brainstorming in a group. The technique sounds so silly that people will become playful when answering. Humor brings down inhibition and encourages people to say things out aloud. People feel less insecure and more open.
- **Find a creative environment**—Find a relaxing or inspiring environment that triggers your creativity. Try different spots until you find some that really bring out the best in you. I alternate between my living room (which I have carefully decorated) and a couple of local coffee shops.
- **Do something fun**—If you're stuck on something, shift your thoughts by going to do something fun and completely different. Come back to it with a fresh mind.
- **Partner**—Find creative partnerships with another. New ideas can surface as a result of two forces that would not have been discovered by a single person. Brainstorm together.
- **Commit to failure**—Commit yourself to taking enough risks that you will fail some of the time. If you're not failing, you're not doing something sufficiently difficult or creative.
- **Talk to someone about it**—I have found that when I try to articulate a particular problem to someone, I'll somehow articulate my solution as well. When explaining my situation, I'm not expecting them to solve my problem, but rather act as a sounding board for ideas.
- **Plan for roadblocks**—Commit to efforts to overcome potential setbacks. It's worthwhile to identify and have a plan for noncreative items that may inhibit creative thinking. Scott talked about the most common roadblocks people face: lost motivation, ran out of money, unable to convince key person.

Creating a Culture of Innovation

My doctoral dissertation was entitled "Effective Leadership for Enterprise Commerce Management." Of the nine-hundred-plus respondents from various industries who completed the leadership behavior description questionnaire (LBDQ), they rated creativity as the most important leadership competency.

Eighty percent said the business environment is growing so complex that it literally demands new ways of thinking. Less than 50 percent said they believed their organizations were equipped to deal effectively with this rising complexity.

Are CEOs and senior leaders really willing to make the transformational moves necessary to foster cultures of real creativity and innovation?

Here are the six fundamental moves I believe they must make. In all my travels, I've not yet come across a single company that systematically does even the majority of them, much less every one.

1. **Meet people's needs**. Recognize that questioning the status quo—the key to creativity—begins with questioning the way people are expected to work. How well are their core needs—physical, emotional, mental, and spiritual—being met in the workplace? The more people are preoccupied by unmet needs, the less energy and engagement they bring to their work. Begin by asking employees, one at a time, what they need to perform at their best. Next, define what success looks like and hold people accountable to specific metrics, but as much as possible, let them design their days as they see fit to achieve those outcomes.

2. **Teach creativity systematically**. I believe leaders are born to be made. There are five well-defined, widely accepted stages of creative thinking: first insight, saturation, incubation, illumination, and verification. They don't always unfold predictably, but they do provide a roadmap for enlisting the whole brain, creating movement back and forth between analytic, deductive left-hemisphere thinking and more pattern-seeking, big- picture, right hemisphere thinking. The best description of these stages that I've come across is in Dr. Betty Edwards's book *Drawing on the Artist Within*. The best understanding of the role of the right hemisphere, and how to cultivate it, is in Dr. Edwards's first book, *Drawing on the Right Side of the Brain*.

3. **Nurture passion**. The quickest way to kill creativity is to put people in roles that don't excite their imagination. As you will learn later, you must energize people with ever-greater challenges. This begins at an early age. Kids who are encouraged to follow their passion develop better discipline, deeper knowledge, and are more persevering and more resilient in the face of setbacks. Look for small ways to give employees at

every level the opportunity and encouragement to follow their interests and express their unique talents.

4. **Make the work matter**. Human beings are meaning-making animals. Money pays the bills but it's a thin source of meaning. We feel better about ourselves when we we're making a positive contribution to something beyond ourselves. To feel truly motivated, we have to believe what we're doing really matters. When leaders can define a compelling mission that transcends each individual's self-interest, it's a source of fuel not just for higher performance, but also for thinking more creatively about how to overcome obstacles and generate new solutions.

5. **Provide the time**. Creative thinking requires relatively open-ended, uninterrupted time, free of pressure for immediate answers and instant solutions. Time is a scarce, overburdened commodity in organizations that live by the ethic of "more, bigger, and faster." Ironically, the best way to insure that innovation gets attention is to schedule sacred time for it, on a regular basis.

6. **Value renewal**. Human beings are not meant to operate continuously the way computers do. We are designed to expend energy for relatively short intervals—no more than ninety minutes—and then recover. The third stage of the creative process, incubation, occurs when we step away from a problem we are trying to solve and let our unconscious work on it. It's effective to go on a walk, listen to music, quiet the mind by meditating, or even take a drive. Movement—especially exercises that raise the heart rate—is another powerful way to induce the sort of shift in consciousness in which creative breakthroughs spontaneously arise.

These activities are only possible in a workplace that doesn't overvalue face time and undervalue the power of renewal.

Becoming a *Strategic hustler*™ requires being a strategic thinker focused on innovation. Innovation in an effective leader requires insight, initiative, influence, integrity, and interpersonal skills. Let's swim out to see what I have to say about being insightful.

Insightful – The Second I of Intelligent Behavior

Insight is the act or result of understanding the inner nature of things or of seeing intuitively. It is an understanding based on identification of relationships and behaviors within a model, context, or scenario. An insight that manifests itself suddenly, such as understanding how to solve a difficult problem, is also known as an epiphany. Call it an "aha" moment.

I have used the words *Street hustler* and *Strategic hustler*™. Why these terms? Growing up in the streets of New Haven, I witnessed people from the surrounding areas of Connecticut, including New York, New Jersey, Philadelphia, Washington, DC, Oakland California, and Massachusetts who would come to my neighborhood to conduct their business, or hustle, with no regard to the mind, body, spirit, or community. **Said another way**, these *Street hustler*s would burn bridges for immediate short-term gratification. The lack of insight contributed to the absence of foresight requiring continuously reinventing the wheel. Their success was short lived. As I matured and worked in corporate America, I saw the same behavior patterns. To quote a good friend whose occupation was food caterer, *"It's the same soup but a different bowl."* Intuitively, or insightfully, I could predict the likelihood of success of the corporation, program, project, or individual based on learned behavior and situational patterns.

On the other hand, *Strategic hustlers*™ channel their hustle based on long-term gratification. They engage in the daily grind of a hustler; however, there is a long-term vision. That vision has a mission, strategy, goal(s), objective(s), plan, and execution. Furthermore, the *Strategic hustler*™ understands the importance of being a bridge builder. Unlike the *Street hustler*, whose moves are just tactical moves, their moves are both tactical and strategic moves. The *Strategic hustler*™ has insight.

Without insight, the discussion on strategic success ends immediately. Recall the innovation discussion on Keane, KnowledgeWare, and Sterling Software, for they all have something in common. They were all acquired by an entity that realized a symbiotic relationship would exist from the acquisition. **That is,** the acquiring firm had insight that it would be mutually beneficial for all stakeholders affected by the acquisition. So you have Keane acquired by Caritor; KnowledgeWare acquired by Sterling Software; and Sterling Software acquired by Computer Associates. The results of mergers that took place because of these acquisitions demonstrate how critical insight is to making strategic moves. Let's dig a little deeper. Caritor, a global IT consulting and systems integration firm that delivers high-quality IT services to leading clients around the world, paid $854 million to acquire Keane. Keane shareholders received $14.30 per share in cash, 19 percent more than the value of the company's stock. The new company was expecting $1 billion in annual revenue.

Sterling Software, a Dallas-based software company that managed data processing center operations and was successful in network management, offered $143 million to acquire KnowledgeWare, which would thereafter conduct business as Sterling Software. After allocating millions for legal fees, and court costs which negatively impacted their revenue, Sterling successfully integrated KnowledgeWare into its growing roster of acquisition results. A Sterling spokesperson was quoted as saying, "We see tremendous opportunity for Sterling and predict excellent growth."

Computer Associates International, Inc. (CA), is one of the largest computer software vendors in the world. The company sells over 1,200 different products, most of which are designed for businesses rather than home computer users. Because the majority of its products are behind-the-scenes workhorses designed to help big computer networks function, CA's specialty is often called "plumbing" in the software industry. CA acquired Sterling Software in 2000 in a stock-for-stock transaction worth $3.3 billion. CA sold Sterling Software's Federal Systems Group to Northrop Grumman.

Allow me to share what insight has done for me during my career. I recall receiving nomination forms from International Who's Who of Professionals and International Biographe Centre (IBC). In my excitement, I shared my good fortune with a couple of close colleagues, one whom I will call Mr. LOI (Lack of Insight) because of his response: "Oh, I received the same nomination, but they wanted money, so I just passed." He never thought about the possibilities of being global under his own corporation. This did not deter me. I had the epiphany. I completed the applications, impressed during the interview, and was selected to both organizations. The fee, which was an investment, was minuscule compared to the exposure and business gained. One of my lessons learned from my athletic career is that to win a championship you have to be in a championship! To be in a championship you need insight to make the sacrifices, do the work, persevere, and take risks. *Said another way*, you must do now what others won't so that you can accomplish later what others can't. Finally, I was my high school Athlete of the Year; in my mind I was different. I was predestined, recalling Pastor D. E.'s sermon "Living Stones." *Recall,* the Book was written for me to be *great!*

As a humbled member of International Who's Who of Professionals and International Biographe Centre (IBC) in Cambridge England, I attended two congresses, or meetings, that oriented me to international business. My first international congress was sponsored by IBC in Portugal. The event was the Twenty-Sixth International Congress on Arts and Communication. Over 160 international Who's Who professionals and intellectuals from Europe, North and South America, Africa, and Asia were present in a gathering that may one day prove to be as important, or more important, to the advancement of humanity as the quantum leap invention of the wheel.

People of achievement (their biographies were astonishing) presented their views to open minds of their peers and colleagues in an atmosphere that drew on the legacy of illustrious past congresses and the fellowship built over the years among people from different cultures around the world who hold a committed resolve to focus on ways to benefit humanity, as well as their communities, their nations, and themselves.

As an ambassador representing the United States, this ten-day event had me thoroughly immersed networking and attending various plenary sessions. This involvement resulted in being selected by the North American (NA) delegation and the director general of IBC to speak on the behalf of the NA delegation in greeting our global peers during a gala affair held the last night of the congress. My seven minute speech concluded by reciting a poem entitled, "Live Your Creed." Upon completion, my eyes filled with tears when the audience honored me with a standing ovation. This poem was a dedication to my late daddy, who told me that one day things like this would happen to me when God remains first in my life. My networking allowed me to meet a Nigerian delegation whose members stated their country needed God-fearing engineers like me to help them out. Seizing the opportunity, I was the only engineer that attended this congress.

I also attended an International Who's Who of Professionals Congress in Orlando, Florida. The networking opportunities during this four-day global event allowed me to meet professionals, executives, and entrepreneurs from all walks of life. My interest peaked while attending a plenary session held by international investment bankers from Belgium, Portugal, Switzerland, Spain, and Bahamas. They invited me to become part of a very exclusive financial network.

Because of my insight to attend these international gatherings, doors opened to global investment and consulting opportunities in not only the places mentioned above but others including: Nigeria, Singapore, United Kingdom, Thailand, South Africa, Ghana, and Benin and a host of others.

To this point, you've learned that being a strategic thinker requires innovation and insight. You can be innovative and have insight but the key is to make strategic moves. The operative word is "moves." You have to do something. *Stated differently,* you have to seize the opportunity by taking the initiative to implement your strategy. Let's look at my views on taking initiative.

Initiative—The Third I of Intelligent Behavior

Revisiting the definition of initiative as a personal behavior, initiative is the ability and tendency to start an action, including coming up with a proposal, and giving or helping without first being requested to do so.

When I think of this behavior, a specific phrase comes to mind: "You gotta wanna or you ain't a gonna." It is not the kind of vernacular you would expect from a PhD, however, it is a phrase that the young and the mature, with a little help, can understand. In fact, it is a chapter in a book entitled *Goal Realization: The Project Management Objective,* written by James Jones, who owns a bachelor of science in operations management and master of science in computer science. He is a forty-year veteran of the IT industry; *Street hustler* turned *Strategic hustler*™ in his own right. James is a role model. I have known him and his family for over twenty-five years. His book is not on the best-sellers' list, but he is one of those unsung heroes that are comfortable with being unnoticed in life. He doesn't toot his own horn but humbly appreciates when others do it for him. The book was once prerequisite reading for James's custom project management course delivery to General Electric's staff. It contains gold nuggets for anyone aspirating to live a success-filled life. Personally, I think it is an excellent book for our youth because it provides them with life building and sustaining skills for success using language and examples they can understand! Remember life is a project.

As I read the book, especially this chapter, it got me to thinking of my rise from *Street hustler* to *Strategic hustler*™. How was I able to rise from my surroundings to where I am today and have the courage to write about it? When I think about my journey, others were exposed to the same opportunities I was. For some reason they chose not to pursue a better way.

I've learned people in general will go out of their way to help you when they see you have initiative. From Main Street to Wall Street, people appreciate a person with initiative. For example, during my initial months in Atlanta, I volunteered my company services to a small business incubator program called GRASP (**GR**eater **A**tlanta **S**mall Business **P**roject). The executive director was a gentleman by the name of Maurice Coakley. This exposure provided the opportunity to demonstrate my company's skills to GRASP clients, covering hardware and software selection, hardware builds, computer programming, and network solutions design and implementation. These efforts earned a Certificate of Merit from GRASP signed by former United Nations Ambassador and then City of Atlanta Mayor Andrew Young. It was nice to receive recognition for a job well done; however, the biggest payback was being selected from a statewide pool of small businesses to participate in a six-month program called "Market Smart!" This federally funded program was designed to provide training and assistance to small businesses, revenues of $1 million to $25 million, in writing an executable marketing plan. The beauty of the program was that each week a marketing professional would lecture and mentor about a specific aspect of marketing. There were twenty-five members in the first "Market Smart!" class. I was honored to be amongst such success. Notice I didn't say "business plan." To highlight my point let's look at the purpose of a marketing plan.

Purpose of a Marketing Plan

Imagine for a moment that the captain and crew of a 747 takeoff with a full load of passengers. After takeoff, they then ask themselves, "Where are we going," and "how do we get there, and how long will it take?" This situation is impossible to imagine. A modern airline would never allow such a thing to happen. If it did, the plane could easily run out of fuel before reaching its destination. It could fly at the wrong altitude and collide with a mountain, or fly directly into a storm which could have easily been avoided.

To avoid these kinds of problems, the captain is required to file a flight plan that will aid all persons concerned to insure that the plane arrives at its destination at the scheduled time. The plan must take into consideration the amount of fuel necessary, head winds, air traffic, and many other factors. It must also consider alternate routes and alternate destinations in the event an emergency occurs.

Marketing is like a successful airline flight. Both need the assistance of a plan. A marketing plan serves as a road map or guideline. The activities of every division and every person involved in any aspect of marketing are given direction through a marketing plan. A marketing plan enables an organization to establish objectives, priorities, schedules, budgets, strategies, and checkpoints to measure performance.

Any business especially needs to focus on creating a demand for its product or service. That is the business! No customers = no business; thus the program name "Market Smart!" was focused on just that, creating marketing demand. I had a number of ideas, but this program required me to write them down, so they now were goals. My marketing plan was complete, critiqued, and well received by my mentor. Having an MBA in marketing from a top-tier school gave me an edge on the formalities of marketing over my classmates. However, the degree just increased my understanding. It took initiative to create and execute the marketing plan that demonstrated I belonged in that first "Market Smart" class!

Earlier during our discussion of goal-oriented behavior, I provided examples of "seizing the opportunity." Consider each of those an example of what happens when you take the initiative. The takeaway, it takes initiative to seize the opportunity.

To this point you've learned that being a *Strategic hustler*™ with intelligence requires innovation, insight, and initiative. You can be innovative, have insight, and have the initiative to make strategic moves; however, as you learned in the previous chapter on adaptive behavior you must influence people to follow you. Simply put, you have to have followers to be a leader. Let's look at my views on being an influence.

Influence—The Fourth I of Intelligent Behavior

I've long been a fan of the art of persuasion. As a *Street hustler*, I could sell you the Brooklyn Bridge—just kidding, but I have been known for my gift to speak and sell. This trait has served me well as a *Strategic hustler*™. One of the books that I've read and have included in my personal library is Dr. Robert Cialdini's fascinating book *Influence: The Psychology of Persuasion*. It has sold over two million copies and has been translated into twenty-six languages. It has been listed on the New York Times Business Best Seller List, and Fortune Magazine lists *Influence* among its "75 Smartest Business Books."

In his book, Dr. Cialdini (formerly a nationally renowned professor of marketing at Arizona State University) describes *six principles of influence* which encompasses every negotiation tactic and act of persuasion utilized in boardrooms, living rooms, and farmers markets the world over. **Said another way**, these are the six "puppet strings" that all of us tug at to gain compliance from those around us. They are vastly and widely applicable, from business negotiations to marketing to disagreements with your significant other. If you look closely, you will notice that all of us employ them every day to achieve our goals and influence those around us. Many of them are particularly applicable to entrepreneurs. I've crystallized the essence of the six principles and share them below.

Cialdini's Six Principles of Influence

1. **Reciprocity**: The concept of reciprocation is pervasive in our society. It's one of our established social rules—if someone does us a favor, we do them one in return. If someone invites us to a party, we put them on the list for our next gathering. It is a fundamental principle that has been ingrained in all of us since the earliest days of human society. It is the concept of reciprocity that allowed our ancestors to freely share food, skills, and protection with confidence that the resources would be returned in kind. The shared web of interdependency and obligation allowed for the division of labor and specialization of skills—reciprocity was truly an evolutionary advantage.

    Accordingly, it's no surprise that our modern culture has socialized us all to carry a sense of indebtedness to those that help us first—the Golden Rule, karma, and "pay it forward" are all reciprocal social concepts that are instilled in all of us from a very young age. We assign harshly negative labels to those that do not follow the cultural norm—mooch, freeloader, leech. It is no wonder that whenever another person does us a favor, we feel obligated to respond in kind. And so, our natural reactions can become a powerful influencer when exploited. Let me give an example.

    In experiencing the reciprocity principle firsthand numerous times in life, I recall all the people in New Haven who took time out of their busy schedules to help me. It prompted me to coach, mentor, and finance youth events. I also recall being a struggling entrepreneur in Atlanta, Georgia. My first client was Thom Davis Construction Company.

It was a family-owned business and they helped keep my business afloat. Well, Tommy, the owner, was moving to a new home and needed help. I immediately felt the need to give up my weekend to help him because of what he had done for me. I will always feel loyal to him because of the opportunity he gave me.

The above are perfect examples of reciprocity in action—I felt compelled to donate my time, wisdom, and finances to philanthropic causes and to Tommy because I had first received something that I valued for life. Think of the things in your life to see how this principle applies to you.

2. **Consistency**: The consistency principle states, "Once we have made a choice or taken a stand, we will encounter personal and interpersonal pressures to behave consistently with that commitment. Those pressures will cause us to respond in ways that justify our earlier decision." In layman's terms, this means that once we have made a small commitment or statement (especially publicly), it becomes part of our self-identity. For example, if I can get you to make the statement "I love helping children" (and who doesn't), you will be more than twice as likely to pull out your wallet when I then ask you to donate to my favorite children's charity—St. Jude Children's Research Hospital. Not donating to the charity would be inconsistent with your previous assertion that you enjoy helping children (a feeling known as cognitive dissonance). You feel compelled to donate to the children's charity. I have also witnessed this tactic used during the negotiation of a payment settlement in the wrongful death of my daddy.

3. **Social Proof**: Of all the six principles, I believe we experience and are influenced by social proof most strongly and most often. Social proof refers to the phenomenon that we are far more likely to do or believe something if we have seen others like us do or believe it first. In *Influence: The Psychology of Persuasion*, Cialdini cities several studies in the book, including one that analyzed reclusive preschool children. Researchers showed each reclusive child videos of other children their age observing a social activity, and then actively joining into the activity. At recess the next day, the formerly isolated children immediately began to interact with their peers at a level equal to that of normal children in their schools. The principle of social proof illustrates that we often copy behaviors simply because others are doing something. We believe it *must* be the correct thing to do. Each child in the experiment perceived that being social was the "normal" thing to do, which gave them the courage to alter their own behavior. The principle of social proof is applicable to far more than elementary school behavior, and there are further examples in the book that examine social proof as an explanation for buying decisions, mass suicide, and traffic jams.

Entrepreneurs also run headlong into the social proof principle when raising capital for the first time. Many venture capital (VC) firms are reluctant to invest until they hear that others have invested as well. If you are able to secure a commitment from a big name VC firm like Kliener, Perkins Caufield, and Byers, which funded a green startup company I worked for, you'll probably not have much difficulty filling out the rest of your funding round. This is due to the principle of social proof—if others are willing to invest, it must be a good deal. Similarly, when you go to raise a second round of capital, any new investors will want to see participation from the firms that initially invested in your Series A. After all, if your original investors are unwilling to commit further capital, why should anyone new invest? This is often called "the VC Signaling Effect" and has been discussed in depth by both Chris Dixon, a seasoned tech entrepreneur, and Mark Suster, who sold his company to Salesforce.com.

4. **Authority**: This one is fairly self-explanatory—if someone in a position of authority commands you to perform a task, you are likely to comply. We will talk more about authority later when covering (position power) in the chapter on effective behavior. This was proved out in the now infamous and controversial Milgram Experiment. Stanley Milgram is a Yale University psychologist who conducted this experience. The following URL will take you to further detail regarding the experiment: http://en.wikipedia.org/wiki/Milgram_experiment. Essentially Milgram proved that despite moral objections and severe emotional distress, subjects were still willing to administer what they thought to be lethal electric shocks to others when commanded by someone in a position of authority. Milgram used his studies to explain the brutal actions of certain German soldiers during the Holocaust which were committed despite stated, strong moral objection by the soldiers themselves.

5. **Liking**: This one seems obvious, but it's very true—we tend to comply with requests from people who we like (friends, family, etc.). We will talk more about liking later when covering (personal power) in the chapter on effective behavior. Amway Corporation has exploited the liking principle to great success. Each day thousands of people invite their friends over for tea and finger food, only to eventually ask them to purchase some Amway products at the end of the party. By relying on the obligation we all feel toward those we like, Amway has built one of the largest direct sales organizations in history. In fact, Amway relies almost solely on parties and the "liking" principle to generate over $10 billion in revenue each year.

However, not only can your friends and relatives exploit the liking principle, anyone can. The liking principle also encompasses arguably the most powerful persuasion method of all—attraction. An attractive, flirty stranger can create the same persuasive "liking" effect that your best childhood friends enjoy. That's the reason nearly every pitchman, model, and TV commercial family is good looking, and all those Bud Light commercials feature women in bikinis. The more attractive the person trying to gain our compliance is, the stronger "liking" that they create, and the better the chance they have of persuading us. "Liking" is the principle that explains what Hollywood has known to be true for years—sex sells.

6. **Scarcity**: "Hurry, supplies are limited! This deal won't last! Call now!"

How many times have you seen slogans like those above plastered on store windows or shouted by TV infomercial salesmen? Probably more than you can count, and it's because of the scarcity principle. We are far more likely to agree to a request if we believe (falsely or correctly) that we will not have another chance in the future. Fear of losing an opportunity can be a very powerful motivator. It is generally true that things that are difficult to obtain are better than things which are easy to obtain— consequently we are subconsciously conditioned to use scarcity as a proxy for higher value. Cialdini mentions a used car salesman that always made sure more than one interested buyer was present whenever he was selling a car. The competition increased anxiety in both buyers and made the car seem that much more attractive, which without fail increased the price the salesman got for the car.

To summarize the aforementioned principles of influence:

1. **Reciprocation**: Doing a favor for someone often gets you a favor in return
2. **Commitment and Consistency**: People hold an ideal of staying consistent with their behavior
3. **Social Proof**: People look to others when they're not sure how to act themselves
4. **Liking**: People do business with others they know, like, and trust
5. **Authority**: People defer to others in authority when making decisions
6. **Scarcity**: People don't like to miss out on something valuable and scarce

Cialdini's book provides far more detail on the above principles than I have included here, including numerous studies and examples ripped straight from current events that illustrate each principle in action. I recommend Cialdini's book to any entrepreneur, product manager, or marketer, as well as anyone looking to be more persuasive in general. It's an absolutely fascinating read.

When I am most successful, it's because the people around me have made me successful. After all, I never scored a touchdown without my blockers. I never delivered a project that met business requirements and was completed on time and within budget without the effort of my team members. It comes down to the fact that success is created by a group of people and not by any single individual. How do you get people to come together around a goal and objective and be great? It's establishing a sense of common purpose. Greatness does not come from a tactical sense of execution. Greatness comes by having a vision that goes beyond you and even beyond the organization. This is what influence is all about.

Okay, you've learned how innovation, insight, initiative, and influence contribute to the intellect of an effective leader, but there is still more required. You have to be a good communicator. Good communicators have admirable interpersonal skills. My dad would always tell me to greet people in a manner that they feel special. His greetings varied to include "Pleased to meet your acquaintance" or, the one I liked the best, "It's been a plum pleasing pleasure and a profound privilege." I've heard one of the greatest motivational speakers in the world, Les Brown, use the latter. I've coined my own greeting building on that phrase: "It's been a plum pleasing pleasure and a *profusely* profound privilege," and would finish with "to teach you" or "to meet you." Seems to be a bit overboard? Try it and see the kind of response you get.

Let's look at another "**I**" of intelligent behavior, interpersonal skills. You must have them to grow into an effective leader.

Interpersonal—The Fifth I of Intelligent Behavior

Interpersonal skills are how well a person relates to other people. They may be also be referred to as people skills or communications skills. You must express yourself freely and effectively in a way that empowers you without compromising the rights of others. The following steps will demonstrate how conflict resolution, anger management, and assertive expression are all interpersonal skills that you can master to improve your relationships with others.

1. Effective Communication

1) Recognize that people want you to listen to them, to hear their perspective. They want and expect this courtesy more than they want you to be in agreement with them.

2) Listen to yourself as you begin to communicate. Make sure that you understand what is being communicated to you by repeating what was said in your own words. Respond rather than react, as this will allow you to address the situation in a positive way.

3) Improve the way you listen. Focus on understanding the words that are being said rather than thinking about your response. Don't speak until you fully understand the words that were just spoken.

4) Summarize your understanding of the communication. Clarify any questions with the other person.
5) Read *How to Speak and Listen Effectively,* by Harvey A. Robbins, PhD. It's a very easy read with a number of exercises to help you improve in this area.

2. Assertive Communication

1) Direct your message only to the person you intend to communicate with. Deliver your message to that person only.
2) Say what you think and feel. Be as clear and specific as possible when you state what you want.
3) Encourage others to give you feedback. Ask them to be specific and clear. This interpersonal skill helps others to understand that you are expressing your opinion or feeling instead of a demand.
4) Read *Influencing Others: A Step-by-Step Program for Success,* by William L Nothstine, PhD. It is an easy read with a number of exercises to help you improve in this area.

3. Conflict Resolutions

1) Ask yourself how conflict affects you and why it is important. The answer will determine what you will say during the confrontation.
2) Maintain a positive attitude and communicate positive intentions. Always include the other party.
3) Discuss the problem, giving the other party time to speak. Employ good communication and listening skills. Respect the needs of the other party.
4) Consider alternative solutions to the problem at hand. Choose the solutions that are beneficial to both parties. Ensure that the solutions are fair and specific.
5) Plan a follow-up evaluation of the solutions. You want to make sure the solutions are working to the satisfaction of all parties.
6) Read *Managing Disagreement Constructively: A Practical Guide for Constructive Conflict Management,* by Herbert S. Kindler, PhD. It is an easy read with a number of exercises to help you improve in this area.

4. Anger Management

1) Become more attuned to your feelings. Learn to recognize the anger as it occurs.
2) Avoid misdirecting your anger toward others who are not causing you to be angry. Be aware if the cause is from someone, something, or inside yourself.

3) Diffuse your anger by first taking a deep breath. Walk away from the situation until you have had a chance to calm down.

4) Express yourself responsibly and appropriately to the person who is causing you to be angry—this is appropriate assertiveness. Help the person to understand why his or her behavior is causing you to react with anger. Do not accuse the other person. Instead, use "I statements" to express yourself in a nonthreatening way. See How and When to use "I" Statement below.

5) Participate in daily activities that help you to deal with anger. Try exercising and meditating, these are good activities for releasing anger.

How and When to use "I" Statements

Before giving golden nuggets on the how and when of "I" statements examples let's look at the definition of appropriate assertiveness:

The essence of appropriate assertiveness is being able to state your case without arousing the defenses of the other person. The secret of success lies in saying how it is for you rather than what they should or should not do. "The way I see it…" attached to your assertive statements, helps. A skilled "I" statement goes even further.

When you want to say something but don't know what will help, "I" statement formula is a good step in the right direction. An "I" statement says how it is on my side, how I see it.

You could waste inordinate quantities of brain-power debating how the other person will or won't respond. Retreat to the nearest corner of dignity. You do need to be sure that you haven't used inflaming language, which would be highly likely to cause a negative response i.e. it should be *clean*; because you don't know beforehand whether the other person will do what you want or not. The cleanest "I" statements are delivered not to force them to fix things, but to state what you need.

Use an "I" statement when you need to let the other person know you are feeling strongly about the issue. Others often underestimate how hurt or angry or put out you are, so it's useful to say exactly what's going on for you - making the situation appear neither better nor worse.

Your "I" statement is not about being polite. It's not to do with 'soft' or 'nice', nor should it be rude. **It is about being clear.** It's a conversation opener, not the resolution. It's the opener to improving rather than deteriorating relationships. If you expect it to be the answer and to fix what's not working straight away - you may have an unrealistic expectation. Furthermore, if you expect the other person to respond as you want them to immediately, you may have an unrealistic expectation. What you can realistically expect is that an appropriate "I" statement made with good intent:

1. Is highly unlikely to do any harm
2. Is a step in the right direction
3. Is sure to change the current situation in some way
4. Can/will open up to possibilities you may not yet see

Sometimes the situation may not look any different yet after a clean "I" statement, it often feels different, and that on its own can change things.

Non-defensive Communication

Pointing the finger and using your messages puts blame onto the other person. When we feel someone is blaming us we often become defensive. Once people become defensive or angry, communication usually breaks down.

When to Use:

1. When we need to confront others about their behavior
2. When we feel others are not treating us right
3. When we feel defensive or angry
4. When others are angry with us

Here are my anger management steps:

Step One: Listen actively
Step Two: Use "I" statements
Step Three: Don't make it personal, focus on the behavior
Step Four: State how the behavior affects you
Step Five: State what you need to happen

For children there is a sixth step, which includes a consequence. However, it is recommended not to use the sixth step until the second time around. It is also at this time that the type of consequences can be discussed with the child if they are old enough. Other ways of getting children to be responsible for their own behavior is to use the "When .... then ...." statement or a behavior reward chart.

For example

"**When** the towels are picked up **then** you can go and play."
Step Six: State that there is a consequence to their actions

Here are a couple of examples:

Example One

Step One: Listen and Repeat	So you feel I interrupt all the time?
Step Two: Use "I" not "You"	Ok...but when I'm.....
Step Three: Behavior	shouted at...
Step Four: Affect of the behavior	I need to feel as if I've been understood so please don't shout at me and I will try not to interrupt

Example Two

Step One: Listen and Repeat	So you're saying I never see the good things that you do and you feel unappreciated?
Step Two: Use "I" not "You"	Ok...but when I'm.....
Step Three: Behavior	sworn at...
Step Four: Affect of the behavior	I feel put down and hurt...
Step Five: Needs	I'd like not to be spoken to in that way...
Step Six: Consequences (For Children)	and if I continue to hear you swear in this house then.....

Being able to deal effectively with people from various aspects (effective communication, assertive communication, conflict resolutions, and anger management) is essential to exhibiting intelligent behavior on your way to becoming an effective leader. Working with them with integrity increases the productivity and quality of your interaction. This brings us to the final *I* of intelligent behavior—integrity. Without integrity, there can be no intelligent behavior. Let's see what constitutes an effective leader with integrity.

Integrity—The Sixth I of Intelligent Behavior

The number one characteristic that people want leaders to demonstrate is integrity—people who walk their talk and lead a life of character. Integrity is more than simple honesty. It's more than being ethical. A person with integrity has the rare ability to pull everything together to make it all happen, no matter how challenging the circumstances. My life's journey has allowed me to cross the paths of thousands of leaders from all walks of life in various parts of the world who were men and women of integrity. These were honest, ethical people of "integrity." Some were and some were not making it in some way. Sounds confusing? Let's swim a little deeper and discuss those who "were not." While we would say they all were people of good character, the reality is their personhood was still preventing their talents and brains from achieving all that was in their potential. Honestly stated, they could not get past the "po in potential." Some aspects of who they were as people, they never seen as important to develop were keeping them from reaching heights that all of the other investments, they had made, should have afforded them. While they met the criteria for having "integrity," they also left behind a trail of falling short in some key areas of performance that left them, their stakeholders and the people who depended on them, wanting more. According to clinical psychologist and best-selling author Dr. Henry Cloud they were unable to successfully:

- Gain the complete trust of the people they were leading and capture their full hearts and following
- See all of the realities that were right in front of them. They had blind spots regarding themselves, others, or even the markets, customers, projects, opportunities, or other external realities that kept them from reaching their goals
- Work in a way that actually produced the outcomes that they should have produced, given their abilities and resources
- Deal with problem people, negative situations, obstacles, failures, setbacks, and losses
- Create growth in their organizations, their people, themselves, their profits, or their industry
- Transcend their own interests and give themselves to larger purposes, thus becoming part of a larger mission

These kinds of issues are attributed to a person's interrelationships between character, integrity, and reality (Cloud, 2006). Growing up in an inner-city red zone has been a blessing. Why? It gave me the street smarts for character growth, allowing me to avoid or quickly recover from the following pitfalls:

1. Hitting a performance altitude that is much lower than my aptitude
2. Hitting an obstacle or situation that derailed me
3. Reaching great success only to self-destruct and lose it all

Through discussing the following six essential qualities that determine your effectiveness in life, business, or whatever you do, I will talk about this "makeup," because, in essence, integrity is the courage to meet the demands of reality:

1. Connect, communicate, coordinate, and collaborate
2. Tell the truth based on the facts, eliminating fiction
3. Finish strong
4. Positively embrace negativity
5. Focus on growing
6. Aim to exceed expectations

Integrity Character Trait #1: Connect, Communicate, Coordinate and Collaborate

Let's look at some formal definitions for connect, communicate, coordinate, and collaborate.

Connect is to join, link, or fasten together; unite or bind.
Communicate is the activity of conveying information and confirming understanding.
Coordinate is the act of coordinating, making different people or things work together for a goal or effect to fulfill desired goals in an organization. *Said another way,* they must cooperate.
Collaborate is working together to achieve a goal. It is a repeatable process where two or more people or organizations come together to realize shared goals by sharing knowledge, learning, and building consensus.

Leaders with integrity connect, communicate, coordinate, and collaborate. *Said another way,* leaders must connect with people before they can effectively communicate; effective communication is necessary for effective coordination; having a coordinated effort (cooperation) is essential for effective collaboration.

Proverbs 4:23 says, "The issues of life flow from the heart." As I meditate on the words in this scripture, I've concluded that trust is about the heart, and someone making an investment in you comes from his or her heart. My experiences as a leader in sports, business, community, and family have shown that when you gain people's trust, their heart, then their desire and passion, follow. During our discussion on Situational Leadership®, we spoke about leadership being the interplay of ability and willingness. Ability is not enough because that speaks to performing a task. You can be an excellent task performer and still not be an effective leader because people find working with or for you difficult. Recall, you are only a leader if you have followers. You must also focus on willingness. Willingness drives the heart, desire, and passion, all crucial to building a relationship. Effective leaders are excellent bridge builders. They value creating relationships with people. Regardless of the task, when people are willing, they are truly committed to giving their best effort. Without 100 percent willingness, at best people will be compliant, which does not capture their best effort. This would require imposing my will on them.

Sounds egotistical, does it not? I'd be fooling myself if I thought that. "Will" is an interesting term. We usually think of it in terms of volition and choice. "Will you do something?" This question is asking if you would choose to do a particular thing.

Having a heart implies being nice. I am sure you can think of many situations where being nice did not produced the desired results. Let me help you deliberate. Why do "nice couples" get divorced? Why do "loving parents" have kids that take detours from the norm and join countercultures? Why can't some really nice leaders capture the hearts of their people? When it comes to human behavior, sometimes being nice is not enough. We have to be connected, and that's a whole different dimension of character. What is that dimension? Keep on reading and you will learn.

Empathetic Trust

What strengthens this component is the relationship with the other. This creates a connection that is the opposite of "detachment," whereby a person is kind of an island unto him- or herself. Now, don't confuse that with being introverted, or extroverted. Those styles can be used in the service of either connectedness or detachment. You can be very extroverted, and even nice to people, and never establish a deep bond. In fact, an extrovert's wordiness can even serve to keep people at bay and never allow them in. *After all,* nobody likes to be around a person who dominates the conversation. Detachment is about not crossing the space to actually enter into another person's world through the curiosity and desire to know them, to understand them, to be with them, to be present with them, and ultimately to care for them. Sadly, a lot of loving and nice people are detached in this way, and their relationships suffer for it.

My success personally and professionally comes from building relationships with people that see me as "being real." *Said another way*, what they *see* and *hear* is what they get. My empathy toward human beings allows people to feel a genuine interest in my knowing them, knowing about them, and having what they know matter. As deputy CIO, I reviewed the personal files of all my staff before meeting with each privately. This homework allowed me to build the trust essential to having a good relationship. One of the senior project managers thanked me for taking the time to get to know him and understand his history with the company. He proved to be one of my star performers in leading and managing large multimillion-dollar projects.

I use the word "empathy," not "sympathy." People have a tendency to confuse the two. So let me digress. Sympathy and empathy are separate terms with some very important distinctions. Sympathy and empathy are both acts of feeling, but with sympathy you feel for the person; you are sorry for them or pity them, but you do not specifically understand *what* they are feeling. Sometimes we have little or no choice but to feel sympathetic for someone's plight or predicament that we cannot can't understand. It takes imagination, work, or possibly a similar experience to get to empathy.

Empathy can best be described as feeling *with* the person. Notice the distinction between feeling *for* and feeling *with*. To an extent, you are placing yourself in that person's place, have a good sense of what he or she feels, and understand his or her feelings to a degree, possibly because you have had the same or similar experience. It may be impossible to be fully empathetic because each individual's reactions, thoughts, and feelings about tragedy are going to be unique. Yet the idea of empathy implies a much more active process. Instead of feeling sorry for, you're sorry with and have clothed yourself in the mantle of someone else's emotional reactions.

As a walk-on scholarship football player at the University of New Haven, I had teammates who had never interacted with a black person, intellectually or socially. Even though my black teammates had issues with our white teammates, I did not. They were impressed with my abilities, including my ability and willingness to play and play hurt, excelling in the process, but they were even more impressed with my intellect. I would engage in conversations that dispelled any myths they may have had about black people. The level of respect I commanded led to being nominated as a varsity team captain. As a corporate trainer/consultant, my ability and willingness to connect with each student to ensure he or she had a productive learning experience led to repeat training and consulting engagements with companies like Wachovia, JPMorgan Chase, Internal Revenue Service, AIG, Citibank, 5/3 Bank, Warner Bros, and Wal-Mart, just to name a few. These relationship-building skills were inherited from my dad. He never met a stranger.

The moral to the stories is; in sports, in work, in marriage, in parenting, in friendship, in business, connection along with trust happens when one person has a true emotional investment in the other, and the other person experiences that and returns it. Until this occurs there is no relationship. To do that requires the character that gets out of oneself long enough to know, experience, and value the other. You have to be empathetic. Being empathetic speaks to your character.

Empathy is one way to connect with people and build trust. There is another level of trust which wants everybody to be successful. It requires looking out for your fellow man.

Street hustler or *Mutual* Trust

This is a different level of trust taken from the life of a *Street hustler*. The *Street hustler* understands and respects a supplier's need to receive fair and reasonable compensation for delivering a product and/or service that adds value to help the *Street hustler* sustain success. It's when the supplier flips the script and performs an act that shows the *Street hustler* that the supplier not only has their best interest in mind but also has *Street hustler's* best interest in mind. The result is a level of trust that extends beyond empathetic trust to *Street hustler* trust. So what does that mean? It means that the *Street hustler* is inclined to reciprocate, recall our earlier discussion on reciprocity, providing favors and revenue generating opportunities to the supplier. ***Thus*** *Street hustler* trust creates a win-win situation for all parties involved.

Let's fast forward to my life as a *Strategic hustler*™. I have worked with consulting companies where everything had to be documented in a contract. In these cases, there were very few contract extensions. Why? The companies could be trusted to do what was agreed to. If the contract stated they were going to provide a product or service in the deal, they most likely would. Clients could trust what they had agreed to. Great, or was it? Clients like the kind of trust that looks out for their interest as well as yours. Unbeknownst to them they like *Street hustler* trust. Earlier I mentioned we would talk more about how *Street Hustler* trust contributed to the successful growth of Sterling Software's Business Intelligence Group. Well now is later. The division was able to exceed sales and revenue projections for a new product launch because I was able to convince marketing and my boss to practice *Street hustler* trust. Of course, to get their buy-in, *Street hustler* trust became *mutual* trust—***it is the same soup but a different bowl***. After all, we were asking our customers to take a leap of faith with us. We had to show them that we were not only looking out for Sterling Software's interest but also for their interest—this made it mutual. ***Said another way,*** we had to reciprocate to show our commitment to their success. The reward for this level of trustworthiness was that Sterling Software's Business Intelligence Group Practice grew to become one of the best business intelligence solutions providers in the software industry.

One of the cardinal principles of my fraternity is uplift—helping a fellow human being. I will talk more about this later. For now, know this *"uplifting"* character reflects my value of people. It is important to value people as people, not objects. What's the difference? Objects are treated as a means to an end, whereas people, when they are valued, are treated as though they really mattered, with care, concerns, and good intent, not harm.

Think about what you can do to gain this level of trust. Are you the type of person who values people?

My life experiences have shown me that incredible things happen when two parties "become vulnerable" with each other. They get open, creative, take risks, learn from each other, and deliver fruit in whatever their endeavor to a much more leveraged degree than if they were in the protected mode. Referring back to my Sterling Software example, we were able to exceed our sales and revenue projections. Our clients were able to get a business solution allowing them to meet their strategic initiatives. This happens in personal relationships such as marriage, friendships, parenting, and in business. To get everything that can come from two people's hearts, minds, and souls, you have to get to openness and vulnerability. You have to have access, and access is only given as trust increases.

Connection, communication, coordination, and collaboration go very differently when defensiveness and protectiveness are not in the way. Once both parties have trust then solutions are discovered and both parties work on the other's needs.

Grace and Leadership

Father God gives us mercy and grace with his "unmerited favor." He gives us grace when he extends favor, not because we have earned it in some way, but because he just possesses it to give. When I think of describing a "person of grace," one word comes to mind: "uplift." I am a proud member of Omega Psi Phi fraternity, with "uplift" being one of our cardinal principles. We as Omega men leave others better off than we found them, even when we get nothing in return. It makes for ultimate trust.

In leadership, this means that you want your staff to do well and to become all that they can be. It also means that you do things for them that are unmerited and help them get there. That does not mean, as we will see, that you do not have requirements and standards of performance for everyone in your life. But what it does mean is that you should make efforts to help them to reach those standards. Intelligent behavior is when an effective leader uses his or her grace to help his or her staff to reach the high standards by providing coaching, training, encouragement, or utilizing other resources to help them get there. They did not "earn" those things, and they are "unmerited," but they serve to help them to reach the standard that is there. Leaders without grace set the demand and do nothing to help people meet it. Then when they don't meet the demand, they turn on them as adversaries.

As a corporate trainer, corporate executive, entrepreneur, and coach, I've participated in the professional and life skills development of thousands of people. Recall the listing of seized opportunities during our discussion on goal-oriented behavior. Each of these required a "person of grace" to help people meet the requirements and standards of performance. Let me give you a few examples:

- As executive consultant/coach, the performance-based training and follow-up project mentoring delivered was authorized by senior management as part of their strategic initiative to "uplift" employees with learning and growth opportunities; learning and growth will be discussed later when covering Balanced Scorecard in chapter 20, "(P)erformance

Management"—strategic projects and operational demands achieved a 50 percent increase in achieving their goals, saving and generating millions of dollars

- As managing director/chief learning officer, I led a corporate mandate to deliver certified Oracle training to qualified professionals who desired a career change or skills upgrade to earn Oracle certifications
- As director of information technology/acting chief information officer for two biotech startups, I delivered solutions enabling both company employees to learn new technologies and ways of doing business benefitting them and the company
- As quality assurance (QA) team lead for PMI's OPM3 project, created an effective on-boarding process and quality assurance processes enabling volunteers to develop or sharpen skills in QA and to make significant contribution to the success of a global standard
- As the deputy chief information officer for the City of Atlanta, the divisional turnaround happened because of a "Retreat, Regroup, and Redeploy" transformation strategy, upgrading abilities and willingness through performance-based training and mentoring
- As founder and program advisor delivered free computer literacy training to more than four hundred students' ages ranging from seven to seventy—students gained essential skills for the information age
- As founder/CEO/president, hired college interns giving them practical skills, knowledge, and experience designing and writing computer software systems to solve complex business problems
- As park-recreational and high school football coach taught and mentored at-risk youth, for twenty-two years; many of these young men are now corporate executives, husbands, dads, entrepreneurs, coaches "giving back" to their communities—this is my MOST valued accomplishment
- As legal guardian, uncle Frank aka daddy, helped raise five children (4 girls and 1 boy) retrieving two from the Georgia Department of Family and Children Services—they have produced thirteen grand's (nieces and nephews) and are raising them to be productive citizens

For readers who are parents, grace works the same way. To achieve is the child's responsibility, but to empower is the parent's responsibility. Setting a standard is not enough. The parent of grace gives support, coaching, teaching, structure, modeling, help, and consequences to empower the child to get there. The child cannot provide these, and so they are unmerited. They are given without being earned, and that is grace. Grace is not removing the standard. The requirements stay, and the person of grace does what is possible to help the child to meet them.

Integrity is having the character to "uplift" another person to help him or her be all he or she needs to be. Doing this allows you to move as a positive force to improve the person. This is the key to long-term, successful relationships and work scenarios. You want to be the calm in the center of the storm, thus meeting the demands and being a redemptive force.

Open Yourself Up

The final characteristic to building trust is through vulnerability. Referring back to my role as deputy CIO, I made a bold move. My "Retreat, Regroup, and Redeploy" strategy required taking key business process consultants away from the daily routines, which meant meetings had to be missed. When presented with this dilemma, I instructed them to inform the director or commissioner of our situation and request that meeting minutes be sent to them. If the commissioner or director had any problem, then he should contact me directly. This "Retreat" move made me vulnerable. What if the action plans developed were not well received? What if the commissioners or their directors would not cooperate with me? Think about it for a second. How much would you trust someone who is powerless, a wimp, or incompetent? Maybe you could trust these people not to lie to you, but what aspects of your life would you "entrust" to them for safekeeping, or to make better for you? My actions were strategically designed to allow my staff, the commissioners, and directors to trust me. Why? Trust has a requirement of strength and power.

But, on the other side, being so strong has its negative effects. People feel that you are unapproachable. That you say you have an "open-door policy" but really don't. In this scenario, there can be no trust. Why? For trust to work in human relationships of any kind, whether leadership, marriage, parenting, or business, we have to be able to see some kind of crack in the armor so we feel that the other person is real. We might fear someone of great power or even admire him or her, but trust is another issue. This tug-of-war between power and trust creates a tension that can challenge you to open yourself up. To quote Dr. Henry Cloud, "not enough power and we can't entrust things of value to the person; too much power, and we can't feel that they could ever understand or relate to our own vulnerability." (Cloud, 2006)

We talked about me being "real." My life journey has taught me that in order for someone's character to be able to negotiate reality, there must be this dynamic tension between power and vulnerability. Chapter 1, "Leaders Are Born to Be Made," briefly covers my challenges growing up in an inner-city red zone. My dad provided me an example of this power and vulnerability balancing act.

I recall going to the hospital on numerous occasions to see my mother or brothers lying in a hospital bed recovering from surgery from an illness, a gunshot, or knife wounds. Well while getting dressed to make another visit to see my brother, I just stopped and froze, half-dressed, as if being stuck in quicksand. I was just standing there for what seemed to be a long time, trying to think about it all, almost unable to think or move. It all felt so heavy. After I had been standing there for who knows how long, my dad walked in.

He was a great listener, and after tearfully explaining my feelings on why I didn't want to do this anymore, I ended by telling him, "I can't." What happened next will remain etched in my memory for life. He hugged me, with tears in his eyes, saying, "Baby, I know how you feel. Sometimes I feel even worse; this is my baby [referencing my younger brother] whom I have to see and I am powerless. All I can do is pray."

The world kind of stopped for a moment. Here I am looking at a man six foot three, three-hundred-plus pounds, shedding tears and telling me he didn't want to go either. I had never seen this side of my dad. He also added that I needed to go because he wanted me to see what happens when you mess in the streets with the wrong people.

We went to the hospital, and I looked at my younger brother, who appeared to be dead, but thank God, he wasn't. At that time, I felt transmuted inside from overwhelmed and unable to overwhelmed and able. I made a promise to myself that I was not going out like that! Courage, perseverance, and hope had somehow been created though this experience.

My dad had given me his courage, perseverance, and strength to identify with and use. When I say "transmuted," that is exactly what happened. "Transmuted" is a term that means that something is changed in form, substance, or nature. In this instance, one emotional state, and a character state, was transmuted or changed to another through an interaction and connection. The technical aspects of how that happens are for psychologists and quantum physics to grapple with, but the reality aspects are available to people every day who have to meet the demands of reality. People's emotional, intellectual, and character states can be changed as they connect with each other. And when you are in any significant relational context, from leadership, to marriage, to parenting, or others, you will hit moments where someone needs transmutation from you. That reality will make a demand on your character. If you do it well, you will build trust.

To this day, grown men and women approach me, thanking me for helping them become the successful individuals they are. They have become productive citizens (doctors, lawyers, businessmen, entrepreneurs, husbands, dads, and mothers). One of the chapters in this book is called "Having a Teachable Point of View." The focus of that chapter is connecting in a way that gives people something that they can use. It becomes mutually beneficial to both you and the person. This is a big part of what leaders, teachers, parents, managers, and coaches do every day. However, to do that, we have to build trust and connection through the key hole of power and balance.

Being able to connect with my dad's feelings allowed me to get my act together. **In retrospect,** all of the emotions that were keeping me from "getting it done" were overcome because he gave me the "courage" to use my abilities to press on. That is why role models who are strong enough to depend on, but vulnerable enough to identify with are so important. They give you power to "get it done." Recall in chapter 3, "(G)oal-Oriented Behavior," how my mentor helped me turn a profanity-laced insult into a promotion to a highly visible position. This person was a former *Street hustler* turned *Strategic hustler*™—this transformation was the strength and vulnerability that made him an ideal role model at such a critical moment in my life.

The essence of the first character trait of integrity is connecting with people to build trust. An effective leader needs this to communicate, coordinate, and collaborate—effectively. The encouraging part as stated in chapter 1, "Leaders Are Born to Be Made," is that we all can grow in this area. This can only happen by having the courage to tell the truth based on sound facts. Let's look at another all important character trait of integrity.

Integrity Character Trait #2: Tell the truth
based on the facts, eliminating fiction

As we saw earlier, whenever the discussion of integrity comes up, the default position is to talk about honesty and ethics. If someone is an outright liar or cheat, then there is nowhere to go with him or her. GE CEO Jack Welch had a rule: if someone is an outright liar or cheat, that type of person was fired—no questions asked. If everyone had that basic honesty, we would not have had the scandals that rocked Wall Street in the huge meltdown of companies like Enron. Telling the truth is the first part of having an orientation toward truth. We all desire to be with honest people.

In fact, another essential characteristic of people with integrity is the ability and willingness to tell the truth based on the facts not fiction. People of good character are people who can be trusted to tell the truth and to give a representation of reality to others as best as they understand it. That is the basic foundation of all life, from business to government to family to commerce to friendship. Without it, we don't have much. Many entrepreneurs who have worked in third-world countries find that communication, coordination, and collaboration is very challenging because it is very difficult to connect and build trust when people entrusted to tell the truth and give an accurate account of reality do not. The corruption and lack of integrity at the basic levels are so rampant; almost no one can invest and do business there.

Everything I've ever read every person whom I've ever talked to, all the events and things I've ever seen around integrity lead me to believe that people of integrity keep their eye on the prize. Van Spruill, my youth league football coach, would always tell me, "Keep your eye on the prize." Knowing what the prize was helped me to determine the reality of fact, and what was fiction. How many times have you read a story where the boss makes drastic moves to increase the sales of the company, only to find out that the product being sold does not fulfill a need? In reality, the target market simply does not like the product. You recall my earlier discussion on developing laser like focus? It has taught me that people who do well have a reason, and those that don't have a reason, too. We will talk about this later.

Seeking Reality

Let me say this: those who think they know it all end up being dumb! I recall my dad telling me this repeatedly, and I have to agree. One of my first tasks when trying to solve a problem is to identify the problem. You really don't know what you don't know. Sometimes when you think that you have identified the problem, you find out something different if you're looking for reality. I recall working with a large client who was implementing a multimillion-dollar solution to help track purchasing patterns across the company. This company had over eighty thousand employees and produced more than fifty-five thousand products, including adhesives, abrasives, laminates, passive fire protection, dental products, electronic materials, medical products, car care products (such as sun films, polish, wax, car shampoo, treatment for the exterior, interior, and the under-chassis rust protection), electronic circuits, and optical films. It had operations in more than sixty countries—twenty-nine international companies with manufacturing operations and thirty-five with laboratories. My responsibility as the engagement manager was to manage the customer relationship and financials with this client. During a meeting with a senior vice president, I got a gut feeling the solution he was expecting would not be delivered. In fact, after listening attentively to him, I remember thinking, "Who is telling him the truth? He needs a business modernization, or reengineering, solution before implementing the technology." Sure, he would get the technology and service to implement his vision of a global tracking of purchasing patterns, but he wanted actionable information. For those of you who may not be familiar with the term, he wanted data that knowledge workers could make fact-based decisions with. It had to be specific, consistent, and credible. I continued to pry, determined to get him to see the same problem I did. I asked him, "Are you familiar with the magical number 7 plus or minus 2?" He answered, "No." I proceeded to explain to him how we as humans have limits on our capacity for processing information. The 7 ± 2 represents the proposed minimum and maximum chunks of information our brains can efficiently process in short-term memory, and the proposed output results would not allow the user to be productive because of information overload. My goal was to get him to realize applying technology to the problem would not fix the problem. I proceeded to discuss the business benefits of a business modernization effort, providing a **P.R.O.G.R.E.S.S.** framework focused on transforming people, processes, information, and technology. Without getting too technical, the benefits would make the company easy to do business with—from the viewpoint of the customer, channel partners, and enterprise strategies. Finally the light bulb came on. He realized though it would significantly increase the project budget, the cost benefit analysis showed a significant payback. The company took aggressive action to remedy the problem. With a competitive mandate and support from more than one hundred top executives, they initiated a strategy to understand each customer and channel partner's business and buying habits. This was the catalyst for an enterprise shift—realigning the organization from fifty disparate business units into seven marketing groups and centralizing information in a global enterprise data warehouse.

Employees, customers, distributors, and suppliers could finally access one common, centralized source of information via the Internet and intranet. The benefit is everyone gets the same version of truth with a unified view of the company's worldwide activity. With the support from the top down through all the realigned business units, the entire company understands its goals and sees the results. Employees get what they need, when they need it—no longer must they wait days, weeks, or months for reports. The IT department's frustration with lengthy backlogs diminished and allowed them to focus on proactive projects.

A project with a projected budget of $3.4 million ended up with an investment less than $50 million, with a total net benefit in the first five years of operation exceeding $100 million. Just think, if the SVP suffered from "arrogance of ignorance," he would have never seen and experienced the reality he was expecting. Having the courage to ask the "7±2 question" challenged this top-level executive's character to seek reality.

The opposite of actively seeking reality is avoidance. The person who avoids finding out what is true may be doing that for a variety of character reasons. Take leaders who engage in "arrogance of ignorance." In their avoidance of seeing the product or service having some major problems, they lose sight of money, manpower, time, and market share. Why would they be so blind? It seems simple to us as we hear the story, but every day, people do the same kinds of things out of basic character problems—basic pride, omnipotence, arrogance, grandiosity, or narcissism.

To admit being wrong about something does not enter their minds. As you can see, not demonstrating the know-it-all behavior allows you to grow into an effective leader who not only seeks feedback, but readily accepts it, knowing that it is bringing you closer to reality. In chapter 2, "(A)daptable

Behavior," Dr. Foresight agreed to jettison a product even though NEWTECH already had paid $1 million for the license to use it. Why? He had the courage to accept the feedback from an employee that his decision was in error and agreed he made a mistake. Personally, I am my biggest critic. We will revisit this topic in a later chapter when we discuss personal mastery. This is important; because of personal mastery, I am always seeking truth from the outside.

My mind-set is that "there is no shame in my game!" For if we are afraid of the truth about ourselves and have a character stance to hide, then we are headed in the wrong direction, away from reality. Think of the character issues that get in the way and create this kind of fear:

- Fear of seeing that I am wrong or have faults that are ugly. Those lead to guilt, or fears that I may lose love, approval, or standing with the people, I care about most.
- A fixed view of myself from experience, either positive or negative. Our early relationships give use a view of who we are, and to look at new input means challenging those views, which leads to anxiety.
- A lack of skills or resources to deal with what I find. If I open Pandora's box, what will I find and what will I do with it?
- A need for a total redo of a life plan or script. What if Mom or Dad made me believe that I was gifted in some area or should be able to do so and so, and the reality is that I am not and I can't? Now what? Or if this was my own dream, am I out of touch with my true areas of giftedness?

I make you aware of these issues so that you can see the character who seeks reality about themselves has the courage to embrace whatever reality discovered. We can face another day knowing we can meet the demands of the external world even better. The one who is true with himself or herself on the inside will be most able to negotiate things on the outside as well. It is the last 10 percent that will always give you the courage to springboard you to your reality—only if you can handle the truth. Let's dig a little deeper.

Give Me the Last 10 Percent

During the summer, I would lift weights and play basketball at the local YMCA in New Haven. My workout coach was a gentleman by the name of Mike Katz. Mike, a former player for the New York Jets, was a former American International Federation of BodyBuilders (IFBB) professional bodybuilder, most famous for his appearance with Arnold Schwarzenegger in the 1977 bodybuilding documentary film *Pumping Iron*. He was known for his role as the underdog in the 1975 Mr. Universe competition, where he refused to give up on himself despite placing fourth in the Tall Man division.

Mike called me "Clyde" because my thick, long sideburns reminded him of New York Knickerbockers Hall of Fame guard Walt "Clyde" Frazier. He would always push me at the end of my weight-lifting sets with the phrase, "Give me the last 10 percent." After a while, I began to understand Mike was encouraging me to make my last rep the best.

It has been over twenty years since our paths have crossed, but when I hear this phrase, he immediately comes to mind. When searching for my reality, teaching, mentoring, or coaching I am always demanding "the last 10 percent." People have a tendency to hold back on feedback that might be difficult for someone to hear and do not always express their full critique of their performance. As a practitioner of Situational Leadership®, handling of the "last 10 percent" would vary depending on the person. For example, recalling the "R1 to R2 to R3 Experience" we discussed in chapter 2, "Ⓐdaptable Behavior," if the person is insecure (R1), then I might say, "It was OK," not "You're best," but "OK." The goal is to encourage them to where they become confident in what they're doing. Knowingly holding back the last 10 percent allows being perceived as honest but not brutally honest. However, if the person is confident (R2) then I would say, "Before you ever do that again, please come to me, or get some help." They may become insecure again (R3), which requires *touching* them with, "We need the last 10 percent to be the best that we can be." There will be a more in-depth discussion on *touching* later. For now, my effectiveness to reaching my goals has been having the character and desire to hear, go after, and deliver "the last 10 percent."

Can You Handle the Truth?

As an effective leader within or of an organization/team, you have the responsibility of facing the unadulterated truths that creep up from time to time. Sometimes they are things most would consider good news. At other times, they are things that give you that special kind of migraine that feels like you were the ball at batting practice. Truth can take any form it likes, whether we are prepared to hear it or not.

I find it amazing the number of leaders who feel when the ugly truth arrives that they have this cosmic responsibility to shield those they're leading from it. Perhaps it could be a genuine concern for their response to bad news, but more often than not, they don't have what they would consider an reasonable, explainable or believable answer for it that moment and so they keep it quiet until they think they do. Like the famous line from *A Few Good Men* with Jack

Nicholson, the mantra of "You can't handle the truth!" seems to govern these decisions.

The reality is that people with integrity hunger for the truth. This comes from reaching outside of the box and being open to hearing it. While there are some things that are sensitive company information and should be closely guarded, this happens less often than people imagine. You have an entire organization whose best interest is to do what is good for their stakeholders. It creates job security for each one of them. My viewpoint is effective leaders with integrity should share with them the truth about challenges they are facing. Why? In a later chapter, we will talk about using stretch goals to energize people through ever-greater challenges. Effective leaders are winners who have to understand that reaching outside for the truth is a good and positive thing. And people sometimes ward off positive reality about themselves because it would mean a lot to take responsibility for it. Do you know people who have some gifts and some abilities that they have not been using? Are they facing a situation where they are going to be put in a position to use them? As a consultant to international companies in the financial, logistics, and real estate industries, I witnessed a number of knowledge workers who, on paper, had the abilities to be considered for a newly created challenging position but lacked the willingness to step up to the table. Truth can be perceived as intimidating, causing people to avoid it regardless of it being positive or negative. Effective leaders seek both, even the kind that would stretch them out of their comfort zone.

Up to this point, our focus was on seeking the truth about ourselves. Effective leaders seek the truth about other people. Not only do we avoid seeing reality about ourselves, but sometimes because of past experiences and sometimes to keep our own internal stability, we do not see others in the reality of who they are. I've used the word "reputation" repeatedly in this book. Reputation consists of two parts:

1. The task
2. The relationship

Earlier in this book, these terms were introduced when discussing Situational Leadership®. Task was associated with *ability*. Relationship was associated with *willingness*. Recall *ability* defines the components that contribute to perform the task and *willingness* defines the components that contribute to formulate the relationship. I spoke of my reputation in high school and college. When a person travels through a few years with an organization, or with a partnership, or any other kind of working association, one leaves a "reputation" behind in these two areas, task and relationship. What did the person accomplish and how did he or she deal with people? We can tell a lot about that person from the nature of the reputation. In terms of the task, what does the reputation look like? Is it a reputation of goals being reached? Is it a reputation of profits being made? Was there growth in the business or the deal that the person was working on with you? Was the mission being accomplished?

Or, is it a different kind of reputation? Was it a reputation of unreached goals and projections, misfires, and missions not accomplished? Was there a lack of completion, disorganization and chaos? Had a large number of unexcused absences?

You can see from a reputation, which is real performance and results, we can tell a lot about the person. Remember according to the trilogy of success; *Results matter.* They are the stuff from which we are evaluated and for which we strive to bring our dreams and plans into reality. When we look at results, the reputation, we are really looking at ourselves and learning something about our character in the same way that the reputation of a ship tells us a lot about the ship.

At the end of the day, we must look back and see if the reputation of our work is profitable or not. If it isn't, it is time to ask ourselves some hard questions. The reputation is the results we leave behind. And the reputation doesn't lie and it doesn't care about excuses. It is what it is. Understand, no matter what we try to do to explain why or to justify what the reputation is—it still remains. It is what we leave behind and is our record.

On the other side of the reputation are the relationships. Just as we leave the effects of our work behind in results, we leave the effects or our interactions with people behind in their hearts, minds, and souls. We leave a reputation of people behind us as we move through their lives whether it is professionally or personally. Therefore we must look out over the transom and ask ourselves, "What does the reputation look like?"

Understanding the effect reputation has on your career is essential to your integrity. In the people side, just as in the task side, there are results. The question I ask myself is, "Did they feel I edified their life?" Notice this is not about you! *Realize* they have the right to ask, "What have you done for me lately?" As a corporate trainer/executive coach, I had to be concerned with my interaction with my students. Were they more trusting after working with me? Were they more fulfilled as people? Did they learn from me and feel lifted up and encouraged? Were they stretched and inspired to become more than they were before they worked with or for me? Did my relationship cause them to produce more?

Or could they have walked away feeling wounded; less trusting, put down, cheated, even manipulated, downright disappointed and let down? On the other hand, were they angry and possibly thinking about how to get even? Did I make some feel inferior, like losers, or did I tarnish my reputation by possibly offending someone making them ashamed for me, or of me, because of how I interacted with them? Ultimately, would they want to do it again or recommend me to others?

While writing this book I am working as a contractor in the role of business process strategist in the Transformation and Process Group of an international bank headquartered in Madrid, Spain. Their mission is to become "the best" universal bank in the country. Prior to being hired, I went through a very challenging interview process. After providing the hiring firm my professional references, I informed my colleagues their names were given as people who could honestly attest to my professional skills—leadership, technology, and relationship management. This was done as a professional courtesy to prepare and prevent them from being blindsided with questions about my reputation on both sides—task and relationship.

We agreed they would contact me at the conclusion of their interviews to give me a heads up on the types of questions asked. They respectfully did; informing me that the interviewer asked questions about my work habits, results, and the feelings that they or people who worked with me had. They indicated that they told the interviewer that they would hire me back without reservations. When I spoke to the interviewer, she repeated back what my colleagues had told me. She said she could tell my "integrity, honesty, and character were beyond reproach." Initially my contract was approved by the client for six-months. It was extended an additional twelve months as a direct result of my performance—of task and relationship. My goal is to build a world-class reputation for the next client.

For those of you who remember Sergeant Joe Friday from the TV drama *Dragnet*, his favorite mantra was, "Just the facts." You've learned the second character trait of integrity, having the ability and willingness to determine what's real (reality) and what's fiction. To quote one of my favorite biblical scriptures (John 8:32), "*And ye shall know the truth, and the truth shall make you free.*" A person of integrity is concerned with just the facts leading to the truth. Let's look at another character trait.

Integrity Character Trait #3: Finish Strong

An effective leader has the ability and willingness to finish strong producing the results which leads to reaching goals, profits, or the mission. This starts with knowing your strengths and weaknesses. Earlier I stated that people who do well have a reason, and those that don't have a reason, too. Now I am going to tell you the reason. It is my experience that people do well when they do what they do well and stay away from what they do poorly. Is that not common sense? Yes, but when did common sense have much to do with people's personal or business practices? And more to the point, what does this have to do with character? It's really that simple.

In chapter 3, "Ⓖoal-Oriented Behavior," we discussed how everyday Americans create organizations that succeeded beyond their wildest imaginations (Glauser, 1998). The common practice by all of the entrepreneur's interviewed is that they grew the business as far as they could before deciding to turn over the reins to an operations manager who was better equipped—i.e., more education, experience, etc.—to grow the business and take it to the next level.

Through interviews, observations, and my experience I've learned behaviors that allow people to finish strong. They are: (a) very successful, (b) came from all walks of life, and (c) from different parts of the world [Pakistan, India, China, Hong Kong and the United States]. I've assembled the following list to help you finish strong.

1. You need to start something before you finish it.

- Go start it; don't wait for that perfect moment. Don't sit on the idea for long, just get started. *Said another way,* "Just Do It," as the Nike slogan suggests.
- If you want to write a book, start by deciding a working title and writing that first paragraph. You can also choose to write a one-page outline. If you want to start an online store, decide on the product line and book a domain name.
- If you need to submit a report to your boss or to your class teacher (depending upon what age group you are in), start by collecting information from the web, books, and various other knowledge sources you choose. If you are an (aspiring) entrepreneur, start by building a demo (prototype) and go out to collect feedback. If you can create a demo, sell it, and build it in bootstrap fashion, who knows, you can be tomorrow's Russell Simmons or Bill Gates. The idea is not to think too much before you start if it is not a high-risk decision.

2. See that you start with a worthwhile idea.

- I am going to talk more about introducing ideas later but for now one word of caution before you start: make sure you are out to live your own dream and not somebody else's. See that you are really keen and interested in the work that you are taking up. Do not start just because doing it is very cool. Remember the earlier lesson on Marketing 101.
- You should have a genuine inclination toward pursuing it and the appropriate skill set and resources (physical energy, availability of time, investment if required) to execute it. Remember, you gotta wanna or you ain't a gonna.

- Do not invest in the stock market just because your friend made a killing investing in equity. Not to doubt the intelligence of your friend, but it is better to be inspired by legendary investors like Warren Buffet. He chose not to invest in technology stocks during the boom before the Internet bubble because he did not understand technology. The moral to the story is to venture into a field that you understand.
- Start something because you are passionate about it and you possess some skill set relevant to the task that you are taking up. Remember that people do well when they do what they do well and stay away from what they do poorly.

3. See that there are some rewards for you.

- Start something that will provide some gain to you. It need not be monetary gain. The gain can be physical (better health through regular exercise); financial (wealth creation through regular saving); mental (clarity of thoughts through regular meditation); or emotional (satisfaction due to having a romantic life that you desired). When you see gain, you will be motivated to take action.

4. Convert your task into actionable chunks.

- If you want to finish a task successfully, just break it into manageable chunks. Think of eating anything big in one bite! Do this by thinking about finishing it one bite at a time.
- Convert your task into goals or milestones. It can be done at ideation stage itself. Remember to create SMART (Specific, Measurable, Attainable, Realistic, and Tangible) goals and you will inch closer to success day after day. This concept will be discussed in more detail in chapter 20, "Ⓟerformance Management."
- It is good to get into a habit of reviewing your plans and actions. It helps you keep on track. Sometimes en route to the finish line, you may miss some targets. Do not panic. Just relax for a while and speed up the accelerator. While speeding up just do a small check that you are headed in right direction. Further, do not fear to change tracks if you feel that you are not moving in the right direction.

5. Make sure that follow-through is not too complex.

- Promise of future gains and goal setting can take you some distance, but if you want to keep on working, make sure that follow-through is not too complex.
- If you are starting an exercise regimen to maintain good health, there is no point beginning with the most difficult form. Start with basic

stretching and gradually move to sets that are more complex. What is complex today will be simple tomorrow. If exercising calls for extreme sacrifices, you are least likely to sustain it. If good health calls for exercising, then you should choose a regime that is practical and can be pursued day after day.

6. Focus on productive action.

– It is important to note that the majority of your actions are productive. You do not need to be bound by any rules here, but just see that your actions are taking you in the direction of your dreams. While you are focusing on productive action, keep allowing yourself regular fun time—time to spend with friends, family, and with self (if you like it that way).

7. Celebrate small victories.

– Celebrating small victories works wonderfully to take you closer to the goal. First, it helps you realize that you are reaching there. This feeling helps a lot when you are pursuing a goal which is taking some time to achieve. Second, it makes sure that follow through is not looking too complex to you, further lowering your chances of quitting.

– In most cases people leave a task unfinished when they see no success in sight. There can be other reasons also, but this is the primary reason. Some of you may cite dogfights between stakeholders as one reason; but such fights appear when success looks far. If you smell success coming your way, you are most likely to stay on track. Celebrating small victories help you realize that success is not very far from you.

8. Stay away from distractions.

– In today's world of excesses, it is easy to come across various distractions. Most of these distractions will come in disguise. The Internet comes in disguise as a source of useful information but can suck your time as a leech sucks the blood. Outings with friends come in the veil of fun and relaxation, but if done in excess can become a major hindrance and keep you away from your goal.

– A useful gadget like the TV remote control can take hours of your valuable time if you choose to sit on the couch and continue flipping channels one after another. Food that satisfies hunger and gives you energy to pursue any task can become a distraction if you choose to indulge in eating too much.

– The best idea is to stay away from objects, gadgets, and individuals that take you away from your goals. Avoid going to extremes with food, sleep, and other essentials for life.

9. Make knowledge your friend and not your shield.

- Many times, people continue to read and act little. Their logic is to have perfect knowledge before they can start. In these fast-changing times, better if you learn the basic stuff and get started. Don't succumb to "analysis paralysis", or over-thinking, a situation such that an action is never taken.

- Books and literature can be a big boost, but they should not serve as a shield to keep you away from working on your real target.

- When I started this personal development book, the idea was to create a resource where people could find pointers to make a positive difference in their lives. It need not be a big change, but just a small idea, a little help.

- I could have read a thousand more books in addition to a big chunk that I have already read. They would have provided me with more ideas and perspectives, but by the time I had finished reading, my inclination to write might have been lost. It is just a scenario, but a highly possible one.

- I felt that I possessed the skill and life experiences to share some unique insights with you. There was no point in waiting till tomorrow, when I may not have the same excitement toward sharing these thoughts with you. I still read books and continue to learn from people I meet. I understand that learning is an ongoing process. There is no full stop in it.

- The core idea here is to make books and other resources (such as the web) your friends—things that take you forward on the path of action. Embellish yourself by reading, learning, and acting to apply what you have learned. Experience is the best teacher. *Said another way*, an ounce of practice is better than tons of theory.

- A favorite phrase is "knowledge is power." I say knowledge becomes power when acted upon. From our earlier discussion on tenacity, we covered tenacity requires doing something; meaning not being afraid to pull the trigger and make a decision. Remember, action is the foundational key to success.

10. Be in touch with your inner self.

- Solitude will keep you on track. Find some time to be with your inner self wherever possible. During this period meditate, read your intentions out loud, make and review goals. It will be great if you can just sit silent and feel your breath going in and coming out. Initially this time of solitude can be a bit tough on you, but later you will tend to enjoy it, as it will be your recharge time. You will feel like being plugged into an energy reservoir and getting charged.

- An energized, fresh human brain works like a fully charged mobile phone battery. It receives the ideas clearly, processes these ideas to perfection, and provides clear output. The (solitude) recharge should provide your brain enough energy to perform its duty effortlessly.

11. Let go and let God.

- There will be times when things may not go as you'd like them to. In such situations, the best strategy is to keep your cool. Realize that there are certain things we cannot control. We can control our actions, our speech, our association with people; but a natural calamity, unfavorable market conditions, or the death of a loved one is beyond our control.
- This understanding will keep you on path when things are not going your way. Be courageous to accept the reality; this is what integrity is all about. If such a situation arises, do the best you can in that situation and march ahead with faith. I love the "Prayer of Serenity" for the message it conveys. It can be your guiding light also. Here, I take liberty and share this prayer with you;

> *God, grant me the serenity to accept the things I cannot change, courage to change the things I can, and the wisdom to know the difference.*

12. Seek advice when required.

- Go out and seek advice when you need it. Make sure to check whom you are seeking the advice from. The person should be someone who has already lived a dream similar to yours. Such a person will be in the state to answer your queries, clear your doubts, and most likely will point you in right direction.
- If you want to become a swimmer, go ask somebody who has excelled at swimming. Similarly, if you want to be the CEO of a Fortune 500 company, go talk to a Fortune 500 CEO—current or past With today's means of communication, you can reach just about anyone. It is best to start with an e-mail, as it is less obtrusive and can be responded to at the receiver's convenience.
- You may say, "Why would a big-time professional respond to my query?" Show your passion for the work you are doing, and most of them will respond. In such situation, it helps if you have a strong personal brand.
- If you cannot talk to a Fortune 500 CEO, go to somebody who is accessible. Go to a person in your town or city who runs a small enterprise or the CEO of a small company.

13. Stay on course long enough and you will succeed.

- Remember this point, quitters never win and winners never quit, I believe make or break when it comes to strongly finishing a task that you have taken up. Make sure that you are in it for the long haul. "Long enough" is the key here. The point being, you have to finish STRONG! Like a heat-seeking missile go until your dream is your reality—then success will be yours.

Let me share a story with you before I summarize the above steps. I worked with one company whose CEO achieved major successes as well as some big failures over twenty years. In a strategic planning meeting with upper management, we charted the success and failure of the company, looking at its strategic initiatives. In each case of colossal failure, it had been entered into as a "rebound project" following a loss of a major project loved by the CEO. When something that he loved had not worked, he immediately came up with a new big idea that he romanticized and entered into as a way of avoiding the natural depression and feelings of loss that followed the last one. But autopsies had not been a part of the corporate mind-set until the board removed the CEO. At that point, they got a leader who was more interested in not repeating past mistakes than pursuing new, "exciting" plans to temporarily keep from being bummed out.

To stumble, bumble, and fumble is natural to the learning process. *Said another way*, failure and loss are necessary for growth and success. Having had my share of failed ventures, I can attest that to understand them, process them, and grieve them takes depth of character. To quote Dr. Henry Cloud, "It takes a well of emotional resources that can fuel the soul and spirit while one is doing that kind of work. The empty person, needing the next manic 'fix' of excitement and optimism, cannot wait. S/he has to jump in. The mature one carries the optimism inside and knows there will be another day, but only after, s/he has fully lived this one. That way, this day won't have to be lived again." (Cloud, 2006)

To summarize the integrity character trait, finishing strong requires you to be selective, realistic, organized, accountable, and determined.

1. **Be Selective**—Don't accept a task just because someone asks you to do it. You can do just about anything in life that you want to do, but you cannot do everything. I want to help everyone and have a very hard time saying no to a request. However, if I were to accept every job offered to me, I would be overwhelmed and would end up doing a poor job on every job. If, instead, by carefully selecting jobs that I do best allows me to deliver and provide a service that meets and sometimes exceeds the client's expectations. Remember point one of the trilogy of success.

2. **Be Realistic**—Allow yourself enough time to be able to complete a task without having to sacrifice quality to be able to finish that job on time. I used to be an optimist, and that's not a good thing when it comes to determining how much time it will take me to finish a job. I always think I can finish a job sooner than I really can, and I end up stressed out when the time comes that the job is supposed to be finished and it isn't. I'm learning to be more realistic and give myself a better take on the time I think I need to finish the task.

3. **Be Organized**—Break a task into smaller portions and set goals for when you will complete each portion. I am a methodologist. The Six Principles of Productivity Management discussed earlier and the **P.R.O.G.R.E.S.S.** approach we will discuss later keeps me organized.

4. **Be Accountable**—Tell someone what you have *and have not* accomplished for your task. There is nothing like having to tell someone what you haven't done to motivate you to get moving! For me, this step means keeping my clients up to date on the progress of their projects, including having to tell them if I am behind schedule (which is very rare!). Having to tell them they will have to wait a bit longer for a deliverable is not a good feeling, and it motivates me to stay on track and keep working.

5. **Be Determined**—Trust me, there will be failures. Remember, Thomas Edison's' words about failure shared earlier. I focus on this because it is so very easy to become sidetracked by obstacles. You have to keep your eyes on the prize. This may mean letting go of things that are working, if they are not the best things. Why? Because they will take up time, energy, and resources that may be good and even profitable, but are keeping you from the best things. I learned in sports, *"the good is the enemy of the best."* This truism applies to business also. In retail, this is why the best organizations move things out at the end of the year, to make way for what is coming. Keeping that entire old inventory, even though you could probably sell it over time, is not a good idea. They need the shelf space and focus. So it must go.

You've learned the third character trait of integrity, having the ability and willingness to finish strong, that an effective leader must have to be successful. There is more to the character aspect of work than a good work ethic. Working hard, consistently, with diligence and perseverance is paramount. But depending on how someone is put together, it is possible to work hard, be committed, sacrifice, and persevere while at the same time not achieving results. Results, as well, are the fruit of other aspects of our makeup.

If fears, narcissism, pride, emotional ties, emotional and spiritual emptiness, or other character issues are in the mix, then the work is going to be mixed up with the fruits of those issues, instead of the fruits of labor. The reputation will be one where the goals were not reached, the mission and purposes sacrificed to the altar of personal immaturity. That is why success and fruitfulness depend as much upon focusing on the "whom" you are as much as the "what" of the work you do. Invest in your character, and it will give you the returns that you are looking for by only investing in the work itself. You can't do the latter without the former.

Let's look at another character trait of integrity.

Integrity Character Trait #4: Positively Embrace Negativity

All enterprising people determine to succeed [hustlers] must positively embrace negativity. This brings us to the integrity character trait—the ability and willingness to embrace, engage, and deal with the negative—which leads to ending problems, resolving them, or transforming them. My journey from a *Street hustler* to an internationally recognized program/project management expert has been attributed to my ability and willingness to embrace negativity and deliver solutions. A person who is always prepared to deal with the "knowns" and the "unknowns" that life and business bring can embrace negativity. The **P.R.O.G.R.E.S.S.** approach that was introduced earlier and will be discussed in-depth later was adopted because it gave me a positive approach to embrace negativity. The name "**P.R.O.G.R.E.S.S.**" creates positive thoughts. To quote one of my favorite TV personalities, Dick Vitale, "*It's Awesome, Baby!*" Friendship or association with positive thinking people contributed also. As the saying goes, *"Birds of a feather flock together!"*

Earlier I mentioned that you would learn the origin of the phrase, *"It's the same soup but a different bowl."* This phrase comes from a first-class individual Mr. Osie Lee Carraway a.k.a. "OC" pronounced *"oh see."* OC the consummate overcomer taught me how to embrace negativity with a smile. How? Keep on reading. An older gentlemen, we had a lot in common in that we both were former *Street hustlers*, former athletes, went to college, coached kids, were spiritual men of the Christ, our middle name was "Lee," and our effectiveness contributed to our success in the workplace. OC grew up in the streets of Philadelphia—and to hear him tell it, he was "a *baaad* boy." He served in the military, and his many professional accomplishments included being the conference coordinator at the Alston and Bird Law Firm, one of the most reputable law firms in Atlanta. He was everything a role model with integrity could be—a loving husband and dad, a great friend and mentor. He and his loving wife, Carsandra, and their kids took care of my kids, which allowed me to travel for business for three years. OC's wisdom kept me in line. With what appeared to be a "sixth sense," he would greet me as I returned from a teaching/consulting trip to pick up my kids from his home and say, "Young man, do you feel like going to school—again?" His conversations were so thought-provoking that I always accepted. He had this phrase that he would say whenever he wanted to communicate that something, though it was different, if you looked real close there were many similarities. The phrase *"It's the same soup but a different bowl"* was coined from his work as a caterer. He, in his "Philly smooth" way, eloquently and succinctly was able to get his point across. This phrase has become a staple in my conversations across the world when I am trying to get people to understand they do not have a monopoly on their particular issue. I would sometimes mix it up by saying, *"It's the same bowl but a different soup,"* and OC would look at me from his six-foot-three-inch frame with his million-dollar smile and say, "Same difference!" he reminded me so much of my dad. Like dad, OC encouraged me to believe in Father God; to acknowledge him in everything that I do; to never settle for less; to always *"notch it upward and onward"*; and to know that I "can do all things through Christ, who strengthens me." This is how you embrace negativity with a smile. **Said another way** having street smarts and book smarts is not enough you need a spiritual connection!

While writing about positively embracing negativity; the last stanza from Edgar A. Guest's poem, *"See It Through"* comes to mind. It states:

> *"Even hope may seem but futile,*
> *When with troubles you're beset,*
> *But remember you are facing*
> *Just what other men have met."*
> *You may fail, but fall still fighting;*
> *Don't give up, what e'er you do.*
> *Eyes front, head high to the finish,*
> *See it through!"*

These words *"But remember you are facing; Just what other men have met"* epitomize the wisdom in OC's phrase. And though my friend has transitioned he left me with a phrase to communicate that though a problem, opportunity, or situation may appear unique; if you peel back layers, like an onion, you will find the similarities that either you or somebody else has already dealt with effectively already. Can you guess what the phrase is? This is *not* a trick question!

Let's look at **P.R.O.G.R.E.S.S.** We will discuss the character it takes to apply this approach to positively embrace negativity. The following explains each letter:

1. **Picking** issues and/or problem identification. It takes character to actively search for issues and/or problems and face them head on. My philosophy is that every problem and/or issue is an opportunity for a solution. It is a chance to make things better and get to a good place.

2. **R**esearching current situations. The devil is in the details. It's one thing to actively search for issues and/or problems, but you have to begin to face the problem. When you don't face the problem, you don't experience the "good" of getting it fixed. The difference is in facing the demand of reality, and having the character to do so, based on experience. Remember the 7±2 discussion earlier? The SVP had to decide that there were other problems that needed to be addressed if he was going experience his reality. Today, he is enjoying the fruit of not only his streamlined solution but also his character.

3. **O**btain the root cause. There are many tools and techniques to use in this step, which will be discussed later. Lacking the discipline to find the root cause of a problem results in solving the symptom(s) of the problem not the real problem. The bottom-line is, the problem is solved only when its root cause is identified and fixed.

4. Generate alternative solutions to resolve the issue or problem. You must always be on the alert for alternative solutions. Visit http://www.problemsolving.net. This website is dedicated to providing you with scores of clear and practical techniques of problem solving for all fields, based on the scientific method of problem solving and presented in nontechnical language in easy-to-follow steps.

5. **R**un a pilot. We discussed how problems are an opportunity to make things better and get to a good place. The operative words are "get to a good place." Alternative solutions need to be tested to determine if they can get to a good place. One of the most important aspects of character in life, without question, is one's ability to confront. If the nature of reality is that there are always problems, if you do not confront them and instead tolerate them, then problems are what you will have. I have never met or observed a person with a truly whole, successful reputation who did not confront well. In this step, you confront on a small scale to see if the solution is an appropriate solution to solve the problem.

6. Examine the results. One of the abilities that make someone able to lean into the negatives, face them, and recover is to be separate from the problem or the negative outcomes. They have the ability to separate themselves from their results. Sounds confusing, yes? Keep on reading and learning. I believe that people's identity is tied to their outcomes; they don't exist in a certain way. They are what happen. So, if things are going well, they are well. But if things don't go well, and the outcomes are bad, they are not well at all. When I coach kids or adults and they hit a slump, one of the ways to get them out of it is to help them get separate from their results. Solving a problem and examining the results provides you information to make a go/no-go decision. It has no bearing on your character. Star performers do not derive their sense of who they are or how they feel from the outcomes of their performance.

Certainly, doing well feels good and contributes to good feelings, but that is different from one's feelings about oneself. The results are the results and the self is the self. That way, achievers improve performance when it is not what it should be by focusing on what they need to do differently and the changes that they need to make. The problem becomes the focus, not "me." **Said another way**, "I need to do A or B" instead of "I am a loser." In the second scenario, A or B never gets addressed because the person is down for the count.

7. **S**et up for the transfer from pilot to larger scale. When I think about this step, the word that comes to mine is "ownership." Once you have decided on the appropriate solution, it now must be made available to the masses. This comes with some bumps and bruises, which leads to some negativity. All scale-ups suffer from this. Effective leaders own the resolution of these when feeling their character or reputation is being damaged. Let's look at a couple of scenarios. I recall an assignment with USAir that made a multi-million dollar purchase of a software development toolset to increase their productivity in writing computer programs to manage critical information for the company. There were a number of problems, so many that the two consulting firms that were hired to straighten out the problems failed. My familiarity with the software toolset and development approach along with my turnaround strategy led to me being hired as a senior management consultant. I led a pilot project involving the areas of profit sharing and revenue management that successfully demonstrated how the software should be configured and loaded on the corporate mainframe computer and then be used by the development teams to conduct the analysis, design, construction, and testing of application programs. It was now time to transfer the software tools and techniques to the technical staffs located in different regions of the United States. I developed and delivered a well-received training session that included senior technical leaders from each location. As mentioned earlier, there were "hiccups," but we were able to get through them successfully.

Another situation occurred while leading the commerce and IT functions for one of the startup biotech firms in the renewable energy space mentioned earlier. The company had significant success in building and running its pilot project. Its patented technology provides a faster and cheaper solution to converting biomass to sugar. Visit www.renmatix.com for more detail. With each scale-up, more opportunities for solutions surfaced. Everyone involved took ownership for resolving the problems/issues. **Said another way**, their positive mental models allowed them to positively embrace negativity. In fact, the CEO/cofounder Srinivas Kilambi, PhD, CFA, would always say, "The only thing around here that is constant is change." I would joke with him and others calling him the reincarnation of the late great Sam Cooke with his "*a change is gonna come*" mentality. With a culture of embracing negativity as the status quo, they are positioned to becoming a dominate player in the renewable energy space.

8. Seek continuous improvement. This requires character that embraces excellence as a journey instead of a destination. I have just mentioned a few of my experiences above but you will see throughout this book how effective leaders always strive for excellence, not perfection. I learned as a high school and college scholar-athlete, parent, godparent, teacher, observer of happily married couples, and philanthropist, there is always room for improvement. However, it does not happen overnight. But it can and will happen with diligence and vigilance.

Ok, I gonna get spiritual with you right now: "*Trouble don't last always,*" (Lamentations 3:18-23), "*Joy cometh in the morning*" (Psalm 30:5). The trials and tribulations of life make you stronger. They build your life muscle. An effective leader with integrity positively embraces negativity with a mindset that believes things are going to get better. This is part of growing and maturing—personally and professionally. Let's look at this integrity quality.

Integrity Character Trait #5: Focus on Growing

Dr. Kilambi, mentioned earlier, is a friend who has one of the most interesting business careers in the areas of biorefineries, biomass, solar, nanotechnology, biotechnology, and clean water. His companies have many intellectual property (IP) technologies in diverse areas such as bioenergy, green chemicals, green materials, biosolar, and water. Another company is a torchbearer for a novel cement manufacturing technology for the first time since the Romans, a compelling solution to manufacture "Kiln and Clinker free nano-cement" using 75 percent less energy, 50 percent lower capital expense, and with 30 percent lower emissions of greenhouse gases than conventional Portland cement. He is the ultimate philanthropist, having authored India's second Food + Energy Revolution blueprint. To quote one of his business partners, "*Srinivas is a scientist, technologist, entrepreneur, and inventor all molded into one whose 'out of the box' thinking has led to several innovative yet practical ideas that have the potential to become viable business entities. He has the innate ability to take ideas from diverse fields and integrate them into a 'project' that could impact various human needs—food, water, building materials, and energy. He is a challenging leader who strives to get the most out of people who work for or with him—and in the process make them 'thinkers,' too.*"

Effective leaders embrace negativity because they have learned channeled in the right way it leads to growth. They energize people through ever-greater challenges. I was drawn to work for Dr. Kilambi because he was challenging. His ability and willingness to be concentrate on growth—were compelling. I have been around effectively successful people, but he was truly unique. There were colleagues who had myths about working with persons from India and questioned my decision to accept a full-time position as director of information technology after a six-month contract working as a senior project management consultant. But as a former *Street hustler,* I loved his boldness, frankness, and energy because it was reality. Working with him required having thick skin, but that was the makeup which allowed him to achieve success. Once he felt you exceeded his expectations, then he had your back! I was the third and last IT director he hired. Sometimes we would butt heads, but it was always professional, and once I provided justification, he would say, "Do it!"

Having an entrepreneur state of mind allowed me to seize this opportunity to direct his company's commercial and IT day-to-day operations. His stretch goals demanded that I engage in strategic development and alignment of IT strategy with "fluid" business objectives and provide thought leadership as a member of leadership team. Lead enterprise IT, including operations, tactical roadmap, infrastructure, networks, telephony, Supervisory Control and Data Acquisition (SCADA)/Program Logic Controller (PLC) software development, architecture, program/project/portfolio management, governance, on-demand/on-premise application development (e-procurement, e-HR, e-commerce, accounting, shop maintenance, and management), outsourcing and support—all with a full-time staff of two people. The challenge was always to exceed his expectations—we will talk about this later.

Dr. Kilambi understood my character and he expanded my role to director of commerce and information technology. He would challenge me, saying, "You have a PhD, which means you are an outstanding thinker and even better doer. That's why I hired you!" The business development executive from the Gartner Group further expanded my role by categorizing me as "acting chief information officer," because compared to her existing client executives in the middle market business space, my responsibilities/authorities equaled or exceeded theirs. Looking at Dr. Kilambi was like looking in a mirror; he was literally unable to not develop and grow. It is about "more," but in a different way from greedy people. That is not his character. The "more" is about becoming more of who he was as a person, in life, in business, and in his relationships. It was the curiosity and drive to develop into more ability, more knowledge, more completeness, and ultimately, more experience.

Drive through Your Last Down

As a football player, I never took a play off. This was attributed to my dependability. My teammates along with the coaches knew I would handle the responsibilities given to me on each play—bring a play into the quarterback, act as a decoy, block an opposing defensive player; run the ball; throw a half-back option pass; or catch the ball. Each play required the type of drive, or effort, as though I was playing my last down. You may have heard a sports commentator, when describing a running back, or halfback say, "He runs angry," "He finishes off the run," or "He runs each play as though it is his last." This is what I am talking about. Remember, I survived the perils of an inner-city red zone—this is instilled in me forever! Intensity and integrity are the keys that have opened the doors to a land of opportunity. This *"ain't no stoppin' me now"* attitude provided the mental toughness to take on the most difficult of assignments in any situation or environment with the determination to succeed. Pushed by this character, allows finding great purpose, passion, performance, and profit.

People with this character trait leave a reputation of making things bigger and better over time. There are some differences in this trait from the previous about solving problems. When people solve problems, they get better, their organizations get better, and their relationships get better. In other words, things improve. If you have a broken leg or an infection and you get it treated, it will definitely work better. You can use it again. But it will only do what it was already capable of, now without problems caused by the hindrance. It will work better, for sure. But it will not be stronger or able to do more than before you broke it. It will just be repaired.

In life, some people are good problem solvers, but are not growers. They clean up all the mess they encounter in themselves and others. As a direct result, they run clean businesses and have clean relationships. Things work, but they don't become more than they are. There good maintainers, as opposed to growers. Business will always need problem solvers, but they are not the ones you turn to for a business to grow. That takes a different skill set. It gets confusing, too, because good operations can add to profits and it will look as if the business is growing, as the numbers are getting better. But that increase is really about all the benefit of what already exists, not building more.

You may be asking, "OK, Dr. Harper, how do I grow?" Approach your growth as if you were playing "your last down." This creates a drive to become the best you can be. Don't take learning for granted—see chapter 5, "Ⓛearning Behavior." Reinvent yourself (remember the trilogy of success). **Focus on growing,** develop new skills or ways to do something to increase your value. View learning the ability to solve different problems as an opportunity to grow.

Based on what you've learned, we can agree that it is pretty tough to solve a problem in a vacuum. Can't we? You have to connect to others and be oriented toward the truth to solve the problem. Dr. Cloud states:

> The more we get into this thing called character, the more
> we see that integration and wholeness is paramount.
> It all goes together, and when we are stuck in one, it
> will certainly affect the other.

In other words, all character traits are integrated to form the behavior perceived as being of integrity—they are all interdependent, and it is difficult to have one really work without the others.

But as integrated as they are, there is still a difference in the creation of new capacities, new skills, and new areas of fruitfulness. To meet the total demands of reality, we must continuously grow. We must always increase our abilities, skills, and capacities, in every area of life. *That is* we must always continue to learn how to "get our hustle on!"

This book shares the life experiences of ordinary people who have done extraordinary things to show you that if they just maintained the status quo; never challenging themselves to grow; their dreams would not have become reality. To realize their dream(s), required notching it upward and outward, with the drive of an athlete playing as if it was their last down—or game. For those of you who never played sports what I am saying is there had to be a force inside that literally drove them to want, find, and be more. The fact that you are reading this book is a strong indication that you want to grow because you want more out of life. *Stated differently,* you want to experience your reality—by getting your hustle on!

Strategic hustlers™ have this drive inside. It is as natural to them as breathing. Everything they put in their hearts and minds is infused with this drive, to make it better and to make it grow. Their relationships grow, their businesses and careers grow, and their personhood grows. The groups and departments they belong to also grow. They can't help it. It is a drive. They have the "*Midas Touch.*" For those of you who may not be familiar with this phrase here is a lesson in Greek mythology. The Midas touch, or the gift of profiting from whatever one undertakes, is named for a legendary king of Phrygia. Midas was granted the power to transmute whatever he touched into gold. *Strategic hustlers*™ have this "Midas Touch" because most of the things they touch turn into gold!

Help Develop Others

The best way to retain anything is to teach it. Part of being a good learner is to be a good teacher. Teaching and sharing is a growth experience.

My growth is attributed to my ability and willingness to invest in the growth of others. All of the star performers in this book share that gift. That gift is called "Having a teachable point of view." We will talk about this later.

My desire to develop others began as a mentor to youth in high school and college. This assignment is a part of fulfilling God's purpose of me. I am inspired to contribute to the success of another individual. To quote the words of my dad's favorite song by the late great Mahalia Jackson:

> If I can help somebody
> As I travel along
> If I can help somebody
> With a word or song
> If I can help somebody
> From doing wrong
> My living shall not be in vain.
>
> My living shall not be in vain
> If I can help somebody
> While I'm singing this song
> My living shall not be in vain.

As the senior vice president and chief operating officer for a startup, First Rate Computer Training Corporation, I developed and executed a turnaround strategy taking the company from $200,000 to a projected $5.6 million in three years. The strategy focused on revising the customer satisfaction policy, growing our people into leaders, fine-tuning the "nuts and bolts" of the business to expand the product and service offerings, and partnering to enhance our core competencies. As the company began to turn around, a large consulting company signed a multiyear, multimillion-dollar contract with the firm to deliver training using a very popular computer operating system. We then entered into a multiyear, multimillion-dollar contract with a municipality in St. Louis, Missouri, to develop and deliver skills development training for vocational jobs. We received proclamations from the governor of the State of Georgia and the mayor of the City of Atlanta, Georgia, for a computer literacy program.

I've received local, state, national, and international acclaim for mentoring people who were doing interesting and helpful things having social value. Leveraging my childhood upbringing, I'd ask questions like: "What are you doing, and why are you doing it?" And, "How can you do it better?" Growth is motivated by the right "whys" and by growing into someone who can do it better. This has nothing to do with business strategy. It is an expression of my character. I must build into other people growing as well as myself. It is just part of who I am.

Having It All Together, Stay Hungry

Have you ever looked at a person and thought, "So-and-so has it all together"? What does "all together" mean? Our view of character has been based on the importance of integration at the macro level. The big picture is where all aspects of character are whole and come together to make for a person who is "all together." But the devil is in the details. In the micro level of this aspect, integration is a telltale sign of character as well. The person who is doing it well is growing not in just one area of life, but all of them. This is how you know it is character and not compensation.

In chapter 8, "(E)nergize People through Ever-Greater Challenges," there are a series of exercises to bring to fruition the point that I'm about to make. So don't worry if this is hard to grasp. To begin, some people just focus on their career and create lopsided growth. While they grow that aspect of who they will be, the rest of their lives lag behind. The fruit shows neglect of an integrated focus of growth. They advance in their profession and lose a marriage. They win accolades, but because of spiritual emptiness end up wondering, "Am I fulfilling my purpose?" They become technically savvy, and relationally inept.

When growth is like that, it is often compensatory in that people rely on strength to become all of life. In that way, they are asking aspects of themselves to do things that they cannot do. Your work cannot fulfill all of your needs as a person. Nor can your relationships. But often when people have character conflicts in one of those areas, they will ask the other area to become their whole life and thus compensate for what they can't do well. That is imbalance, and it always leaves its own reputation.

The integrated character feels the same hunger and awareness of the drive in all areas—the relational, spiritual, intellectual, and other aspects. In that, they create balance, and growth in one area fuels growth in another. Lopsided growth is a symptom of some aspect of disintegration in the person.

Consequently putting it all together means that for growth to happen, people must be fully alive, hungry for more, and not afraid to go out and seek it. Like my friend Dr. Kilambi in the seeking, in all areas, they become more than they were yesterday and pass that on.

Integrity Character Trait #6: Aim to Exceed Expectations

Earlier, you recall we talked about the trilogy of success:

1. Deliver results that exceed expectations
2. Reinvent yourself
3. Assimilate into the social culture of the organization

These points are the focus of this final character trait. How have I been able to deliver results that exceed expectations? It's one's ability and willingness to be transcendent—which leads to enlargement of the bigger picture and oneself. In chapter 12, "Ⓡespect Diversity," I talk about the effects of self-confidence—either you have it or you don't. Without stealing the thunder of that chapter, here is a snippet of what you will be receiving. One of the conversations lays the foundation on having an attitude that "I can walk on water" vs. "I won't drown." The conversation borders on being humbly self-confident as opposed to being arrogant. I want to put this attitude in context. To live and flourish, we must bow to the things larger than us. Father God, my parents, my grand-parents, teachers, and mentors are just a few of the people to whom I attribute my growth. When I think about how 80 percent of my growth is attributed to them, the words from the great Bobby Womack come to mind: "No matter how high I get, I still be looking up to you!" Seems like common sense right? And that is where character enters the scene and will determine everything about a person's reputation.

Keeping It Real, Get In Where You Fit In

I have been blessed and fortunate to travel the world meeting very interesting people. The people who are really grounded in who they are don't suffer from trying to be the center of the universe. They do not believe that every-thing and everyone exists to serve them and their purposes.

In its worst form, this is the ultimate sickness, akin to what psychologists refer to as narcissism. It is marked by such traits as grandiosity, omnipotence, extreme selfishness, exploitiveness, lack of empathy, an overestimation of one's talents or importance, feelings of entitlement, and egocentricity. People feel they are "special." You know the traits and have seen them. Descriptions of them make it into the vernacular of our culture, such as T-shirts that say, "It's all about me."

But aside from such jokes that more normal people make about themselves when they see themselves as a little self-centered, most of the time we do not like the trait at all and don't want to be identified with it in any manner. We see it as immature at best and arrogant, selfish, or prideful at worst. Being self-centered is not admirable because it craves the very admiration that is not earned. In chapter 2, "Ⓐdaptable Behavior," the discussion on negative com-munication team traps can be directly tied to self-centeredness. How? This siloed thinking takes away from the systems thinking that is required to being authentic and being perceived as a team player.

Psychologists say the opposite of this kind of self-centered behavior can be described in many ways. I like to think of it as a quality of "keeping it real." It is the person who has gotten beyond, above, or transcended ordinary human selfishness, self-centeredness, and lives in a very different reality from thinking life revolve around them. I have had the experience and blessing of helping to raise fourteen godchildren, nieces, and nephews (four boys and ten girls), along with a younger brother and sister. In watching them grow and their unique personalities form, I've witnessed the self-centered attitudes change as they realize there are things much bigger than them, and that their existence is really not just about them and their interests, but ultimately about the things larger than they are. They have learned their life is about fitting into those things, joining them, serving them, obeying them, and finding their role in the big picture. Ultimately they become part of them and find meanings much larger than a life that is just about them. Life is about blending in with things that transcend us. This, my friend, is getting out of one's own way and "keeping it real!" Oh, by the way, recall the point made earlier about "assimilating into the social culture of the organization." *It's the same soup but a different bowl. Said another way*, we all have to learn how to "get in where you fit in."

Being Emotionally Aware

In chapter 12, "(R)espect Diversity," we will discuss *emotional awareness,* the recognition of how our emotions affect our performance, and the ability to use our values to guide decision making.

It is not only the megalomaniacs and those with Napoleon complexes who think it all exists for them. There are milder versions as well; the ones that we usually battle within ourselves and in people with whom we associate. Often this trait is just annoying, but if someone has a lot of responsibility, or if we are connected to them in a significant way, the results can be devastating.

Instead, we long to be around those who are willing to take one for the team. They have a servant mentality. I recall countless situations when delivering information to my staff that those individuals who see the glass as being half empty would ask "What's in it for me?" questions. Almost in an instant, the people who see the glass as being half full would give them a look as if they were saying, "It's bigger than you; look, get over it."

Working with some of the largest companies in the world or volunteering on some of the largest initiatives in the world supports that big things, not ourselves, are the things that make us large. My joining these initiatives made me larger. The paradox is that to join things bigger than us, we have to humble ourselves and become "smaller," in a sense. My ability and willingness to realize that I am smaller than the transcendent things, and I exist for them and not them for me, allow me to be excellent and grow into greatness. When my dad told me, "Don't be afraid to be great," I had to learn how. I've come to the final conclusion. The greatest people are the ones who have not sought greatness, but served greatly, the causes, values, and missions that were much bigger than they were. And by joining and serving those, exceeding expectations, greatness emerges.

I want the reader to be emotionally aware that if we think we are "bigger" and that everything is about us, then we are reduced to a little world of our own making. And we see everything only in terms of what it means for us. The results are always shallow, smaller, or even toxic, destructive, and poisonous.

Recall the earlier discussion on adaptive behavior. A major reason for the contents of this book is to encourage you that if a man like me can come from where I come from, survive what I've survived, and humbly accomplish what I've accomplished, then so can you. Just know that it is always "bigger than you!" I can't tell you where you are in life, but I can hopefully provide you with the T-N-T (Tools and Techniques) on how you can exploit the positive attributes of integrity and courage to meet the demands of reality. After all, this is a key to exceeding expectations. Another key is daring to be different.

Dare to be Different

Let's talk about Blue Ocean Strategy (BOS). An in-depth discussion is beyond the scope of this book. I strongly suggest you visit www.blueoceanstrategy. com for more detail. Here are a couple of epic quotes from the authors of *Blue Ocean Strategy*, W. Chan Kim and Renée Mauborgne:

Quote #1: "Stop benchmarking your competition. The more your benchmark your competition, the more you tend to look like them."
Quote #2: "There is no such thing as a permanently great company, or permanently great industry. But there are permanently great strategic moves."

With a little imagination these can be applied to your personal life.

Quote #1: Stop following the crowd be a leader.
Quote #2: If my success is to be it is up to me!

What is Blue Ocean Strategy (BOS)? The following are ten key points to define BOS:

- BOS is a proven strategic planning approach based on research of 150 strategic moves spanning over more than a hundred years and thirty industries
- BOS dares you to be different at a low cost
- The aim of BOS is not to outperform the competition in the existing industry, but to create new market space, or a Blue Ocean, thereby making the competition irrelevant—this is *key*!

- Value innovation is the hallmark of BOS as it is accomplished using systematic and reproducible methodologies and processes in pursuit of Blue Oceans by both new and existing firms
- Creating a BOS requires using the following T-N-T: the strategy canvas, value curve, four actions framework, six paths, buyer experience cycle, buyer utility map, and Blue Ocean idea index
- The visual focus of the T-N-T effectively builds the collective wisdom of the company, improving communication for effective strategy execution
- BOS covers both strategy formulation and strategy execution
- In addition to value innovation other key conceptual building blocks of BOS are tipping point leadership and fair process
- While competitive strategy is a structuralist theory of strategy where structure shapes strategy, BOS is a reconstructionist theory of strategy where strategy shapes structure—we will talk more about these concepts later
- As an integrated approach to strategy at the system level, BOS requires organizations to develop and align the three strategy propositions: value proposition, profit proposition, and people proposition

As you see, to be a **BOS**ist, or **B**lue **O**cean **S**trategist, requires intelligent behavior to dare to be different. We talked about structuralist theory of strategy and reconstructionist theory of strategy. For those of you who may not be familiar with strategic decisions processes, let me give you some insight on strategy's relationship to the organizational structure.

How Strategy Shapes Structure

When executives develop corporate strategy, they nearly always begin by analyzing the industry or environmental conditions in which they operate. They then assess the strengths and weaknesses of the players they are up against. With these industry and competitive analyses in mind, they set out to carve a distinctive strategic position where they can outperform their rivals by building a competitive advantage. To obtain such advantage, a company generally chooses either to differentiate itself from the competition for a premium price or to pursue low costs. The organization aligns its value chain accordingly, creating manufacturing, marketing, and human resource strategies in the process. On the basis of these strategies, financial targets and budget allocations are set. We will talk more about value chains during our discussion on **G.R.I.P.**

The underlying logic here is that a company's strategic options are bounded by the environment. *Its* structure shapes strategy. This "structuralist" approach has dominated the practice of strategy for the past thirty years. According to it, a firm's performance depends on its conduct, which in turn depends on basic structural factors such as number of suppliers and buyers and barriers to entry. It is a deterministic worldview in which causality flows from external conditions down to corporate decisions that seek to exploit those conditions.

Even a cursory study of business history, however, reveals plenty of cases in which firms' strategies shaped industry structure, from Ford's Model T to Nintendo's Wii. Blue Ocean Strategy reflects the fact that a company's performance is not necessarily determined by an industry's competitive environment. The Blue Ocean Strategy framework can help companies systematically reconstruct their industries and reverse the structure-strategy sequence in their favor.

Blue Ocean Strategy has its roots in the emerging school of economics called endogenous growth, whose central paradigm posits that the ideas and actions of individual players can shape the economic and industrial landscape. *That is* strategy can shape structure. Kim and Mauborgne call this approach "reconstructionist."

While the structuralist approach is valuable and relevant, the reconstructionist approach is more appropriate in certain economic and industry settings. Indeed, today's economic difficulties have heightened the need for a reconstructionist alternative. The first task of an organization's leadership, therefore, is to choose the appropriate strategic approach in light of the challenges the organization faces. Choosing the right approach, however, is not enough. Executives who are effective leaders then need to make sure that their organizations are aligned behind it to produce sustainable performance. Most executives understand the mechanics of making the structuralist approach work, so we will focus on how to align an organization behind the reconstructionist approach to deliver high and sustainable performance.

Intelligent Behavior is Asking, "What is the Right Strategic Approach for You?"

There are two factors that determine the right approach to win: the structural conditions in which an organization operates its resources and capabilities, and its strategic mind-set. When the structural conditions of an industry or environment are attractive and you have the resources and capabilities to carve out a viable competitive position, the structuralist approach is likely to produce good returns. Even in a not-so-attractive industry, the structuralist approach can work well if a company has the resources and capabilities to beat out the competition. In either case, the focus of strategy is to leverage the organization's core strengths to achieve acceptable risk-adjusted returns in an existing market.

But when conditions are unfavorable and they are going to work against you whatever your resources and capabilities might be, a structuralist approach is not a smart option. This often happens in industries characterized by excess supply, cutthroat competition, and low profit margins. In these situations, an organization should adopt a reconstructionist approach and build a strategy that will reshape industry boundaries.

The question is, "What is the right strategic approach for us?" Let me extend the question, "What is the right strategic approach for us—to win?"

How Blue is Your Company

- Is your company facing heightened competition from domestic and international rivals?
- Do your sales representatives increasingly argue they need to offer deeper and deeper price discounts to make sales?
- Are you finding you need to advertise more to get noticed in the marketplace, yet the impact of each advertising dollar spent is falling?
- Is your company focused more on cost cutting, quality control, and brand management at the expense of growth, innovation, and brand creation?
- Do you blame your slow growth on your market?
- Do you see outsourcing to low cost companies or countries as a principal prerequisite to regain competitiveness?
- Are mergers and acquisitions the principal means your company sees to grow?
- Is it easier to get funding to match a strategic move made by your competitor than it is to get internal funding to support a strategic move that allows you to break away from the competition?
- Is commoditization of offerings a frequent worry of your company?
- List your key competitive factors; now list your competition's. Are they largely the same?

According to Kim and Mauborgne, if you answered yes to a majority of these questions, then your company is stuck in the red ocean.

Blue Ocean strategy offers you a way to swim out of the red ocean filled with sharks. It presents a theory, tools, and frameworks to allow your company to break away from the competition and create a blue ocean of new market space.

Summary

You can't be a strategic thinker, or *Strategic hustler*™, without innovation, initiative, insight, influence, and interpersonal skills (communication), or without integrity! The 6 *I*s are the essentials to intelligent behavior. Being a BOSist requires using this behavior to go where no one else has. This intelligence motivates great leaders to have the propensity to learn and leverage what they have learned to grow and teach others. You have to share the wealth. *Said another way*, you have to learn, or take, and teach, or give. This leads to the next chapter, which discusses the Ⓛ in **A.G.I.Ⓛ.E.**—Ⓛearning behavior.

CHAPTER 5

Learning Behavior

Introduction

This is a book for the ages. I was the founder and advisor for an award-winning educational program called CompuKamp™ that provided computer literacy and personal development instruction to students ranging from age seven to seventy. The objective of the four-week course was to expose students to various computer applications—including but not limited to: computer engineering, robotics, simulations, communications, desktop publishing, etc—and basic learning and leadership skills. The course motto was "Cyberculture is a social structure and way of life in which wealth, power, and success belong to the computer literate." Many students completed this very demanding curriculum providing me with the life-long teaching lesson—communication barriers can be overcome. Also, delivering training to thousands of professionals from all walks of life fueled this truism. These experiences reinforced one of the most valuable lessons learned growing up in an inner-city red zone: that leaders are born to be made.

During my doctoral studies, I completed courses entitled "Philosophy of Wholism" and "Ecology." My appreciation of these courses centered on the enlightenment given that though theories sound dramatically new and different, closer scrutiny reveals that they recycle previous ideas. The courses also required reading practical and applicable books in philosophy. As a professional trainer, I was particularly intrigued with literature focused on the philosophy and practices of organizational learning, performance, and change. This chapter stresses the importance of being a learner for practicing and aspiring managers and leaders. Let's start the discussion with my viewpoint: learning leaders create learning organizations by teaching.

The Learning Organization

Learning organizations are:

Organizations where people continually expand their capacity to create the results they truly desire, where new and expansive patterns of thinking are nurtured, where collective aspiration is set free, and where people are continually learning to see the whole together.

The basic rationale for such organizations is that in situations of rapid change only those that are flexible, adaptive, and productive will excel. For this to happen, it is argued, organizations need to "discover how to tap people's commitment and capacity to learn at all levels." (Senge, 1990)

It is a well-documented fact, or common knowledge, all people can learn providing they are placed within an environment and given the tools and guiding ideas that facilitate learning, and, most importantly, they *listen effectively.*

Being part of a great team is a meaningful experience. Listening to former college teammates and coaches who experienced careers in the National Football League (NFL), former staff members, students, fraternity brothers, sorority sisters, and professional colleagues they all talk about being part of something larger than themselves, of being connected, or being generative. It becomes quite clear that, for many, their experiences as part of truly great teams stand out as singular periods of life lived to the fullest. Some spend the rest of their lives looking for ways to recapture that spirit.

Real learning gets to the heart of what it is to be human. We become able to re-create ourselves—recall point number two of the trilogy of success—the ability and willingness to reinvent. This applies to both individuals and organizations. Thus, for a learning organization, it is not enough to survive.

"Survival learning," or what is more often termed "adaptive learning," is important—indeed, it is necessary. But for a learning organization, "adaptive learning" must be joined by "generative learning," learning that enhances our capacity to create. (Senge, 1990)

The dimension that distinguishes learning from more traditional organizations is the mastery of certain basic disciplines, which are innovating learning organizations. These disciplines are systems thinking, personal mastery, mental models, building shared vision, and team learning.

Systems Thinking—the Cornerstone of the Learning Organization

Ecology teaches us that every person, place, or thing has an inherent interdependency on its environment. This is synonymous to systems thinking.

Systems thinking is a formal discipline of management science that deals with whole systems, their interconnections, and interactions of individual parts. For example, can you imagine holding up your hand a foot in front of your face and blocking your view of the earth, the entire earth? Astronauts have been able to do that. The world looks drastically different from their perspective. They see the whole earth. Unfortunately, we only see bits and pieces of our company and industry in our earthly day-to-day work. Systems thinking provide a wholistic approach to learning.

Let's dig a little deeper. We learn best from our experiences, but we never directly experience the consequences of many of our most important decisions with regard to organizations. We tend to think that cause and effect will be relatively near to one another. Thus, when faced with a problem, it is the solutions that are close by that we focus upon. *Said another way*, we make decisions like a *Street hustler*. Like the *Street hustler*, we look to actions that provide short-term benefits. We don't consider the consequences of our decisions downstream. However, when viewed in systems terms, short-term benefits often involve very significant long-term costs. For example, cutting back on research and design can bring very quick cost savings, but can severely damage the long-term viability of an organization. Part of the problem is the nature of the feedback we receive. Some of the feedback will be reinforcing (or amplifying), with small changes building on themselves. This small action snowballs, with more and more and still more of the same, resembling compound interest. Thus, we may cut our advertising budgets, see the benefits in terms of cost savings, and in turn further trim spending in this area.

In the short run, there may be little impact on people's demands for our goods and services, but, in the long term, the decline in visibility may have severe penalties. An appreciation of systems will lead to recognition of, use of, and problems with such reinforcing feedback, also in addition to an understanding of the place of balancing (or stabilizing) feedback. A further key aspect of systems is the extent to which they inevitably involve delays—interruptions in the flow of influence that make the consequences of an action occur gradually.

The systems viewpoint is generally oriented toward the long-term view. That is why delays and feedback loops are so important. In the short term, you can often ignore them; they are inconsequential. They only come back to haunt you in the long term. The *Strategic hustler*™ understands and embraces this.

I am going to introduce a tool and technique (T-N-T) that allows you to graphically illustrate key elements of systems and how they interact—system maps. System maps provide a way to take a journey of "seeing" systems using a picture. Note it's challenging to "seeing" systems, and it takes work to acquire the basic building blocks of systems theory and to apply them to your organization. On the other hand, failure to understand system dynamics can lead into cycles of blaming and self-defense. As I recall my dad admonishing me, "Expect the unexpected." Failure to understand the big picture makes you reactive, fueling these cycles. Later you will learn two types of system maps—super system map and strategic maps. For now let's examine the core disciplines.

The core disciplines

Alongside systems thinking, there stand four other disciplines. My view of a "discipline" is a series of principles and practices that we study, master, and integrate into our lives. The five disciplines can be approached at one of three levels:

- Practices—what you do.
- Principles—guiding ideas and insights.
- Essences—the state of being those with high levels of mastery in the discipline

Each discipline provides a vital dimension. Each is necessary to the others if organizations are to be learned. The following pages will cover each of these disciplines: Personal Mastery, Mental Models, Shared Visions, and Team Learning.

Personal Mastery

Organizations learn only through individuals who learn. Individual learning does not guarantee organizational learning. But without it, no organizational learning occurs. *Personal mastery* is the discipline of continually clarifying and deepening our personal vision; of focusing our energies, of developing patience, and of seeing reality objectively. It goes beyond competence and skills, although it involves them. It goes beyond spiritual opening, although it involves spiritual growth. Mastery is seen as a special kind of proficiency. It is not about dominance, but rather about calling. Vision is vocation rather than simply just a good idea (Senge, 1990).

People with a high level of personal mastery live in a continual learning mode. Consider them ultimate lifelong learners. They never arrive. Sometimes, language such as the term "personal mastery" creates a misleading sense of definiteness, of black and white. But personal mastery is not something you possess. It is a process and lifelong discipline. People with a high level of personal mastery are acutely aware of their ignorance, their incompetence, and their growth areas. And they are deeply self-confident. You recall in chapter 4, "Ⓘntelligent Behavior," our discussion on integrity, "Seeking Reality?" The essence of that topic was, "*The opposite of actively seeking reality is avoidance. People do the same kinds of things out of basic character problems—basic pride, omnipotence, arrogance, grandiosity, or narcissism. To admit being wrong about something does not enter their minds.* "This may seem paradoxical, but only for those who do not see the journey is the reward.

Earlier I introduced the term "self-directed" during the discussion on the R1 to R2 to R3 phenomenon. To further develop the importance of being self-directed, I'll start by saying self-direction is a discipline. This is an important term, because the key to being a lifelong learner is developing this discipline. The discipline entails developing personal vision; holding creative tension (managing the gap between our vision and reality); recognizing structural tensions and constraints, and our own power (or lack of it) with regard to them; a commitment to truth; and using the subconscious (Senge, 1990). *In other words,* self-directed learners set their own goals and standards and the path to attaining them—with or without help from experts. They use experts, institutions, and other resources to pursue these goals. Being independent does not mean being a loner; many independent learners are highly social and belong to clubs or other informal learning groups. A self-directed learner is both able and willing to take responsibility for his or her learning, direction, and productivity. He or she exercises skills in time management, project management, goal setting, self-evaluation, peer critique, information gathering, and use of educational resources. He or she can learn from any kind of teacher, but most thrive in an atmosphere of autonomy. Some learners become situationally self-directed; some become self-directed in a more general sense.

I am a self-directed learner. In earning my PhD in administration and management, the learning philosophy of Columbia Commonwealth University was based on having students who would excel as self-directed learners. Some may call this nontraditional learning. I'm inclined to include this in the category called experiential learning. Personal mastery requires understanding one's mental model.

Mental Models

Experiential learning results in people having their own unique mental models. To further develop the term "experiential learning," it is learning acquired through life journeys. A mental model is an explanation of someone's thought process about how something works in the real world (reality). It is a representation of the surrounding world, the relationships between its various parts, and a person's intuitive perception about his or her own acts and their consequences. Our mental models help shape our behavior and define our approach to solving problems (akin to a personal algorithm) and carrying out tasks.

How? These are "deeply ingrained assumptions, generalizations, or even pictures and images that influence how we understand the world and how we take action" (Senge, 1990). This is our professional "repertoire." We are often not that aware of the impact of such assumptions etc. on our behavior – and, thus, a fundamental part of our task is to develop the ability to think on our feet. Just reflect on a situation where you had to provide an answer to a question that you had not prepared for.

The discipline of mental models starts with turning the mirror inward learning to uncover our internal pictures of the world, to bring them to the surface and hold them carefully to inquiry. It also includes the ability to carry on meaningful conversations that balance inquiry and encouragement, where people expose their own thinking effectively and make that thinking open to the influence of others.

The learning leader must understand that for any organization to develop a capacity to work with mental models, it will be necessary for people to learn new skills and develop new orientations, and the necessity for institutional changes, they must promote such changes. The key point to understand is that entrenched mental models thwart changes that could come from systems thinking. This is why point two of the trilogy of success is so critical. Moving the organization in the right direction entails working to transcend the sorts of internal politics and game playing that dominates traditional organizations. It also involves seeking to distribute business responsibly far more widely while retaining coordination and control. This can only happen when the teams within the business are focused on the same goal. This requires building a shared vision.

Building Shared Vision

Let me start by stating that if any one idea about leadership has inspired organizations for thousands of years, it is the capacity to hold a shared picture of the future we seek to create. Leadership with vision has the power to be uplifting—and to encourage experimentation and innovation. Creating a common vision and common purpose fosters a sense of the long term, which is fundamental to systems thinking.

Let's dig a little deeper into vision and purpose. Since this book covers leadership, the essential leadership act is to create visions that bring people together and give them a sense of common purpose. Those who create the vision are "visioning." Purposing is continuous stream of actions by an organization's formal leadership that has the effect of inducing clarity, consensus, and commitment regarding the organization's basic purpose (Cohen, 1993). When there is visioning and purposing, people excel and learn not because they are told to, but because they want to. But many leaders fail to make the connection between visioning and purposing. Their visions never get translated into shared visions that fire up an organization. What has been lacking is a discipline for translating vision into shared vision—not a "cookbook," but a set of principles and guiding practices.

The practice of shared vision involves the skills of finding shared "pictures of the future" using visioning and purposing that foster genuine commitment and enrolment rather than compliance. In mastering this discipline, leaders learn the counter productiveness of trying to dictate a vision, no matter how heartfelt. This point is driven home in the book, *Goal Realization: The Project Management Objective*, by James J. Jones—an adjunct professor and corporate trainer/management consultant. The chapter entitled "They Gotta Wanna Or They Ain't A Gonna" eloquently highlights the pitfalls of trying to influence people who can't answer the question, "What's in it for me?" This brings us to the next discipline—team learning.

Team Learning

Such learning is viewed as "the process of aligning and developing the capacities of a team to create the results its members truly desire" (Senge, 1990). It builds on personal mastery and shared vision—but these are not enough. People need to be able to act together. As a person who has benefited from leading and being an individual contributor on teams–athletic, community, and business—for over forty years, I can attest that team learning, is mutually beneficial for the organization in that it provides favorable results, and for each member as their professional and personal growth is accelerated than what would occur individually.

The discipline of team learning starts with "dialogue," the capacity of members of a team to delay assumptions and enter into a genuine "thinking together." *To the Greeks,* dia-logos *meant a free flowing of meaning through a group, allowing the group to discover insights not attainable individually.... [It] also involves learning how to recognize the patterns of interaction in teams that undermine learning (Senge, 1990).*

Recalling my learning experience from the "Ecology" and "Philosophy of Wholism" classes, when dialogue is joined with systems thinking, there is the possibility of communicating in a language that is more suited for dealing with issues wholistically rather than being diverted by questions of personality and leadership style. Hence the journey from thinking like a *Street hustler* to a *Strategic hustler*™ begins.

Thus, you've learned that embracing the disciplines of systems thinking, personal mastery, mental models, building a shared vision, and team learning are keys to acquiring the behavior trait of being a learning leader. You now have the foundation to leading a learning organization. But leaders lead from differing perspectives and roles.

Leading the learning organization

As a learning leader, understand that leaders come in three flavors: design-ers, stewards, and teachers. They are responsible for *building organizations* where people continually expand their capabilities to understand complex-ity, clarify vision, and improve shared mental models—they are responsible for learning. Learning organizations will remain a good idea...until people take a stand for building such organizations. Taking this stand is the first leadership act, the start of *inspiring* (literally, "to breathe life into") the vision of the learning organization. Let's look at the responsibility of each role.

Leader as designer

As an executive, manager, and trainer/coach I have had to create learning approaches to develop leaders and employees. The focus was to design a learn-ing process that would allow each job performer to effectively and efficiently resolve the critical issues they face and develop their mastery in the learning disciplines. ***Thus,*** the learning goal was to design a system to make the leader and employee more productive. Integrating the five disciplines is fundamen-tal. However, the first task entails designing the governing ideas—the pur-pose, vision, and core values by which people should live. The leader should start with building a shared vision, as it fosters a long-term orientation and an imperative for learning. Other disciplines also need to be attended to, but just how they are to be approached is dependent upon the situation faced. Let's look at a couple of examples.

As the chief learning officer for a leading Oracle consulting firm I devel-oped and implemented a professional development plan by understand-ing the company's work dynamics; identifying mission-critical positions and gaps in organizational competencies, then identified curriculums leading to Oracle Certification at Associate, Professional and Master level in various disciplines.

As an executive coach/trainer delivering proprietary performance-based training in: technology management; project leadership; process improve-ment; risk management; systems design; and earned value business manage-ment, students were required to create an action plan detailing how they would use the skills acquired during the training to drive improved produc-tivity throughout their organization. Follow-up mentoring and consulting allowed me to help many students achieve their plans delivering technology, process improvement, organizational change management solutions resulting in millions of dollars in savings and revenues.

Leader as steward

As an IT executive with a startup company in the biotech renewable energy space, I worked closely with the associate vice presidents of projects and business development and supply chain management. With each potential business partner or employee, they were told purpose stories about our organization. As I listened to the stories shared by each leader, I came to realize that they were doing more than telling stories, they were relating the story; the overarching explanation of why we do what we do, how the organization needs to evolve, and how that evolution is part of something larger. I realized that such *purpose* stories provide a single set of integrating ideas that give meaning to all aspects of the leader's work—and, not unexpectedly, the leader develops a unique relationship to his or her own personal vision. He or she becomes a steward of the vision.

An important point to grasp here is that stewardship involves a commitment to, and responsibility for, the vision, but it does not mean that the leader owns it. It is not his or her possession. Leaders are stewards of the vision; their task is to manage it for the benefit of others. Leaders learn to see their vision as part of something larger. Purpose stories evolve as they are being told, in fact; they are as a result of being told. Leaders have to learn to listen to other people's visions and to change their own where necessary. Telling the story in this way allows others to be involved and to help develop a common vision that is both individual and shared.

Leader as teacher

Leaders must have a teachable point of view. I will cover this more in detail later in the book. But the first responsibility of a leader is to define reality. While leaders may draw inspiration and spiritual reserves from their sense of stewardship, much of the leverage leaders can actually exert lies in helping people achieve more accurate, more insightful, and more *empowering* views of reality. Let's consider these statements from Gail Sheehy's *New Passages: Mapping Your Life Across Time*:

Each of us tells our own personal life story to ourselves, every day. The "mind chatter" that rushes through our brains at two hundred words per minute when we're not concentrating on something else becomes the story we are living. I should have done this, or I'll never get over that.

The mind is formed to an astonishing degree by the act of inventing and censoring ourselves. We create our own plot line. And that plot line soon turns into a self-fulfilling prophecy. Psychologists have found that the way people tell their stories becomes so habit-ual that they finally become receipts for structuring experience itself, for laying down routines into memory. (Sheehy 1995:169)

I came across these profound statements studying the philosophy of wholism. Recall the discussion on mental models? There our professional repertoire of how we understand the world and how we take action. These statements helped me to self-assess my mental models by turning the mir-ror inward, learning to uncover my internal pictures of the situation to bring them to the surface, and exercise my ability to ask questions to understand the truth and to carry on learningful conversations that bal-ance inquiry and encouragement, and make my thinking open to the influ-ence of others. A good practice is to seek to understand and then to be understood.

The Pinnacle: Profound Learning/Teaching Requires Commitment

As a lifelong learner, I believe true learning takes place when the leader/ teacher invests the time and the emotional energy to energize those around them in a dialogue that produces mutual understanding. You can command behaviors by issuing orders. But developing effective leaders who will continue to teach others requires a serious commitment to teaching.

Figure 5-1 leverages earlier lessons in Situational Leadership® behaviors to communicate various approaches to leading and teaching. At the lowest level, the learner uses a command (S4—Delegating) approach to lead and teach. At the highest level the learner uses a teaching (S3—Participating) approach to lead and teach. Notice the similarities for the Sell Them (S2—Selling) and Tell Them (S1—Telling). Recall situation leadership addresses the level of interaction between task and relationship. As a learner, effective leaders must force new leaders to constantly teach and learn this way of teaching leadership renews the team, group, or organization. According to leading experts, there are four critical factors to consider (Tichy, 2002):

1: Depth of Learning

The depth of learning that occurs both for the leader and the follower varies significantly depending upon the leader's approach. At the most superficial level, command and control leaders do not create much learning for them-selves or their followers. At the other end of the spectrum, both the leaders and the followers learn from each other.

Figure 5-1: Approaches to Leading and Teaching

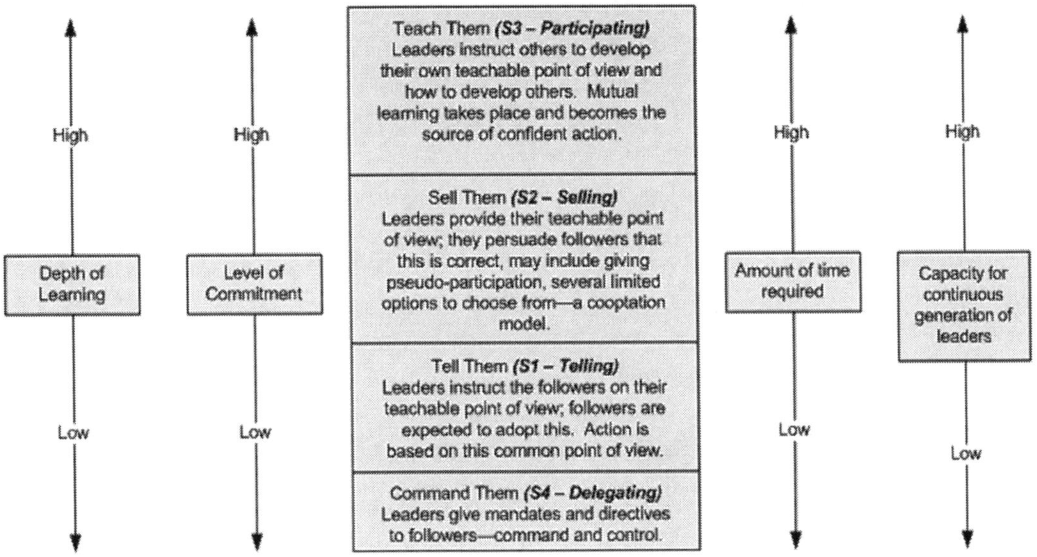

High — Depth of Learning — Low

High — Level of Commitment — Low

Teach Them (S3 – Participating)
Leaders instruct others to develop their own teachable point of view and how to develop others. Mutual learning takes place and becomes the source of confident action.

Sell Them (S2 – Selling)
Leaders provide their teachable point of view; they persuade followers that this is correct, may include giving pseudo-participation, several limited options to choose from—a cooptation model.

Tell Them (S1 – Telling)
Leaders instruct the followers on their teachable point of view; followers are expected to adopt this. Action is based on this common point of view.

Command Them (S4 – Delegating)
Leaders give mandates and directives to followers—command and control.

High — Amount of time required — Low

High — Capacity for continuous generation of leaders — Low

2: Commitment

Commitment is another critical factor. Teaching entails a serious commitment on the part of the leader to nurture his or her own personal development and other individuals and a serious commitment on the part of the followers to wrestle with the teacher's point of view and develop their own.

3: Time

It takes a little time to command and much time to teach.

4: Continuous Generation of Leaders

Later in the book, you will see that when there is genuine teaching, a positive cycle is created. Learners have developed their own points of view and are energized to help others as they have been helped. They consequently make good teachers. By contrast, the command model launches cycles that range from blind obedience to open revolt.

Your Own Leadership Lessons

Effective leaders are great teachers who are also great learners. The rite of passage is before you can teach, you must learn. Effective leaders have teachable points of view because they reflect on their lives and experiences. I have dedicated a later chapter, "(H)aving a Teachable Point of View," to this topic, but for now, I'll say you will see that they know what they know and they can tell you where they learned it. When I started to think about writing this book, it required taking the time to examine the important leadership, management, and learning events in my life. It helped me to begin to bring to the surface some of the tacit knowledge—the lessons I carried around with me—and make it explicit in this book. I attributed this to some of the following exercises, which you should do. Take each exercise in turn. At the end, you'll be asked to record some elements from your teachable points of view that have grown from your life experiences.

What is Your Proudest Leadership Moment?

In chapter 1, "Leaders Are Born to Be Made," it showed no matter where start in life *(Street hustler)* through honesty, hard work, prayer, and being in the right place at the right time you will finish at great heights *(Strategic hustler™)*. With reflection, meditation, constant learning, and practice you can improve your leadership abilities. Everyone has enjoyed leadership success at some point. At some time, whether in high school or college, on the athletic field, in a community or church group, or at work, we have all made things happen through other people that otherwise would not have occurred. We have all been leaders. Looking back over your life, what is the moment that you are *most* proud of as a leader? Use the space below to capture the details of that moment:

_____

_____

_____

_____

_____

_____

_____

_____

What is Your Worst Leadership Moment?

Similarly, just as all of us have enjoyed success, we've also experienced the pain of leadership failure. Learning to be a leader requires looking back and learning from past mistakes so that you don't repeat errors in judgment or mistreat people. As you review your life, what was your most disappointing experience as a leader?

_____

_____

_____

_____

_____

_____

_____

Learn from Past Experiences

One of the characteristics of effective leaders is that they consciously think about their experiences. They roll them over in their minds, analyze them, and tie them together into teachable points of view. They constantly update and refine these views as they acquire new knowledge and experience. And they store them in the form of stories that they use not only for guiding their own decisions and actions, but also for teaching and leading others.

This book is about the life experiences of effective leaders. You need to identify the actual experiences, the impact they had on you at the time and what you have learned from them that shapes your teachable point of view. Yes I am telling you to take notes.

Lifelong Leadership Lessons

Review your life as a series of emotional learning experiences. Take a few minutes to consider the lessons you have learned in the past. Start with your first important leadership experience, whether as a child, young adult, or businessperson. Then, after you have brought yourself to the present, record some of your major lessons.

The distillation of ideas, values, edge, and methods for energizing others will be needed to further define your teachable point of view. These are the lessons you've drawn from your experiences that you can articulate and teach to others. The remainder of the chapters in this book will provide you with the information to further define each of these as you prepare your teachable point of view.

Experience	Leadership Lessons I Learned
1.)	
2.)	
3.)	
4.)	

Summary

In closing, the major takeaway is that we learn from experiences. The more effectively we listen the better we learn. As a leader, you should always learn what creates value and how to deliver it. Learning and growing excites everyone, motivating people to want to make the business the best it can be. They accept criticism and new ideas. They see the wisdom in them and apply what they learn to themselves and the value chain. Again, you can only *learn* if you *listen*!

Effective leaders are learners who consciously think about their experiences. They roll them over in their minds, analyze them, and draw lessons from them. They constantly update and refine their view as they acquire new knowledge and experience. And they store them in the form of stories that they use to not only guide their own decisions and actions, but their team and to lead others. The learning organization must have leaders who learn. Leaders who learn are successful because they are effective. Use the following **L.E.A.R.N.E.R.** acronym to recall the major points in this chapter:

L = Listen effectively; it is the key to learning
E = Exhibit enthusiasm about contributing to something bigger than yourself
A = Aspire toward excellence
R = Recognize the importance of being a lifelong learner

N = Nurture personal development in yourself and others
E = Enjoy self-directed learning
R = Review your life as a series of emotional learning experiences

I used the word "Effective" purposely throughout this book instead of "Winning" or "Successful." Why? Keep on reading to learn as the next chapter discusses the Ⓔ of **A.G.I.L.Ⓔ. L.E.A.D.E.R.S.H.I.P.**—Ⓔffective behavior.

CHAPTER 6

Effective Behavior

Introduction

A leadership scholar practitioner is enlightened by scholar and practical lessons in leadership. Personally my growth as a scholar came from years of researching numerous leadership literatures in uncovering, studying, and documenting the "Literature Review" chapter of my doctoral dissertation. As a practitioner, over thirty years of experience in athletic, community, and professional endeavors provided real-world leadership knowledge.

No one has a monopoly on knowledge. And although I have read a lot, it is impossible to read it all. And although I have a wealth of experiences, it too is impossible to experience it all. **My goal was to strive for excellence, *not* perfection. This is the intellectual underpinning of an effective leader.**

Tens of thousands of books have been written on leadership, and there are several academic journals devoted entirely to the subject, including *The Leadership Quarterly* and *The Journal of Leadership and Organizational Studies*. Perhaps the most definitive review and integration of the leadership literature was Bass and Stogdill's 1,200-page *Handbook of Leadership*, which was published in 1990 (and still does the best job of making sense of the literature, for my money). And if you *really* want a long book on leadership, you can get the four-volume *Encyclopedia of Leadership*, which checks in at 2,120 pages, weighs fifteen pounds, and, as of this writing, cost a whopping $800. Clearly, the task of reviewing the leadership literature—and acting on it as leader—isn't to understand it all (that is impossible), but to develop a point of view on the few themes that matter most.

In my reviews of the writings and research, I kept bumping into an old and popular distinction that has always interested me: leading vs. managing. The highly regarded leadership scholar Warren Bennis, quoted earlier in this book, has likely done more to popularize this distinction than anyone else has. He wrote in *Learning to Lead: A Workbook on Becoming a Leader* that "There is a profound difference between management and leadership, and both are important. To manage means to bring about, to accomplish, to have charge of or responsibility for, and to conduct. Leading is influencing, guiding in a direction, course, action, opinion. The distinction is crucial." And in one of his most famous lines, he added, "Managers are people who *do things right* and leaders are people who *do the right thing.*"

Another thing that interested me was making the distinction between effective and successful. Is an effective leader successful? Is a successful leader effective? Is the distinction between leading and managing important to answering these questions? Let's tackle the effectiveness and successful question then we will deal with leading and managing. The following sections on effectiveness are based on research findings and are summarized.

Determining Effectiveness

One of the most important issues facing the applied behavioral sciences is that of human productivity—the quality and quantity of work. Productivity concerns both effectiveness (the attainment of goals) and efficiency (resource costs, including those human resource costs affecting the quality of life). In this section, my primary focus is on effectiveness. Peter Drucker, a founding father of management theory, wrote, "Effectiveness is the foundation of success—efficiency is a minimum condition for survival after success has been achieved. Efficiency is concerned with doing things right. Effectiveness is doing the right things" (Drucker, 1973).

Management Effectiveness vs. Leadership Effectiveness

In discussing effectiveness, we must once again distinguish between management and leadership. As we discussed earlier, leadership is a broader concept than management. Management is thought of as a special kind of leadership in which the accomplishment of goals is paramount—more specifically; these goals are at the organizational level, process level, and job performer level. They also focus on resources, interfaces, and performance. This focus is the essence of **G.R.I.P.** management. You will learn more about the management practices used to control each later. Leadership is an attempt to influence people, individually and in groups, for whatever reason. Influence and leadership may be used interchangeably. Not all leadership behavior is directed toward accomplishing organizational goals. In fact, many times when you are trying to influence someone else, you are not even part of an organization. For example, when you are trying to get some friends to go someplace with you, you are not engaging in management, but you certainly are attempting leadership. If they agree to go, you are an effective leader but not an effective manager. Even within an organization setting, managers may attempt to engage in leadership rather than management because they are trying to accomplish personal goals, not organizational ones.

For example, a manager may have a strong personal goal to become a senior or executive level manager. In attempting to achieve this goal, this person may not be concerned with organizational goals at all, but only with undermining the plans of the person whose position he or she desires and others who may be contenders for the job. The manager may accomplish this personal goal and, in that sense, be a successful leader. However, this individual cannot be considered effective because these actions were probably disruptive to the effective operation of the firm.

Parkinson's "law" suggests a clear example of a person's placing personal goals before organizational goals. His law states that in bureaucracies, managers often try to build up their own departments by adding unnecessary resources such as human power, equipment, facilities, etc. (Parkinson, 1957). Although this tendency may increase the prestige and importance of the managers, it is often lease to "an organization environment that is not only inefficient but also stifling and frustrating to the individuals who must cope with (it)." (Carvell, 1970). Therefore, in discussing effectiveness, we must recognize the difference between individual goals, organizational goals, leadership, and management.

Successful Leadership vs. Effective Leadership

I struggled with this concept in naming my doctoral dissertation, but thanks to the help of a couple of psychology and organization books, I was able to understand there is a difference. Allow me to share this wisdom. Any attempt by you to have some effect on the behavior of another is called *attempted* leadership. This attempted leadership can be successful or unsuccessful in producing the desired response. A basic responsibility of managers in any type of organization is to get work done, with and through people, so their success is measured by the output or productivity of the group they lead. With that thought in mind, Dr. Bernard M. Bass suggested a clear distinction between successful and effective leadership or management (Bass, 1960). Let's dig deeper into his suggestion.

Suppose manager **A** attempts to influence individual **B** to do a certain job. **A's** attempt will be consider successful or unsuccessful depending on the extent to which **B** accomplishes the job.

Let's assume that **A's** leadership is successful. In other words, **B's** response to **A's** leadership stimulus falls at the successful end of the continuum which ranges from successful to unsuccessful. We still don't know the whole story of effectiveness.

If **A's** leadership style is not compatible with the expectations of **B**, and if **B** is antagonized and does the job only because of **A's** position of power, then we can say that **A** has been successful but not effective. **B** has responded as **A** intended because **A** has control of rewards and punishment. This is position power—not because satisfying the goals of the manager or the organization also satisfied **B's** needs.

On the other hand, if **A's** attempted leadership leads to a successful response, and **B** does the job because it's personally rewarding, then we consider **A** as having not only position power, but also personal power—the person has a charisma about them. **B** respects **A** and is willing to cooperate, realizing that **A's** request is consistent with some personal goals. In fact, **B** sees these personal goals as being accomplished by this activity. This is what effective leadership means, keeping in mind that effectiveness also appears as continuum that can range from very effective to very ineffective, as illustrated below.

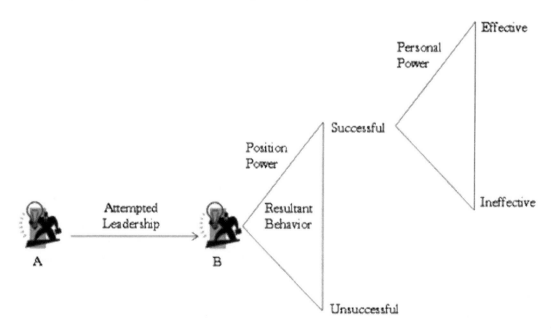

Success has to do with how the individual or the group behaves. On the other hand, effectiveness describes the internal state, or predisposition, of an individual or a group, and hence it is attitudinal in nature. Individuals who are interested only in success tend to emphasize their position power and use close supervision. Effective individuals, however, will also depend on personal power and use supervision that is more general. Position power tends to be delegated down through the organization; personal power is generated upward from below through follower acceptance.

A four-year observational study to determine the similarities and differences between successful managers (those who were rapidly promoted) and effective managers (those who had satisfied, committed employee and high-performing departments) by Fred Luthans, a professor of management at the University of Nebraska (Luthans, 1988), inspired me to conduct a similar study, during the period of 2000 to 2004, and compare the results. Thus while working on my doctorate and consulting for various companies around the country I observed the similarities and differences between successful managers and effective managers using the same criteria as Luthans. What I observed amazed me. Luthans' study reported that successful managers spent more of their time and effort networking with others inside and outside the organization than did effective managers. Politicking and socializing occupied most of their time, with less time spent on the traditional activities of managing—planning, organizing, directing, and controlling. This is exactly what I had observed too. Having served as State Advisor to the United States Congressional Advisory Board, the behaviors witnessed reminded me of those demonstrated by the congressman, senators, representatives worked with. **Said another way,** they behaved similarly to *politicians.* In contrast, the effective managers spent most of their time in communications, that is, managing workflow [people, process, information], and in human resource management i.e. motivating/inspiring, appraising/counseling, nurturing/developing, guiding/setting goals, educating/training, recognizing/rewarding/reprimanding. These activities contributed most to the excellence achieved in their high- performing departments. All *Strategic hustler*™ behavior qualities.

What I learned from both studies is that more attention needs to be paid to designing systems to motivate and inspire effective managers, not those with the most successful political and social skills. By rewarding effectiveness, organizations will increase their abilities to compete and excel in the twenty-first century.

In the management of organizations, the difference between successful and effective often explains why many supervisors can get a satisfactory level of output only when they are right there looking over a worker's shoulder. But as soon as they leave, output declines and often such things as horseplay and scrap loss increase.

Call centers realize this phenomenon that is why you will invariably hear the proverbial message, "For quality control purpose, this conversation may be recorded or monitored." By monitoring incoming calls, the supervisor can rapidly determine if service representatives are answering calls quickly and professionally. If the representatives perceive the monitoring in a negative fashion and view the supervisor as ineffective, their performance can deteriorate when the monitoring is stopped. A supervisor who uses the monitoring as a tool to assist the representatives in achieving business goals and who rewards positive improvements in call answering and order placement will find that performance stabilizes or improves even when the monitoring is discontinued. The supervisor has used effective leadership to help the representative meet business goals.

I am going to switch gears to discuss how this occurrence applies to education and business organizations but also to less formal organizations such as the family. If parents are successful and effective, having both position and personal power, their children accept family goals as their own. Consequently, if the husband and wife leave for the weekend, the children behave no differently than if their parents were there. If, however, the parents continue to use close supervision and the children view their own goals as being stifled by their parents' goals, the parents only have position power. They maintain order because of the rewards and the punishments they control. If these parents went away on a trip, leaving the children behind, upon returning they might be greeted by chaos.

So you see managers could be successful but ineffective, having only a short-lived influence over the behavior of others. On the other hand, if managers are both successful and effective, their influence tends to lead to long run productivity and organizational development. This really is what leadership and management is all about.

Now that I've dealt with the distinction between successful and effective, let's look at leading and managing.

The Essence of A.G.I.L.E. L.E.A.D.E.R.S.H.I.P. with a G.R.I.P.

The remainder of this chapter focuses on being an effective leader minimizing the gap between leadership and management. The previous information laid the foundation that being successful only comes from being effective. You can be successful and have the same short-term results as the *Street hustler*, or you can be effective and enjoy long-term success, as the *Strategic hustler*™.

Earlier I mentioned leading the commerce and IT departments for a couple of biotech companies producing alternative energy using biomass (wood/corn). They were funded by world-renowned venture capitalist Kleiner Perkins Caufield and Byers. While researching real-world advice on being a *Strategic hustler*™, I came across a July 27, 2010, interview that appeared on the *Fast Company* website, www.fastcompany.com, between Kermit Pattison and Randy Komisar—a partner at Kleiner Perkins Caufield and Byers. Having met some key partners from KPC&B, I am delighted to share the interview with you in a summarized form. It embodies **A.G.I.L.E. L.E.A.D.E.R.S.H.I.P.** with a **G.R.I.P**.

Fast Company Interview

Randy Komisar is a veteran Silicon Valley venture capitalist (VC) and entrepreneur who has spent the last twenty-five years launching technology startups. Komisar is a partner at Kleiner Perkins Caufield and Byers, where he specializes in working with technology entrepreneurs. "I'm not attracted to them because of the bottom line," he says. "I'm attracted to them because of the top line–the change they can make." His own pedigree: co-founder of Claris Corporation, CEO of LucasArts Entertainment, CEO of Crystal Dynamics, founding director of TiVo, senior counsel at Apple Computer, author of two books, and "virtual CEO" to an array of fledgling companies. In this Q&A, he warns of the classic mistakes of manager-wannabe-leaders, the perils of too many bullets and not enough Zen, and why CEOs are like dogs.

Kermit Pattison: What are the classic pitfalls you see entrepreneurs making over and over again?

Randy Komisar: Mistaking the difference between leadership and management. A lot of people believe the two are the same and believe that, because they have been effective or excellent managers, that they're capable of leading. While the two ideally come together, the qualities and attributes of a leader and a manager are not exactly the same.

Kermit Pattison: In your mind, what's the difference between management and leadership?

Randy Komisar: Management is more operationally focused. It's more of a supervisory role of setting priorities, allocating resources, and directing the execution. Leadership is more forward thinking, more about enabling the organization, empowering individuals, developing the right people, thinking strategically about opportunities, and driving alignment. Mind you, the line is not black and white. But it's a classic mistake to think that because someone is a good manager that he'll necessarily be a good leader.

In early stage projects, the CEO oftentimes is effectively a project manager. I've seen some of those people over think leadership—literally start to compound the challenges by thinking too big and not immediate enough.

Kermit Pattison: They start to think, "Oh, I've got to be a leader; I've got to start reading books and learning theory"?

Randy Komisar: Exactly—I need a vision statement; I need to define my culture in five bullet points. When I started running companies twenty-something years ago, I learned that the first thing to do was to define my culture, which meant sitting down and writing up a cute little vision statement. What I realized, after being involved with enough companies, is that these vision statements all look alike, the words are gobbledygook, and they're not very meaningful.

Now what I usually say is, "We're going to come up with a culture statement a year after we formed." Put it on the calendar. Why after a year? Because then we can actually see what our culture is—what we don't like about it and what we do like about it.

Kermit Pattison: How much of leadership is natural vs. a discipline that can be learned?

Randy Komisar: The first thing to realize is how many different styles of leadership can be successful. There isn't one style of leadership that is innately more successful than others are. There are certain skills sets, which are learnable, that are very important. You need to be able to communicate. If you can't communicate well, you won't be able to inspire, motivate, and attract the resources necessary for success. Prioritization is a really important skill. You've got to know what's more important than the other thing. It's amazing how many truly smart people can't prioritize. Only a minority of people can effectively prioritize and focus.

And you need to have effective interpersonal skills. That doesn't mean you need to be social and it doesn't mean you need to be outgoing. But it means that when you sit down in your office with somebody who's relying on you for leadership, you've got to be able to emphatically communicate with them around their challenges, figure out how to help them be more successful and resolve their conflicts so they can do their job better than they thought they could.

Kermit Pattison: You say companies need different breeds of leaders at different stages. How are CEOs like dogs?

Randy Komisar: I call the first CEO the retriever—the leader who has to go out and assemble the resources. He has to go out and find the people, the money, and the partners. That person is really great salesperson—he has to sell the vision every day. He's asking people to believe in something that doesn't exist and take a substantial leap of faith.

The next is the bloodhound CEO. You got to find out where that value proposition is going to find pay dirt so you can actually build a business around it. You've got something now, but how do you optimize it? You've got to sleuth that out.

The husky is the next one. Now you've got a product, a value proposition, and you've figured out your business model. Now you've got to pull this sled, as it gets heavier with people, products, and customers up a hill, which is essentially the hill of building a big successful business. The one dog you never really want pulling your company is the St. Bernard.

Kermit Pattison: The rescue dog.

Randy Komisar: Right. Because at that point you know, you've got big trouble.

Kermit Pattison: Even a great leader, if the wrong breed at the wrong time, can be a mismatch?

Randy Komisar: Absolutely. There are different talents in the *creation* of businesses and *running* of businesses that need to be taken into consideration. A mistake often made in the venture investment business is rushing to bring in a big CEO into what is still a small venture. The mismatch of skills is severe. The big CEO needs resources, needs a strong sense of direction and momentum, and is not very effective day to day with a bunch of people putting bits and bytes together. The other mismatch that's harder to foresee is the small company with momentum. You say, great, let's bring in the guy who can grow it to $100 million and take it public. The problem is that you may face yet another significant right or left hand turn in your business which that CEO may be completely unqualified to do. I liken it to a story a friend of mine told me many years ago about driving through the Sahara. For three nights, the road through the sand was dead straight to the south. On the third night, there was a right hand turn. At the base of that turn, it's full of crashed trucks. I think about that CEO the same way. If you're not an agile, venture CEO, you are very likely to end up crashing at that turn.

Kermit Pattison: What episode earlier in your career were formative experiences on leadership?

Randy Komisar: At Go Corporation I worked for Bill Campbell, who has absolutely been formative to me. Bill showed me, first and foremost, that business was worth doing. At that point, I was a lawyer and I certainly had no inclination to go into business. To me, business was about buying low and selling high–a fun game, but not an interesting life. Bill taught me the high art and that what was interesting are the people you work with, the people you sell to, the constituents and stakeholders you bring together, the art of being able to manage them all together to succeed, and to create potential beyond the obvious. I just found that mesmerizing– that's why I do what I do today.

Kermit Pattison: If you look at the ranks of CEOs today, who strikes you as being particularly thoughtful about leadership?

Randy Komisar: When I read interviews with CEOs lately around leadership, I've got to tell you, the stuff that gets published seems awfully conventional. I'm not seeing any brilliant insights about leadership lately from the leaders who get a following out there.

I've given up on the guru model and think more in the Zen model: things will change and that's okay. What we need is a set of constant provocations. What I like to read are those things that really challenge my assumptions, authors who are willing to think differently, no matter whether I agree with them or not, because they at least broaden my own thinking. What I don't like reading is the pabulum—the ten habits of great leaders or whatever. Those are constraining and not very effective for the average person.

Kermit Pattison: Speaking of bad advice, what's the worst advice about leadership you ever heard?

Randy Komisar: One of the most important lessons I learned is that people are not fungible. I've had bosses who said, "We're not going to pay well, invest, or develop our people because there's always somebody to take their place." The problem with that logic is, while it might be statistically true, it fundamentally indicates a culture that is not going to invest in anybody. Nobody is going to become very effective.

The other piece of leadership that somebody tried to teach me, which I dismissed, is manage by the numbers—if you manage by the numbers everything else takes care of itself. Just get people to execute, measure, hold people accountable, and that's enough. That's *not* enough. Yes, it is important to instill accountability in organization, it's important to have good metrics, to discipline the process, reward people, and withdraw those rewards when they're not being effective. But that won't get you greatness.

Kermit Pattison: So what does get you greatness?

Randy Komisar: When I am most successful, it's because the people around me have made me successful. It comes down to the fact that success is created by a group of people and not by any single individual. How do you get people to come together around a goal and objective and be great? It's establishing a sense of common purpose. Greatness doesn't come from a tactical sense of execution. Greatness comes having a vision that goes beyond yourself and even beyond the organization.

I hope you enjoyed this interview. Personally, working for a startup is great experience, especially when the owners are serial entrepreneurs. You learn that the only constant is change. The startup I worked with had three CEOs; each brought a certain level of expertise to bring it to the next level. Leaders in this type of environment must always keep their fingers on the pulse to be proactive, in control, and adaptive. *Said another way*, they must master the Knowing-Doing gap to be effective.

The Knowing-Doing Gap

In *The Knowing-Doing Gap* (Sutton, Robert and Pfeffer, Jeffrey, 2008), one of the themes of the book equates to the goal of "knowing the terrain" mentioned during my discussion on goal-oriented behavior. This book provides examples where leaders use various reasons distinguishing leading (knowing) and managing (doing) to avoid the hard work of learning about the people they lead, the technologies their companies use, and the customers they serve.

I remember hearing of a cell phone company CEO, for example, who never visited the stores where his phones were sold—because that was a management task that was beneath him—and kept pushing strategies that reflected a complete misunderstanding of customer experiences. (Perhaps he hadn't heard of how often the late Steve Jobs dropped in at Apple stores.) That story is typical. "Big picture only" leaders often make decisions without considering the constraints that affect the cost and time required to implement them, and even when evidence begins mounting that it is impossible or unwise to implement their grand ideas, they often choose to push forward anyway. One of my favorite reality shows entitled *The Boss*, in which CEOs took a page from Job's book and visited various operations of their business looking for process improvement and people enrichment opportunities.

As a certified project/program management trainer/consultant/mentor, I have had hundreds of conversations with project managers who have been assigned tasks by naive and overconfident leaders—things like implementing IT systems and building software. When they couldn't succeed because of absurd deadlines, tiny staffs, small budgets, and in some cases because it simply wasn't technically possible to do what the leaders wanted, they were blamed. Such sad tales further reinforce my view that thinking about what could exist, and telling people to make it so, is a lot easier than actually getting it done. I call this Management by Blue Sky.

Please do not misunderstand me, I advocate dreaming. The extraordinary acts of ordinary people start with a dream. But one characteristic of the dreamers I admire—Reginald Lewis, Dr. Bill Cosby, Oprah Winfrey, Steve Jobs, Tom Joyner, Russell Simmons, Bernie Marcus, Dr. Srinivas Kilambi,

Dr. Yamille Jackson, folks at Pixar like Ed Catmull and Brad Bird—is that they also have remarkably deep understanding of the industry they work in and the people they lead (recall my discussion in goal-oriented behavior, "Knowing the Terrain"), furthermore they are willing to get very deep into the weeds. This ability to go back and forth between the little details and the big picture is also evident in the leaders I admire most who aren't usually thought of as dreamers. Lee Iacocca's efforts to turn Chrysler around were successful in part because of his in-depth knowledge of the company's operations; he was very detail oriented during the crucial early years of his leadership. I recall reading that Bill George, in his first nine months as CEO of Medtronic (a medical device company), spent about 75 percent of his time watching surgeons put Medtronic devices in patients and talking with doctors and nurses, patients, families, and hospital executives to learn the ropes.

Summary

I am not rejecting the distinction between leadership and management, but arguing that the best leaders do something that might properly be called a mix of leadership and management. At a minimum, they lead in a way that constantly takes into account the importance of management. Meanwhile, the worst senior executives use the distinction between leadership and management as an excuse to avoid the details they really have to master to see the big picture and select the right strategies.

Therefore, harking back to the Bennis theorem earlier, let me propose a corollary: "To do *the right thing*, a leader needs to understand what it takes to do things right, and to make sure they actually get done." When you glorify leadership too much and management too little, there is great risk of failing to act on this obvious but powerful message. This is the essence of **A.G.I.L.E. L.E.A.D.E.R.S.H.I.P.** with a **G.R.I.P**.

The following provides an example on the importance of having behavior that is adaptable, goal-oriented, intelligent, learning, and effective. While serving on a executive advisory team—CIO, CTO, VP of Information Management, and myself—leading a process excellence program with a $55 million budget for a global leader in the reinsurance industry, we used a cultural-learning model for effective collaboration on various projects staffed with team members from: London United Kingdom, Dublin Ireland, Zurich Switzerland, Johannesburg South Africa, Toronto Canada, and the United States. Effective leadership begins with effective relationship building. This requires being **A.G.I.L.E.** Let's look at how a Global Index Project—which provided the company investable measures of the global stock market—benefited from its use.

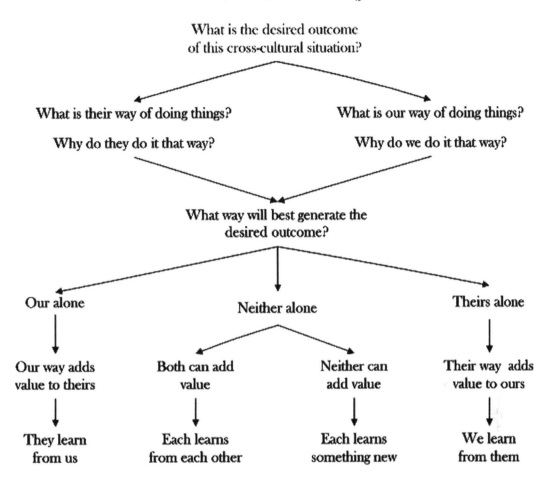

A Model of Cultural Learning

What is the desired outcome
of this cross-cultural situation?

What is their way of doing things?

Why do they do it that way?

What is our way of doing things?

Why do we do it that way?

What way will best generate the
desired outcome?

Our alone   Neither alone   Theirs alone

Our way adds
value to theirs

Both can add
value

Neither can
add value

Their way adds
value to ours

They learn
from us

Each learns
from each other

Each learns
something new

We learn
from them

The A.G.I.L.E. Benefits of a Cultural Learning Model

The model provided a decision tree that accelerated moving the team beyond cooperation to collaboration and increased the value of lessons learned from each other, resulting in a better solution. It took us beyond tolerance and cooperation toward building cultural synergies at the project level and strategic level. This process transformed from a discrete event to one that was continuing and evolving. Recalling an earlier discussion on integrity, the model allow us to connect, communicate, coordinate, and collaborate.

Here are some insights using the model. The relationships created during the project life cycle were more powerful than technical quality. Therefore be especially aware of the "not invented here" syndrome. The surest sign of a great network player is their willingness to let go of their own standard (especially if it is superior) and adopt someone else's to leverage the dynamics of the network. The effective leader must be **A.G.I.L.E.** to establish teams with winning characteristics from a strong sense of purpose and progress to continuous learning, all of which are vital and all must be present. For the remainder of this book *Strategic hustler*™ and effective leader are used interchangeably.

We've concluded our journey on what it takes to be **A.G.I.L.E.** *It's all about being* flexible. We now will focus our attention on **L.E.A.D.E.R.S.H.I.P.—** *or being upfront.* A leader looks to change or challenge the status quo. The next chapter begins the Ⓛ.**E.A.D.E.R.S.H.I.P.** journey starting with Ⓛ.

CHAPTER 7

(L)ook to Change/Challenge Status Quo

Introduction

Reflecting back over my career, past and present, I begin to recall the names of many great leaders in the community, business, entertainment, academics, and sports. The question I asked myself was, "What behaviors made them leaders?"

There are probably a few reasons, but one that comes to my mind is that leaders are the people who decide what needs to be done, and make things happen. I consider myself a change agent. From the streets of New Haven, Connecticut, to all points around the world, my success has been attributed to my ability to personally master revolutionary and evolutionary change. This is my general theory in business and life. I've also realized that a key to being a successful change agent is to "seek first to understand, then to be understood" (Covey, 1989).

Leaders look to change or challenge the status quo. This book is about a mix of leadership and management, coined as **A.G.I.L.E. L.E.A.D.E.R.S.H.I.P.** with a **G.R.I.P.**, being applied to help you win in your everyday life. I share my life experiences to help you move from concept to reality, hopefully removing any speculation. I challenge you along the way to reflect on your situations. Develop a habit of meditating on the words you read and applying them to your life. The topic of this chapter is a popular saying for entrepreneurs and leaders. After all, management experts have been telling would-be entrepreneurs and leaders to challenge the status quo for almost as long as there's been a status quo. But sometimes we get so used to hearing a phrase—I know I do—that it becomes obvious—something we take for granted as true, even when it shouldn't.

Let me put this phrase in the proper context, because I learned the hard way that telling people to challenge the status quo, without qualifiers, can send the wrong message. Here are some interpretations to illustrate what I mean:

- *Do things different.* Doing things differently doesn't mean doing them better—the same goes for change, which, for its own sake, is disruptive
- *Don't be a yes man.* Nobody should be a yes man or woman; stating what you believe to be true without fear of consequences is called being a good manager or leader—it's not about challenging anything
- *Be a contrarian.* Then you're a constant PITA, or Pain In The A–, an impediment to the coalescence of ideas, strategies, and plans, a thorn in everyone's side
- *Challenge management.* Sure; and when you become "management," then upstarts can challenge you; the result is a never-ending us vs. them battle—it's silo behavior and it's dysfunctional
- *Take a stand against authority.* This shouldn't apply in a capitalistic economic system. And it can be construed as supporting disruptive childish behavior, i.e., acting out
- *Take risks.* Well, sure, risk is a necessary ingredient for growth of any kind, but the status quo may already incorporate an excellent growth plan
- *Think outside the box.* Successful entrepreneurs do look at old ideas in new ways. But if you take it too far, you can end up with fringe ideas and impractical solutions to problems

Look, there are no quick fixes for anything important. Well, challenging the status quo is no different. It's more about the process—how you do it—than it is about simply challenging the norm. So by all means, challenge away, but keep three things in mind when you do:

1. **The goal.** Never lose site of the goals of your company, group, business, whatever it is you're evaluating and "challenging"—that should be your guiding light
2. **The customer.** Whoever your customers are—those who buy your products or services or another organization within your company—stay focused on meeting their needs
3. **The organization.** Every so often, stop and take a look around to make sure folks are actually following your lead—if not, you may have some internal selling to do

Stories on status quo

I am going to share a few stories to highlight points made above. As you read each story, ask yourself, "Am I challenging the status quo?"

Shopping

This story is about a shopping experience. By now, you have gathered that throughout this book, my teachable point of view is reinforced through the leadership stories told. I have a tendency to look for leadership everywhere I go—especially when I shop (always looking to be wowed with great leadership and customer service).

One summer weekend I was shopping at DSW shoe store with a good friend. After selecting a pair of shoes to purchase, I made my way to the counter to check out. The cashier asked if I wanted to use my DSW charge card to save 10 percent. I did, but I didn't have the card with me.

Politely she offered to look up my information offering me a pen to write down my Social Security number on a nearby piece of paper. A co-worker over hearing the conversation and request politely intervened suggesting having me type the information into the computer screen.

I instantly felt relieved not having to write down my Social Security number and thought that was a very helpful tip offered by the co-worker. How would you have responded if you were informed of a better way to do something? Hopefully not like the cashier, who replied, "But that's the way I have always done it!"

This leads me to a very important point that needs to be made. *Just because you have always done something a certain way does not make it the right way.* In this case, her co-worker offered a better way of handling the situation—one that protected my identity. Unfortunately, the cashier zoomed in on being challenged to change vs. the benefit of change. Strive to be receptive to feedback when given. More importantly, strive to challenge yourself to find ways to provide better leadership and service by being more effective and efficient in all that you do.

While I am on a roll, here is another question for you. *What have you been "doing as you always do" that you can strive to improve upon this week?*

Creating change, accepting change, making change work, being rewarded by change—all are resisted by that condition called the status quo. And most of the times we don't even realize it.

The following stories on hiking and blogging were reprinted with permission from Andy Cox, acox@coxconsultingroup.com.

Hiking

I was out hiking in the Phoenix Mountain Preserve—one of my usual routes—and thinking about the subject of change. As I came to the place on the trail where I always stop and drink some water, and prepare for the climb forward, it hit me that everything about this hike was predictable—and that felt good. But, at the same time, I had my eye on a distant trail that looked pretty challenging—but every time I thought about taking it, I would rationalize my decision by telling myself I didn't know where it went, I needed to get back in an hour, I had lots of alternatives that I had already discovered. My feet kept me on the same old trails—every time. In my defense, I do have five different trails that I take at different times—it's not as if I only have one.

But I know people that have been hiking and jogging for years who wouldn't think of trying a different trail.

With a conscious effort, I turned my feet to the new trail, and away I went. The desert is a funny place—it looks so blank—but it isn't. Go around a bend and a new view presents itself. Go further and a narrow trail to the top of a mountain shows up. A particularly beautiful tree or cactus—a saguaro with a really distinctive shape—a coyote that crosses the trail—all reward the senses when seen for the first time.

My exercise in challenging my personal status quo had a great reward—a new trail to add to my alternatives—a fresh view of an old friend that is full of surprises. And I had overcome my resistance to change—if only a little. The status quo is a subtle enemy—it presents itself in little ways. And it presents itself day after day—it always will. And when the challenge of change is imposed on us, all those little acts that have reinforced the comfort of doing the same things the same way can keep us from accepting and benefiting from change—we see it is an intrusion on our comfort zone.

How to overcome the effect of the status quo? I challenge you to examine just one way you do things—it doesn't matter what. Then do it a different way—just to see what happens. And every day after that, try to seek out change in your own life. The practice of looking for and trying new ways can be one of the most powerful personal skills you can have. Honor the status quo—routines are important—but routines can also create an illusion of comfort, and it is an illusion.

Blogging

I just finished checking the status of articles I post. I check to see how many views and downloads have taken place since I posted them. I noticed a symbol on my summary page—what could that mean? Inspired by my new quest to try different things, I clicked on it. What was the result? I found a way to check statistics on all my articles more quickly. Wow—that's neat! T h i s w a s a little triumph in my ongoing battle to challenge my personal status quo.

Try it yourself—do it today—it will enrich your life. Look for those little discoveries that can make life, careers, relationships that much more meaningful. It will prepare you for those inevitable changes that hit all of us—sometimes without warning—and make dealing with them an advantage, rather than a threat.

Challenging the Status Quo—Transforming a New York City's Public School System

As former vice chairperson of Towers High School's School Council, located in Decatur, Georgia, one of our jobs was challenging the status quo in school policies and practices. I want to share the following story that appeared in the May 2006 issue of *Educational Leadership*. I am paraphrasing this story written by a New York City Department of Education district administrator.

In 2002, about the time that No Child Left Behind (NCLB) became law, New York City elected a new mayor, a self-made man who deeply believed in the transformative power of free markets to remake lives. During the next thirty-six months, with the help of a schools chancellor selected from outside the ranks of the education establishment, Mayor Michael Bloomberg put into motion a wholly remarkable—and to its critics, deeply troubling—remaking of the largest school system in the United States. "*At its center was a centralized, businesslike bureaucracy and controversial, uniform curriculum designed not merely to challenge the status quo, but to end it.*"

A special bill approved in 2002 by the New York State Legislature made the mayor "*solely accountable for school performance to the New York State Department of Education (National School Boards Association, 2002). He was free to do whatever he saw fit to turn around what was widely viewed as a dated and broken system plagued by a gamut of problems that ranged from low test scores to patronage-riddled schools and districts.*" Bloomberg went from being founder and head of media giant Bloomberg LLC to CEO of "*a new corporation of 1.1 million children, 134,000 employees, and 1,400 schools.*" I want the reader to understand that challenging and changing the status quo, when appropriate, requires having a *can do* and *will do* mentality. Bloomberg demonstrated this *universal* attitude I've learned that is required to turn around any situation

Later we will discuss the importance of capturing metrics to validate the achievement of desired outcomes. Here the desired outcomes were the selected results from standardized tests administered in spring 2005. They seem to indicate that the mayor's business-inspired model of school reform was successful. "*State reading measures demonstrated a 9.9 percent increase for New York City fourth-graders, the greatest gain since the test was initiated in 1999. City reading scores for third-, fifth-, sixth-, and seventh-graders demonstrated even larger gains. Fourth-grade math scores for 2005 likewise rose an impressive 9.3 percent."*

But hold up, wait a minute, these apparent gains told only part of the story. Spring 2005 scores for 8th graders in reading, math, and social studies fell to historic lows, and high school graduation rates, already depressed, remained stagnant. Moreover, it became unclear whether the gains were the result of Bloomberg's reforms or the result of pedagogically sound policies put in place over the last several years by the two previous school chancellors. Critics also noted that across the entire state of New York, 4th grade standardized test scores in both reading and math inexplicably soared in the spring 2005 assessments.

Bloomberg's critics challenged him to task *"on purely curricular grounds— for prescribing system wide use of a progressive whole language curriculum (Balanced Literacy) and a matching constructivist math program, and for including hours of test preparation in the curriculum each week."* The Bloomberg reformers' standardized mandate dictated almost everything classroom teachers did— *"from where they stood in the classroom to how they sat students to how they taught, (using textbooks or chalkboards were no longer allowed). School principals enforced these new policies, which applied to all but 250 exempted schools in the system."*

Not surprisingly, the reorganization has produced strained relations throughout the chain of command as workers at all levels are forced to implement an education program whose validity many question. Recall what was mentioned earlier about people wanting things to be better but not different. *"More than 9,000 teachers filed grievances in the first year of the reorganization. In June 2005, 60,000 of the system's 80,000 teachers, responding to a union poll, gave the Bloomberg reformers an F for failing to respect the judgment and professionalism of the school workforce."*

The New York City Department of Education district administrator who wrote this article served in this role from *"2003 to 2005."* This allowed witnessing firsthand the results of applying business-style management borrowed from the private sector to schools, teachers, and students. Such an implementation leads to the question of whether an education reform steeped in unquestioned centralized sovereignty can prosper and thrive in any school culture deeply rooted in the ideals of social service, community building, and responsiveness to the individual. Let's dig a little deeper to learn a little more about challenging/changing the status quo.

Them Vs. Us

When a system is ineffective in the business world, you attempt to replace it with one that works. Bloomberg did just that. Choosing former Justice Department antitrust lawyer Joel Klein as the new schools chancellor, the

Bloomberg team set about buying advice on what a totally new approach to education should look like. All key players in the reorganization planning came from outside the New York City school system; it was clear from the start that the new organizational structure would consist of policy shapers and policy followers—them vs. us.

According to the administrator, *"they—the policy shapers—were nonunion, highly paid, and often short on education credentials. Although they set policy, they refused to engage in any discussion of what the problems with that policy might be. Their vision was global and sweeping, envisioning that all problems could be remedied through strict, uniform adherence to policies designed by experts. They were all about the Big Picture, eschewing the daily details.*

"We, the policy followers, worked in district offices or as school principals or teachers. We dealt in education quagmires, such as how to meet accountability goals with students whose parents chronically pulled them out of school. Now, inexplicably, we were part of the problem."

Recall our earlier discussion on the ADKAR® Individual Change Model it appears this tool would have been helpful in this situation. Let's continue to swim a little deeper to revisit the importance of a leader having adaptive behavior.

Losing Job Ownership

Later you will learn about the components of the Human Performance System. Here is a situation where there is a misalignment between measurements and desired outcome(s). Rather than measuring their professional success against such business indicators as quarterly gains or cost containment, educators tend to obtain work satisfaction from the impact that they have on their immediate work environment. Teachers and administrators thrive in environments that value staff members' input in problem solving, that enable them to work with students as they see fit, and that promote a sense of kinship in the school community. *Said another way*, teachers and principals enjoy the autonomy of their work, as well as the community recognition that comes from doing a good job.

I collectively identify these intrinsically motivating factors that educators value as indicators of *job ownership*. These are central to why good teachers flourish and why dedicated school principals rarely miss a day of work. When Bloomberg usurped many of these job ownership factors from the New York City Public Schools' workforce, he inadvertently caused an enormous morale implosion.

Let's keep it moving. Before discussing Bloomberg's actions which resulted in this enormous moral implosion, I am going to share the following status quote with you.

"There are two kinds of fools: one says, 'This is old, therefore it is good'; the other says, 'This is new, therefore it is better.'"—*William Ralph Inge*

Stranded

Bloomberg left almost every principal stranded on an island when, during the spring and summer of 2003, he eliminated approximately three thousand jobs by dissolving the school system's entire central administrative staff as well as thirty-two community district offices, Almost everyone principals had relied on for routine or organizational advice—friends, mentors, supervisors, and secretaries—no longer had jobs. These cuts severely limited the principals' ability to safely and effectively manage their schools. *"As a result, by September 2004, approximately one-quarter of the system's existing principals had retired, quit, or reverted back to assistant principal positions."*

The New York City Department of Education district administrator states, *"We who remained in the district offices were uncertain of what our jobs entailed, given the wholesale firing of our far more experienced predecessors just weeks before. We were fearful to take almost any stand without authorization from the central staff, which not only was located miles away but also, had a mind-set light-years from our own. The new central administrative staff rarely returned our phone calls or e-mails, leaving us stranded in matters as important as how to manage the suspension of a dangerous student or as routine as how to order supplies."* Recall our earlier discussion on courage and integrity here is another example where the lack thereof minimizes a leader's effectiveness.

When we discuss **G.R.I.P.** you will learn T-N-T (tools and techniques) that will help you prevent or solve the problems and issues you are about to read.

By the start of the 2004 school year, the new district offices had begun to function in much the same way as the old, but far less efficiently. Gone were dozens of workplace fundamentals, such as resource libraries and resource centers, sufficient office equipment, and a well- functioning interoffice mail system. Further, in their rush to consolidate and centralize, the reformers had eliminated the school-based position of special education supervisor. In the process of sending the terminated administrators' files to new headquarters, hundreds of student records across the city were misplaced or mistakenly tossed out. If you are a school administrator, I challenge you to revisit this section after completing the chapters on **G.R.I.P.** prepared to deliver a solution!

According to the district administrator there was a steady exit of *"angry"* principals and district-level supervisors resulting in the loss of the system's best and most experienced school leaders having vital institutional knowledge.

The Instant Principal

The Bloomberg reformers had devised their own corporate-style training program to replace departing principals. In 2003, they launched the $75 million Leadership Academy to develop new principal talent and to reform licensure requirements. Private business supporters, notably California billionaire/education reformer Eli Broad, funded the program. The academy's purpose was to train new principals, bypassing the time-honored and up-through-the-ranks career ladder of the old system. Whereas previously a principal may have followed a lengthy service and time investment reminiscent of trade guilds, the new system would speed matters up. Hmmmm…sounds like what the National Football League attempted to do with the replacement refs. We all know how that worked out.

Research proved that despite all efforts of the fast-track principal training: (a) executive training in team building, management, and leadership; (b) competitive salary; (c) learning how to implement the Bloomberg pedagogies of choice—balanced literacy and constructivist math—and how to conduct walkthroughs to monitor for classroom compliance; (d) case studies, role playing, and shadowing a master principal—*"of the 180 aspiring leaders only 113 worked as New York City principals in two years of operation."*

Inexperienced leaders, in any field, can have on negative effect on morale. In this case the moral I am referring to is the school and community. For example, a well-qualified assistant principal was bypassed by a young and inexperienced Academy principal for a principal position that opened when the incumbent resigned. The local instructional superintendent, who under the reform, *"was a kind of super principal in charge of monitoring up to ten schools succumbed to unexpected pressure from the chancellor's office to place the candidate in the position rather than the assistance principal"*—much to the chagrin of parents and staff. As time progressed, many in the school found it difficult to take direction from someone who had far less school experience than they had resulting in many, the assistant principal included, deciding to look for work elsewhere.

Of course, many principals under the old system were unfit to lead, and many teachers were unfit to teach. A strong candidate, such as the aforementioned assistant principal, could just as easily have been pushed aside under the old system by a patronage hire. Yet many had hoped that the Bloomberg reform would improve school leadership, not merely replace one problem-riddled system with another. What had begun as a bold challenge to the status quo was increasingly looking like a familiar copy dressed up in new clothes. *Said another way, it's the same soup but a different bowl!*

The Cost of Reform

Bloomberg applied the most extreme measures in disbanding an operable system that required thoughtful reform, not dissolution. His actions may have brought him the immediate results he sought—namely, strict compliance and silence from those working in his schools and districts—but these came at a heavy price. An education system built on fear, distrust, and lack of job ownership is an unlikely candidate for success.

Whatever the original intent, it seems clear that the plan to challenge New York City's education status quo has resulted in a human resources quandary. Bloomberg may have found that in education, it is easier to change practices than to change minds. *Remember a person convinced against their will is of the same opinion still.*

Summary

Looking to challenge/change the status quo is the Ⓛ in Ⓛ.E.A.D.E.R.S.H.I.P. When done in proper context, positive things happen. When done out of context, negative things happen. You need to consider both sides to make an informed decision to challenge or change the status quo. As I ponder the words to use to end this chapter, President Barack Obama is delivering an address on education at the Urban League's One Hundredth Anniversary Convention highlighting the steps his administration has taken over the past eighteen months since he assumed the presidency to improve the education system in America. The president stated that education reform is a top priority for his administration because the "status quo is morally inexcusable, it's economically indefensible, and all of us are going to have to roll up our sleeves to change it."

Thanks, Mr. President! For not only helping me to end this chapter but to begin another one focusing on a behavior that you displayed so gallantly in becoming the first African-American President of these great United States of America. Leaders inspire followers by displaying an energy that is contagious. President Barack Obama was able to energize people with ever-greater challenges with the phrase, *"Yes We Can!"* He continued this energizing in running for re-election with the phrase, *"We're Not Going Back. We're Moving Forward."* The next chapter explores the Ⓔ in L.Ⓔ.A.D.E.R.S.H.I.P.—Ⓔnergize people with ever-greater challenges.

CHAPTER 8

(E)nergize People with Ever-Greater Challenges

Introduction

You've seen the phrase, "(E)nergize people with ever-greater challenges" used repeatedly in this book. Leaders are not only highly energetic people themselves, but they actively work to create positive emotional energy in others. They do this by structuring the organization to get rid of bureaucratic nonsense, and by stretching and encouraging everyone they meet. My former pastor, Reverend Dr. Curtis M. Cofield, helped thousands of people in inner-city New Haven escape from lives of dependency by following one simple formula: energize people through ever-greater challenges.

A future discussion will cover how **A.G.I.L.E.** leaders use ideas and values to promote leadership at all levels of their organizations. But for now, ideas and values unify people and allow them to act independently in ways that effectively move the organization toward a common goal. The ideas and values are themselves strong motivators because they inspire people to action. However, ideas and values alone are not enough. Winning teams do their jobs better than their opponents. In a highly competitive world, this means they work faster and with greater energy. Therefore, winning leaders not only encourage people to have good ideas and develop strong values, they also take deliberate actions to generate and channel to productive uses.

All organizations inherently have energy because they are made up of people, and people have energy. In **A.G.I.L.E.** organizations, people have more energy and use it productively. While non- **A.G.I.L.E.** waste their energy on negative activities such as internal politics and resisting changes demanded by the marketplace, the winners use theirs positively to overcome problems and meet new challenges. The *"speed of the leader is the speed of the group,"* my college football coach would always say. My thirty years of experience shows that top

163

leaders understand that positive energy produces positive results. They use energy, like ideas and values, as a competitive tool. And they consciously work at creating a positive energy in everyone else in the organization.

During the journey through this chapter, I will talk about how effective leaders use their own enormous energy to work longer, harder and more effectively to win. I will discuss a number of methodologies and resources that **A.G.I.L.E.** leaders use to create positive energy in others. These include everything from personal face-to-face interactions that inspire confidence and determination, to designing processes that encourage independent action to eliminating bureaucracies and time-wasting activities that foster inaction. But most importantly, I will talk about how effective leaders transform negative energy into positive energy, and how they harness the energy that is generated in times of distress so that their organizations not only survive difficulties that destroy other institutions but emerges stronger for the experience.

Energizing Nonenergizers

My experience as a senior executive for the City of Atlanta illustrates this phenomenon. When assuming the role of deputy chief information officer (CIO) of the Business Strategic Services Division of the Information Technology department, the jobs were in jeopardy, and the staff had plenty of stress-induced energy. They were investing their energy in bickering, bemoaning their fate, and resisting the opinions of key executives. They were underperforming. My objective was converting the problem into an opportunity for solution. The focus of my transformation strategy was to provide opportunities to take responsibility for their own fate and give them confidence and hope, the team rechanneled their negative energy into positive energy transforming from a group of self-perceived victims into a team of take-charge winners. Now I must admit that not all came along as willing participants. But recall my discussion on teamwork earlier: in short, some can, some should not, and some cannot take the journey.

As a former player and coach of winning sports teams, we won because we thought we could win. The understanding of the possibility of achieving a desired goal is the very ingredient that generates the energy required to achieve that goal and to tackle new ones. Therefore, one of the most value things that effective leaders do is build the determination and self-confidence in others to help them become leaders as well. Remember, *"Leaders are born to be made!"* Later in this chapter, I'll show you how I systematically do that.

Effective Leaders Are Highly Energized Themselves

You can probably guess that I am a very energetic person. Remember an earlier statement, *"The speed of the leader is the speed of the group!"* In studying other effective leaders, I've mirrored my behavior after them in throwing myself wholeheartedly into everything I do. To quote David J. Wess, M.Ed, "Remember no half effort; no 'good-enough'; only the best will do in whatever you undertake!"

"Good, better, best. Never let it rest.
Until your good is better and your better is best."
St. Jerome, Father of the Latin Church 340-420AD

In reality, perfection is in the eye of the beholder. But excellence is attainable by anyone. Understand, delivering value does not require one to be perfect, but it does require one to be excellent. Show determination in delivering value and career aspirations will happen. Top performer's competitive nature drives them to focus on the successful completion of a task. They seize opportunities to change and grow by working longer and harder than most people can even imagine. Never thinking about slowing down. *Said another way*, they are willing to do now what others won't so they can accomplish later what others can't.

As a *Strategic hustler™*, the long hours and laser like focus may appear to keep me from things that others may view as sacrifices. However, my dad always told me that there is a time and place for everything. I recall my college football playing days at Virginia State College when practicing in 103-degree weather; while working the team would chant, "Work hard and you won't work long!" And you know something? We loved it. Consider this experience an example of how important it is to be passionate about what you do. In the example, this uplifting environment caused each person's passion to motivate and inspire them to work hard to achieve individual and collective rewards they valued. *Said another way*, their passion energized them and their teammates. The moral to this story is showing passion is essential to being an energizer. Later we will talk more about passion as [**P.A.S.S.I.O.N.**]. Interesting? Keep on reading and learning.

In fact, "fun" is a word that often crops up with **A.G.I.L.E.** leaders. As deputy chief information officer (CIO) for the City of Atlanta, I had a tough job of turning around a faltering division. I was the third deputy CIO heading this division, but my boss loved my performance, work ethic, and integrity. He could see in me the edge to make the tough decisions. He would ask how things were going and I would smile and say, "I am having fun." He would smile and encourage me to keep up the good work. I encourage you to being the go-to person in business-as-unusual situations. Let me share some memorable lessons in energizing.

Energizing Lessons from Childhood

Tichy asked the question, "Where does this delight in tackling the difficult and this single-minded devotion come from?" (Tichy, 2007). I am going to rephrase this question to ask, "Where does this quest to be the best come from?" To answer this question, I need to take you down memory lane. Beginning in elementary school, we already discussed my "Coming from hell to get to Yale." In high school, when I won the school's top physics student award, the Harold Cohen Physics Award, my physics teacher, Mr. Mays, told me, "You can go very far in life if you continue to learn to apply yourself." I was later chosen to receive the Bausch & Lomb Honorary Science Award as one of the most outstanding high school science students in the United States. The awards continued to pour in, culminating with being named to National Honor Society and Who's Who among American High School Students. Additionally, there were the sports awards mentioned earlier. Do you get my drift? All of these successes humbled me and taught me that by applying myself I could achieve anything. I became a self-motivator. This was a critical trait, being a first-generation high school graduate who was now attempting to duplicate that feat in college. I spoke earlier of my family challenges; thus my quest to be the best drove me! Thanks to Mr. Mays, I learned to apply myself to not be afraid to go after ever-greater challenges. Start thinking about your childhood energizers. What energized you?

Energizing Lessons from College

When discussing seizing the opportunity in chapter 3, "Ⓖoal-Oriented Behavior," we briefly covered my trials and tribulations transferring from Virginia State College (VSC) to the University of New Haven (UNH) and playing college football at UNH. The head coach Tom Bell would not let me quit without a fight. Overcoming the obstacle during this period of time was my energizing experience. Good leaders invest in their people, learning what motivates and inspires them. Coach Bell learned my past and knew what buttons to push. We met while I was recovering from a basketball knee injury. Before going any further, allow me to digress to help you get an understanding of my emotional awareness.

The result of transferring to UNH from VSC caused me to lose two semesters of college course credits, because UNH's computer curriculum was engineering focused whereas VSC's computer curriculum was business focused. Making this paradigm shift was a struggle. Being home didn't help things because of the many distractions—thank God for a persistent dad. To add insult to injury, I had a knee injury—prior to the injury, I considered myself invincible! All of this put me in a state of mind of just wanting to do the necessities to graduate—after all, that is why I went to college. I thought, "Forget football!" Then reality set in—*it takes money to make money!* Sure, I got financial aid from UNH, but when I received the bill for the cost of tuition and books, I had an epiphany—quickly. I said to myself, "There is no way!" I had to get out of my emotional state of mind and get back into my business state of mind. ***Said another way***, I had to get out of my feelings and get into the game. We will talk more about this phrase later. I recalled what it took to become a walk-on football scholarship recipient at VSC— I was a "$6 million man with a $6 knee." We will also talk about this later. The point now is that in addition to my academic woes, I had personal issues, financial concerns, and this damn knee injury. The challenges were there. I had football skills, and it would have been ignorant, stupid, and dumb of me to not use them to help pay for my education. That decision turned out to be one of the best I have ever made.

Now back to my initial meeting with Coach Bell—on crutches. I approached him, introduced myself, and humbly requested a tryout for the team. My *Street hustling* instincts took over and immediately, I began to negotiate getting financial aid—*when* I made the team. Coach looked at me, making the comment that I looked like the "$6 million man that had a $6 knee." We later met to further discuss my goals. He helped me understand the challenges of: knee rehabilitation and making the team because of the prized recruits being lured to the football program. He added that an NCAA rule limited what he could do but that he would do all that was humanly possible to help me. This was the energizing news I needed to hear. It was time to "get my hustle on!" My goal was to do whatever it took to make the football team.

That summer I survived a grueling rehabilitation program which prepared me to compete for a position on the team. Though my knee was not 100 percent, I needed money for school and felt 80–90 percent of me would have to be enough to make the team. One of the lessons learned from past coaches and NFL players was that excelling in sports requires 80 percent physical ability and 20 percent mental prowess. I rationalized the odds were on my side, which made me more determined to make valuable contributions as a defensive back and special teams player. I was having a stellar camp. My best performance involved me returning four interceptions for touchdowns during an intrasquad scrimmage game. That performance prompted the coaching staff to unanimously convince Coach Bell that my ball-catching and running skills would best serve the team on offense. I was switched to running back/flanker. This switch would prove my return was premature. While running an agility drill, my knee was reinjured. This caused me to miss the first game against

Framingham State University in Framingham, Massachusetts. The injury lingered, resulting in me losing my confidence and laser-like focus as the knee became progressively worse—to a point where I ran with a limp. I also made a bad decision resulting in disciplinary action from Coach Bell. Enough was enough! Embarrassed, frustrated, injured, and deenergized, my mental and physical state prevented me from making the positive contribution to the team's success. Finally, swallowing my pride; and taking a dosage of integrity; I met with Coach Bell to apologize for my behavior and requested his permission to leave the team. I joked that the "$6 million man still has a $6 knee and a $6 attitude." He agreed but simultaneously praised my character, courage, and talent, encouraging me not to give up because he hadn't. Coach Bell remembered that I transferred to UNH as a dean's list student. He energized me by issuing a challenge to get back on the dean's list. Knowing my athletic goals, Coach energized me to come back the next season ready to pursue my goals of helping UNH to its first winning football season and becoming UNH's first All-American football player. Coach Bell loved the fact that despite what he called "man among boys" talent, I always put the team first. I thank Van Spruill, my midget football coach, for this lifelong lesson.

Keeping my promise required renewed focus on my schoolwork. After two mediocre semesters (2.3/2.6 GPA), I obtained a 3.6 GPA and the first of many dean's list honors. I was also selected as a summer intern to work at E. I. DuPont in Wilmington, Delaware. This opportunity allowed me to grow in many ways. This was my first job, and to work for such a world-renowned company was humbling and a blessing. In meeting various interns from all over the country, DuPont officials let us know our selection was attributed to being the best of the best—what an honor and privilege. Secondly, I spent the summer competing, either outshining or holding my own, against top-notch football players attending leading Division I, Division I-A, and Division II college programs. My tenacity, ability, and willingness to compete, prompted my newfound friends to nickname me "Sweetness Too." We challenged each other and they helped me get in *"First Team Shape."*

My hard work paid off as the only opponent that slowed me down was badly bruised ribs. Though starting off playing junior varsity that is not where I ended. With a *"Get Your Hustle On!"* attitude, I outperformed prized recruits and established letterman to become a junior varsity captain/starter and eventually a varsity starter leading the team, junior varsity and varsity, in almost every rushing/receiving category. I was named Most Improved Player and Outstanding Offensive Back by the coaches. They also nominated me as a team captain my senior year. Most importantly, I was awarded a financial package that more than covered my tuition and books. This allowed me to finished UNH debt free! Then it happened again. I reinjured my knee during an off-season basketball game. It occurred just before summer break. The knee injury lingered the whole summer. I called Coach Bell to inform him of my decision to use my senior year to concentrate solely on graduating with honors. He told me that after what I accomplished my junior year; he would not let me "quit." This man was a motivator—a persistent energizer. It proved contagious as persistence and perseverance allowed me to brave another grueling rehabilitation program. Again the hard work paid off as I found myself in head-to-head competition with a prized recruit for the starting running back position. It was a *"split decision"* that was made on the day before the first game. He won, eventually becoming an All-American candidate, but he had to earn it! Disappointed with the decision I remembered the hard work that put me in position to win—and kept this experience as a lesson learned. The dream senior year eluded me. However, I was a small part of the first winning varsity football season in UNH's history. And that's what it is all about—winning and being part of something that is bigger than you! In the end, my biggest victories achieved included being named to *Who's Who Among Students in American Universities and Colleges* and graduating cum laude from a top-tier private university—debt free.

Sharing Your Energy Energizes Others

I share these stories not to impress you, but to show where my energy to help others emerged from. My involvement in these activities (sports, academics, and community) taught me self-confidence, persistence, perseverance, pursuit of excellence, teamwork, respect for diversity, leadership, and faith in God—oh yes, I learned to be a praying man. Energizing myself has allowed me to continue to make a difference. It did not didn't end after twenty years of coaching and mentoring at-risk youth. It continues to this day, as I travel the world edifying both young and mature with **A.G.I.L.E. L.E.A.D.E.R.S.H.I.P. with a G.R.I.P**.

Many effective leaders display their energy physically. They are action-oriented people. It shows not only in their decisions but also in their physical presence. I recall seeing films of Jack Welch white hot with intensity for hours as he paced the stage talking to and answering questions from GE workers. In Dr. Noel Tichy's book, *Leadership Engine,* he speaks of a number of leaders' experiences, but the two that impressed me the most were members of the United States Armed Forces. Retired General Wayne Downing, the former commander of the Special Operations Forces, completed West Point, served two tours in Vietnam in airborne units, and has completed two ultramarathons with lungs scarred so badly from childhood asthma that he only has half the lung capacity of healthy humans; and the late Rear Admiral Chuck LeMoyne, Downing's deputy commander, who continued to run three miles a day and swim while undergoing radiation and chemotherapy after the removal of his larynx. After the cancer surgery, he stayed on the job as deputy commander right up until his retirement, rather than accept less-strenuous duty.

The enormous physical energy of leaders excites and energizes everyone around them. Recall, the speed of the leader is the speed of the group. Still, as impressive as leaders' physical energy is, it is their emotional energy and their ability to evoke emotional energy in others that truly marks them as a breed apart. How they display it isn't as important as the simple fact that they are supremely engaged by their work, and it shows. An effective leader can turn even the most mundane of meetings into an exciting, fire-in-the-gut building encounter.

When I formed my company Intelligent Systems Services Corporation in 1989, its branding label was "Delivering Intelligent Solutions through People, Process, Information, and Technology." The key to my success was to energize people from all walks of life in various parts of the globe. For over twenty-five years, I've realized that some people become leaders no matter what their chosen path because their positive energy is so uplifting. Even in tough times, they always find a way. They seem to live life on their own terms even when having to comply with someone else's requirements. When they walk into a room, they make it come alive. When they send a message, it feels good to receive it. Their energy makes them magnets attracting other people.

Effective leaders share a passion for people. They draw their energy from helping others get excited about improving their lives or businesses. And they energize their people at every opportunity with stimulating ideas and values. We will talk more about this later.

Equally important, leaders model the intensity and energy that it takes to stay ahead competitively and meet goals that are ever more ambitious. In part, they do this because they love what they do. They also know how to stay engaged in what they are doing at the moment. Leaders focus on how they make people feel after each interaction. Personally, I feel that at the end of the day, every person has got to come away edified from my meetings. Objectively speaking, they must feel better than they did before the meeting.

You must be candid and honest but with compassion. Here is a lesson learned from the street, be able to step on a person's shoes and still leave a shine. I offer self-confidence to pursue the opportunities that **C.H.A.N.G.E.** offers.

Being an effective leader means tapping a deep reservoir of emotional energy. This drive and motivation mixes needs for accomplishment, power, and, most importantly, institutional legacy. This is the essence of transformational leadership; namely, leaders are energized not just by the goals of the team or the organization, but also by transforming and coaching individuals to be leaders themselves.

Simply put, an effective leader's job is to energize others. When I was promoted to deputy CIO, Business Strategic Services (BSS), I delivered a group presentation addressing transforming BSS. The goal was to energize the group.

This full-time job focused on my staff, CIO, and chief operating officer. In chapter 3, "Goal-Oriented Behavior," when discussing the goal of team building, it was stated that the dynamics of building a team are going to either positively energize team members or negatively energize them. In either case, they will decide whether to take the journey or not. This experience also reinforced using the power of ideas and values, which I will talk about in a later chapter, to energize people. I don't always win every time, but I have a very high percentage of success and continuously employ my "good, better, best" focus.

What's "Energy" Have to Do with It?

Just plain energy is a neglected dimension of leadership. It is a form of power available to anyone in any circumstances. While inspiration is a long-term proposition, energy is necessary on a daily basis, just to keep going.

Leveraging our earlier discussion on integrity, I have identified three things that characterize the people who are energizers. You will see they have integrity.

1. A relentless focus on the bright side, in chapter 4, "Intelligent Behavior," this was an integrity quality called "Focus on Growing." Energizers find the positive and run with it. A state government official in a state that doesn't like government overcomes that handicap through her strong positive presence. She dispenses compliments along with support for the community served by her agency, making it seem that she works for them rather than for the government. She greets everyone with the joy generally reserved for a close relative returning from war. I can see skeptics' eyebrows starting to rise, but judging from her success, people love meeting with her or getting her exclamation-filled emails. She is invited to everything.

The payoffs from stressing the bright side can be considerable. In her book, *SuperCorp* (Kanter, 2009), she tells the story about how Maurice Levy, CEO of the global marketing company Publicis Groupe, tilted the balance in his company's favor when his firm was one of several suitors for Internet pioneer Digitas. At one point in a long courtship, Digitas hit problems, and the stock collapsed. One of Publicis's major competitors sent Digitas's head an e-mail saying, "Now you are at a price that is affordable, so we should start speaking." Levy sent an e-mail the same day saying, "It's so unfair that you are hurt this way because the parameters remain very good." Levy's positive energy won the prized acquisition.

2. Redefining negatives as positives, in chapter 4, "Intelligent Behavior," this was an integrity quality called "Positively Embrace Negativity." Energizers are can-do people. They do not like to stay in negative territory, even when there are things that are genuinely depressing. For example, it might seem a stretch for anyone to call unemployment "a good time for reflection and redirection while between jobs," but some energizers genuinely stress the minor positive notes in a gloomy symphony. A marketing manager who was laid off by his company that was hit hard by the recession saw potential in people he met at a career counseling center and convinced them that they could start a service business together. He became the energizing force for shifting their definition of the situation from negative to an opportunity.

A contract ended rather abruptly leaving me without work for eight months. During that time, I answered an advertisement for free Oracle training. Already an Oracle Certified Professional, this was an opportunity for me to re-invent myself. I impressed the technical interviewers and my leadership background sparked the interest of the CEO—who was equally impressed. In fact, instead of becoming a student I was hired to lead strategic projects; and because of my trilogy of success earned a promotion to managing director/ chief learning officer for this large training/consulting firm. Like the marketing manager, I became the energizing force for helping this company meet its strategic goals.

"Positive thinking" and "counting blessings" can sound like naïve clichés. But energizers are not fools. They can be shrewd analysts who know their flaws and listen carefully to critics so that they can keep improving. Studies show that optimists are more likely to listen to negative information than pessimists are, because they think they can do something about it. To keep moving through storms, energizers cultivate thick skins that shed negativity like a waterproof raincoat sheds drops of water. They are sometimes discouraged, but never victims. These are *Strategic hustler*™ studies but these are lessons learned as a *Street hustler. **Said another way, it's the same soup but a different bowl!***

Let me share another story with you. An entrepreneur who built numerous businesses and incubated others had a strong personal mission to raise national standards in his industry. He began that quest by meeting individually with the heads of major industry organizations, all of whom told him that he would fail. He nodded politely, asked for a small commitment to one action anyway, just as a test, he said, and went on to the next meeting. Eight or nine meetings later, he was well along on a path everyone had tried to discourage him from taking.

> *"Our greatest glory is not in never falling but in rising every time we fall."*
>
> ~ Confucius

3. Fast response time: energizers don't dawdle, in chapter 4, "Ⓘntelligent-Behavior," this was an integrity quality called "Aim to Exceed Expectations." Energizers don't tell you all the reasons something can't be done. They just get to it. They might take time to deliberate, but they keep the action moving. They are very responsive to e-mails or phone calls, even if the fast response is that they can't respond yet. This helps them get more done. Because they are so responsive, others go to them for information or connections. In the process, energizers get more information and a bigger personal network, which are the assets necessary for success.

The nice thing about this form of energy is that it is potentially abundant, renewable, and free. The only requirements for energizers are that they stay active, positive, responsive, and on mission.

Let's Get Busy—Personal Energy/Energizing Others

As an effective leader, you must first start with self-awareness of your own sources of emotional energy. Self-awareness plays a large role in respecting diversity which will be discussed later. What are the activities that energize you most, and which activities strip you of your emotional energy and leave you feeling angry, frustrated, bored, or tired?

What energizes you the most? (Specify activities.)

_____

_____

_____

What deenergizes you the most? (Specify activities.)

_____

_____

_____

How I can raise my level of positive emotional energy:

_____

_____

_____

Energize Others

Okay, what is it you have done or plan to do that energizes people with ever-greater challenges? It could be to give your kids an assignment that they don't think they can complete and you coach them to get the job done. It could be giving your staff stretch goals and helping them achieve them.

Balancing Energy in One's Life Space

Variety is the spice of life. All work and no play makes for a dull life. Transactional Analysis (TA) studies the intervention of three ego-states consistently used by people: Parent, Adult, and Child using an *"Ego-State Model."* I am going to repurpose those lessons with the following exercises. Examine your life space by drawing three circles: one for self, one for work, and one for family. Let the size of each circle represent relative investment of time in that activity; let's say over a typical week. Overlap the circles to the extent that the activities do or do not overlap. For example, the drawing below represents a family business where the individual is working with family members and doing things with the family and work colleagues of a recreational nature as well. What the drawing does not tell us is whether or not this is energizing or deenergizing. A dysfunctional family may be sucking energy from all domains of their members' lives.

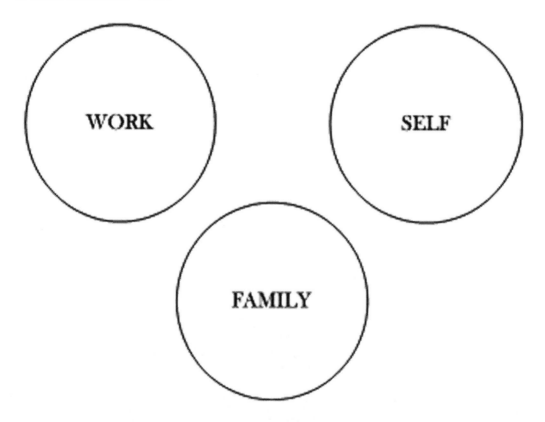

The second example is from a consultant who shared an illustration of his life space in a workshop. Basically, his life is dominated by work, with a little time spent on his own recreations and friendships and almost no time for his family (a wife who is also a consultant, no children).

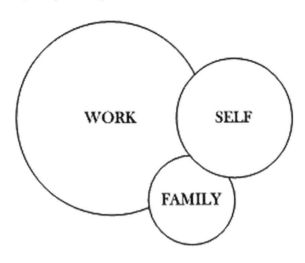

Your Life Space

Using the examples above, draw three circles to show how much overlap exists between your personal, family, and work activities. Use the size of the circles to represent the relative amount of time you spend in each area.

1. Identify energy conflicts (work/family, self/work, self/family).

_____

_____

_____

2. Identify energy synergies (self-renewal through work-related activities, family involvement with work groups, etc.).

_____

_____

_____

The Effective Leader Developing Leaders Challenge

As mentioned in chapter 5, "Learner Behavior," effective leaders need to help and coach others. The life spaces exercise is a great activity to build into either individual coaching or workshop settings. I've even used it on my kids because it legitimates people taking ownership and control of how they spend their time. Your challenge as an effective leader is to be a listener and learner, to help others deal with these issues as you grapple with them yourself.

Effective Leaders Energize Others through Transitions

Story #1: Business Transition

The balance of life issue is one way to help each individual deal with personal energy. You will learn in chapter 9, "Ⓐcknowledge the Burning Platform," that the bigger problem is getting the large group of people energized around the change—current or future. In the twenty-first century, this is radical, revolutionary change.

Change in general unleashes, or opens the gates, to a lot of mixed emotions: fear, hope, anxiety, uncertainty, elation, sadness, excitement, etc. Deal with the emotional energy in a positive way while still recognizing the realities of the struggle. You have to get in the trenches. *Said another way*, you have to be a hands-on leader. This implies giving inspiring speeches, pep talks, helping people see the opportunities that lie before them, and creating an environment that supports fulfillment of the group's mission. The most critical part is leading people through transitions laden with deeply mixed emotions.

You will have to use your creativity to channel these mixed emotions into a positive force. Prior to appointing me to lead the Business Strategic Services (BSS) as deputy CIO, the CIO was considering outsourcing the division to a Big Four consulting firm. I convinced the CIO his vision for the division was achievable providing he had the right leader to bring it to fruition. My predecessors were productive, but change was needed. We spent hours reviewing my plan to leverage their successes in executing a "retreat, regroup, and redeploy" strategy to turnaround the division. He was very detailed in the questions asked finally giving his approval to present my strategy to his boss the chief operating officer (COO). She liked the innovative approach and agreed with the CIO in granting her approval. My belief is that to have successful transformation, it must be transparent to all parties that will be impacted. I met with my staff to discuss the current situation and the alternatives executive management was considering. The fact executive management was considering outsourcing the division created a bonding, "we will show them" attitude. This didn't come easily; as my staff felt their performance assessment was inaccurate. I gave them my "get out of your feelings and get into the game" pep talk. We will talk more about this in chapter 16, "Ⓟersistence and Perseverance." The new mission statement shared with the group was made public on the corporate website. I initiated a formal process excellence program targeted to save the city $50 million–$60 million over a five-year period and generate over $100 million in revenues during that same period. The plan required me to provide hands-on coaching and mentoring to each member of the staff to perform their new assignments. Though politics keep me from seeing the plan through to completion, the legacy left behind allowed delivery of key process excellence initiatives. *Said another way*, having the ability to energize people established the momentum to deliver the desired results in my absence. Later we will talk about delivering results through effective delegation. For now here are some recommendations from star performers formerly on my staff:

Star Performer #1

"Dr. Frank is the true meaning of "lead by example." Given his diverse knowledge and expertise in process improvements, within six months he resuscitated a dying division. It was his project management and work products that became the standard for all to follow. Under his direction, he mentored, coached, and demanded from us the same as himself... excellence. Because he is a lifetime learner, his success is predicted, and repeated. I am a witness that Frank is naturally born for this, and I attribute much of my success and furthered education to him. Thank you for being such an asset worth the investment to be "linked in" to!"

Star Performer #2

"Frank is a superb leader, excellent motivator, great communicator, and always delivers significant results. He can make a big difference in any organization. He is a future CIO and the organization that picks him to lead their IT group will be both lucky and grateful for the results he delivers. He has the highest professional and personal integrity, has a winning attitude, and commands a vast array of knowledge of every relevant IT and business framework. He is a first-rate problem solver, innovative thinker, and is a driven, analytical, astute, and business-savvy executive. As a PMP, Frank is tactically focused, while his entrepreneurial spirit and a well-rounded business leadership keep a longer-term strategic vision in mind.

He has done it all in IT. He has risen through the ranks from developing applications, training and coaching application development teams, apps management, project and program management, heading up a PMO and Shared Services organization, leading business analysts though business process reengineering, and being a deputy CIO. I have firsthand experience observing his successful delivery of these services and working with him on all these facets of IT when Frank hired me in the PMO where he was deputy CIO at the City of Atlanta.

In 2002, I first started working with Frank at GE, where we learned Six Sigma quality methodology. In starting a PMO at GE, we combined Six Sigma with RUP and PMBOK Guide processes. We still continue our conversations about PM processes and methods and have matured this thinking into thought leadership positions. Frank has proved this leadership with his work heading the Quality Assurance section of PMI's OPM 3 standard.

If you are looking for someone to establish credibility with clients and internal organizations, who is comfortable challenging the status quo but mature enough to know when to fight and when to align, and who can design and deliver on critical IT initiatives, then Dr. Frank Harper should lead your critical initiative as a transformation program manager or CIO. Frank is someone you want to work with over and over again."

Story #2: Community Transition

Under the leadership of Reverend Dr. Curtis and Elsie Cofield, Immanuel Baptist Church (IBC), the state of Connecticut's oldest and largest black Baptist church, had consistently extended its generosity, becoming a model for social action. Mrs. Cofield, known as "the Mother Teresa of Connecticut," was the co-founder/president of AIDS Interfaith Network, Inc. (AIN), a twenty-one-room treatment center that also runs a day program for AIDS and HIV patients. The center also sponsored programs such as a teen hotline, substance abuse counseling, and the Sunshine Corner for children affected by HIV/AIDS and other illnesses. This was accomplished during a period when churches in the Afro-American community were shying away from so many of the controversial social issues, the Cofields were out in the streets trying to pull people together without imposing their religious values on those they were trying to help. They were effective and successful because they were able to direct to their work the same energy that people had directed toward shying away from controversial social issues, resulting in IBC becoming a model for social action.

How to Energizing People through Transitions

The above stories imply that an effective leader has the job of helping others master transitions. What do I mean by "transitions"? I am speaking of the emotional transitions life brings when humans are faced with change. To explain this further, I am going to use a transitions framework developed by William Bridges, a highly regarded development consultant who has studied personal and professional changes for over twenty years. His theoretical framework says that all successful transformations, or transitions, involve three distinct phases. There is the "ending" phase, when people disengage from the past and "the way things were." There is a neutral zone, which he calls the "transition" phase, when people have let go of the old but haven't yet figured out how to live with the new. And, finally, there is a "new beginning" period during which people learn to feel at home with the new identity and to be productive with the new way of doing things. Bridges also draws a distinction between a "change" and a "transition." He explains it this way: "A change is a shift in the world around us. A transition is the internal process we go through in response to that shift. Changes are events and situations; transitions are experiences. [Each change] will put the people it affects into transition." Bridges concludes that many organizational change efforts fail not because people fear the change itself, but because they resist the unpleasant process of transitioning. As an effective leader, you need to inherently understand these psychodynamics of transitions and be able to help others through them. This ability to capitalize on transitions and use them to create productive, positive energy is one of the keys to effective leadership.

Bridges' theory is excellent, but how can an effective leader apply it to energize real-world transitions? My street smarts and athletic competitiveness has served me well during my professional career. Having been to a New England Patriots free-agent tryout camp, I was elated when attending a CIO Summit in Boston, Massachusetts. Super Bowl winning Head Coach Bill Belichick of the New England Patriots was a guest speaker. While listening attentively to Coach Belichick, I began drawing comparisons to my experiences as a football player and coach. As we discussed earlier the words of my friend OC's summarized analogy, *"It's the same soup but a different bowl."* Leadership was required to:

1. Create a sense of urgency
2. Define a mission that is inspiring and worth achieving
3. Set goals that stretch people's ability
4. Build a spirit of teamwork
5. Create the expectation that goals can be met

Let's see a real-world application of these to transform the Business Strategic Services division.

A Sense of Urgency

I informed my staff that executive management was considering outsourcing the division. For those of you who may not be familiar with the term outsourcing that means your job is given to someone else, **said another way**, you have no job! I also delivered them my "get out of your feelings and get into the game" pep talk. The essence of the talk was to convince them that I thought they were more capable than management gave them credit for, and they needed to demonstrate it and thereby save their jobs.

An Inspiring Mission

Having the mission statement posted publicly on the web presented the prospect of an unquestionably better future. The stronger the attraction of the future, the greater the energy people exert to work toward it.

Stretch Goals

To get my staff to work harder, the operations excellence program implemented targeting to save the city $50 million–$60 million over a five-year period and generate over $100 million in revenues during that same period. There were a number of process improvements when implemented would achieve this goal. What was needed was a structured, documented, implementable approach to make it happen.

Teamwork and Hope for Success

To make the goals seem attainable and to build up my staff's confidence and determination, the plan required me to provide hands-on coaching and mentoring to each member of the staff to perform his or her new assignments. Recalling "When It Comes to Teamwork," discussed during the "Building Teamwork" section in chapter 3, "Ⓖoal-Oriented Behavior," not everyone should, can, or shouldn't make the journey. The hope for success hinged on this fact. As the leader, I still have to create an environment that "we're all in this together" teamwork.

Goal Realization

To instill confidence that goals can be reached. I instituted project management and work products that become a standard for all to follow. My mentoring and coaching aim was to help everyone produce the appropriate deliverables that were timely, accurate, and within budget.

Energizing People Through Change

Take a few minutes to think through how you will use each of the five elements above to energize people about change.

Create Urgency

How will you give people a sense of urgency? Think of competitive threats and opportunities. Think of drawing the dire consequences of inaction in a verbal picture people will immediately understand. See step 4, "Communicate the Change Vision," in chapter 2, "Ⓐdaptable Behavior," for ideas.

_____

_____

_____

Inspiring Mission

How will you craft an inspiring mission? How will you connect your mission to people on a level that is important to them individually without being so vague that it loses meaning?

Stretch Goals

What goals and objectives will you set? How will you make your stretch goals seem worthy of striving for?

Teamwork

How will you instill a sense that you are all (including yourself) preparing for change?

_____

_____

_____

Confidence

How will you give people the confidence that can help them overcome their fears?

_____

_____

_____

Energizing Individuals

As an effective leader working with and developing others, you need to think about how the combinations of the five factors above affect people. Each individual deals with change and emotions differently (more on this will be discussed during our discussion titled "Respect Diversity"). The goal is to use whatever combination of these factors each person needs to help him or her work through transition.

Team Member	Urgency	Mission	Stretch Goals	Teamwork	Confidence

Think about each individual on your team. Record what you do with the person individually in order to energize them.

Summary

Energizing people with ever-greater challenges is the first Ⓔ in **L.Ⓔ.A.D.E.R.S.H.I.P.** Earlier we discussed the speed of the leader is the speed of the group. The leader with speed is an energizer. Great leaders need to be an energizer to energize people to stretch and desire to make a significant, valued contribution to the team effort. An energizer knows when a change must occur. In addition to the world-class behaviors discussed to this point, they must also Ⓐcknowledge the burning platform. The next chapter covers the Ⓐ in **L.E.Ⓐ.D.E.R.S.H.I.P.**

CHAPTER 9

(A)cknowledge the Burning Platform

Introduction

The CIO Summit mentioned in the previous chapter was an IT executive event attended while serving as deputy chief information officer for the Business Strategic Services IT Division of the City of Atlanta. Its theme was "IT-Enabled Business Transformation: From Vision to Reality." During this event, the opportunity presented itself to meet and briefly talk with John P. Kotter, professor of leadership, and emeritus at Harvard Business School and widely regarded as the world's foremost authority on leadership and change. Well-respected corporate trainers have the ability to leverage their many years of subject matter expertise and presentation skills to develop and deliver a concise, complete, economical training experience that engages students. These skills served me well during a brief encounter with Professor Kotter, since as guest speaker, everyone was trying to talk to him after hearing his inspiring presentation. I cornered him to validate my summary of his epic book, *Heart of Change*. Another good habit is seeking and validating knowledge from the best in the world, when possible. This is inspecting what you are expecting.

To his and my delight, in two or three minutes we discussed the core message of his book. I concluded by stating to him, "*Said another way*, you must acknowledge the burning platform. Without the heart leading the mind, there will be no change, because a person convinced against his or her will is of the same opinion still." He looked at me with a broad smile and said, "Never heard it put that way, but you've got it!" My dear readers, this made my stay at the conference priceless. Allow me to share what it means to acknowledge there is a burning platform and then how to proceed with implementing change.

The Burning Platform

The term "burning platform" comes from a true story in which four men were left stranded on the burning platform of the Piper Alpha oilrig fire in the North Sea in 1967. The men faced the choice of staying where they were and facing certain death, or taking the risky step of jumping into the freezing ocean and risking death from hypothermia. The two men who decided to remain behind perished.

There are two elements to the story. The two who stayed put died. The unacceptable option is staying the same and hoping things get better. Against the odds, the two who jumped into the sea survived. The message is that sometimes radical, risky change is essential. We need to communicate both elements. Ask yourself, what is our "burning platform" issue that requires urgent and courageous attention? What are the negative consequences of no change? Identify both elements.

Implementing Change

Once you have acknowledged the burning platform issues, as a leader you have to do something about it. Below is Dr. Kotter's eight-step process for implementing change. We will discuss an alternative approach to implementing change that leads to same steps—in chapter 11, "Ⓔxhibit Emotional Energy and Edge." For now, let's examine each step.

Step 1: Create Urgency

"Orchestrating pain messages throughout the institution is the first step in developing organizational commitment to (major) change."—Rosabeth Moss Kantor, former editor, *Harvard Business Review*

In order for people to change, they need to have some sense that it's important. You need to think about how you will create an awareness that change is urgent to achieve. You need to create a pain message. Insightfully, you need to create a feeling that makes people very uncomfortable to a point that they want to change.

Step 2: Create the Guiding Coalition

The second action step is to assemble a group with enough power to lead the change. Managing the human element of change is central to the success of the change. There are two elements.

Guiding: This change group doesn't need to know all the answers. It doesn't even need to be the most senior group of people in the organization. (Maybe the people who created the challenge can't fix it.) It does need to accept responsibility, and have authority, to guide.

Coalition: Get the group to work together like a team. It may be a mix of managers, board, staff, and even donors. Sometimes it's a specific staff team asked to deliver the change and working to a plan developed by a senior grouping such as the board.

Typically, a change team is a group charged with a specific task to help with a change process. It is often small in number, perhaps a maximum of eight people, often working alongside a consultant. Members normally meet regularly for a limited time—normally three to six months. They usually carry on doing their normal jobs, so they need some staffers or consultants to help deliver the change action. Importantly, they are often chosen for their attitude or mind-set—not their representative status or seniority.

To be successful they need:

- A clear understanding of what they have to tackle and clear guidelines to follow
- To be clear on their role—to act as a means of consultation on a change, to sell the change, etc
- The backing of the most senior group and the time and resources to deliver the project

Change teams often benefit from some training in change processes. For example, I leverage my PhD work and training experience to teach the business process consultants how to implement technology process improvements.

Step 3: Develop a Vision and Strategy

The guiding coalition only provides you with a *vehicle*. To help them deliver change, you need them to come up with or ferret out two other elements:

- **Vision**: Recalling our discussion on building a shared vision in the learning-leader chapter. The vision has to be created to help direct the change effort. Here the vision has to be reinforced via purposing. You need to be able to articulate this positive state as clearly as the burning platform

- **Strategy**: You need to know broadly how you are going to get to this vision and roughly how long it will take. Your strategy should involve phasing in changes in the process. So, for example, "first we will have the consultation, then redundancies, then the restructure, and then people will have new development opportunities"

The vision and strategy should be written down and agreed upon. It can be changed as events change. But it should be a formal plan.

Step 4: Communicate the Change Vision

You need to communicate the vision once you have developed it.

A formal or informal communication plan should be developed. At minimum, it should include what needs to be communicated; why it needs to be communicated; between whom the communication should take place; the best method for communicating with that person(s); who's responsible for sending the communication; and when and how often the communication should be sent. Using interpersonal skills, the stakeholders, those individuals impacted by the change, need to be kept in the loop and well informed.

When Sterling Software was in the process of acquiring KnowledgeWare, they communicated information internally through town-hall type meetings and externally to the press that this was a tremendous opportunity for Sterling and a prediction of excellent growth due to KnowledgeWare position and reputation as the number one CASE tool vendor in the world.

As an executive consultant with one of the world's largest wholesale reinsurance providers, I collaborated with a Big 4 Consulting firm in leading a business transformation project streamlining a $ 400 million quote/treaty business with projected savings of $36 million over a five year period. This required changes in various operations that permeated down to specific job/performer tasks. The theme communicated for this project and others targeted at other areas of the business was BoF (Business of the Future).

It is always best to communicate the change vision in terms of *Think, Feel, Do* because change is most successful when it starts as a thought but comes from the heart. ***Said another way,*** change is most effective when a person's heart and mind are committed to creating a healthy and new growth to excellence—[**C.H.A.N.G.E.**]. Figure 9.1 Think-Feel-Do illustrates this emotional sequence.

Figure 9.1 – Think Feel Do

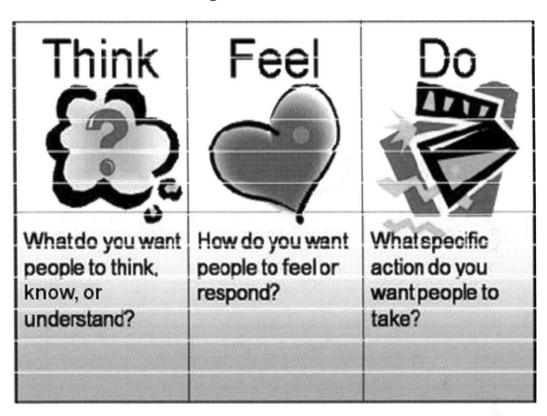

Think	Feel	Do
What do you want people to think, know, or understand?	How do you want people to feel or respond?	What specific action do you want people to take?

Your change message should create an emotion to want to do something different to improve the situation. If it does, it will be powerful and targeted.

Step 5: Empower Others to Act

Realistically, the senior management team cannot control the whole change process. And in order for the change to spread out, even the most skillful and competent change team can't do it all. To gain broad acceptance, others throughout the organization need to feel they too have a part to play and are trusted.

So you need to break the change up into smaller projects and allow people to add to the process—for example, Sterling Software, though they acquired KnowledgeWare, allowed the KnowledgeWare leaders who were not let go to contribute to developing a new business model, resulting in new divisions within Sterling. The result was that staff felt better about the change in terms of broad-based action—they had a role and a part. This is the Ⓓ in **L.E.A.Ⓓ.E.R.S.H.I.P.**, which means deliver results through effective delegation. We will talk more about this in a later chapter.

This empowerment can involve a number of different approaches, but the best way is simply to give small groups specific projects to do that will help contribute toward the change. These projects need to be relevant, limited in scope, and capable of being delivered in a reasonable time scale autonomously.

Step 6: Create Short-Term Wins

Steps 5 and 6 are strongly linked. You need to ensure that the change is still seen to have momentum even when it encounters difficulties or challenges. Small wins help with this.

The wins need to be:

- Enough so that it feels like things are happening
- Clear wins or successes
- Communicated widely and celebrated

The wins can be *external*—for example, a new major donor signs on to your ideas—or *internal*—the restructure is finished and the new teams start work.

Make sure you make time to acknowledge and celebrate the wins. Don't keep looking up the mountain.

Step 7: Consolidate Gains and Produce More Change

Step 7 involves summarizing what has been achieved—perhaps through a mid-term review or conference. You then need to make sure you keep the pressure on and ask for another "chunk" of change which will help make more progress toward the vision in Step 2.

Don't rest or get complacent. Step 7 is a key message—you do need to keep the pressure on to deliver the vision.

Step 8: Institutionalize Changes in the Culture

People have a habit of slipping back into old ways of doing things after a period of "being good." Think about how many people lose weight, then put it on again, or give up smoking only to start again. Organizations can do the same thing:

- The customer care initiative fizzles out after a few months since the customers don't seem to appreciate it and it is hard work

- The commitment to open communication proves to take a long time, so is abandoned and we go back to secret squirrel
- The merger ends up involving two "tribes" agreeing to work alongside each other rather than developing a shared new approach to work

So the final step is to ensure that the changes you need are actually embedded in the corporate or organizational culture.

Summary

The *Strategic hustler*™ stages transformations. Employing the skills of intelligent behavior, they orchestrate the *"Why"* of **C.H.A.N.G.E.** [**C**reating a **H**ealthy **A**nd **N**ew **G**rowth to **E**xcellence]. They are constantly challenging the status quo with a laser-like focus on maximizing throughput, operational efficiency, customer service, and competitiveness. From a personal perspective they want to get to a better place. And, most importantly, when they identify change opportunities, they have the courage to do something about it. They lead and manage the following *"How"* of **C.H.A.N.G.E.**:

- Create tension
  - Define a purpose
    - Ensure sponsor commitment
  - Create a shared need
    - Establish a sense of urgency
    - Voice the vision
- Harness support
  - Mobilize commitment
    - Form a guiding coalition
  - Design the future state
    - Refine the vision
- Articulate goals
  - Build investment
    - Empower others to act on the vision
    - Connect, communicate, coordinate, and collaborate
- Nominate roles
  - Transition to the future state
  - Monitor results and learning
    - Plan for and create for short-term wins
  - Build systems and Structures
    - Consolidate improvements and produce still more change

- Growth capability
  - Improve individuals and organization to master the change
    - Institutionalize new approaches with adoption and learning
- Entrench changes
  - Continuous effort to master the change
    - Consistent Lessons learned

Seize opportunities to make anything [project, business, team, one's own life] better. A great leader accomplishes this with the help of others. Understand there must be a willingness to ask for help. Said another way, they can only to deliver results through effective delegation. The next chapter discusses the Ⓓ in L.E.A.Ⓓ.E.R.S.H.I.P.

CHAPTER 10

Deliver Results through Effective Delegation

Introduction

The surest way for an executive (leader) to kill himself or herself is to refuse to learn how, when, and to whom to delegate work. Since benefits are delivered via programs and projects, this chapter will discuss delegation within the context of program/project management. The delegator will be referred to as the *leader*. The delegatee will be referred to as the *follower*.

As a project/program management professional, I can attest that although project management concepts are simple, their application can be very complex, whether they are being applied to an existing organization or to a newly organized project. Ineptly conceived or poorly executed project management concepts lead to failure. Therefore, a delegating leader must have the right structures in place in order to prevent projects from failing.

Projects are of a wide variety; however, effective leaders must design their project organization by analyzing and evaluating issues of responsibility, authority, reliability, and accountability, and by balancing these to optimize human interactions with minimum barriers. They must be able to organize the project participants and their activities in a manner that facilitates open communication, successful delegation, and effect team building. Before we can talk about delegation, let's talk about the keys to being an effective delegator.

After witnessing the misunderstandings of the dynamics of effective delegation, I concluded reliability and accountability exist only when sufficient authority is granted to fulfill a responsibility. Because these elements are critical for the flow of work to proceed smoothly, they must be in balance in order to be effective. Briefly:

- *Authority* confers the right to impose some degree of obedience
- *Responsibility* confers the obligation on the recipient to act with or without detailed guidance or specific authorization
- *Reliability* refers to the degree to which the recipient of authority and responsibility can be depended upon, i.e., to respond with sound and consistent effort
- *Accountability* in the project context is the extent to which the individual or team of individuals are answerable and must provide visible evidence of their actions—I call this holding their feet to the fire

These four elements are highly interrelated. For example:

- When authority is granted to someone, accountability must be required

and

- When responsibility is assigned, reliability to accomplish must be expected

These interrelationships should be understood in order to justify giving rewards or recognition to motivate participants. You recall rewards and recognition are inherited by a leader who has position power.

Therefore, authority and responsibility (that refers to acting and accomplishing) must be balanced by an appropriate level of accountability and reliability (that refers to accomplishing and then deserving proper rewards or recognition). An effective delegator understands, people can be held accountable only if proper authority and responsibility are given and if they get appropriate recognition/rewards for fulfilling their responsibilities. I will use the following two scenarios—sports related and personal experience—to illustrate my point.

An athletic coach cannot play the game. His or her effectiveness is based on their ability to delegate the right task, to the right people, at the right time, to get the right results. The coach must get his or her players to trust each other by executing their assignments and having confidence that their teammates will do the same. When everyone does their job, the probability of success is increased tremendously. Of course, there are risks that the wrong play was called for the specific situation. But that is why adjustments must be made. Hence, you have a quarterback of a football team that exhibits trust and confidence in his teammates to block for him, catch and/or run the ball, and pick up a crucial first down or score a touchdown. Then there is the point guard of a basketball team having trust and confidence in his or her teammates to execute on a pick and roll, hit the open jump shot, or get a crucial rebound. They all are leaders who realize they cannot do everything themselves. These scenarios have one thing in common—the game. The game represents the project environment. If you agree with these truisms, then you realize that as a project leader, you cannot do everything yourself.

In my role as director of commerce and information technology/acting CIO for a startup alternative energy company, there were no formal policies, procedures, or processes in these areas. As with any ad-hoc process, work was done haphazardly so the product was produced using inefficient and expensive means. Having had practical experience on effective delegation, I had to convince my bosses, who were very wealthy serial entrepreneurs, that giving me the responsibilities with creating these areas with common sense practices was not enough. They were tying my hands because I didn't have the authority to make the tough decisions. I always had to go to my boss, a cofounder who was the executive vice president and chief strategy officer for IT decisions, and to the associate vice president of business development and supply chain management for commercial/supply chain decisions. Both of their challenges were delegating the authority to allow the critical decisions to be made. Through my coaching, they were able to see the errors of their ways; through compromise they granted the authority, enabling me to deliver solutions. These solutions proved to be cost-effective, efficient, and timely.

The moral to these scenarios is you must delegate your work and responsibility by passing your authority in part or in total to another person. Delegating is not easy, yet it is one of the most important skills that effective leaders must learn. It requires effective communication, negotiation, and interpersonal skills.

What delegation involves

Delegation is the process by which authority is distributed from the leader to individuals working on the project. This leader is in the role of project manager. Any project team member accepting an assignment through this delegation accepts new authority and the responsibility for it. The expectation is that the person will be reliable and will be held accountable for performance of the assignment. When project managers delegate authority for any task, they still have the ultimate responsibility for the results. They also agree to be held accountable for the decision to delegate (i.e., the way the project managers have chosen to handle their responsibility). The act of delegation, therefore, creates a duality of responsibility and accountability that is related to the same task and its execution.

What delegation is not (Verma, 1995):

- It is not "passing the buck"

- It is not "dumping"
- It is not "puppeterring"
- It is not "dealing with trivia"
- It is not "ego gratification"

Delegation involves (Verma, 1995):

- Giving responsibility (obligation to perform the assigned tasks)
- Gaining acceptance (the team member's agreement to be responsible)
- Granting authority (the right and power to accomplish the tasks)
- Expecting reliability (assurance of best and consistent effort)
- Requiring accountability (accepting responsibility for success or failure)

You'll recall our previous discussion on these key elements of delegation. I would describe the relationships between authority, responsibility, reliability, and accountability in the delegation process of a project environment as:

- The leader grants authority and requires accountability from the follower
- The leader assigns responsibility and expects reliability from the follower

Simply put, when accountability is met, it leads to accomplishments. When responsibility is fulfilled in a reliable manner, i.e., reliability is demonstrated by quality results, it leads to recognition. The delegation process, used in this way, creates positive reinforcement and enhances motivation in both the leader and the follower to further increase performance.

To make delegation a "full package," it is important that the delegated work be accepted by the follower and that, whenever possible, leaders delegate in terms of "objectives and products" rather than "process or procedures." Earlier I mentioned a profanity-laden outburst from my boss because we didn't agree on a solutions delivery approach. He was an ineffective leader who violated the rule of delegate a "full package." That is, he did not delegate in terms of "objectives and products" but in "process or procedures." I am the type of person who is not offended by being told, or collaborating on, *what* to do. However, I require very little to no guidance on *how* to do it. Do you see the cause of the conflict? You learned in chapter 2, "Ⓐdaptable Behavior", an effective leader chooses the appropriate leadership style based on the readiness of the follower. The following paragraphs provide golden nuggets of information on becoming an effective delegator. For over twenty-five years, this process has served scores of others and me very well.

Delegation Process

The process of delegation is illustrated by a "4Ds" decision making model (Drop, Defer, Delegate, and Do), which is based on four questions:

1. *What can be dropped?* Certain items can be easily dropped without serious consequences
   To prioritize:
   - Choose the activities with low payoffs
   - Decide on things not to be done on a priority basis
2. *What can be deferred?* Certain items can be easily deferred without serious consequences
   To prioritize:
   - Try to be effective rather than efficient
   - Use a file folder marked BAW (Bells And Whistles). I call items in this folder BAW because they are essentially nonessentials features and benefits. They are "nice to haves." Most of the time events occur that render these items unimportant. It is a practical way to approach time management by doing important things first
3. *What can be delegated?* The answer to this question gets to the real heart of the delegation process. The ability of a leader to delegate effectively and distribute work to others determines two things:
   - Their overall worth to the organization in getting things done through others
   - Their overall achievements in life, which give them self-satisfaction

     However, the important question here is, *Does the leader have someone to delegate to?*

     These days it is becoming difficult due to downsizing, scarce resources, and tight schedules. In such cases, leaders have to depend upon real teamwork (I help you; you help me)

4. *What must I do?* This is an important point in the delegation process. Here leaders decide what they can do and what they must do. They should concentrate on things that are the most important, urgent, and have high visibility and payoffs. These are the things in the projects for which they will be remembered and recognized. On smaller projects, leaders should address this question at the start and do whatever is necessary to kick off the project and set the stage for success

Why delegate?

Recall the sports analogy made earlier. Every game, or project environment, has constraints and scarce resources that have to be managed to be effective. For example, in football you have to put the football in play within a specific time or be penalized for delay of game. Additionally, the offense is limited to playing eleven players at a time, and of those eleven, only a maximum of seven can be used to advance the ball. Basketball gives the team with the ball twenty-four seconds to shoot the ball into the basket or they lose possession. Only five players can be used to score the basket. Baseball requires nine players on defense and only one batter and one pitcher can interact during play. The batter gets three strikes and four balls to try and get on base. As stated earlier, the coach has to delegate the right task, to the right people, at the right time, to get the right results. So you can see that effective delegation is essential in a project environment because of tight schedules and scare resources. It is important to delegate work in order to increase effectiveness and efficiency in managing a project, reducing the crisis atmosphere.

In each of the above scenarios, each player has an opportunity to shine. Why? Delegated task provide stimulus and opportunities to project team members, improving their participation and interest in the project and possibly opening new horizons for them. One only has to look at the free agent market value a player creates when he or she "puts up the numbers" and shows he or she is a team player. In addition, delegation creates more free time for the leaders to work on the most important and critical tasks, as well as, simply, more time to think. Creative thinking by the leader and interested, challenged project team members helps to avoid the "one-person-band" syndrome.

What should or should not be delegated? To avoid delegation paralysis, leaders must evaluate what to delegate and what they must do themselves. Mark Towers suggests leaders as project managers should delegate the following (Towers, 1993):

- Routines (to get out of comfort zones)
- Tasks that require technical expertise (to offer ever-greater challenges)
- What someone else can do better (to increase morale)
- Some enjoyable things to others (to motivate)
- Tasks or challenges to vary the routing of those who have boring jobs
- Activities that will allow people to cross-train one another so that they can manage their day-to-day crises (to increase self-confidence)
- Projects involving the critical, visible issues of quality, quantity, cost, and timeliness to self-managed project teams or self-directed teams. The team will accept the challenge, do a good job, and spread the workload evenly

What should not be delegated? Leaders, project managers, should not fully delegate (Towers, 1993):

- Long range planning (although they should involve others)
- Selection of key team players
- Responsibility for monitoring the team's key project or key function
- The task of motivating fellow team members (people value how much the leader cares for them)
- Evaluation of team members (performance appraisals)
- Opportunity to reward team members
- Rituals such as funerals, groundbreaking ceremonies, and celebrations (successful people suit up and show up!)
- Touchy, personal matters or crises
- Items that set precedents or create future policies

A rule of thumb in delegation: always delegate to increase productivity and quality. Put on your Adaptive-Leader hat and evaluate the amount of task and socioemotional support the follower will require. Effective delegators know what their limits or boundaries are when delegating, and what they must handle themselves.

Now that you understand the reason for delegating, the next few pages will expose you to what leading experts are saying about obstacles to the delegation process and then conclude with how to delegate effectively.

Obstacles to the Delegating Process

This topic swims deeper in exposing behavior traits of leaders and followers. Earlier we discussed Readiness Levels, Effectiveness and Position Power, and Effectiveness and Personal Power. Of the many projects and programs I have been affiliated with, there are three general categories of obstacles that can make delegation in a project difficult.

Obstacles related to the project manager. These obstacles vary from project manager to project manager and are mostly related to management style and level of confidence in the team members. Recall our discussion on being adaptable and effective. For example, project managers may enjoy using personal authority and therefore resist delegating to project teams members, perhaps fearing that others may do a better job. Or they may fear that surrendering some of their authority may be seen by others as a sign of weakness. Other obstacles include:

- Subjects are too confidential to involve others
- Team members are not sufficiently qualified and capable
- It takes too long to explain the job to someone else ("it's faster to do it myself")
- "I can do it better"
- "I already delegate enough"
- "I cannot take the risk of getting unsatisfactory results"
- "I will lose track of the progress"

Obstacles related to project team members. Sometimes, even if the project manager wishes to delegate, he or she may encounter some roadblocks from project team members. Team members may be reluctant to accept delegated authority due to fear of failure or lack of self-confidence.

The additional responsibility may substantially increase their workload and thus complicate working relationships. Even initially cooperative teams can resist delegation if the project manager does not provide sufficient guidance and support once delegation is made. Recall the discussion on Situational Leadership® in the chapter 2, "Ⓐdaptable-Behavior"—the R1 to R2 to R3 Phenomenon. The leader must evaluate the followers' readiness and understand the human dynamics going from leader directed to self-directed.

Obstacles related to organization. The overall climate of the organization may encourage or discourage the delegation process. For example, in a very small organization, the project manager may have no one to whom to delegate. Or, project team members may be suspicious if top management generally does not encourage delegation and a project manager wants to initiate a change.

How to Delegate Effectively

Effective leaders carry a heavy burden of responsibility. They cannot do everything themselves and therefore must delegate some of the tasks to others. Effective delegation depends upon interpersonal skills, especially communicating and negotiating skills. This section outlines a practical method and guidelines to delegate effectively.

Practical Method for Effective Delegation

There are eight essential ingredients of effective delegation, which can be represented by the acronym (2 x ETFP) which stands for Easy to Follow Procedures. Effective and successful delegation involves four steps, each having two major ingredients. (Towers, 1993)

E = Entrust and Enlist
T = Teach and Touch
F = Familiarize and Follow Up
P = Praise (the Process) and Participate (in Feedback)

Entrust and Enlist. *Entrust* means to select the right individual for the task and show full confidence in the capacity and the ability of that person to perform. Recall the earlier sports analogy: the coach must select the right people to perform an assignment. *Enlist* means to gain that person's partnership. An effective leader uses adaptive behavior to assess the readiness of the subordinate and then chooses the appropriate leadership behavior to guide him or her. Therefore the adaptive leader must connect, communicate, and coordinate to ultimately collaborate. Inform the person how important the task is to achieving the company or project goal(s) and involve him or her in the planning. This helps the effective leader to gain the follower's acceptance and hence commitment to perform the task to the best of their ability. This "buy-in" creates an open flow of quantum and incremental ideas amongst the team. We will talk more about quantum and incremental ideas later. But for now, delegating in terms of objectives rather than in procedure encourages the creativity. I've found team members who are delegated in this manner feel challenged, motivated, and instilled with pride and commitment. ***This is an example on how a*** person is energized with ever-greater challenges. Earlier we covered what can happen when the leader delegates in terms of process and procedures instead of objectives and products. Remember, *Entrust* the right person whom you can count on to get the job done. Then *Enlist* by explaining that the task being delegated is critical and important to the project; by demonstrating that you only delegate tasks that you are willing to do yourself; and by approaching the person with, "I need your help"—expressed genuinely, not as lip service. The "I need your help" is key because even though you can perform the task, you have to be able and willing to admit that the follower brings new insight—we talked about this earlier—which increases the likelihood of achieving the project's quality, schedule, and cost objectives.

Teach and Touch. When delegating, leaders may need to teach (or model) certain behaviors to help the follower succeed:

Time: Agree on a time line or a deadline ("ASAP" is too vague!)

Tools: Provide the necessary tools. If necessary, teach the follower to use those tools

Troubleshoot: Help the follower to identify boundaries and possible sources of trouble. Confirm your availability to help when problems arise

The concept of "touch" implies empowering people so that they feel a sense of ownership and accomplishment. People need to be "touched" (not literally, but mentally) and excited about the challenges and opportunities of jobs delegated to them. Touching can also be a part of effective communication. While delegating work to someone else, the leader should touch that person figuratively with his or her eyes. Good, solid eye communication signals dedication, compassion, and seriousness (Towers, 1993).

Familiarize and Follow Up. From my experiences in sports and business, to work together in a true partnership, partners must be familiar with each other's work processes, workloads, and personalities. If leaders show interest in their staff's work situations, interests, and workload, they will likely return that interest and finish the delegated tasks effectively and efficiently.

The second half of this step emphasizes that old delegations axiom: "people respect what you inspect and therefore you should inspect what you expect." Note that sufficient time must be provided to enable the person to accomplish the task. The degree of inspection or follow-up will depend upon his or her maturity and competence.

Praise the Process and Participate in Feedback. Delegating work to others involves some risk because it may not be done the way you would have done it. But it is important to praise the process. As a spiritual person, I am always thankful for everything—good, bad, or undecided. Here is some spiritual advice, stay mindful to always give praises. Praise the effort of the person—no matter how successful or unsuccessful the overall outcome of delegation turns out. Thank him or her for their efforts and give positive reinforcement. Any shortcomings can be pointed out later (after the positive aspects), along with suggestions for correcting them. It is your responsibility as the leader to make a list of things that went well as well as those that did not go so well. Remember an effective leader is a learner and a teacher. So give feedback. Why?

Feedback is a very healthy concept and will help everyone in the project to change, improve, grow, challenge, and become more creative and an effective leader and staff member. You should encourage your staff to give their input in planning and implementing the delegated task, and they should be given an opportunity to appraise your delegation skills.

Effective delegators of tasks ask three simple questions of the people to whom they delegate projects or tasks (Towers, 1993):

1. What helpful things can I do for the person being assigned the task?
2. How do I avoid interfering with the process of delegation?
3. What else can I do to be an effective delegator?

Below is a [S.I.M.P.L.E.] guide to Accountability—Holding Feet to the Fire!

During my doctoral studies, I came across this acronym for making and holding people accountable. It is another way of stating what we have already covered—hence ***said another way***. Holding a person's feet to the fire, or making them accountable, is S.I.M.P.L.E. I hope your find this helpful in being an effective delegator.

S = Set Expectations
I = Invite Commitment
M = Measure Progress
P = Provide Feedback
L = Link to Consequences
E = Evaluate Effectiveness

S = Set Expectations

- The success of any organization comes down to one thing: how well it organizes its members to focus on and work toward the same purpose
- The employees need to know what is expected of them before they can be held accountable for anything
- The more clearly the expectations and goals are set up front, the less time will be wasted later clarifying—or worse, arguing about—what was really expected

I = Invite Commitment

- Just because your employees know what to do doesn't mean they will do it. After goals and expectations are set, employees need to commit to achieving them
- Employees are more likely to do this when they understand two things: how the goals will benefit them personally, and how the goals will help move the organization forward
- Once this connection is made, they are more likely to buy into the goals, and actually welcome your holding them accountable for the results

M = Measure Progress

- Information is needed to hold your employees accountable. Measure their ongoing performance and gauge whether or not they meet the goals and expectations to which they had previously committed
- Goals are only measurable when they are quantified. Measure the results and compare them to the employees' goals to discover the gaps that require further attention

P = Provide Feedback

- Feedback will not solve problems by itself, but it will open the door for problem-solving discussions and follow-up actions
- The employees need feedback to do a good job and improve in areas where performance is falling short of expectations. Most of the time, giving objective, behavioral feedback is all it takes. Setting expectations followed by quality feedback is the backbone of holding someone accountable for results

L = Link to Consequences

- Sometimes employees need a little external motivation to live up to their commitments
- When they struggle to reach their goals, they can be helped by administering appropriate consequences

E = Evaluate Effectiveness

- Review how the process has been handled
- Put a systematic and consistent method in place and you'll find that when people are held accountable for work that must get done, it gets done

Let's Get Busy on Practicing Effective Delegation

Being an effective delegator has been to the key to my success. Being a Situational Leadership® practitioner draws me to leadership and management practices that have a foundation is this approach. If you keep on reading and learning you will understand why. The following Tools and Techniques (T-N-T) were adopted from the Bruns Leadership Group (www.brunsconsult.com). I've leveraged them to lead, manage, and teach thousands from all walks of life during my travels in business, athletics, and community. Table 10.1 highlights "Five Critical Questions to Guide Your Delegation" which references figure 10.1 the target delegation model and table 10.2 the delegation level definitions.

Five Critical Questions to Guide Your Delegation

Table 10.1 Five Critical Questions provides a critical thought process to guide your delegation decisions. It identifies the area of focus (topic); the questions you need to think about (critical question); and your delegation action plan (to do).

Table 10.1 Five Critical Questions

TOPIC	CRITICAL QUESTION	TO DO
VISION	1. What is the overall goal you are trying to achieve?	a. Describe success in detail b. Determine key stakeholders
ANALYSIS	2. What are the critical and relevant aspects of the situation that must be addressed?	c. Articulate as much of the situation as time and importance dictate d. Decide what stake you have in the successful outcome of the task
IMPORTANCE	3. What is your interest and involvement in the situation?	e. Decide and inform that person(s) to whom you are delegating of your "must haves" vs.. your "nice-to-haves" vs. your "non-directeds" (See Target Delegation Model)
CAPABILITY	4. What level of delegation will be appropriate with the person(s) to whom you are delegating?	f. Evaluate the person you are proposing to delegate to and determine the appropriate level of delegation: tell/sell /test/consult/ delegate (see Delegation Level Definitions)
FOLLOW THROUGH	5. How do you plan to follow up on the delegated task?	g. Determine your own work plan for follow-through, depending upon the level of delegation you've identified

Source: Bruns Leadership Consulting. Copyright and all rights reserved. Material has been reproduced with the permission of Bruns Consulting Leadership.

Figure 10.1: The Target Delegation Model

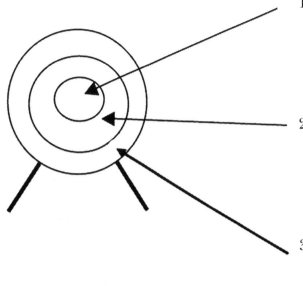

1. List your "must haves" –there is no room for error; the follower is told what and how to do the task to achieve the desired outcome

2. List your "nice to haves" –you are concerned how these tasks are accomplished but you can allow some leeway to the follower on how they are done

3. List your "nondirecteds" –how the task is accomplished is left entirely up to the follower

Delegation Level Definitions

Table 10.2 applies Situational Leadership® discussed in chapter 2, "(A)daptable Behavior" to delegation. The level of delegation is based upon the follower's ability and willingness. Through-out this book competence and commitment will be used interchangeably with ability and willingness respectively.

Table 10.2 Five Critical Questions

Tell: Use when	■ Follower(s) are low in ability and low in willingness ■ You have no options yourself – it must be done a specific way ■ Your "must have" target zone in nearly total ■ There is a very high cost of non-performance ■ There is low trust and no surprises can be tolerated
Sell: Use when	■ Follower(s) have moderate ability but low willingness "buy-in" is very important to the outcome ■ Your "must have" target zone is large ■ There is a high cost of non-performance ■ You are beginning to build trust and desire no surprises
Test: Use when	■ Follower(s) have ability and willingness ■ You welcome other ideas and insights to compare with yours ■ You are open to being questioned ■ Your "must have" target zone is moderate ■ Trust is developing and you don't expect any surprises
Consult: Use when	■ Follower(s) have moderately high ability and willingness ■ You want subordinates to have high buy-in to the project or task ■ Others might have innovative ideas or know more than you do ■ Your "must haves" target zone is quite small ■ You can define the vision but need to know the *how* ■ There is high trust and you know there will be no surprises
Delegate: Use when	■ Follower(s) have high ability and willingness ■ You belief your subordinate has high ability ■ You're sure others have good ideas or know more than you do ■ Your "must haves" target zone is quite small ■ You can define the vision but need to know the how ■ There is high trust and you know there will be no surprises

Summary

In a highly competitive market of the twenty-first century, the ability to delegate effectively is the true challenge of the leader's personal time management. In a project environment where all participants are under constant pressure to meet objectives within scope, time, cost, and quality constraints, they must work as partners with each other. In such an environment, people have to work interdependently, and therefore delegating becomes an essential skill to get things done. Delegators must be adaptable, goal-oriented, intelligent, a learner, and effective when delegating.

Effective delegation is vital to a well-functioning organization, project team and project organization. The process of delegation involves the effective assignment and acceptance of responsibility and includes a clear indication of the tasks to be performed and the results expected. Communicating these points clearly is crucial to effective delegation.

Our journey toward **A.G.I.L.E. L.E.A.D.E.R.S.H.I.P.** brings us to the second (E) in **L.E.A.D.(E).R.S.H.I.P.** This is (E)xhibit Emotional Energy and Edge. Too much emotion can lead to undesirable results. Too little emotion can result in the same. Then how do you determine the appropriate mix? Read on and see.

CHAPTER 11

(E)xhibit Emotional Energy and Edge

Introduction

Early in my career, I was a direct distributor in the Amway business. My motto was, "It takes guts to leave the ruts!" This motto gave me an edge, as you will later see. Prior to starting this business, I was employed as a lead programmer/analyst in the Housewares and Audio Business Division of General Electric. My performance and career goals had me on track to enroll in GE's most prestigious Financial Management Program (FMP). Excited about the opportunity, I reviewed every piece of FMP collateral—videos and literature—I could get my hands on in preparation. Here is background on this program.

FMP develops leadership and analytical skills through classroom training and key assignments. The program combines coursework, intensive job assignments, and interactive seminars in the areas of financial planning, accounting, operations analysis, auditing, forecasting, treasury/cash management, and commercial finance. The program is led by senior GE professionals and mentors and is committed to developing world-class financial leaders for various careers.

It was during my research that I came across the word "edge." One of the special qualities of FMP graduates would be having the foundation to make tough decisions. Dr. Jack Welch, GE's CEO, called this leadership quality "edge." My interpretation of having the "edge" was analogous to having the "guts" to make the decisions to "leave the ruts!". In *Leadership Engine*, by Noel M. Tichy, PhD, "edge" is defined as the courage to see reality and act on it.

As a former football captain and football coach, I learned that having edge without emotional energy is like a little child sitting down getting ready to bite into what they think is their favorite peanut butter and jelly sandwich only to discover there is no jelly. I guess you can tell my admiration for a nice gooey peanut butter and jelly sandwich. Yes, it is gooood!!!! Seriously, emotional energy and edge are critical to **A.G.I.L.E. L.E.A.D.E.R.S.H.I.P.** with a **G.R.I.P.** In fact, edge is my short way of saying emotional energy and edge. So when I mentioned edge think of emotional energy and edge.

This chapter will cover the importance of edge, its relationship to integrity, and how you can develop edge in yourself and others.

What's Edge Got to Do with It

Effective leaders "win" by making tough decisions in both life and business. They have edge and integrity. Achieving your dreams will require you to face hard realities, to cut through conflicting currents and ambiguities and to stake out clear positions.

Dr. Welch exposed me to this direct, take-no-prisoners style of action, which, as a *Street hustler*, winning football player, and coach, I was all too familiar with. The world-class behaviors discussed in this book are practiced by people from all walks of life and different parts of the globe, however, for various reasons they are not able to make the tough calls. Top performers have this learned ability. A noted point, a *Strategic hustler*™ needs courage to make the tough decision(s) to turn their dreams into reality—personally and professionally. Keep on reading and learning.

Earlier, when speaking of energizing people I cited various examples of mastery at creating positive energy. I talked about how, through a carefully calibrated combination of stretch goals, support, and team building, negative energy was turned into positive energy. This is what emotional energy does. Having an ability to create positive energy is only one of the reasons that my teams and clients succeeded in turning dreams into reality. Let's revisit some of these examples.

Sterling Software displayed their edge in a number of ways. The one that sticks out like a sore thumb is the way they integrated acquired companies into the Sterling culture. They had a mature, disciplined process in which they sought to understand the current culture of the acquired company. By probing department heads, the Sterling transition team unearthed the logic behind their choices. The dismissals, though done with integrity, were painful. Remember, not everyone should, could, or can make the journey to a championship. Sterling was focused on building a winner, and if, during the probing session, the department head did not measure up to the Sterling inquiry, he or she simply didn't make the team. The integrated project team resulting from this exercise would then be charged with developing a new business model integrating the acquired company into the Sterling business model.

Like so many in New Haven, Connecticut, I have been a great fan of Reverend Dr. Curtis and Elsie Cofield for years. After all, Dr. Cofield baptized me and also honored me at a Little League football banquet. Years later, our paths crossed again at a Baptist Church convention in Texas. What an example they have been for so many who seek to exemplify strong ministry in the context of strong family. Civic and religious leaders said that under the Cofields' leadership, Immanuel Baptist Church (IBC), the state's oldest and largest black Baptist church, has consistently extended its generosity, becoming a model for social action. Mrs. Cofield, known as "the Mother Teresa of Connecticut," is the cofounder/president of AIDS Interfaith Network, Inc. (AIN), a twenty-one-room treatment center that also runs a day program for AIDS and HIV patients. In addition, the center sponsors programs such as a teen hotline, substance abuse counseling, and the Sunshine Corner for children affected by HIV/AIDS and other illnesses. In the '80s, when churches in the Afro-American community were shying away from so many of the controversial social issues, the Cofields displayed edge as they were out in the streets trying to pull people together without imposing their religious values on those they were trying to help. This took a lot of courage.

The key element in exercising edge, however, isn't that it hurts, but rather that it takes courage. Edge is a complex combination of two factors. The first is an incredible drive to seek the truth and to find reality and base decisions on it. The second is the courage to act on this truth and make tough calls. And it is in the management of IBC and AIN as an organization and the design of its program that the Cofields have displayed their edge even more sharply.

At IBC/AIN, from the very beginning, Dr. and Mrs. Cofield have shown edge not only in their willingness to face an unpopular reality, but also in their defiance of conventional wisdom in responding to it. The unpopular reality is that churches should not be considered safe havens but rather places to take action. Thus, programs exist to try to decrease the strains of poverty, drugs, and crime. It took having edge to develop the models for each of these.

Edge and Integrity

Edge is the courage to see reality and act on it. Integrity is having the courage to meet the demands of reality. My dad used to always tell me that you can tell the content of people's characters by the kinds of decisions they make when they are under pressure. From a leadership perspective, one way to tell if a leader really has edge and integrity is if he or she is willing to publicly admit his or her mistakes. Overlooking this revealing sign is easy because it really pains no one but the leader. But for the effective leader, it's the ultimate test of edge and integrity: the edge to admit he or she was wrong, and the integrity to admit publicly that he or she was wrong. It is also a positive sign that the leader will accept the honest mistakes of others as well.

I have made my share of mistakes, as we all have. The key is having the integrity, or courage, to publicly admit them when appropriate. Earlier I spoke of my good friend and mentor "OC." I would always discuss my challenges of being a single parent raising a teenage boy and girl. OC, the consummate over-comer, would provide his advice by telling me a story on how he dealt with his teenagers—one a boy and the other a girl. He would tell me there were times when he would approach his son or daughter and admit to them he was wrong in his actions. Listening to him, I would have a revelation, because I remember times when my dad would do the same to me. Maybe this was the Holy Spirit speaking to me. As I meditated on his words, thoughts of how much integrity that man had crossed my mind. Man his courage and edge was awe-inspiring!

Dr. Michael "Doc" McCrimmon was another man of integrity. Doc is one of the most educated and experienced IT professionals in the world, endowed with an aura of integrity that embraces your total being when in his presence. I got a taste of the integrity and edge of this friendly man, who happens to be an ordained minister, when being recruited to join KnowledgeWare for a consultant job. Prior to Doc getting involved, I was recruited by an operations director, whose name escapes me. I verbally accepted the offer and was waiting on the offer letter. When the offer letter arrived, the salary offer was $10,000 less than the verbal offer. Thinking that it was a slight oversight by the Human Resource Department, I immediately contacted them. They refused to change the offer, stating that for the position, the salary was at the top end of the pay scale. The offer was refused.

I talk about "reputation" in this book to let you know that it precedes you. Here is an example. Months later Dr. McCrimmon, who replaced the operations director at KnowledgeWare, called me. He mentioned that my name kept surfacing when discussing with his peers, superiors, and staff, in his words, the "first-round draft choices" who would excel as consultants. We discussed the circumstances that led to my refusing the original offer to join KnowledgeWare as a senior consultant. He assured me that he would do what was necessary to bring me on board. He stated, "My goal is to hire the best CASE tool consultants in the world to build this consulting division." I passed the phone screen interview and was invited for a face-to-face meeting. When I walked into the room, there was this impeccably dressed African American with a faded hair-cut. In addition, he had a PhD! I thought to myself that he was worthy to be my boss. He introduced himself as Dr. Michael McCrimmon in a down-to-earth manner. He engaged me in a thought-provoking conversation, grabbing my attention with his visioning and purposing statements using them to explain how he was going to help the company achieve its strategic goals. We discussed how my skills, knowledge, and experience might benefit the company and how working for a world class company would benefit me. Dr. McCrimmon scheduled interviews for me with directors, senior managers, senior consultants, and instructors.

After the interviews, we met briefly and agreed I was a first-round draft choice. He wanted to meet with the others to get their opinions, but I knew the job was mine. A few days later, I received an offer letter to join KnowledgeWare Consulting Division as a *principal* consultant, a promotion from a senior consultant. Additionally, he increased the offer by $20,000! My reputation got me in the door and my communications skills earned me this position. But Doc's edge and integrity closed the deal. I accepted the offer, and it proved to be a smart, strategic career move for KnowledgeWare and for me. Doc's star-performer qualities of "edge" and integrity allowed him to build a world-class consulting organization for the leading Computer-Aided Software Engineering (CASE) tool vendor in the world. As you continue to read, you will learn these same qualities that allowed this amazing man to experience his reality.

Let's Get Busy Practicing Edge

Because "Leaders Are Born to Be Made," edge can be learned. Learning edge starts with having the courage to recognize when tough times require tough decisions. Once this is done you must think before you react. Plan you actions by asking yourself, "what will I do and by when;" react by pulling the trigger and making a *tough* decision. Consider the following a planning exercise in goal-setting—with edge.

	What I Will Do	By When
1.	_____	_____
2.	_____	_____
3.	_____	_____
4.	_____	_____
5.	_____	_____

This next activity involves developing edge using a triage approach. The key is getting people to face increasing levels of complexity, stress, and risk/reward consequences. A nursing practitioner who owns a doctorate in nursing along with twenty-plus years of experience explained how triage nurses are trained in emergency rooms. They start as understudies, or protégées, and then are given more responsibility, along with more stress. At every step, experienced doctors and nurses coach and mentor them. They help them work through technical issues as well as emotional ones. The point is to make sure they realize the importance of making balanced decisions and have the skills and courage to do so.

Every senior or executive level position held or contract won required me to prove my edge during a probationary period. Just like football, these *tests* were my tryouts for the team. I seized the opportunity, after all, if I had to entrust my life to a triage nurse, I would do my best to make sure they had successfully operated under fire in a big-city emergency room where they gained significant experience taking immediate action under stress.

Personally, developing edge personally and in others is often stressful but relatively straightforward. Put yourself and others in situations where such behavior is called for and then keep increasing the stakes. I believe this is what Father God was doing to me as he brought me through life's trials and tribulations. It never gets easy, and the goal is not to make you immune to the pain that tough decisions can create for you and others, but to practice facing difficult decisions that will give you the self-confidence to act on your beliefs and values. This process will test your conviction to those ideas and values. Later in the book, we will talk more about ideas and values.

Enhancing Your Edge Development

Consider what you can do to improve your capacity for triage. What assignments and experiences would help you? Who would be a good mentor? Think of some creative ways of dramatically enhancing your triage capability.

1. _____
2. _____
3. _____
4. _____
5. _____

Enhancing Edge in Others

Demonstrating the first quality of integrity I had to team with key staff members to develop an action plan to help them develop more edge. It would start with me looking at my staff roster and asking the questions: What is my action plan for the key people on my staff who need to develop more edge? How will I teach edge and triage? How will I give them difficult experiences that test them? How will I ensure that a failure does not irrevocable hurt the company while I keep stress in the situation?

Key People	Edge Enhancing Experiences
1.)	
2.)	
3.)	
4.)	

Communication Edge

As a student and practitioner of strategic decision making, I know decisions are never made in a vacuum. Your decisions will impact how you feel about yourself and how others perceive you. Let me share with you a situation when edge was necessary and how the decisions were handled with compassion.

One of the challenges inherited as the newly appointed deputy CIO, Business Strategic Services, was managing a project portfolio budgeted at $165 million. Everyone had their pet projects but with limited resources and minimal executive support. I now had the responsibility to make critical business decisions, some would be unpopular. As a proponent of fact-based decision making and making appropriate change, I required answers for each project to the following questions:

1. What business processes need to be managed?
2. Why do they need to be managed?
3. What are the critical success factors?
4. What is the proposed solution?
5. What is the payback period?

This line of questioning removed any politicking allowing me to restate the project budget for the fiscal year to a more realistic and attainable amount.

Answering these *project war story* questions proved to add value, be efficient and produce the same results as Dr. Kotter's—Eight-Step Change Management process discussed earlier. The following table shows the relationship between both approaches.

Project War Story	Kotter's Change Management Process
1. What business processes need to be managed? 2. Why do they need to be managed? Answering these questions required creating a sense of urgency and a guiding coalition. Note: A process has to mature from standard to measurable to be managed.	1. Create a sense of urgency 2. Create the guiding coalition
3. What are the critical success factors? The vital elements for a successful strategy must be determined and articulated with a vision statement and a "call to action" "all-hands-on-deck" mandate	3. Develop a vision and strategy 4. Communicate the change vision 5. Empower others to act
4. What is the proposed solution? 5. What is the payback period The solution must allow the company to respond dynamically and effectively to change. It must be implemented incrementally supporting a continuous process improvement philosophy.	6. Create short-term wins 7. Consolidate gains and produce more change 8. Institutionalize change to the culture

Summary

I am not hard-pressed to find real life examples of people who face difficult situations and deliver the truth when making the tough calls with the understanding of the pain and risk the decision brings. They demonstrate courage making life's journey on a tough road and tell the truth despite all odds. This is having the courage to see reality and act on it. Edge is a difficult quality to judge from the outside because only the individual knows at the moment if he or she has a firm grasp of reality and is sincerely acting for the good of something bigger than them. Here I am going to recall one of my favorite biblical scriptures (John 8:32) states, *"And ye shall know the truth, and the truth shall make you free."* **Said another way**, over time, the rightness or wrongness, the pettiness or nobility of a leader's actions will become apparent. Nevertheless at the time when the decisions are made, it isn't always easy to tell the smooth-talking gamblers and charlatans (*Street hustler*) from the gifted, visionary leaders (*Strategic hustler*™). Only the individuals know for sure—which is one of the reasons that having values is so integral to having edge. The final test of edge is whether the leader can, in total honesty, say, "I acted when I should have. I've had the courage of my convictions." Remember, it takes guts to leave the ruts! Let's examine the Ⓡ in **L.E.A.D.E.Ⓡ.S.H.I.P.** as we look at how effective leaders Ⓡespect diversity.

Ⓡespect Diversity

Introduction

Transitioning from a *Street hustler* to a *Strategic hustler*™ provides a unique view on life. It gives another way to view the world. Daniel Goleman, PhD, author of the *New York Times* and *Wall Street Journal* best-selling book *Emotional Intelligence*, defines "the Emotional Competence Framework" as consisting of self-awareness, self-regulation, motivation, empathy, and social skills. This book deals with each of these. I choose to talk about self-awareness in this chapter because it is our inner rudder to respect diversity. What do I mean by inner rudder? Keep on reading. What matters most is not academic excellence, not a business school degree, not even technical know-how, or years of experience. It is nice to have these things. However, one's ability to respect diversity and embrace one's social environment is the key. You recall the points of *your* trilogy of success:

1. Deliver results that exceed expectations
2. Reinvent myself
3. Assimilate into the social culture of the organization

The first two focused on the hard skills necessary to become a star performer but have no impact on respecting diversity. We will further continue to sharpen your trilogy of success later. But for now, the third point focuses on the soft skills needed to respect diversity. Being able to assimilate or blend into the social culture of an organization requires an emotional intelligence. We start by making a case for soft skills—a key ingredient to respect diversity.

The Case for Soft Skills

At Sikorsky Aircraft, a team was assigned to perform time and motion studies to uncover process improvement opportunities in a manufacturing process for assembling an electrical wire harness. Before conducting the studies, the shop personnel were interviewed to get their insight on process improvement opportunities. Successfully completing this project required more than technical know-how—it required skills in listening and understanding, flexibility, and teamwork. There would also be the ability to energize others, make commitments, and gain the confidence of those they work with.

The National Association of Insurance Commissioners (NAIC) is the US standard-setting and regulatory support organization created and governed by the chief insurance regulators from the fifty states, the District of Columbia, and five US territories. For superior performance in rolling out a program/project management methodology, technical expertise and analytical skills were invaluable, but so are emotional competencies such as, interpersonal skills, innovation, and effective leadership, building partnerships, and networking.

At South African Federal Reserve Bank, the central bank of South Africa, technical expertise and analytical skills are invaluable, but so are emotional competencies like self-confidence, flexibility, an achievement drive, service orientation, and teamwork, cooperation, wielding influence, and developing others.

My portraits of competence, sharing personal experience, summarize the reality of millions of people at work. They represent shared values on how critical respect for diversity contributes to adding value and demanding excellence for these and many other organizations. Having the ability and willingness to lead and manage people who look, think, and/or act differently contributes to the effectiveness and success of any person—professionally or personally. It's also a good thing for the organization—or initiative. Remember, you are not a leader unless people are willing to follow you. These people will come from all walks of life.

The Leadership Edge

Respecting diversity is central to effective leadership. An inability to manage diversity impedes the productivity of people. You recall in chapter 2, "Adaptable Behavior," we talked about Situational Leadership®, which is a leadership approach based on interplay among (1) the amount of guidance and direction a leader gives; (2) the amount of socioemotional support a leader provides; and (3) the readiness level that followers exhibit in performing a specific task. This concept was developed to help people attempting leadership, regardless of their roles, to be more effective in their daily interactions with others. It provides leaders with some understanding of the relationship between effective styles of leadership and the level of readiness of their followers. The key word "readiness" is the extent to which a follower demonstrates the ability and willingness to accomplish a specific task. I restate again that you are only a leader if you have followers. A leader's strengths or weaknesses in emotional competence can be measured in the gain or loss to the organization of the fullest talents of those they manage.

Diversity applies to culture, skill, knowledge, gender, age, etc. People tend to be at different levels of readiness depending on the task they are being asked to do. Readiness is not a personal characteristic; it is not an evaluation of a person's traits, values, age, and so on. Readiness is how ready a person is to perform a particular task. This concept of readiness has to do with specific situations—not with any total sense of readiness. All persons tend to be more or less ready in relation to a specific task, function, or objective that a leader is attempting to accomplish.

Handling an emotional situation demands troubleshooting skills: being able to establish trust and rapport quickly, to listen well, and to persuade and sell a recommendation. As Dr. Goleman puts it, *"You need capacities like self-awareness, perspective taking, and a sense of presence so you're the person at the table everyone is going to rely on."*

As deputy CIO for the City of Atlanta, assuming the responsibility of an underperforming division, with the staff of twenty-five comprised of different genders, mixed races, varying education and experience levels, charged with ensuring the business value delivery of IT solutions citywide—thousands of city employees and millions of citizens. Having worked with diversity professionals raised my awareness on how important having respect for diversity would be in leading this transformation. It gave me the emotional competence to realize that people from different cultures with different work experiences and different viewpoints would have to be coached and mentored through individual transitions discussed previously. Respecting diversity is essential to leveraging the strengths of people to get the job done.

Minority women staffed the team responsible for delivering innovation/ change management. This area was on the hot seat, and it took skillful negotiation to prevent the CIO and COO from outsourcing the area. Feelings in the division meetings ran high because they felt the negative perception was unjustified. Let me share with you a formula that eventually turned the division around. As a former Army ROTC student at Virginia State, I was introduced to the "divide and conquer" strategy. As a doctoral student reading the *Art of War*, I was reacquainted with this strategic approach in further detail while serving in various leadership roles. Additionally, while performing consulting work at

Fort McPherson, an army base in East Point, Georgia, I came across an acronym, **R.E.S.O.L.U.T.I.O.N.,** written on a board for a conflict resolution class. Each letter represented a step in resolving conflicts. The letters were as follows.

R = Respect the right to disagree
E = Express your real concerns
S = Share common goals and interests
O = Open yourself to different points of view
L = Listen carefully to all proposals
U = Understand the major issues involved
T = Think about probable consequences
I = Imagine several possible alternative solutions
O = Offer some reasonable compromises
N = Negotiate mutually beneficial agreements

I don't recall the course instructor or company delivering the training, but that's not important. The advantage of working for different organizations worldwide is that you are given many opportunities to learn. I have used this acronym as the foundation in many conflict resolution situations where it involved training or an actual negotiation.

Applying the "divide and conquer" approach, I conducted one-on-one meetings with each team member, allowing me to devise and implement a turnaround plan focused on: 1) retreating, 2) regrouping, and 3) redeploying to successfully change the course of the division.

Retreating

The myriad of opinions on the group performance was the basis of conflict. The mayor's office, including the chief information officer (CIO), was of the opinion the group was underperforming, whereas the group felt they were performing and stated a number of accomplishments. I felt it was time to retreat to the nearest corner of dignity. Using the **R.E.S.O.L.U.T.I.O.N.** formula, specific key members of my staff and I retreated from going to various meetings and worked on redefining the work objectives of the group, ensuring alignment with the strategic objectives of the Information Technology Department and mayor's initiatives. We went back to the basics of acquiring the diversity to become change agents. Through a series of lunch-and-learn sessions, I presented the new transformed view of the division.

- Technology and process roll-out must be owned throughout the organization—process owners

- Implementation teams must be comprised of managers and line personnel
- Implementation must be sponsored by senior executives
- Implementation teams must not ignore existing culture
- Constant feedback is imperative
- Assumptions must be challenged
- Strategic initiatives must have a champion

To become an essential professional member of the Business Strategic Services (BSS) team, each member needs to make personal and professional changes. In chapter 3, "Ⓖoal-Oriented Behavior," we discussed team building and teamwork mentioning the characteristics of a team member who fit into one of the following categories:

1. Not everyone will take the journey
2. Not everyone should take the journey
3. Not everyone can take the journey

My challenge was to identify which members, if any, of my staff fit into these categories. The good news was everyone was excited about the renewed direction of the division. More importantly there seem to be no personal reasons or personal agendas which allowed me to authenticate their behavior as sincere. In short, they were the real deal! Thus that eliminated categories 1 and 2. The bad news, or opportunity for solution, was that key members lacked ability to deliver the products and services required by the *new* BSS. Thus they were in category 3. You recall people in this category are weak leaks. They must be traded or trained. I decided to train them. This is where the regrouping happened.

Regrouping

As a corporate trainer in areas of technology management, process improvement, and systems analysis and design, I taught performance-based courses as opposed to information-based courses. The difference was that the performance-based training required the knowledge workers to attend class with a real-world problem, and they had to produce a course deliverable, which was an action plan detailing how they would apply what was learned to solve their unique problems. The action plans were the basis of project schedules that would later be developed along with subordinate-superior evaluations. Information-based training does not require an action plan; thus, the knowledge workers may forget what they have learned in class since there is no practical application to reinforce the material.

By applying a "divide and conquer" strategy, I focused on the process improvement group, program/project management group, and business analysis group, in that order. The process improvement group received top priority because this was where the most displeasure resided. It was a major focus of the division, but despite having a solutions delivery methodology, it was not communicated and reinforced as a standard. This became evident in witnessing the business process consultants' (BPC) unique approaches to delivering solutions. Their approaches were ad-hoc which contributed to a lack of consistency and predictability in translating problems into solutions. To mature their approach from ad hoc to standard, the BPCs were assigned to a project to consolidate the city's call center using a similar approach. I purposely put them in situations where they had to collaborate to leverage each other's strengths and compensate for any weaknesses. My role was to coach and mentor them, realizing that if this did not work, it could lead to career suicide, but my goal was to change the status quo and build a collaborating team.

The repeated use of the "divide and conquer" strategy allowed developing well-received frameworks for process improvement/organization change management, a Program Management Office and a Center of Excellence for Business Analysis. There were other capabilities needed—i.e., enterprise architecture—but my immediate goal was not to "boil the ocean."

My emotional intelligence contributed to the success of this project. Relying on my gut feeling allowed me to make decisions after collaborating with Human Resource and my boss on an action plan should a team member continually fail to meet expectations despite uplifting efforts involving training, coaching, and mentoring. Recall a team leader cannot avoid dealing with weak links. Team members who don't carry their own weight not only slow down the team, they impact your leadership. This proved critical during the redeployment stage of my turnaround plan.

Redeploying

As a *Strategic hustler*™, my gut feeling allows me to look for effective resource utilization to ensure the success of any initiative. I call these the five *M*s. We will have an in-depth discussion on them later in chapter 18 "(R)esource Management." They are as follows:

Man (Human) Power
Money
Materials
Methods
Machinery

Though I rolled out a team equipped with a new approach, the emotional intelligence was lacking. In chapter 10, "Ⓓeliver Results through Effective Delegation," we discussed the old delegations axiom: "people respect what you inspect and therefore you should inspect what you expect." You see the most important resource is man (human) power. Through inspection, I was able to determine where my weak links existed. The key question was having the emotional intelligence, which starts with a gut feeling, to appropriately deal with them.

The Source of Gut Feelings

I am going to share with you how your brain works to create your gut feeling. The ability to read your gut feelings has primordial roots in evolution. The brain areas involved in gut feelings are far more ancient than the thin layers of the neocortex, the centers for rational thought that enfold the very top of the brain. Hunches start much deeper in the brain. They are a function of the emotional centers that ring the brain stem atop the spinal cord—most particularly an almond-shaped structure called the amygdala and its connected neural circuitry. This web of connectivity, sometimes called the extended amygdala, stretches up to the brain's executive center in the prefrontal lobes, just behind the forehead. Figure 12.1 illustrates these "Gut" emotional centers.

Figure 12.1 The Gut Centers of the Brain

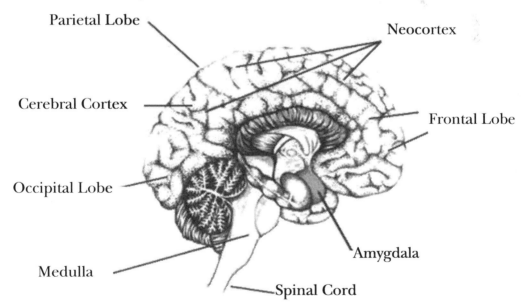

Your brain stores different aspects of an experience in different areas—the source of a memory is encoded in one zone, the sights and sounds and smells in other areas, and so on. The amygdala is the site where your emotions and experience recall are stored. Every experience that you have an emotional reaction to, no matter how subtle, seems to be encoded in the amygdala.

As the repository for everything you feel about what you experience, the amygdala constantly signals you with this information. Whenever you have a preference of any kind, whether for ordering the salmon rather than the tilapia special or a compelling sense that you should not take a particular course of action; that is a message from the amygdala. And via the amygdala's related circuitry, particularly nerve pathways that run into the viscera (the internal organs of the body, specifically those within the chest, such as the heart or lungs, or abdomen, as the liver, pancreas, or intestines), you can have a somatic response—literally, a "gut feeling"—to the choices you face.

This capacity, like other elements of emotional intelligence, can grow stronger with the accumulating experiences life brings us. *Said another way,* the longer you keep living; the more you experience and learn; the stronger your intuitions become. It's like your gut tells you things and there's a chemical reaction that's going on in your body, which is triggered by your mind, and tightening your stomach muscles, so your gut is saying, 'This doesn't fell right.'

From a spiritual viewpoint, I call this guiding sensibility *wisdom.* We all have seen that people who ignore or discount messages from this repository of life's wisdom do so at their peril.

The Value of Intuition

My life journey from *Street hustler* to *Strategic hustler*™ has allowed me to witness the power of intuition in many situations: young people choosing not to take a course of action that would have undesirable consequences; offensive coordinators who must manage all offensive players and assistant coaches, design specific offensive plays, develop a general offensive game plan, and call the plays for the offense during the game; credit managers who must sense when a deal might go bad even if the numbers look fine; executives who have to decide whether a new product is worth the time and money it takes to develop, people who must make an educated guess about who among a field of candidates for a job will have the best chemistry in a working group. All such decisions demand the capacity to fold into the decision-making process our intuitive sense of what is right and wrong.

Many years being in the trenches leading and contributing to the success of various programs/projects has allowed me to acquire a repository of knowledge and experience that gave me that gut feeling to ask the right question(s), resulting in changing their course to allow completion on time, within budget, and according to customer requirements, resulting in millions to billions of dollars in savings and revenues.

Intuition and gut feeling bespeak the capacity to sense messages from our internal store of emotional memory—our own reservoir of wisdom and judgment. This ability lies at the heart of self-awareness, and self-awareness is the vital foundation skill for three emotional competencies.

Respecting Diversity and Self-Awareness

Self-awareness is the capacity for introspection (introspection is the self-observation and reporting of conscious inner thoughts, desires, and sensations) and the ability to reconcile oneself as an individual separate from the environment and other individuals. Think of it this way, respecting diversity requires self-awareness. The competencies of self-awareness include: emotional awareness, self-assessment, and self-confidence. Let's go deeper into these competencies

Emotional awareness: Knowing when emotional feelings are present in us and others and having the ability to use our values to guide decision making

Accurate self-assessment: A truthful evaluation of one's own talents; with the courage to understand where improvements are needed and desire to learn from experience

Self-confidence: The knowledge that you can do something and do it well

Competency #1—Emotional Awareness

Do you recognize your emotions and their effects? How do you know that this competence exists within a person? With respect to diversity, people with this competence:

- Recognize which emotions they are feeling and understand why
- Understand the connection between their feelings and behavior
- Identify how their performance is impacted by their feelings
- Knows what to say and do (behavior) in a specific social setting
- Recognize that each of the above has a direct impact on their existence in a diverse society

Being aggressive in the pursuit of professional and life goals necessitates a "take-no-prisoners" attitude. This requires a virtue of conquering everything and everyone in the way. As the football team captain, I would get too easily irritated, without any sense that this anger was making me treat people in an abrasive way. My coaches helped me get control of my emotions because they could see that I was distancing myself from the team. No one wanted to work with me. As a youngster, I did not have the slight bit of awareness of how my emotions were pushing me around. My nieces would say, "You Betta Recognize!" I have witness this lack of emotional control in managers who become so focused on getting ahead or parents who desire to prove a point. Consequently, people don't want to work with them or for them—you'll recall an earlier statement that you are only a leader if people are willing to follow you. How about a parent whose behavior distances him/her from the rest of the family?

That awareness—of how our emotions affect what we are doing—is the fundamental emotional competence. Lacking that ability, we are vulnerable, like the football captain or manager, to being sidetracked by emotions that are out of control. Such awareness is our guide in fine-tuning on-the-job performance of every kind, managing our unruly feelings, keeping ourselves motivated, tuning in with accuracy to the feelings of those around us, and developing good work-related social skills, including those essential for leadership and teamwork.

Remember leaders are born to be made. People can be trained to be more emotionally self-aware and to have more empathy for their clients or colleagues, which is essential to being able to build long-term, trusting relationships. From our discussion on influence, we know people have a tendency to buy anything from people they like.

Emotional awareness starts with a stream of feelings, which runs in perfect parallel to our stream of thoughts that is a constant presence in all of us and with recognitions of how these emotions shape what we perceive, think, and do. From that awareness come our feelings that affect those we deal with. *Said another way*, your emotions can reverberate in the interaction with followers—for better or worse. It's all about perception.

Respecting dignity requires excelling in this competence. This shows an awareness of your emotions in any given moment—often recognizing how those emotions feel physically. You can articulate those feelings, as well as demonstrate social appropriateness in expressing them. Emotional awareness on a continuum ranges from those who are unable to know their feelings to those who are self-aware. People who are unable to know their feelings are at a tremendous disadvantage. In a sense, they are emotional illiterates, oblivious to a realm of reality that is crucial for success in life as a whole, let alone work. This shows when comments or behavior may be perceived as being offensive to others who don't look, talk, or think like them.

Meditation has proven to be a great way for me to stay in tune with my feelings and thoughts. With the ups and downs of life, to relieve the mental pressure, I've chosen this technique as a means for cultivating my self-awareness. You'll recall at the start of this book my discussion on meditating on Pastor D. E.'s sermon. This approach is a time-honored way to get in touch with my deeper, quieter voice of feeling: taking time out to "do nothing." Do-nothing productivity means not only taking a *timeout* from working, but also not filling the time with idle time wasters: watching TV, or doing something else while watching TV. Instead, it means putting aside for the time being all other goal-oriented activities and doing something that opens our minds to a deeper quieter sensibility—like dreaming of the pink sand of Bermuda along with its turquoise water beaches. To use a quote from a multilevel marketing presentation, "That, my friend, is a hint, hint, clue, clue."

Self-Awareness: Life's Inner Rudder

A rudder is a device used to steer a ship, boat, submarine, hovercraft, aircraft, or other conveyance that moves through a medium (generally air or water). Our self-awareness is an inner rudder that moves us through life. You have to force yourself to spend some time away from the hustle and bustle of your job in order to get down to reality again. If you don't spend enough time doing that, you can lose hold of the reins and get into all kinds of trouble.

What kind of trouble? The trouble starts with drifting away from our guiding values, or what is important to us. Personal values are not lofty ideas, but intimate credos that we may never quite articulate in words so much as feel. Our values translate into what has emotional power or resonance for use, whether negative or positive.

Self-awareness serves as an inner barometer, gauging whether what we are doing (or are about to do) is, indeed, worthwhile. If there is a discrepancy between action and value, the result will be uneasiness in the form of guilt or shame, deep doubts or nagging second thoughts, queasiness or remorse, and the like. Such uneasiness acts as an emotional drag, stirring feelings that can hinder or sabotage our efforts.

The choices we make in keeping with the inner rudder are energizing. They not only feel right but also maximize the attention and energy available for pursuing them. In his book *How to Be a Star at Work*, Robert Kelley, PhD, provides a study where star performers make career choices that let them work with their own sense of meaning intact or enhanced, and where they felt a sense of accomplishment and believed they make a contribution. While average workers were content to take on whatever project they were assigned, superior performers thought about what project would be invigorating to work on, which persons would be stimulating to work under, which personal idea would make a good project. They knew intuitively what they did best and enjoyed—and what they did not. Their performance excelled because they were able to make choices that kept them focused and energized. In chapter 8, "Ⓔnergize People through Ever-Greater Challenges," I argued that before you can energize others, you have to energize yourself.

People who follow their inner sense of what is worthwhile minimize emotional static for themselves. Unfortunately, too many people feel they cannot speak up for their deep values at work, that such a thing is somehow impermissible.

The silence about values skews the collective sense of what motivates people. Making money alone seems to loom much larger than it actually is for many of us. Highly successful entrepreneurs rarely show flashy displays of their wealth. What motivates them more than money were things like the excitement and challenge of starting a business, the freedom of being the boss, the chance to be creative, and the opportunity to help others find themselves. These are my goals for writing this book. Sharing with you gold nuggets of knowledge gained from my personal experiences and from the words of friends, colleagues, and world-renowned experts are my driving force. Hopefully you, the readers of this book, will share it with others just as I've shared it with you.

Except for the financially desperate, people do not work for money alone. What also fuels their passion for work is a larger sense of purpose of passion. Given the opportunity, people gravitate to what gives them meaning, to what engages to the fullest their commitment, talent, energy, and skill. And that can mean changing jobs to get a better fit with what matters to us.

Effective leaders must understand that self-awareness offers a sure rudder for keeping career decisions in harmony with our deepest values. As the saying goes, "If you don't know where you're going, any road will get you there." The less aware we are of what makes us passionate, the more lost we will be. Moreover this drifting can even affect our health; people who feel their skills are not being used well on the job, or who feel their work is repetitive and boring, have a higher risk of heart disease than those who feel that their best skills are expressed in their work.

Competency #2—Accurate Self-Assessment

Effective leaders' respect for diversity begins with recognizing their emotions and their effects, or emotional awareness; they also must know their inner resources, abilities, and limits. They must have the courage to accurately assess themselves. With respect to diversity, people with this competence are:

- Familiar of their strengths and weaknesses in dealing with people whom don't look, act, or think like them
- Insightful, learning from experience working with people whom don't look, act, or think like them
- Open to receive the "Last Ten Percent" from others whom don't look, act, or think like you

- Able to laugh at themselves with others whom don't look, act, or think like you

Let me put it this way. Before you can lead others in a diverse environment, before you can help others in a diverse environment, you have to respect diversity. I will say this repeatedly throughout this book. Effective leaders lead by example. *The key point being*, if you want a creative explosion to take place, if you want the kind of performance that leads to truly exceptional results, you have to be willing to embark on a journey that leads to an alignment between an individual's personal values and aspirations in addition to the values and aspirations of the company—or the environment.

Can You Stand the Rain?

I worked with an international company in Calgary, Canada on a major transformation project that included flattening the corporate hierarchy and giving employees the authority to make critical decisions. The executive sponsor, a top manager named Tom, had all the right rhetoric about "sharing power" and delegating authority—he just couldn't do it when any hint of a crisis arose. *Specifically,* when the rain started to fall and disruptions caused by the rain surfaced, Tom's leadership behavior changed from "sharing power" to dictator.

When things were going well, Tom was fairly good about handing down responsibility, accountability, and authority to his extremely competent staff. But at the least appearance of an emergency, Tom grabbed the reins, overturning anyone else's advance or efforts. This not only undermined the company's initiative to push power down the ranks, but it damaged the self-confidence of Tom's staff. As a direct result, his incessant talk about the virtues of sharing power while actually taking it back corroded his credibility.

Tom was blind to the contradiction, even though I pointed it out to him. As stated earlier, the first step to improving one's performance is to identify a need for improvement. But in Tom's case, such self-knowledge can be extremely difficult to come by.

As a former *Street hustler* turned *Strategic hustler*™, I can attest that such blindness in problem areas can be risky to one's health, and to one's career. Regardless, of what type of hustler, both have weaknesses, and those who did not succeed failed to learn from their mistakes and shortcomings. The unsuccessful executives were far less open to acknowledging their own faults, often rebuffing people who tried to point them out. This resistance meant they could do nothing to change them.

There have been many studies involving thousands of managers from many organizations that produced findings indicating that accuracy in self-assessment was a hallmark of superior performance, something poor performers lacked. It's not that star performers have no limits on their abilities, but that they are aware of their limits—and so they know where they need to improve, or they know to work with someone else who has a strength they lack—regardless of that person's race, color, creed, sexual preference, and religious persuasion. In the latter case, they aren't afraid to deliver results through effective delegation.

Know Yourself, Know Your Team

As an athlete and a coach, I prided myself on knowing the strengths and weaknesses of my opponent, staff, team, and myself. This has benefited me tremendously during my professional career uncovering strengths and weaknesses in technical areas, corporate culture, and organizational politics. Self-assessment classes and tools fueled the fire to know myself, and then my team. This has contributed to my effectiveness as a leader because people in leadership too often view their need to change as a sign of failure or weakness. The competitive striving that got them to the top can also stop them from admitting their shortcomings, if only out of fear of their competitors in organizational politics.

Psychologists indicate we all share this tendency toward denial, an emotionally comfortable strategy that protects us from the distress that acknowledging the harsh truth would bring. Defensiveness takes many forms: minimizing the facts, filtering our crucial information, rationalizations and "good excuses"—anything to rob the facts of their emotional truth.

This illusion of harmony and effectiveness is what is wrong with organizational life. Instead of facing the truth that could open the way to genuine improvement, people act as though everything is fine when in fact it is not. This creates the blind spots we discussed earlier.

Effective leaders need to be able to "handle the rain"; you must know yourself and your team. There are a number of blind spots. I am going to share with you research by Robert Kaplan, a professor of management practice at Harvard Business School and a former vice chairman at Goldman Sachs Group Inc., who studied the effects of damaging behaviors by senior level leaders. In an intensive study of forty senior executives whose drive to excel was actually damaging their performance and prospects, he identified eight behavior styles which were threatening to derail their teams.

These managers were unaware of the negative impact they were having on their teams: something psychologists often refer to as "blind spots."

- **Blind ambition:** This leader has to win or appear "right" at all costs; competes instead of cooperates; exaggerates his or her own value and contribution; is boastful and arrogant; sees people in black-and-white terms as allies or enemies

- *Unrealistic goals:* This leader sets overly ambitious, unattainable goals for the group or organization; is unrealistic about what it takes to get jobs done
- *Relentless striving:* This leader is compulsively hardworking at the expense of all else in life; runs on empty; is vulnerable to burnout
- *Drives others:* This leader Pushes other people too hard, burning them out; micromanages and takes over instead of delegating, comes across as abrasive or ruthless and insensitive to the emotional harm to others
- *Power hungry:* This leader seeks power for his or her own interests, rather than the organization's; pushes a personal agenda regardless of other perspectives; is exploitative
- *Insatiable need for recognition:* This leader is addicted to glory; takes credit for others' efforts and puts blame on them for mistakes; sacrifices follow-through in pursuit of the next victory
- *Preoccupation with appearances:* This leader needs to look good at all costs; he or she is overly concerned with appearances and public image, and makes decisions more on the basis of how it will "look" rather than what is best for the organization or the team; they crave the material trappings of prestige
- *Need to seem perfect:* The leader who becomes enraged by or rejects out of hand, any form of criticism, even if it is realistic; they have a tendency to blame others for their failures and find it impossible to admit mistakes or personal weaknesses

The irony is all eight "blind spots" we have discussed can actually motivate people to avoid self-awareness – because by acknowledging themselves they would have to admit to failings they cannot bear to acknowledge. This need to deny often makes such leaders resistant to any or all feedback. Moreover, it makes them a nightmare to work for!

Everything that you do in life is a learned habit. Thus, you can learn to undo any inefficiency. We all have them because nobody is perfect. Being a lifelong learner means consistently working on self-improvement. The arrogant and impatient person can learn to listen and consider other views; the workaholic can slow down and find more balance in life. It takes guts to leave the ruts! Improvements have to be pursued, which means you have to take the initiative. Organization change management professionals spend a great deal of time helping clients become aware of how bad habits damage the person and the organization, resulting in ruined relationships. With no understanding of what these behaviors do to us and others, there can be no motivation for change. Lack of awareness makes one clueless.

During the research for my doctoral dissertation, entitled "Effective Leadership of Enterprise Commerce Management," there were telling discrepancies between how managers rated themselves on abilities like adaptability and learning, and how their peers rated them. The lesson learned was that whenever such discrepancies exist, how our peers see us is the more accurate predictor of our actual performance.

For the most part, such discrepancies averaged out, with managers rating themselves more leniently than peers on some competencies, and more harshly than peers on others.

Evaluating yourself takes integrity. Everyone needs improvement because we all are human, thus *we are not perfect.* Any person who admits no flaws, exaggerates his or her abilities, and dodges feedback, not wanting to hear about any of his or her deficiencies, will never be an effective leader.

Roads to Good, Better, Best

To turn your dreams into your reality understand that "good enough" is not good enough. Good enough cannot compete against a passion for excellence coupled with a deep understanding on how to achieve that excellence.

Recall the motto "Good, Better, Best" mentioned earlier. Learn it, for its purpose is to encourage and inspire you to always continue to improve until you've reached excellence—your reality. **Said another way,** being excellent is your best! I am going to share with you a small, inventive step taken to help me become a more effective communicator. While reviewing course evaluations received from my students, I came across one where the student indicated that my insertion of "you know" into sentences was distracting and confusing. Guess what? I am not the only one with that problem.

My colleagues had told me the same. I started recording my lectures and monitoring—"you know" came up time and again without my having intended it or even realizing I was speaking the words. I had become utterly oblivious to this disquieting habit. Determined to change, I took a bold step, asking my students to raise their hands whenever they heard the words. With four hundred hands making me fully conscious of this habit, I changed in no time. However, I do make an occasional slip, "you know!"

Superior performers intentionally seek feedback; they want to hear how others perceive them, realizing that this is valuable information. I can attribute my success to being self-aware. I am always asking, "How do I look?" "Am I communicating effectively?" Again, "Good, Better, Best"; this self-awareness keeps me in a process of continuous self-improvement.

And self-awareness in itself is an invaluable tool for **C.H.A.N.G.E.,** as we discussed earlier, especially if the need to **C.H.A.N.G.E.** is in line with the person's goals, sense of mission, or basic values—including the belief that self-improvement is a good thing. I am a living witness to this. You will be also!

Knowing my strengths and weaknesses in respecting diversity, and approaching my work accordingly, is a competence that is shared among star performers. Virtually every star performer I've ever met realizes this is a key skill to competing in a global environment.

The moral compass being, star performers know where they must get better to be an effective leader in the twenty-first century.

Competency #3—Self-Confidence

Do you have a strong sense of self-worth and capabilities in a diverse society? If yes, then you:

- Have a charismatic and self-assuring presence
- Can voice views that are unpopular and can "*stand the rain*" for what is right
- Are decisive, able to engage in intelligent risk taking and innovation
- Are very comfortable working with others whom don't look, act, or think like you

We've talked about events that contributed to my growth in the area of self-confidence. It is time to revisit some behavior theory combined with real-world application in laying a practical foundation for building self-confidence. You will read about effective leaders from all walks of life whose self-confidence mirrors mine. I lecture kids, including my own, and adults consistently about having self-confidence. Why?

Self-confidence gives us the requisite self-assurance for forging ahead or stepping in as a leader. Let's look at the continuum of self-confidence—lack of self-confidence and extreme self-confidence. For those who lack self-confidence, every failure confirms a sense of incompetence. During my senior year in high school, I experienced my first losing football season. I had never lost at anything! My self-confidence was gone and it manifested itself in feelings of helplessness, powerlessness, and crippling self-doubt. Extreme self-confidence, on the other hand, can look like arrogance, especially if the person lacks social skills. And self-confidence is not to be confused with brashness; to have positive impact self-confidence must be aligned with reality. For this reason, a lack of self-awareness is an obstacle to realistic self-confidence. As a consultant, I accept the fact that my clients hire me because they expect me to "walk on water" in solving their problems. And I do! This is my self-confidence controlled with excellent social skills that have afforded me the opportunity to provide services to some of the largest companies in the world. Understand this, humility opened doors to tremendous opportunities.

Presenting to an audience in person, by television, or radio requires self-confidence. Highly self-confident people can seem to exude charisma, inspiring confidence in those around them. Super performers have higher levels of self-confidence than average performers.

People with self-confidence typically see themselves as high achievers, able to take on challenges and to master new jobs and skills. Let's continue to sharpen your trilogy of success. Earlier we discussed point number one and point number three now we are going to discuss point number two.

Point number two talks about reinventing yourself. Learn new skills to exploit new opportunities. The statement made earlier, "And I do!" is not one of self-aggrandizement, but one of self-confidence. Effective leaders have an inner strength allowing them to ably justify their decisions or actions, staying unfazed by opposition. Good leadership traits are not to be intimidated or easily pressured. Executives appreciate my candor and drive. They love the **J.U.I.C.E.** (**J**oyful personality, **U**nique capabilities [competence], **I**ntegrity [beyond reproach], **C**ommitment to excellence, and **E**nergy and edge) I bring to deliver solutions.

My life experiences, to make a tough decision or follow a course of action unpopular to those in authority or work in a diverse environment required an inner strength called self-confidence. People with self-confidence are decisive without being arrogant or defensive, and they stand by their decisions. The best performers in sports are the ones who did what others wouldn't so they could accomplish what others can't. All the preparation boils down to processing the information, setting up an execution strategy, and delivering. This same truism applies to business—good leaders vs. average leaders bring information together, set up a timetable, and execute.

Having Talent—and Believing It

In chapter 2, "Adaptable Behavior," I spoke of the R1 to R2 to R3 Experience. Let's talk about this experience within the context of respecting diversity. You can revisit chapter 2 for a more detailed discussion and examples for any clarity needed.

People go from being insecure (R1) to confident (R2) and then become insecure again (R3). This is because at the lower levels of readiness (R1, R2), the leader is providing the direction enabling followers to learn how to apply their talents to a given situation. This leader directed behavior is done to build the follower's confidence. As the transition is made to the higher levels of readiness (R3, R4); the follower's decisions become *follower directed* or *self-directed* as the leader empowers them to make task decisions. This transition from leader directed to self-directed may result in apprehension or insecurity. Eventually one's confidence has to kick in. I've witnessed this phenomenon as a *Street hustler*, athlete, and *Strategic hustler*™. **Face it,** having talent is half the battle, but you must believe it. A major reason for a high round draft choice being labeled a "draft bust" is the inability to showcase the talent because of the lack of confidence brought on by the Human Performance System (HPS). In chapter 20, "®erformance Management," we will discuss this in more detail when addressing job/performer level performance management. The following will prepare you for what is in stored for you in this chapter.

When I started to "get my hustle on" with shining shoes on the Yale University campus and other areas in downtown New Haven, Connecticut, I had to get my presentation together in order to solicit business. But when it came time for me to put my plan in action, I lacked the confidence to approach people. As a high school football coach, some of my players were fantastic practice players. But when given the opportunity to perform during a real game, they failed to seize the opportunity. In both scenarios lack of self-confidence was common. My experience teaching and mentoring thousands of professionals has allowed me to witness the same lack of self-confidence in applying new-found knowledge.

Of course, over a period of time with systematic efforts to be assertive, I grew in confidence to approach people with a well-rehearsed, "Shine, sir?" or "Shine, ma'am?" Sounds good, does it not? The practice players eventually grew in self-confidence to perform on game day as they performed in practice. And the professionals grew in self-confidence to apply the tools and techniques learned in class to solve a specific business problem. While some people seem born with a natural self-assurance, even those who are shy and timid can become bolder with practice. Remember, leaders are born to be made!

Closely related to self-confidence is what psychologists call "self-efficacy," the positive judgments of one's own capacity to perform. Self-efficacy is not the same as the actual skills we have, but rather our belief about what we can do with the skills we have. Recall according to Situational Leadership® theory having skills is not enough to guarantee our best performance—we need the willingness, which consists of motivation, confidence, and commitment to apply our skills. **Confidently,** we have to believe in our skills in order to use them at their best.

When teaching computer literacy, I could tell which students felt confident in their ability to complete a difficult task. Those with self-efficacy gladly stepped up to the challenge; those with self-doubt didn't even try, regardless of how well they might actually do. You can conclude, self-confidence raises aspirations, while self-doubt lowers them. It only makes sense that the more confidence you have the better job you will do.

There is a tight link between self-knowledge and self-confidence. Our mental model provides us an inner map of our disposition, abilities, and deficiencies. For example, my nephew viewed himself as skilled at playing the French horn, able to carry a tune and march with precision in the band, but felt shy in his personal life, whether at clarifying events or speaking to adults on challenging matters. Our sense of self-efficacy, then, is domain-specific: how well we think we can do the job does not necessarily match how well we believe we might do in a parallel activity elsewhere in life.

The professionals in this book or workers in general, do better in part because they believe in their ability, which motivates them to work harder longer and to persevere through difficulties. They positively embrace negativity in accepting failure as part of the learning process, are not afraid of being inept, and don't give up on their own opinions and judgments—even their good ideas—when challenged. As mentioned earlier, they go from being insecure (R1) to confident (R2) and then become insecure again (R3). Eventually our self-knowledge and self-confidence reach a point where we can perform the task with confidence. Everybody goes through this progression. I say this because we are not born knowing what we know. The R1 to R2 to R3 Experience is more pronounced in a diverse environment. Why? In a diverse environment, we *all* have to learn it from somewhere, somebody, and/ or something.

When diverse individuals in a company or organization can work together shift happens, production increases and it results in a more positive work environment. This fuels personal growth in positive self-knowledge and self-confidence. The end result is the courage to face the demands of reality (integrity). Let's look at the relationship between courage and self-confidence.

Courage and Self-Confidence

I am going to share this personal story with you because it touches my heart. My daddy was killed due to hospital and nursing home neglect. During the deposition, I realized that a number of nurses and doctors—from various cultures—lacked the courage to speak out, which would have spared him and my family the pain and suffering. *Said another way*, they lacked the courage because they lacked the self-confidence to speak out on the abnormalities of the treatment provided. This experience inspired the following story, about a different yet similar situation, showing the relationship between courage and self-confidence—to speak up.

It was out-of-control blood pressure—a result of neglecting to take his hypertension medication—causing an elderly man to suffer a massive stroke. Now he was in the intensive care unit in a hospital that specialized in brain injury, and the next few days would tell whether he would live or die. Frantic treatments focused on assessing the amount of brain damage and trying to control any further bleeding.

His visitor, a close friend who was a registered nurse working in the same hospital, happened to see the man's medical chart and noticed that of the many medications he was being given, none was for controlling blood pressure. Concerned, she asked the neurology resident poring over the results of a brain scan at her friend's bedside, "Is he taking his blood pressure medication?"

Irritated at the interruption, the brain specialist snapped, "We only treat them from the neck up here," and stormed out of the room.

Now alarmed that a medication crucial for her friend's recovery seemed to have been overlooked, the nurse marched into the office of the hospital's chief of medicine. She waited for him to finish a phone call, apologized for the interruption, and explained her concern. The order to resume the patient's blood pressure medication came immediately.

"I knew I was going outside proper channels by going to the chief of medicine," the nurse explained. "But I have seen stroke patients die because their blood pressure wasn't properly controlled. It was too urgent to let protocol get in the way."

The attitudes that the rules and standard procedures can be bent without disrespecting cultural differences, and the courage to do so, are hallmarks of self-confidence. Indeed, in a study of 209 nurses at a large university hospital, those who had the strongest sense of self-efficacy where most likely to speak out when confronting inadequate or medically risky situations. Nurses high in self-confidence would confront the physicians directly or, if that failed to correct things, go to their superior.

Such confrontation or protest is an act of courage, especially given the low status of nurses in the hospital hierarchy. The self-confident nurses believed that if they dissented, their opinions would carry weight in changing the problem for the better. The nurses who lacked self-confidence had another inclination: rather than protest or make efforts to right the wrong, they said they would quit.

Nursing may be a special case, because nurses as a rule are highly employable. In occupations where the job market is tighter—teaching, social work, or middle management, for instance—it may take a particularly high level of self-confidence to see a similar degree of courageous, open dissent. But no matter the kind of job or organization, it is those with the greatest self-confidence who will be most willing to take the risk of speaking up and pointing out problems or injustices that others only grumble about—or quit over.

Courage and Spirituality

I chose to share this story with you because of my spiritually. I would not be writing this book if it were not for my personal relationship with Father God. He has giving me the ideas and words to write this amazing book on leadership and management using my unique learning experiences.

During a doctorial philosophy course, I read and studied *The Tao of Physics: An Exploration of the Parallels between Modern Physics and Eastern Mysticism,* by physicist Fritjof Capra. Though some of Mr. Capra's colleagues were offended that any physicist would compare the science of modern physics with the religious practices of Eastern mystics, he had the courage to challenge the status quo and compare the science of modern physics with the religious practices of Eastern mystics (primarily the beliefs and practices of Hinduism, Buddhism, and Taoism). The reality is that there are some very striking similarities with the intuitively Eastern mystical view of reality and the experimentally rational view of quantum theory. Quantum theory, also known as quantum physics or quantum mechanics, is a branch of physics providing a mathematical description of much of the dual particlelike and wavelike behavior and interactions of energy and matter.

A past experience increased my understanding of the Islamic religion. While on a consulting engagement in Kansas City Missouri I had the opportunity to reconnect with a childhood football hero and friend, Rasool Ahmed, an IBM executive, and his lovely wife Gwen—both graduates from the University of Connecticut and *Strategic hustler*™ *extraordinaire.* Devoted Muslims, they invited me to celebrate the Thanksgiving holiday with them and their well-mannered and disciplined children. I witnessed the Muslim way of life-the respect, love, friendship, discipline, and spirituality. Yes, spirituality! Let me tell the readers, ***"it is the same soup but a different bowl."*** I then recalled the late Archbishop Earl Paulk's pioneering kingdom-teaching quote, "For whosoever will!" I started to follow God's lead and began to connect the dots, realizing that from a doctorial course and a visit with a friend, he was giving me a revelation on what the archbishop was saying!

This leads our discussion about a young man from the Paulk family whom I've known of for over twenty years. His two kids were in my four-year-old Sunday school class, which I taught for twelve years. I've watched him grow into a spiritual man with strong conviction and courage. He used to be called "Donnie Earl," named after his famous dad and uncle, but prefers "DE" to eliminate all the questions that go with having a name such as Donnie Earl—to hear him tell it.

I had the chance to meet with Pastor DE to discuss some spiritual issues, but we just started talking about everything. I got to know the man whom I had admired and respected from a distance. He reminded me of Joe "GI Joe" Gallagher, a good friend and college football teammate of mine who was a true gentleman off the field but a fierce competitor on the field. Joe, a six-foot-three-inch, 235-pound offensive guard with model looks, was a "kick butt and ask questions later" type of guy. Hence, I gave him the nickname of "GI Joe."

He was largely responsible for creating the holes that allowed me to average 115 yards rushing per game. Oh, by the way, like Pastor DE, he was white. Let me tell you some things about my pastor and friend. Pastor DE was raised in Decatur, Georgia, in south DeKalb; is a faithful husband; loving dad; a former Division I college basketball player; has an honorary doctor of divinity; has authored a few books, including *The Holy Bible of Inclusion*; serves as the only white member on the board of the Southern Christian Leadership Council (that was founded by Dr. Martin Luther King Jr.); grew up with people from all around the world, most of whom were black (which his rhythmic dancing can be attributed to); plays a mean guitar; has a singing voice as smooth as silk; and at six foot two, 230 pounds, bench pressing 400 pounds, the only thing that keeps those who don't know him from being intimidated by his presence is his warm, friendly smile and greeting. He is one of the most down-to-earth men on the planet. As far as being a man of the Spirit, his humility is beyond reproach, but he is a student and scholar-practitioner of the word of the Spirit! All this makes him one of the most thought-provoking, innovative SPRITUAL pastors in the world—who happens to be my friend! Knowing him, when he reads this, his face will turn red from blushing—he may even shed a tear! But that is why so many people love him. His life and ministry is a great example for respecting diversity and courage.

Pastor DE's courage, displayed in the midst of a storm, is an inspiring story for all to know. I am blessed to share it. As a series of scandals stripped away everything he had—his church, his financial resources, even his dad—he found the courage to speak his truth.

"I don't know how to say this, but the scandal didn't make me inclusive; it took away my fear," Pastor DE says. "Before that I was saying that I'll preach about gay inclusion and just sort of mention it here or there. When you lose everything, you have nothing to lose. I looked at my wife one day and said, 'All I have left is me, and what God is speaking to me.'" Man, this statement embodies everything that self-awareness is about: emotional awareness, self-assessment, and self-confidence! In 2006, Pastor DE moved from a church he started in Stone Mountain, Georgia, to become the senior pastor at Chapel Hill Harvester Church, located in South Decatur, Georgia. Built by his dad, Don Paulk, and his uncle, Archbishop Earl Paulk, the four-thousand-member church was one of the largest independent, racially diverse churches in the nation.

Soon after Pastor DE took over as senior pastor, he faced what he collectively called "the scandal": a number of women came forward alleging Archbishop Earl Paulk used his influence as bishop to coerce them into sexual relationships. As part of the legal proceedings, Archbishop Earl Paulk was forced to undergo a paternity test to see if he had fathered several children in the church.

The paternity test revealed that Archbishop Earl Paulk, the man Pastor DE grew up believing was his dad, was actually his biological dad. Yet it was as these scandals rocked the church that Pastor DE found the courage to say what was in his heart.

"The thing that really hurt me the most, during the time that I was coming back here and beginning to speak about gay inclusion, we were going through, my goodness, a scandal of epic proportion. I think there was in all thirty-six stories—and there was still one last week—but the majority of our church stayed," he says.

"They stayed through the adultery allegations, the racketeering charges, there's been all sorts of things they've accused us of, some true, some not true, but the majority of the people stayed," he adds. "It wasn't really until I started teaching gay inclusion and other religious thought [that people began to leave]."

Pastor DE was taking his congregation into a new train of thought, which created some uneasiness in his congregation with his teaching and the damage done by his family's legacy. These almost caused him to leave and start over somewhere else. "I think if I had the money, we probably would have left, but all we had was what we had, so let's put our feet down," he says. "We had nothing left, we had no reputation, and that's maybe the best thing that ever happened to us because it freed us from all the fear. The trying to garner votes from congregants, and tithes, and saying let's just be ourselves, it's all we have left."

Pastor DE began to focus on his core principles and beliefs as he moved toward what he calls "radical inclusion" and away from Christianity. He founded the organization Pro-Love in 2004, which has sponsored inclusion marches every year since. He also began work on his new book, *I Don't Know…The Way of Knowing.*

The book outlines his beliefs, a multinational mixture of Hindu, Buddhist, Daoism (Taoism), and other religious thought, combined with quotes from an array of historical and cultural figures. Throughout the book, Pastor DE demonstrate a true effective leader is one who can admit to not knowing the answers but believes collaboration is needed to look for the answers together. This reinforces an earlier point that a diverse group of people focused on a common end goal is the most effective and efficient way to solve problems.

"This is kind of playing my cards here; in several years we probably won't be called a church anymore, we'll just be called a community," Pastor DE says of his congregation, which now has about one thousand members and is now called Spirit and Truth Sanctuary. "I think we'll just be a community of seekers."

Pastor DE never ceases to amaze me with his conviction and courage. A couple of well-known bishops were made public spectacles because of their socially and spiritually unacceptable practices. Pastor DE has an agenda that's all about God's love. He requested the entire congregation show support by attending the services at each of these bishops' churches. We really impressed the members of these congregations, because *no* pastor who went through what Pastor DE did *publicly* would have had the courage to show his face in another man's house of worship. This effective leader's self-awareness and courage were instrumental in the Spirit and Truth Sanctuary's healing from "the scandals" and leading the trendiest, friendliest, most radically inclusive worship in Atlanta, Georgia.

Summary

Ⓐs an effective leader, if your team members all look, talk, and think the same, then there is no respect for diversity. Throughout my career, I have either been the first or the only African American in my collegiate and professional settings. I am drawn to diversity because where there is a bold declaration of respect for diversity, a healthy dose of self-awareness exists. The stories shared in this chapter about the experiences of my friends and colleagues peels back the layers of self-awareness, exposing *emotional awareness, self-assessment, and self-confidence*. **Said another way**, self-awareness exudes courage.

Emotional intelligence (EQ) taps into a fundamental element of human behavior that is distinct from your intellect. There is no known connection between IQ and emotional intelligence; you simply can't predict emotional intelligence based on how smart someone is. Intelligence is your ability to learn, and research shows it's the same at age 15 as it is at age 50. Emotional intelligence, as you've learned, is a flexible set of skills that can be acquired and improved with practice. Although some people are naturally more emotionally intelligent than others, you can develop high emotional intelligence even if you aren't born with it. Remember leaders are born to be made.

Personality is the final piece of the puzzle. It's the stable "style" that defines each of us. Personality is the result of hard-wired preferences, such as the inclination toward thinking or feeling. However, like IQ, personality can't be used to predict emotional intelligence. Also like IQ, personality is stable over a lifetime and doesn't change. IQ, emotional intelligence, and personality each cover unique ground and help to explain what makes a person tick.

Effective leaders demonstrate intelligent behavior when they respect diversity because they embrace the personalities, IQ, and EQ of different people creating a diverse environment required for optimum problem solving and solution delivery. The end result is a self-managed team which collectively adds value and sustains excellence. The next chapter provides my view on these. Keep on reading to learn about the Ⓢ in **L.E.A.D.E.R.Ⓢ.H.I.P.**—Ⓢustain success by achieving excellence.

CHAPTER 13

Ⓢ ustain Success by Achieving Excellence

Introduction

To be truly successful, one has to strive for perfection. *Said another way,* we all have to strive to get a little closer to excellence. Hopefully, passion for the work being done drives our need for perfection.

We all do things, with respect to our work that mimics an athlete not performing to best of their ability. However, the twenty-first century is a new era of intense competition with countries [globalization] that strive for excellence. Indeed, they demand it!

In the era of globalization, "Get Your Hustle On!" takes on a global dimension. The multinationals are smart and hungry, and want our jobs, customers, money, etc.

They study America's masters—Peter F. Drucker, W. Edwards Deming, Joseph Juran, Philip Kotler, Bruce Henderson, Tom Peters, Jim Collins and newcomer's like me and dozens more. Earlier I mentioned that "good enough" is not good enough. The words, "*Good, Better, Best*" appear throughout this book for this reason.

Good enough cannot compete against a passion for excellence coupled with deep understanding of the necessary tools, techniques, tactics, and technologies required for success.

This chapter is about sustaining success by achieving excellence. *Think of it as* success is adding value and demanding excellence. *Note: Excellence is a value, culture, or outcome which means it has a different meaning depending on the eye of the beholder. Remember this when dealing with point three of the trilogy of success.* The lesson will comprise of stories that demonstrate the behaviors that comprise this acronym—**S.U.C.C.E.S.S.F.U.L.** When you read this acronym, or the word, *"successful"*, think of the following behaviors to achieving excellence [adding value and demanding excellence]:

S = See your goals
U = Understand the obstacle(s)
C = Clear your mind of doubt
C = Create a positive mental picture
E = Embrace the challenge
S = Stay on track
S = Show the world you can do it
F = Faithfully confess your goals
U = Understand that you have the victory
L = Learn humility

It bears repeating that everyone's life is filled with experiences—traumatic, frustrating, or exhilarating—that can be the source of valuable learning. Having worked for numerous world- renowned companies, my successful track record was earned because of my ability and willingness to meet their needs. My goal-oriented behavior focused on adding value and demanding excellent performance from everyone who came in contact with me—including myself!

My successful journey in business started in 1977, as a sophomore at the University of New Haven, participating in an internship program at E.I. DuPont in Wilmington, Delaware. For twelve years, I was successful in various leadership roles with companies mentioned earlier. In 1988, I made a life decision to move south to Atlanta, Georgia. The *Wall Street Journal* (*WSJ*) had named the city of Atlanta, Georgia, as the number one city in the country to start a business. It was the third year in a row that Atlanta had earned this distinction by the *WSJ*. Armed with high aspirations and a proven product, I moved to this wonderful city. It has taken over twenty years to fill in the blanks with real-world lessons for each letter of the **S.U.C.C.E.S.S.F.U.L.** acronym. Keep on reading to learn the stories and lessons that it taught me.

S—See Your Goals

In chapter 3, "Ⓖoal-Oriented Behavior," recall you cannot have far-reaching goals without first generating awe-inspiring ideas. This is the "see your goals" challenge. It is your purpose. In Stephen Covey's *Seven Habits of Highly Effective*

People, one of the habits is to "Begin with the end in mind." To be successful you must "see your goals." That is easier said than done.

Recall people always come into your **life** for a **reason**, a **season** and a **life-time**. Well, during the first ten months in Atlanta, whether they were friends, relatives, or associates. They showed up and showed out—providing me with room and board, food, money, good times, business leads, knowledge, wisdom, and understanding. The names include but are not limited to: Roosevelt Council, Henry Skrine, Tyrone Johnson, and Freddie Wilson, all esteemed Omega Psi Phi fraternity brothers; my cousins Mattie Jo Hendrix and her husband Bruce and son "Roddy"; my childhood friends Bruce and his wife Mary Grant—another fraternity brother and Delta Sigma Theta sister. Their acts of kindness fueled my drive to stay focused on my goals and overcome life's obstacles —i.e., car repossession, apartment evictions, robberies, family issues/tragedy, lost contracts, business failures, slow paying/no paying customers, bankruptcy. My biggest inspiration, my dad was a phone call away, and, as always, would offer to send money—mind you, as a Social Security recipient he was on a fixed income. Our conversations covered God's purpose for me along with quoting various biblical scriptures to inspire me. We will talk more about them in a later chapter. He would end the conversation with, "Baby remember where you came from and how blessed you are to be in Atlanta." There were other Omega brothers, Robert Vaughn, a brilliant entrepreneur helped keep me focused, and Mitchell Dirton, a consummate friend, always had edifying words and expected greatness from me. What little money earned came from my Connecticut based clients; they kept me afloat. Atlanta based contacts/clients like Tom Walton, Owen Montague, Maurice Coakley, mentioned earlier, along with Lance Herndon helped me penetrate the Atlanta market. Yes, my goal was clear; deliver with excellence; value adding solutions enabling my customer to sustain their success—Marketing 101. However, without this support and my prayers to Father God—*I would have never made it!*

U—Understand the Obstacles

Once you see your goals, identify obstacles that could prevent you from achieving them. These are risks. Trust me, they can come from anywhere. The key is to *identify* [know them], *plan* [know how you will eliminate, accept, or minimize them] and *execute* [monitor and attack them when they occur]. You have to mitigate them! To help you I am going to share a tool called an uncertainty spectrum for project risk management. The continuum of project risk management lies between the two extremes of total certainty and total uncertainty.

Table 13.1: The Uncertainty Spectrum

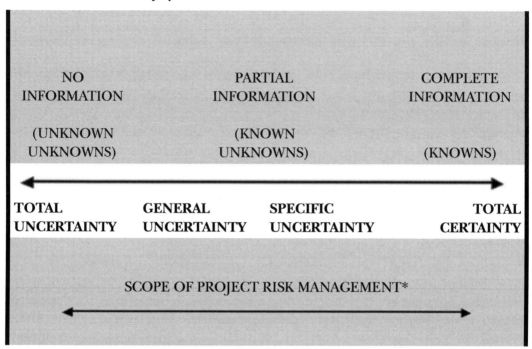

Source: Project Management Institute Project & Program Risk Management: A Guide to Managing Project Risks and Opportunities, Project Management Institute, Inc. (1992). Copyright and all rights reserved. Material from this publication has been reproduced with the permission of PMI.

According to the above diagram; there will be risks where you have no information (Unknown Unknowns); where you have partial information (Known Unknowns); and where you have complete information (Knowns). This contributes to the degree of certainty—total uncertainty, general uncertainty, specific uncertainty, or total certainty—to understanding obstacles. Whether you are a student or seasoned professional; take the steps [identify, plan, and execute], to mitigate them.

During a project planning session at a global biopharmaceutical, it was understood that the roadblocks that would prevent an enterprise data governance project from being successful would be lack of top management support. This led to the development of short-term and long-term adoption & learning strategy, resulting in a successful rollout of their enterprise data governance program.

C—Clear Your Mind of Doubt

The obstacle may be daunting, but you must not doubt yourself. Recall the discussion in the "Ⓖoal-Oriented Behavior" chapter about having a mentor. I stated, "You need encouragement because you will face very discouraging times." Spiritually my faith was grounded in these biblical verses:

- *All things work for good to those who love the Lord and are called to his purpose. (Romans 8:28)*
- *If God be for you, who can be against you? (Romans 8:31)*
- *Trust in the Lord with all your heart and lean not on your own understanding. (Proverbs 3:5)*
- *For God hath not given us the spirit of fear; but of power, and of love, and of a sound mind (Second Timothy 1:7)*

The bottom line: seeking an encouraging mentor will prevent you from letting naysayers steal your dreams. In this case, the naysayer is *you!* The stories shared concerning such notables as the John Keane, former founder of Keane, Inc.; Jack Welch, former CEO of GE; the late Robert Goizueta, former chairman of the Coca-Cola Company; Sterling Williams, former CEO of Sterling Software; Bernie Marcus, cofounder of Home Depot' and Floyd Little, Hall of Fame running back for the Denver Broncos confirmed that taking intelligent risks and learning from failures are the keys to being successful! It's all right to be doubtful, just deal with it as being a healthy part of becoming successful.

When making the decision to move to Atlanta, essentially to start all over, I had my doubts. What if this does not work or that does not work? You may ask "what got me pass this?" It started with putting God first. Earlier we talked about the importance of having a spiritual connection. Well all I had to do is recall where He brought me from and what He has brought me through. This gave me the confidence that He would not let me fail! This history encouraged removing the doubt replacing it with an "*ain't no stopping me now!*" swagger because I *knew* God had my back. My concentration turned from mental obstacles to physical execution. *Said another way,* it was time to "get my hustle on!"

C—Create a Positive Mental Picture

You see your goals, understand the obstacles, clear your mind of doubt, and now you must create a positive mental picture. Create a mental model of yourself achieving, not just seeing your goals. How do you do that? Meditate visualizing a picture of success. As an effective leader, you have to see the solution and, if necessary, provide a compelling argument to influence the appropriate people needed to make it happen.

Once you've trained yourself to create a positive mental picture, you begin to view all problems as opportunities for solutions. Depending on your mental perspective, a half a glass of water is either half full or half empty. In either case your perception will be that progress is being made.

E—Embrace the Challenge

Street smarts and athletic competitiveness fueled my *"ain't no stoppin' me now!"* attitude to embrace the challenge. The previous items talked about getting your mind right to achieve *greatness*! However, a path is created only by walking. To achieve *greatness* you have to *do something*! The leadership journey my friends, colleagues, and I have taken has been full of overcoming challenges—technical, political, and cultural. We embraced the challenge doing whatever it took to survive, learn, and perform. Let's face it. Whether you are playing sports, working, dating, or just trying to make a difference, life is full of challenges that must be overcome. The bigger the reality the more challenges you will have to overcome. **Said another way**, *"the bigger the headache the bigger the pill."* Keep on reading to learn the importance of this statement.

S—Stay on Track

Staying on track requires maintaining laser-like focus. This is very hard to do without first achieving the previous mentioned. A key task of an effective leader is to use a project management tool and technique for tracking the progress. During our previous discussion on goal-oriented behavior, we spoke of working with tenacity covering my experience as a lead technical consultant for Keane Consulting.

At Keane Consulting, my tenacity landed me in leadership roles on multimillion dollar projects for GTE, the City of Bridgeport, Blue Cross Blue Shield, and C.H. Dexter Corporation. Keane's "Six Principles of Productivity Management" was their business philosophy for staying on track. Staying on track to Keane meant delivering projects that meet customer expectations, on time, and within budget. To accomplish these goals, the following had to be done:

1. Define the job in detail
2. Get the right people involved
3. Estimate time and costs

4. Deliver tangible deliverables in eighty hours or less (eighty-hour rule)
5. Define a change procedure
6. Agree upon an acceptance criteria

Applying these six principles along with conducting daily, weekly, and, when appropriate, monthly meetings to discuss progress, issues, and risks has allowed me to ensure program, projects, and tasks stay on track.

S—Show the World You Can Do It

One my favorite entertainers the late, great James Joseph Brown's vocals and dancing earned him titles as the Godfather of Soul, Mr. Dynamite, Soul Brother Number One, and the Hardest-Working Man in Show Business. As a seven-year old, I would entertain the community with my imitations of Mr. Brown's dancing. During one of his songs, Mr. Brown would sing, "Let yourself be heard!" This resonated with me in everything I did. These four words would help inspire me to want to be great. Colleagues and students have called me the "the Hardest-Working Trainer in the Business." The bottom line is that your opportunity to show the world you can do it will present itself. The world could be your school, community, company, organization, etc. The Strategic hustler™, must seize the opportunity and exploit the benefits it brings.

In elementary and high school, seizing the opportunities, despite my circumstances, to demonstrate outstanding leadership and performance in athletics, academics, and community involvement led to the accomplishments previously mentioned.

In college, applying the same formula learned in high school, despite getting sidetracked, allowed me to make history and be named one of the top students in America.

As a professional, an unsuccessful attempt to make the roster of the New England Patriots of the National Football League allowed me to seize the opportunity to continue to reinvent myself by enrolling in the dual masters program at UNH. You recall the challenging courses listed earlier, one of which was an operations research (OR) course. There was a major class project requiring using an OR technique called linear programming to solve a widespread problem in manufacturing industry regarding minimizing trim waste cost. Linear programming (LP, or linear optimization) is a mathematical method for determining a way to achieve the best outcome (such as maximum profit or lowest cost) in a given mathematical model for some list of requirements represented as linear relationships. LP is a specific case of mathematical programming (mathematical optimization). The project required a group of which we each contributed key sections of the study. My team chose me to present the findings to the class. The results of our effort earned an A grade. Upon the encouragement of my OR professor, a former NASA scientist, I submitted the paper in response to a call for papers request issued by the Operations Research Society of America (ORSA) for a joint meeting involving the Institute of Management Science (TIMS) and ORSA. He knew something that I didn't, because the paper, "Determining Trim Waste Costs Using Linear Programming," was selected to be presented at the international meeting. It was well-received by a global audience, validated by copy requests for the paper from major universities and companies in Africa, Canada, Greece, South America, and throughout the United States.

During the course of my career, showing the world I could do it required exploiting numerous opportunities. You recall the trials and tribulations during my initial business experience in Atlanta; well, as my dad would always say, "It's not how you start, it's how you finish." That experience led to accomplishments that included earning a PhD with distinction; a cover-page article in the prestigious *Atlanta Tribune* magazine; a front-page "City Life" article in the Atlanta *Journal Constitution*; numerous articles in various trade magazines; appearances on leading Atlanta community-based radio talk shows; selection to *International Who's Who of Professionals*; invitations to attend the International Congress of Arts, Communications, and Science, held in Lisboa, Portugal, Oxford England, and Dublin, Ireland; being named to *Who's Who in the Twenty-First Century and the list goes on.* All while being a caretaker of elderly parents, volunteer coach to thousands, active godfather or legal guardian to fourteen children and Sunday school teacher to four-year olds.

With humility, I ask, "Not bad for a brother from the hood, yes?" This was attributed to persistence and perseverance, which we will visit in a later chapter.

F—Faithfully Confess Your Goals

You have to claim your goals by including them in your daily conversations. Remember our discussion on creating a positive mental picture and the analogy to the half of a glass of water? I am going to use a verse from the scripture: "Speak those things that are not as though they were."

You have to be fully convinced that your goals will be achieved. As an effective leader, your ability to influence others is largely based on the words that come out of your mouth. Persistence, perseverance, prayer, and planning allowed me to raise over $3 million to fund an overseas investment. I believed in my goals and sold them to my investors. Once you're fully convinced, stop asking for validation of your goals. Put your plan into motion and just do it! Here is another example:

- As principal consultant/engagement manager for Sterling Software mentioned earlier. I ignited the startup of a new division exceeding revenue projections. To be more specific, we exceeded the five-year project goal of $20 million by achieving $40 million in three years. My goal was to build the largest business intelligence group in the world! The plan orchestrated was designed to do just that by delivering a well-received presentation to a global audience demonstrating how existing technology could be repurposed to build a software application that would create a large repository of data that customers could access to find answers to pressing business problems using a variety of business intelligence tools.

My current goals are financial, personal, educational, professional, and philanthropic. I have confessed these goals that line up with what Father God has in store for me because, as Pastor DE stated, *"What God produces, God parents and purifies, because I am predestined."*

U—Understand That You Have the Victory

Being an effective leader increases your chances of winning. Remember you are predestined for success. *Thus,* you have the victory. As executive consultant/coach, my delivery of performance-based training and follow-up project mentoring contributed to the success of many projects. These projects were executed at firms in various industries such as financial, oil and gas, logistics, entertainment, telecommunications, health care, and governments—city, state, federal and international.

I received many e-mails and course evaluations from student/protégées attesting to their success utilizing skills learned and thus rated me an "excellent" instructor and mentor. The phrase "great job" is the norm for my leadership on any sized program or project.

The bottom-line is that if *you* don't think *you* are going to have the victory then *you* won't! Let me share some spiritual wisdom with you.

L—Learn Humility

Effective leaders know they are humble servants. I reflect on my rise from a *Street hustler* to a *Strategic hustler*™ surviving the perils of an inner-city red zone to acquire the experiences to share with you in this book. In my childhood, as an all-star/champion midget football player scoring touchdowns and making game saving interceptions and tackles, knowing that my teammates did their job enabled me to do mine. This lesson amplified itself during high school, college, professional, and personal journeys.

No one person is bigger than the team. My team consisted of my ancestors, parents, relatives, friends, students, coaches, teachers, and even naysayers. All of the accomplishments, awards and accolades mentioned in this book were not for self-aggrandizement but a testimony of no single team member is bigger than the team, but because of my team I was able to develop personally and professionally.

My humility has afforded me the opportunity to meet some of the world's most influential people. This chapter on success would not be complete without me sharing with you a story of a truly great leader. This global leader embraced the **S.U.C.C.E.S.S.F.U.L.** philosophy.

Success Begins with Selling Image

Of all the leaders, I've been privilege to meet, the late Robert Goizueta, former chairman & CEO of the Coca-Cola Company, who increased its value more than any other CEO in the history of the business, is one of my favorites. His story is worth mentioning in any discussion on how sustaining success is adding value and demanding excellence. I had the opportunity to meet Mr. Goizueta and recall him telling me, "I like your image." When he took the helm of Coke it was already one of the nation's most successful and respected businesses. Nonetheless, during his tenure, Goizueta's image as an effectively successful leader grew as the company experienced unprecedented growth in both profits and market value. His success reflected a business philosophy that he said he learned on his family's sugar plantation in Cuba, where he also learned an almost unlimited willingness to take risks, which he got from Fidel Castro. Mr. Goizueta's learning experiences are well known because he often talked about them publicly, and his actions demonstrated the lessons that he had learned. Here we talk about the relationship between success and image. In the next chapter you will learn more about the unique teachable points of Mr. Goizueta, as well as those of another gentleman I've been blessed to meet—NFL Hall of Famer Floyd Little.

I was a consultant on assignment at the Coca-Cola Company when this impeccably dressed mild-mannered executive approached me giving me a handshake and compliment. Though he appeared to be gentle my street smarts told me otherwise. When selected to be Coke's chairman, his quiet, understated demeanor made him seem an odd choice to lead a company where the image of excitement plays such an important role. Goizueta himself once told *Fortune* magazine, "We don't know how to sell products based on performance...Everything we sell, and we sell on image." Upon reading this, recalling his compliment to me; reinforced what my dad had taught me *image* sells! But behind the unassuming façade was a determined and thoughtful man who created a winning philosophy out of his many varied life experiences.

Goizueta's first actions showed that a clear underlying business philosophy wasn't always immediately apparent. Earlier we discussed the importance of learning from failures. During his journey he made a number of missteps and repeatedly backtracked. When he first took over as head of Coke, he pushed its diversification into the fruit juice market, only to reverse himself and later sell off most of the business. He acquired Columbia Pictures, which proved to be a profitable but diverting investment that he also offloaded after just seven years. Additionally, he committed what many considered one of the biggest follies in business history by abandoning the hundred-year-old formula for Coca-Cola's flagship product and introduced New Coke, which proved to be a colossal failure. Appearing to be a man who didn't know which way to turn; he overcame these diversions; and steadily led Coca-Cola to new heights of profitability and shareholder value. Reading his published interviews and his annual letters to shareholders, I could see that he did this by following a philosophy developed through years of examining and learning from his experiences. Like other effective leaders, he is a man who knew what he knew, and where he learned it.

Goizueta was a great believer in cash flow. He understood that earnings were man-made but in the end investors were interested in *showing me the money*. This perspective is sensible to me because the larger the company, the less it understands cash flow. He was epitome of having an innopreneur state of mind in a corporate environment as he made business decisions adding value as if he owned all Coke stock even though he didn't. Using the performance measures of Market Value Added, which measures the difference between a company's market value—what investors could get out of a business by selling—and the capital that investors have put in over the company's lifetime, and Economic Value Added, that calculates returns on invested capital. He evaluated expenditures from the point of view that if a project earns 10 percent but the cost of capital is 15 percent, the project has destroyed economic value. According to Goizueta, "You borrow money at a certain rate and invest it at a higher rate and pocket the difference. It is simple," he stated. As a Yale University graduate, Goizueta was given the opportunity to really test himself and build a life out of nothing when Fidel Castro took over Cuba, forcing the Goizueta family to flee to the United States. Goizueta, who was employed with Coca-Cola as an entry-level chemist in Havana, arrived in Miami with his wife and their three children, $40 in cash, and one hundred shares of Coca-Cola stock held in trust in New York.

His rise to CEO taught him it is possible to survive and prosper even after you have lost everything. The stories shared throughout this book are testimonies to this. In a very real sense, Castro taught him to be fearless about taking risks. You can create opportunities if you are willing to go out on a limb. As a result, from his first day as CEO, he routinely asked questions and suggested experiments just to see what might happen if things worked differently [Looking to challenge or change the status quo]. Again with an innopreneur state of mind, he laid out a strategy that stated, "Our behavior will produce leaders, good managers, and—most importantly—entrepreneurs. It is my desire that we take initiatives as opposed to being only reactive and that we encourage intelligent individual risk taking."

When reflecting on Goizueta's intelligent risk taking, it manifested itself with such successful product introductions as Diet Coke and caffeine-free Coke products. It also led to New Coke. New Coke is a good example of how the pieces of Goizueta's philosophy came together and has become part of the Coca Cola culture today. His fearlessness about risks allowed him to dare to change the old formula. And then, when it proved to be such a disaster, he recognized that the public had provided him with invaluable pieces of information. His grandfather had told him to focus on "things that mattered," and the public's reaction made it abundantly clear to him that the thing that mattered most for Coca-Cola was its unique, original product. I spoke earlier on having an epiphany; well, this was Goizueta's, which accelerated his assault on non-core business units (business units that didn't sell Coke products), generally selling them for a profit, and reduced the company basically to its trademark. Now, the Coca-Cola Company exists almost solely to sell Coca-Cola.

To say that Goizueta returned Coca-Cola to a singular focus on its primary assets isn't to say that he stopped challenging the status quo. On the contrary, his intelligent risk taking and innopreneur state of mind led to the adoption of a global sales strategy focused on increasing the total fluid intake of Coca-Cola products by everyone in the world. Later we will talk about Big Bold Audacious Goals (BBAGS). For now, his BBAGS focused on increasing the consumption on a daily basis of Coca-Cola products among the billions of people in the world—each person consumed 64 ounces of liquid a day with Coca-Cola products accounting for only two of those ounces. He challenged his troops to exploit growth opportunities not limited to emerging markets where Coca-Cola's products were not available, but also in the densely populated where the remaining sixty-two ounces remain to be captured. His consistent visioning and purposing translated to innovations such as marketing partnerships with retailers in the United States and equipping special taxis in South Africa to sell Coca-Cola products.

Mr. Goizueta's larger-than-life image was created from a life journey filled with high expectations and sudden loss, followed by even higher rewards. His effectiveness at Coca-Cola was attributed to sustaining success by adding value and demanding excellence. Because of his image, these are the hallmarks of The Coca-Cola Company today long after his death.

Summary

Demonstrating the behaviors of the **S.U.C.C.E.S.S.F.U.L.** philosophy allows the effective leader to sustain success by adding value and demanding excellence. See your goal(s), understand obstacles, clear your mind of doubt, create a positive mental picture, embrace the challenge, stay on track, and show the world you can do it, faithfully confess your goals, understand that you have the victory, and learn humility. The stories shared in this chapter reinforce that it doesn't matter where you come from; it matters where you end up. They also demonstrate another behavior trait, to be discussed, of **A.G.I.L.E. L.E.A.D.E.R.S.H.I.P. with a G.R.I.P.**, having a teachable point of view. The following quotes embody the essential of this chapter. I hope they inspire you as they did me.

- *"Success is to be measured not so much by the position that one has reached in life as by the obstacles which he or she has overcome." –Booker T. Washington*
- *"Obstacles are like wild animals. They are cowards but they will bluff you if they can. If they see you are afraid of them...they are liable to spring upon you; but if you look them squarely in the eye, they will sink out of sight." – Orison Swett Marden*
- *"It isn't the mountains ahead to climb that wear you out; it's the pebble in your shoe." –Muhammad Ali*
- *"In order to succeed, you desire for success should be greater than your fear of failure." – Dr. Bill Cosby*
- *"Action is the foundational key to all success." –Pablo Picasso*
- *"You can have unbelievable intelligence, you can have connections, you can have opportunities fall out of the sky. But in the end, hard work is the true, enduring characteristic of successful people." – Marsha Evans*
- *"Success is a state of mind. If you want success, start thinking of yourself as a success." – Dr. Joyce Brothers*

Let's examine the Ⓗ in **L.E.A.D.E.R.S.Ⓗ.I.P.** as we look at how effective leaders Ⓗave a teachable point of view.

CHAPTER 14

Have a Teachable Point of View

Introduction

As an effective leader, realize that a point of view does not contribute to the success and excellence of a person, place, or thing unless it is teachable. This is how winning companies build leaders. Each of us tells our own personal life story to ourselves, every day. The "mind chatter" that rushes through our brains at two hundred words per minute when we're not concentrating on something else becomes the story we are living: "I should have done this," or "I'll never get over that."

The mind is formed to an astonishing degree by the act of inventing and censoring ourselves. We create our own plot line. That plot line soon turns into a self-fulfilling prophecy. Psychologists have found that it finally becomes a recipe for structuring experience itself, for laying down routes into memory, and finally for guiding their lives (Sheehy, 1995).

Having talked about mental models as deeply ingrained assumptions, generalizations, or even pictures and images that influence how we understand the world and how we take action. This gives us our worldview of ideas, values, and assumptions about how the world operates. We all have fundamental beliefs, for example, about whether people are naturally generous or greedy, or whether we are victims of fate or controllers of our own destinies. Our experiences shape our responses to the world. But most people don't consciously recognize these views and can't trace their origin. In my experience, effective leaders not only can, but also do.

Effective leaders consciously think about their experiences. They meditate on them and draw life lessons from them. From my years of writing computer software programs, this is analogous to a well-developed computer software program that is designed to interact with a database. Effective leaders constantly update and refine their views as they acquire new knowledge and experience, storing them in the form of stories they use not only to guide their own decisions and actions, but also to teach and lead others. When you hear effective leaders talk about their lives, you learn their teachable point of views.

Winning leaders draw from their life experiences as the source of important ideas and values, and the time when they began to develop emotional energy and edge. Events early in life shape lessons that they use in the future. They consciously capture these lessons and use them as guides. Leaders' stories reveal their teachable point of view. For example, my mentor James Jones taught me, "You gotta wanna or you ain't a gonna!" Fidel Castro taught Robert Goizueta to take risks. As you read this chapter, always remember that everyone has a usable past; effective leaders just use theirs better. They recognize the defining moments of their lives and can communicate the lessons through words and actions. Let me share some more experiences demonstrating having a teachable point of view.

Delivering "Priceless" Training

As a corporate trainer working with Professional Development Services (PDS), LLC. a registered education provider (REP) for the Project Management Institute (PMI), the leading professional project management organization in the world, I delivered technology management training to major corporations and the federal government. The keys to my success were my energy, delivery, and my ability to integrate my experiences into the class. This was critical because most of my students ranged from executives to senior level technicians who were amongst the best in their fields or the company.

My ability to tell a story turning abstract concepts into practical reality made me the go-to person for classroom delivery in addition to on-site consulting and mentoring. My services were requested repeatedly. This was a lifelong professional goal—to be able to go into any organization in the world to deliver a product that adds value and sustains excellence.

I recall one very difficult student, a vice president at a major bank, who questioned whether I could deliver the course agenda covering twenty years of information within the allotted three days. A twenty-five-year veteran of information technology (IT), he was at the top of his game. The course focused on managing the gathering and writing of business requirements. As I began to deliver concept upon concept intertwined with my life stories, he, like the thousands of other students I've trained, began to look at me with astonishment. I have coined the phrase, "*Said another way*," which I used repeatedly throughout this book, as an orthodox technique to grab a person's attention. I follow with delivering stories that support my teachable point of view.

At the end of the course, this student came up to me in amazement, stating how the class was impressed with my teaching skills. Throughout this book, I use the term *great* to describe myself. This is not for self-aggrandizement. Recall that in being **S.U.C.C.E.S.S.F.U.L.**, the **"F"** is "Faithfully confess your goals." My goal was to be great, and if you believe you're great, then others will follow suit. ***Said another way***, greatness begins with you and ends with the customer. This difficult student greeted me and labeled me in front of the entire class a "great" instructor. Here are the excerpts from e-mails sent to his boss and me.

"Good Morning, Frank,

Thank you for your lively presentation of your class material.
I know you have done what you were teaching. As MasterCard says, "This is priceless."
You have put twenty years into three days. I did not think it could be done—boy, was I mistaken. I hope we can have you back in the future."

He later adds in a following e-mail:

"I highly recommend Dr. Harper as a great instructor who presented a very complete course."

Get Right Back Up

I recall two events that taught me when you get knocked down, get right back up. The first occurred while on the old campus of Yale University. The campus is landscaped with tall, thick, beautiful trees. The students would usually play football and baseball on the campus. One day some friends and I were throwing the football around. Tony Defranco, a good friend, could throw a football with accuracy fifty yards. He told me to "go deep," which, for those of you who may not be familiar with football jargon, means to run a "post" or "fly" pattern of at least twenty-five yards. I chose to run a fly pattern, so, using my blazing speed and hard head, as you will see, I took off sprinting. We both misjudged the location of the biggest tree on the old campus. Well, he threw it and I went after it. I made a nice over-the-shoulder catch, and when I took my next step to run up field, it took me full speed into that tree, head *and* face first. *Bang!* The next thing I knew, I was on my back looking up at the sky. Still holding the football, dazed but unfazed, I got up with the help of a passerby and some friends. Tony rushed to my aid with a look of devastation. I didn't know why. I mean, we didn't intend on me testing my toughness by running head *and* face first into what had to be one of the biggest trees in the world! My head was okay—I actually chipped off some of the tree bark, just kidding.

But my face and mouth were a pretty sight, if you know what I mean, and I felt sick to my stomach. Finally, bending over, I began to vomit blood—a whole lot of it! I was rushed to the Yale Infirmary still holding the football. In fact, the doctor had to take the football from me as he stitched my lips—inside and out. When my parents saw my face, they were livid. Life is full of "in-the-moment" experiences. This was surely one of them, but the life lesson learned from it would not be apparent until I met this next gentleman.

Floyd Little is a Pro Football Hall of Fame running back who played for the Denver Broncos, and a former three-time football All-American running back at Syracuse. He and I attended the same high school, James Hillhouse High in New Haven, Connecticut; played for the same head coach in different eras; and achieved All-State recognition. During my senior year in high school, while visiting our former coach, he graciously granted an interview to a newspaper colleague and me for an award-winning article written for the school newspaper. Mr. Little had a compelling story to tell. The analogies he made between football and life were unforgettable. He was describing the year where he led the entire NFL in rushing, an amazing feat. However, Mr. Little stated, "I carried the football 284 times for 1,133 yards and scored only six touchdowns. That means I got knocked on my butt a whole lot but I got right back up!" Can you image that? By relating his successes to his failures, Mr. Little was teaching us humility. He certainly inspired me and my colleague to not be afraid to strive for *greatness*! Almost thirty years after that interview, I still recall how important he viewed risk and failure as keys to his success. I recall him telling me, "You've got it, so go do it!"

If it is not obvious from the above stories, the lesson learned is, "When you get knocked down, as long as your eyes are open, you can get right back up!"

Taking Intelligent Risks

It would be remorse of me to not revisit the earlier story on Robert Goizueta, former chairman of the Coca-Cola Company, when discussing having a teachable point view. He is my inspiration because like me he lost it all, survived and prospered. Also I admired his courage in taking risks, sharing his downfalls and his rise to greatness. Let's examine some key events that demonstrate his teachable views.

Earlier I mentioned my dad telling me, "It's not how you start, it's is how you finish." Goizueta's rise from rags to riches is an example of this truism. Fidel Castro caused him and his family to flee from Cuba to the United States causing them to losing everything. His recovery reminded him that it is possible to survive and prosper even after you have lost everything. In a very real sense, Castro taught him to be fearless about taking risks. Armed with this life lesson, he routinely asked questions and suggested experiments to challenge/change the status quo. This leads us to the Goizueta's next teachable point of view.

Earlier we spoke of the Six *Is* of Intelligent—one of them being Initiative. This next statement supports my argument. Upon becoming CEO of the Coca-Cola Company, Goizueta laid out a strategy which stated, "Our behavior will produce leaders, good managers, and—most importantly—entrepreneurs. It is my desire that we take *initiatives* as opposed to being only reactive and that we encourage *intelligent* individual risk taking." Keep reading and learning that he not only talked the talk but also walked the walk.

Goizueta overcame colossal failure involving introducing New Coke to increase the value of his company more than any other CEO in the history of the business. His fearlessness about risks allowed him to dare to change the old formula—we talked about one of the behaviors of a leader is to challenge/change the status quo. And then, when it proved to be such a disaster, he recognized that the public had provided him with invaluable pieces of information. He spoke of the lesson his grandfather had told him to focus on "things that mattered," and the public's reaction made it abundantly clear to him that the thing that mattered most for Coca-Cola was its unique, original product. This accelerated his assault on noncore business units (business units that didn't sell Coke products), generally selling them for a profit, and reduced the company basically to its trademark. Now, the Coca-Cola Company exists almost solely to sell Coca-Cola.

Let's continue to look at the New Coke debacle for there is another example of having a teaching point of view. At part of the conversation when discussing this experience Goizueta stated, "It is extremely important that you show some insensitivity to your past in order to show the proper respect for the future." As I reflect on this statement a certain football analogy comes to mind. Having played and coached defensive backs for over twenty-two years I understand the statement a TV announcer makes when they say a defensive back must have a short memory. For those of you who may not know what a defensive back is, they are the defensive player responsible for keeping the opposing team's offensive receiver(s) from either catching the ball or scoring a touchdown. Well every defensive back is going to get beat resulting in the receiver either catching the ball for: a long gain, first down, or touchdown. In either case they have to have a short memory. **Said another way**, they can't dwell on the negative experience of what *had* happened, they must learn from it and leverage that lesson to defend the receiver(s) *better* in the future. They must continue to embrace the challenge—positively.

Goizueta had no regrets regarding the New Coke debacle. He states, "Whether or not we were smart or dumb, right or wrong was and is irrelevant.... The job of management is to provide results, and those have been produced in spades" (Morris, 1986). As for his teaching to others, Goizueta would offer,

"An old boss once told me I was too much a man of action. But I like to quote the poet Antonio Machado, who said, 'Paths are made by walking.' "

Mr. Goizueta's success at the Coca-Cola Company and his community endeavors are attributed to him being such a great teacher.

The Bigger the Headache, the Bigger the Pill

I promised you earlier in the book that you would have the opportunity to see how Dr. McCrimmon was able to achieve his reality. Well, now is later. Dr. McCrimmon is the CEO and managing partner of M2Synergistics, Inc., a firm that specializes in coaching (executive), consulting (management), and conveying (motivational speaking). He is not only a former colleague and mentor but also a close friend who served as my proctor during the defense of my doctoral dissertation. He is the consummate effective leader, having worked in information technology for thirty years for companies such as Eastman Kodak, Federal Express, and the Atlanta Committee for the Olympic Games while holding executive roles at Digital Equipment Corporation, KnowledgeWare, Price Waterhouse, and IBM.

Dr. McCrimmon was named the first chief information officer of the Black Data Processing Associates in 2001, an organization that he has been a member of for thirty years. Michael has founded numerous chapters of the BDPA, served as the organization's national vice president, and has served as a member of the board of directors for over twenty years. He has been a pastor for ten years at churches ranging from two hundred members to eight thousand in the Atlanta area. Along with pastoral responsibilities, based on his corporate expertise, he served as chief operating officer, often overseeing day-to-day operations and financial performance. He has a PhD in Computer Science, a Doctor of Divinity in Theology, MBA in International Finance along with a plethora of professional certifications. Needless to say Doc is a "*baaad*" but extremely humble man.

He is the consummate storyteller. It is one thing to read about the importance of telling a story to convey your point, but actually doing it is truly an art in its application and a science that can be learned.

I am very critical of people who can rightly divide the word of truth in preaching the gospel. Having grown up around spiritual men allows me to be quite attuned to wolves in sheep's' clothing. Dr. McCrimmon invited me to hear his first sermon. Doc is a man of integrity and I've always enjoyed hearing him speak. So I decided to attend my friend's inauguration into spiritual greatness. His teaching was epic. Being a former *Street hustler*, athlete, and a *Strategic hustler*™, I listened and watched this anointed man of God deliver a sermon that was awesome. His usage of props to get his point across was on point.

Using the story of David defeating Goliath, Dr. McCrimmon's sermon message focused on, "When you can't run, what do you do?" He concluded with, "If we can't get along, sometimes we got to get it on!" Those readers who understand the street understand this lingual. To align his message to biblical principles he quoted scriptures from the Bible to highlight the following points:

1. Replay old game tapes
2. Don't fight with weapons that you don't know how to use
3. Trash talking (for God) is OK
4. Give headaches, don't get them

As I meditated on his message, this is what it meant. Playing the game of sports is the same as playing the game of life. Obstacles (people, places, things, events, etc.) always surface trying to prevent you from achieving your goals. As a half-back, when I carried the ball, there were eleven obstacles (players) trying to keep me from scoring or getting a key first down. Or, as Floyd Little put it, "I carried the football 284 times for 1,133 yards and scored only six touchdowns. That means I got knocked on my butt a whole lot, but I got right back up!" I immediately thought of these when personalizing the statement "When you can't run, what do you do?" Let's look at the last part, "what do you do?" Well, that depends on whether you have prepared yourself. You see, when preparing for an opponent, to understand his or her strengths and weaknesses, one must study game films, or, **said another way**, "replay old game tapes." Studying old game tapes helps me determine my action plan. Am I going to reverse field, am I going to lower my shoulder and deliver a blow, how should I hold the football—as a student of the game all of these scenarios are played out in my mind before the confrontation. **Remember,** failure to replay old game tapes will not allow you to control your destiny but will allow others to do it for you. It may mean getting knocked down "284 times," knowing that you will get right back up and keep trying. Are you getting my drift?

In preparing to play the game, or do battle, you want to use plays that you're familiar with. To be prepared, you have to "replay old game tapes" and practice executing using the right tools to be successful, or "don't fight with weapons that you don't know how to use." The weapons were the plays that would be executed to exploit the team's strengths and weaknesses. Weapons have both a figurative and literal meaning. As a *Street hustler*, the literal meaning would be things that bring physical pain and suffering. But as a *Strategic hustler*™, you've graduated from the literal meaning to the figurative meaning—those tools and techniques (T-N-T) that allow you to become an effective leader. In this sense, they allow you to become a *great* leader and person that is a benefit to society.

I've mentioned that God has given me a gift of gab. In fact, I've talked so much as a hustler, both *Street* and *Strategic*, I've coined the terms "IntelliSpeak" and "Garbarzz" to make the distinction between them. IntelliSpeak is trash talk for God. Garbarzz is trash talk for the street. In the book of First Samuel, chapter 17, verses 1 to 16, and the book of Romans, chapter 8, verse 31, these scriptures promote, "If God be for us, who can be against us!" Now what does that really mean? Using street vernacular, it means God's got your back no matter what you are up against. So when you are up against a Goliath, or a problem you feel is too big for you to handle, then it is OK to engage in "trash talking for God" because he will take you through your problems, *In this case,* it is OK to engage in IntelliSpeak. I will talk more about this in the chapter on Perseverance. These scriptures, along with my ability and willingness to use Intellispeak, were instrumental in writing this book.

When you "replay old game tapes," "don't fight with weapons that you don't know how to use," and "trash talk for God," you are ready to "give headaches, not get them." Let's talk about being a defensive cornerback in the National Football League (NFL). I am not an avid fan of the NFL, but there are a handful of players I would pay to see. One of them is Darrelle Revis, who has earned the nickname "Revis Island" for the way he prevents opposing team's top wide receiver from catching passes—by himself. He is not perfect, but he is excellent. Why? Mr. Revis is a student of the game of football because he prepares for opponents, so that he can be a thorn in their side. *In short,* Darrelle Revis gives headaches, he does not get them. In the biblical story of David and Goliath, David hit Goliath in the head with a stone that was so big that it sunk into Goliath's forehead (First Samuel, chapter 17, verse 49). Do you think Goliath got a headache? The moral of the David and Goliath story is, "The bigger the headache, the bigger the pill."

Whatever you do in life, live for something higher, bigger, and better than you! The obstacles will be big. But the trouble and tribulation that go with them don't last forever. Just remember: "The bigger the headache, the bigger the pill."

A Mother's Love

Dr. Yamile Jackson, PhD, PE, PMP, is another friend and business associate whom I've collaborated with on planning international business ventures in Africa and other third-world countries. She is part of my LinkedIn family. I am impressed by the woman, mother, teacher, volunteer, entrepreneur, pioneer, and effective leader. Dr. Jackson is the CEO and founder of Nurtured by Design (formerly Zakeez, Inc.). Her credentials include four engineering degrees, with her PhD in ergonomics and human factors engineering; licensed professional engineer in TX (PE), certified project management professional (PMP), and certified Kangaroo Care professional in the USA, "Kangaroo." She emigrated from Colombia in 1988 and worked in the engineering and construction business for twelve years before founding Nurtured by Design.

Nurtured by Design is the global leader in neonatal ergonomics applied to newborn evidence-based developmental care (physical, psychological, neurological, and psychological development). Among the awards she has won, include: Groundbreaking Latina Entrepreneur of the Year (*Catalina* Magazine), Ultimate Latina of the Year Award–Health Category, (United States Hispanic Chamber of Commerce), Outstanding Woman-Owned Small Business of the Year Award (SCORE Foundation, sponsored by Constant Contact, Washington DC), and several awards for product design. Her company and/or personal story have been featured internationally including by Reuters, the *Rachael Ray Show*, the *Today Show*, BBC, Jay Leno, Fox, and *Reader's Digest*, and her son's story was the inspiration for the made-for-TV movie *14:Hours*, aired on TNT.

Prior to Nurtured by Design, she worked in a Fortune 200 company and then opened her own international consulting and training firm in 1998, working mostly for the energy industry. Dr. Jackson was also the first Latin American professional to be elected as director at large of the Project Management Institute (PMI). She currently serves on the board of directors and board of advisors for numerous organizations. Her speaking engagements have included the March of Dimes, the Construction Industry Institute, PMI, the Institute of Industrial Engineers, and the US Institute for Kangaroo Care, etc.

I am especially honored to share my friend Dr. Jackson's story with you because, if you haven't figured it out, she is a children safety advocate. Her actions epitomize my motto, "Every Child Deserves a Chance!" She is truly a humble and remarkable woman. Like all-star performers, Dr. Jackson uses her life experiences in developing her teachable point of view. In her words, Dr. Jackson explains how her life influences how she leads her company:

"Looking back in retrospect, my life has been all about challenges and obstacles: losing my father at a very young age, born and raised in Colombia (a developing country trying to do what was best for its people), raised by a single mother (that has a PhD and worked hard to make all of her three children well-rounded and educated professionals), and choosing a technical profession that has few Hispanic females. While it may seem odd, it is only in reflection that I begin to realize that my life has been all about transforming those challenges and obstacles into something positive. At the time I was too focused on what I wanted to do with my life and how to get there. My thoughts included: emigrate to the United States of America (the land of professional opportunities, especially for a woman in a technical field), become an engineer, finish both master's and doctorate degrees, work for a global and influential company, ultimately to run a company, have a family, and be a world-class mother and wife. I was able to identify opportunities, and those opportunities and ability to perform became my sole focus. My mother always said that I could do and be whatever I wanted, but only if I worked hard to achieve it (and not all at the same time). Had I focused on those obstacles and

challenges, my objective could have been easily deviated and I would not be anywhere close to where I am today."

As stated earlier, effective leaders draw from their pasts. They consciously capture events early in life to shape lessons that they use in the future and use them as guides. Dr. Jackson states, "*By some solid reflection, my own path taught me invaluable lessons on how to lead people, whether in my own company, colleagues, or my customers. In fact the largest focus of my early years in my young company have been providing leadership and education in new ergonomic solutions for newborn babies that complement the medical care to not only save the lives of babies, but ensure the best quality of life possible. The most valuable lesson I have learned personally to drive innovation is to have a crystal clear 'call to arms' as to what you individually and as a company are all about. Focusing on that 'call to arms' rather than the obstacles is the only way to ensure success. By living the message, your employees, customers, and suppliers see the value of what you are doing and ultimately join you in a big way.*"

Effective leaders recognize the defining moments in their lives. **Said another way**, they recognize the "aha" moments creating an epiphany. For Dr. Jackson, the genesis of the "call to arms" for Nurtured by Design was: "*In 2001, I gave birth twelve weeks prematurely to my son Zachary. He was born weighing only one pound, fifteen ounces, and survived the most incredible odds including surviving the shutdown of his life-support equipment, caused by a flood. I went home without him for the 155 nights that he was in the Neonatal Intensive Care Unit in the Texas Medical Center in Houston, Texas. I made a promise to him that his pain and struggle to survive were not going to be in vain, and at Nurtured by Design we work on his behalf helping babies around the world, especially those born prematurely like him. Zachary is our company's chief inspirational officer.*"

To experience Dr. Jackson's, teachable point of view, one only has to visit her company website, www.nurturedbydesign.com, to learn about the products and services they provide. She elaborates, "*More than a portfolio of commercial products that help babies sleep and bond with the parents, we create devices inspired on human nature and maternal instinct that actually save lives and improve the quality of the life of babies, families, and society at large—for a lifetime.*

"*For those born prematurely, many conditions are thought to be 'normal'; for example, the baby's association of touch with pain (which may prevent the baby from enjoying human touch for the rest of his life), of movement with stress (which may prevent proper development of joints and muscles), the detachment or inability to bond with the mother or other family members (we all know the implications of this), some musculoskeletal deformities, or even apnea (baby stops breathing) or bradycardia (heart rate slows down) of prematurity. I have worked for over a decade to design devices that provide a better environment for the baby, and we are starting to prove that while they may be 'common,' they are far from 'normal.'*

"*With our devices, nurses and parents are able to significantly decrease and in some cases even eliminate these life-threatening events like apnea/bradycardia while significantly improving the baby's ability to self-regulate, all without the need of expensive equipment, stimulants, medications, or invasive procedures.*

"Why is this significant? Because with the work we do, we are shedding light on the possibility that apnea and bradycardia of prematurity are not caused by the immaturity of the brain, heart, and respiratory system (as defined in the literature) and that we can prevent them instead of needing stimulants like caffeine to treat them."

Creating a Teachable Point of View

This book describes basic building blocks for **A.G.I.L.E. L.E.A.D.E.R.S.H.I.P. with a G.R.I.P.** Colleges and universities who offer experiential learning are in great demand. Why? Have you ever heard the phrase "Experience is the best teacher"? Skill is important, knowledge is critical, but experience brings both skill and knowledge together under one roof to produce star performers. Furthermore, instructors who have real-world experience can provide teachable points of view to bring theory to life with real-world examples that students can relate to. The end result is an engaged student who enjoys a remarkable learning experience. This truism applies to both a *Street hustler* and *Strategic hustler*™. We have talked about how being [**S.U.C.C.E.S.S.F.U.L.**] allowed providing a product and/or service that added value and demanded excellence to sustain success in the marketplace. In this chapter, I shared examples of linking key "aha" moments to create a teachable point of view. We discussed edge, the ability to make tough decisions. Now you have to pull the other elements together, or integrate them, into compelling stories that motivate others to reach for a better future. But in order to do that you need to understand how ideas and values close the loop to having a teachable point of view. The next chapter will cover ideas and values. So keep on reading and learning!

A point of view is valuable only if it can be taught. Can you teach? Of course you can. In chapter 5, "Learning Behavior," we spoke about being able to teach and learn. Everyone has a real-life story to tell. Something or someone during your lifetime has inspired you to be who you are. This book is full of life stories. Nothing worthwhile in life comes easy. There is no simple playbook for teaching or learning any of these abilities. There are tools, practice exercises, and approaches that can help you improve your own leadership abilities, teach others to improve theirs, and build effective leaders. This is a book for the ages, so I am going to provide you with some pointers to help you develop your teachable point of view. There are a variety of thoughts from leading experts on leaders teaching leadership. As a teaching practitioner, I will say true learning takes place when the leader/teacher invests the time and the emotional energy to engage those around him or her in a dialogue that produces mutual understanding. Recall the story I shared with you from one of my students earlier. He called the training "priceless" because I accepted the challenge to engage students with ten to twenty-five years of relevant experience in a "lively presentation." *Said another way*, learning and teaching occurred because of commitment to [**C.H.A.N.G.E.**]. Recall commitment is an emotional feeling that starts in the heart igniting the mind to do something.

Summary

Having a teachable point of view requires sharing your experiences to motivate and inspire others. You'll need to deliver a customized message of behavior comprising **A.G.I.L.E. L.E.A.D.E.R.S.H.I.P. with a G.R.I.P.** — to be [**S.U.C.C.E.S.S.F.U.L.**] in the twenty-first century.

Earlier we talked about how mental models are the results of experiential learning, which is learning acquired through life journeys. A mental model is an explanation of someone's thought process about how something works in the real world. It is a representation of the surrounding world, the relationships between its various parts and a person's intuitive perception about their own acts and their consequences. Our mental models help shape our behavior and define our approach to solving problems and carrying out tasks.

How? These are deeply ingrained assumptions, generalizations, or even pictures and images that influence how we understand the world and how we take action. This is our professional repertoire. We all have worldviews, complex webs of ideas, values, and assumptions about how the world operates— thanks to our mental models. We all have fundamental beliefs, for example, about whether people are naturally nice or nasty, or whether we are victims of fate or controllers of our own destinies. And we develop these views, which shape our responses to the world, out of our past experiences. But most people don't consciously recognize these views and can't trace their origin. In my experience, effective leaders not only can, but also do.

Effective leaders are winners because they consciously think about their experiences. They roll them over in their minds, analyze them, and draw lessons from them. They constantly update and refine their views as they acquire new knowledge and experience. And they store them in the form of stories that they use not only to guide their own decisions and actions, but also to teach and lead others. Now you know when you hear leaders talk about their lives, it is an opportunity to learn their teachable point of view. Seize it!

Figure 14.1 illustrates having a teachable point of view requires ideas, values, emotional energy, and edge.

Figure 14.1 The Components of A Teachable View

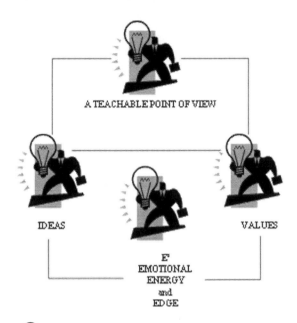

We've discussed (E)motional energy and edge (chapter 11). The next chapter will cover (I)ntroducing ideas based on uplifting values. Let's look at the (I) in **L.E.A.D.E.R.S.H.(I).P**

CHAPTER 15

Introduce Ideas Based on Uplifting Values

Introduction

Effective leaders link their ideas to goals, which are birthed from their dreams. Recall dreams become goals only when written down. Once goals are documented, productive ideas on how to achieve them can flow. The *Strategic hustler™* introduce ideas that uplift society. *Street hustlers* introduce ideas that uplift themselves at the expense of others. Corporate *street hustlers* are those leaders who contributed to the financial meltdown that negatively impacted millions of people and billions of dollars. Let's talk more about why it is important to introduce ideas based on uplifting values.

Phil Knight a favorite *Strategic hustler™*. When Knight started a little athletic shoe company, he named it Nike for the Greek goddess of victory. Knight chose the name not so much as a statement of aspirations for the company as a statement of its purpose. Nike, he declared, would be dedicated to helping athletes win. If this meant pouring resources into the best design department in the industry, Nike would do it. If it meant paying Michael Jordan and other talented athletes millions of dollars to serve as product testers, confidence builders, and role models, Nike would do it. Nike would become a winner by helping its customers become winners. Every decision and every action by every Nike employee would be aimed at furthering that goal. Nike's game would be making its customers winners, or at least feel like them.

This singular idea that Phil Knight articulated at the inception of Nike continues its acceptance today and has propelled Nike to become the premier athletic shoe and sportswear company in the world, with a market value over $15 billion. It has served as the organizing principle that guides all of its activities. Like its customers, Nike's markets are fast-paced. Every day brings new demands and challenges that require instant responses from Nike's workforce.

But because everyone at Nike clearly knows what he or she is aiming for, the company continues to create the right innovative responses needed to get there. It's what makes Nike a winner.

Ideas provide the intellectual underpinning of every human activity. **Said another way**, ideas springboard the goals that lead to the actions we as human beings take. This applies to sports, business, and personal life. In chapter 3, "(G)oal-Oriented Behavior," recall my dad wanting to know where I was going and what I planned to do when I got there. He wanted me to clearly state my ideas.

My life journey has taught me that winners are always firmly grounded in clearly stated ideas. They have an explicit central idea that explains why they are in business and how they intend to add value and demand excellence. My cousin Clyde Powers, my dad's nephew, gave me my first lesson on introducing ideas based on uplifting values. He was only seventeen years old, but before going off and becoming a Vietnam War hero (two Purple Hearts, one Silver Star) he introduced me to building model cars, planes, and boats. This proved to be an uplifting experience. Clyde was a unique teenager. He graduated from high school in Charlotte, North Carolina, and came to live with us in New Haven, Connecticut. My dad made a wise decision when he invited his nephew to stay with us, because having gone through some traumatic experiences; Clyde was the role model everybody needed. He tried to keep us all out of trouble. He was polite, clean cut, drug free, smoke free, liquor free, well-dressed, handsome, smart, athletic, and so very friendly. Clyde found a job working for Armstrong Rubber Company, which allowed him to reward us for good behavior. He was impressed his "little cousin" attended Yale University, and so would make a special attempt to get me involved in thought-provoking things. One of Clyde's hobbies involved building model planes, cars, and boats. He was very meticulous and good at building them, from reading the instructions to separating the parts to painting them and then gluing them together. He would tell me that he would use the picture on the box in which the model was packaged as a guide to select the paint colors. Watching my cousin build those models inspired me. Clyde offered to help me learn how to build models. Once I accepted the offer, it was on! I recall all of the ideas that flowed through my head when building my first model *PT-109*. Clyde, who is brilliant in his own right, would buy me models that had a history lesson behind them. *PT-109* was a PT boat (patrol torpedo boat) last commanded by Lieutenant Junior Grade (LTJG) John F. Kennedy (later president of the United States) in the Pacific Ocean Theater during World War II. Kennedy's actions to save his surviving crew after the sinking of the *PT-109* made him a war hero, which proved helpful in his political career. You see, I was not only developing the skill to build authentic-looking models but also expanding my knowledge base on very interesting things and events of the world. At that time, unbeknownst to me, my cousin was giving me a world-class education. As I reflect on this, my cousin's uplifting values inspired his ideas to purchase me models. Completing my first model and getting his nod of approval made me so proud of myself. This uplifting hobby helped build my self-esteem.

Organizations have ideas also. They determine how the various parts of the organization will interact with each other. Organizations must have well-defined values about what constitutes desirable or undesirable behavior—you will learn more about this later in this chapter. As I recall working for Sikorsky Aircraft, analyzing the assembly line for the electrical wire harness, the most important thing about an idea is that it is shared and understood by everyone working to produce the product. This provides every member with an intellectual framework and an internal yardstick for measuring the rightness of his or her actions. Like an athletic event, the game has to be defined and rules established, allowing ideas to be acted upon individually and collectively to allow everyone to move together toward success.

When Van Spruill decided that he wanted to dethrone the six-time Albie Booth Midget Football Champions, he had to mobilize a team of players around this central idea. Each player focused his efforts toward this goal. When Sterling Software decided they wanted to enter into the business intelligence area, the consulting division of the company had to mobilize hundreds of consultants, trainers, developers, marketers, and salesmen around this central idea. Henry Ford started Ford Motor Company on a central idea he stole from the textile industry, namely, mass production. Ray Kroc founded McDonald's on an idea stolen from Henry Ford, namely, mass production of food. When Senator Barack Obama decided to run for the presidency, he had to mobilize thousands of voters around the central idea "Yes we can!" When Tom "Fly Jock" Joyner decided that he was going to sponsor an annual cruise to raise money for the Tom Joyner Foundation, which offers scholarships to historically black colleges and universities, he had to mobilize a team of his colleagues around this central idea. You get my point! In each case, these fundamental ideas served as the organizing principles for getting thousands of people to achieve a common goal.

I want you to understand that ideas are an essential tool for shaping and motivating anything that breathes—an individual or an organization. My success has been because my ability and willingness to generate ideas. They come from any and everywhere. I am an out-of-the-box thinker. As my dad told me, everybody is ignorant of something. Ignorance is not intended because no one is a know-it-all. However, some successful people get to a level and then, become immune to new knowledge; their attitude is "I know what I know...and don't bother me with more." Now they've displayed a behavior that is intended. This is being arrogant. *Said another way*, these people display a behavior that shows an arrogance of ignorance.

Earlier we talked about the **P.R.O.G.R.E.S.S.** problem solving approach. This approach served me well in allowing the delivery of a cost-reduction research paper, "Determining Trim Waste Cost Using Linear Programming," presented at major universities and corporations in North America, South America, Europe, Africa, and Australia. **P.R.O.G.R.E.S.S.** requires transitioning through these steps: **P**ick the problem/issue, **R**esearch current situation, **O**btain the root cause, **G**enerate alternative solutions, **R**un a pilot, **E**xamine results, **S**et up for transfer, and **S**eek continuous improvement. The "Generate alternative solutions" step is an exercise in generating ideas using brainstorming sessions. Everyone involved is encouraged to submit ideas. I would embrace them, share them, and used them to encourage others to have good ideas. I will talk about using the Balanced Scorecard for Strategic Planning Management in the final chapters on Performance management. But for now, it deserves mentioning, since it is an idea-generation tool that effective leaders should be familiar with because it cascades the organization, which is essential for winning organizations. The Balanced Scorecard allows workers at each level to draw off the central ideas of the company to develop ideas for improving their own operations and to generate ideas for the units under them. Enough on Balance Scorecard; you will get a heavy dosage when I talk about performance later. Just know that goods ideas at all levels drive organizations to success.

The Value of Ideas

Nurtured by Design, evolved from Zakeez Inc., is the worldwide pioneer company that successfully makes ergonomics and human factors engineering and the family the best allies of neonatal developmental care, thanks to ideas of its founder, leader, and CEO, Dr. Yamile Jackson. Earlier we talked about Dr. Jackson's teachable point of views. Now let's dig into the details previously omitted to uncover her ideas based on uplifting values that drives her company.

You recall Dr. Jackson gave birth, 12 weeks prematurely, to her son Zachary who weighed less than two pounds. Let's look at the events that inspired the ideas of this amazing woman for her company.

Three weeks after his birth, Zachary survived the deluge of Tropical Storm Allison that flooded Houston and shut down all power to his hospital, including his life-support equipment. His parents and the Neo-Intensive Care Unit (NICU) staff kept him alive "by hand" for nine hours until he was evacuated. Dr. Jackson held him skin-to-skin to keep him warm while her husband, Larry, and nurses took turns giving him breath manually. The doctors were working extremely hard finding hospitals to which they could evacuate the seventy-nine babies in the NICU. It was then when Yamile prayed for the opportunity to help babies on Zachary's behalf. She promised Zachary that his pain and struggle to survive were not going to be in vain.

Recall Zachary was hospitalized for 155 nights. For each and every one of those nights, Dr. Jackson's goal was to use her knowledge in ergonomics not only to save his life but also to provide him with the best environment possible for healing. Every day she joined the staff in providing proper intervention strategies, individualized care, and family involvement. She quickly recognized the importance and effectiveness of neonatal developmental care practices in comforting, nurturing, and healing critically ill, premature, and low birth weight infants.

She experienced firsthand how important the hands were in properly performing developmental care intervention strategies that she knows contributed to the healing of her critically ill son, Zachary. She learned from the neonatal nurses early on how to effectively use her own hands to comfort her son by placing her hands gently over her son to provide containment and boundaries.

She was with Zachary ten to twelve hours a day, but her agony was leaving her son every night. She wished she could leave her scent and loving touch so her baby would not feel alone. That is how the Zaky was born.

Upon Zachary's departure from the hospital, Dr. Jackson made it her mission to leverage her personal experience and her education and training to redesign the Zaky to make it the most comprehensive, useful, and effective neonatal developmental care device that would make it easier for neonatal nurses and family members to help properly manage the developmental care needs of the infants.

After three years of research and onsite testing, leveraging the help of local neonatal health-care professionals, Dr. Jackson launched the Zaky. The first and only commercial and evidence-based developmental care device designed to keep the parents' scent and to mimic a human hand and forearm, adding a level of functionality that outweighs and replaces virtually every developmental care device on the market today.

More than just inspiring products, Zachary inspires his mother to design ergonomic devices that effectively facilitate evidence-based developmental care around the clock while engaging the parents' natural instincts to nurture and heal. It has earned him the title of CIO (chief inspirational officer). The Zaky and the Kangaroo Zak (which facilitates skin-to-skin contact) are the most comprehensive neonatal developmental care devices designed to make it easier for neonatal healthcare providers to properly perform multiple evidence-based neonatal developmental intervention strategies that have been proven to comfort, soothe, and heal critically ill, premature, and low birth weight infants in the NICU.

To date, the Zaky and Kangaroo Zaks are used by hundreds of neonatal units, both for preemies and healthy babies, in over three hundred hospitals located in the United States and around the world, and Zachary is a healthy and smart boy who keeps inspiring his mother and others to work to help the most vulnerable of our society.

Nurtured by Design's mission statement is to apply ergonomic engineering principles and high doses of natural and parental instinct to the development of products that improve the quality of life of newborn babies, including those hospitalized, setting a higher standard of care for neonatal developmental care.

Its vision is to be the global leader in the development of evidence-based products that truly benefit newborn infants, their families, and professionals responsible for their developmental care. The vision supports being the experts in neonatal ergonomics with a relevant difference: human touch and involvement.

The Relationship of Ideas: Incremental and Quantum

Dr. Jackson's precepts that drive Nurtured by Designs' mission and vision are called quantum ideas. They are big, overriding principles that set direction and are essential to keeping everyone working toward a common goal. But by themselves, they wouldn't be enough to make Nurtured by Design the worldwide pioneering company it is, because they don't suggest a strategy or any specific actions that people might take to reach that goal. For that purpose, every business unit in the company must come up with its own incremental ideas.

For leaders, the need for quantum and incremental ideas presents something of a paradox. A paradox is "holding two seemingly inconsistent truths simultaneously to discover a deeper truth." For the leader, one truth argues that a lot of incremental ideas drive continuous improvement, the evolutionary model of change. Another truth argues that you need big, frame-breaking ideas to create revolutionary changes, a transformational model. The overriding truth, which effective leaders have learned to embrace, is that you need both. You need incremental ideas and quantum ideas, and the two must work in concert. Quantum ideas provide the framework on which incremental ideas hang, and incremental ideas shape the actions that get the quantum ideas implemented.

What I've learned is that many companies spend too much time on incremental ideas, and nobody engages in systems thinking. They lose sight of the quantum ideas. In chapter 5, "(L)earner Behavior," we discussed the importance of systems thinking. Let me give you a reality check with a history lesson. This behavior pattern can be tracked to the Toyota production system, where all line personnel are expected to stop their moving production line in case of any abnormality and, along with their supervisor, suggest an improvement to resolve the abnormality, which may initiate a kaizen. For those not familiar with the term *"kaizen"* here is a formal definition:

"Kaizen, Japanese for "improvement", or "change for the better" refers to philosophy or practices that focus upon continuous improvement of processes in manufacturing, engineering, and business management. It has been applied in healthcare, psychotherapy, life-coaching, government, banking, and other industries. When used in the business sense and applied to the workplace, kaizen refers to activities that continually improve all functions, and involves all employees from the CEO to the assembly line workers. It also applies to processes, such as purchasing and logistics that cross organizational boundaries into the supply chain. By improving standardized activities and processes, kaizen aims to eliminate waste."

The cycle of kaizen activity can be defined as*:*

- Standardize an operation and activities
- Measure the standardized operation (find cycle time and amount of in-process inventory)
- Gauge measurements against requirements
- Innovate to meet requirements and increase productivity
- Standardize the new, improved operations
- Continue cycle *ad infinitum*

If this is challenging to understand chapter 20, "①erformance Management" will give you a clearer perspective—so keep on reading and learning! The problem was every company in the world wanted its just-in-time manufacturing to be as lean and flexible as Toyota's. Toyota's bottom line was in great shape, but the company wasn't generating the kind of quantum ideas that produce bold new products and top-line growth. Only after Honda took the lead with the innovative Accord and Acura did Toyota wake up. Soon, however, a wiser Toyota introduced its successful Lexus and Camry lines, proving itself to be a master of the quantum and incremental paradox.

While consulting on a project with an international bank, I discovered quantum and incremental ideas are needed at all levels of leadership. The project required a team of process redesign professionals to collaborate with the change management team and senior operational management to assist in the successful rollout of new systems. The approach being used prior to my joining the team was laborious and time consuming, which put the project at risk in meeting its deadline. The major challenges required developing new strategies for: processes, procedures, and training. This represented a quantum change (a total rethinking of delivery approach) from a traditional waterfall project management framework to an iterative project management framework to accelerate production of deliverables, drive accountability and make the entire process transparent to teammates and department managers. The quantum ideas were:

- Self-directed, cross-functional work teams
- Iterative development in short cycles continuous improvement
- Ready visibility of work in progress

Once the quantum ideas were understood, the team leader then mobilized people to work on incremental ideas to achieve the needed improvement. The incremental ideas resulted in dividing the work into operational work streams with a three-member team which was led by the process redesign expert who served as the project manager/methodologist and was charged to drive the completion of deliverables.

Let's look at this from a *Street hustler* making the transformation to *Strategic hustler™*. The quantum change I made consisted of changing my environment—see chapter 1, "Leaders Are Born to Be Made," "Coming from hell to Get to Yale"—by attending Yale University's Ulysses S. Grant Foundation college preparatory program, which jumpstarted my additional quantum and incremental ideas to get a college education and become a world-class professional. As I reflect on these, I've realized that just as leaders are born to be made, good ideas are teachable.

Good Ideas are Teachable

I was one of one hundred corporate trainers selected from a pool of 10,500 applicants who attained certification from Learning Tree International as federal acquisitions program/project management (FAC-P/PM) instructors who would deliver training and follow-up support to the federal government in the areas of program/project management, business management, acquisition management, and leadership. Obtaining the certification required successfully completing all phases of the selection process which consisted of a phone interview, vetting interview, and a five-day on-site interview. The phone interview was a screening process. For those of you who may not be familiar with the vetting process, it involves a subject matter expert (SME) for specific areas questioning your abilities and willingness in that area to evaluate your level of competency in generating good (incremental) ideas that would be teachable to the class. ***Think of it as,*** the SME wants to see if your real-world experience, or incremental ideas, would bring value to the class and subsequent consulting/mentoring. I was selected to be vetted in the areas of program/project management and business management for government applications (earned value management). The SMEs were the authors of the courses—they defined the quantum ideas the needed to be taught. They were asked in conjunction with the vetting process for the FAC P/PM curriculum that each request is inclusive of all three levels (I, II, and III) within each specific category of the certification process. Upon successful completion of the vetting process, I would be enrolled in the FAC P/PM T3—Train-the-Trainer Boot Camp. This was the five-day on-site interview process mentioned earlier. Below are my results for the Business Management for Government Applications Level I and II:

Greetings Dr. Harper! Hope all is well!
Below are the criteria used for each vetting for your review.

I have listed the results and comments from Tony Smith, subject matter expert for business management for government applications Level I and II, for your review, file, and action below. Please summarize your reactions to this candidate and select one category for this candidate:

> *1—I do not recommend this person for any Learning Tree course (please explain in detail).*
> *2—I do not recommend this person for this course (please explain).*
> *3—I am willing to review this person after he/she has more experience (please explain specifically how much, with what, etc.).*
> *4—I recommend this person with some reservations (please explain in detail).*
> *5—I recommend this person without reservation for this course.*

Vet Result Comments—Tony Smith—EVM—Level I &II

4—I recommend this person with some reservations (please explain in detail).

***Details for Improvement**—Needs to become familiar with GAO Cost Estimating Guide before delivering first course. This candidate may also be a good choice for the following Learning Tree courses: PM III based on eight-plus years' experience with ANSI/EIA 748 compliant systems approved by DoE and HHS.*

Positives:

*   *Advanced Education: PhD, Administration and Management Specialization, Columbia Commonwealth University*
*   *Professional Certifications/Licenses: PMP, ITIL Foundations, Six Sigma Green Belt*

- *Five-plus years of experience in projects greater than $100 million in value*
- *Fifteen-plus years of experience in projects greater than $10 million in value*
- *Twenty-five-plus years of experience in projects greater than $1 million in value*
- *Fifteen-plus years of experience in training environment*
- *Fifteen-plus years of experience in training*
- *Eighteen-plus years of direct cost estimating experience*
- *Sixteen-plus years of direct EVM experience, eight-plus years in formally accepted EVM Systems (DOE, HHS)*
- *Twenty-seven-plus years of experiences related to the planning for establishing Performance Measurement Baselines (PMB)*
- *Five-plus years of experience with OMB 300 CPIC or similar, congressional level, budgetary processes*
- *Six-plus years of experience in non-DoD agencies*

Challenges:

- *Not a veteran (cousin in the Army)*
- *Not familiar with the GAO Cost Estimating Guide*

The FAC P/PM T3—Train-the-Trainer Boot Camp was challenging but fun. The candidates represented some of the best training/consulting professionals with government experience in the country. We had to deliver multiple two- to five-minute presentations to our peers, senior managers, and directors. Each presentation was videotaped and recorded. We were evaluated by our peers and the master trainer. Let me say this: knowing a subject matter and not having the ability to teach it is like having a point of view that is not teachable—it provides no value. Of the eight candidates in my class, six, including myself, received FAC P/PM instructor certification. I studied the GAO Cost Estimating Guide well enough to make it a nonissue in delivering, to use the words of my evaluators, "a very unique presentation." I attribute my presentation skills to the gentleman, whom I've introduced earlier, in the next paragraph.

At Professional Development Services, I worked with James Jahim Jones (3J), an accomplished course developer and trainer, who has a special talent to clearly formulate ideas and present them so that *anyone* can learn them and teach them. He is an example of a SME who as an effective leader values introducing a core set of quantum ideas about a specific subject matter. For example his course, "Project Management for Quality and Productivity," has been taught at such companies as General Electric and AIG, to name a couple. This course would be of no value if he had not been able to effectively train trainers, allowing them to deliver the material as effectively as he. Winning organizations succeed because leaders at each level draw off the ideas of those above them to frame both large quantum and more specific incremental ideas that help their units reach the desired goal. In order to do this, they must clearly understand and embrace the underlying ideas themselves.

Instructors would audit his classes at least three times before teaching the sections they felt most comfortable with, in the process they were coached to tailor their delivery using their unique professional and life experiences. Additionally, they were encouraged to use their personality to engage the students to create a collaborative and interactive learning environment. The incremental ideas to developing an informative engaging delivery style were required to achieve the priorities and objectives birthed from the quantum ideas. The phrase *"Said another way"* is my signature statement for presenting multiple views on the same topic to ensure students understand the lesson. The students really appreciated those words because they knew I was giving a different perspective to help bring to life an important concept. Keep on reading and learning.

Earlier I mentioned no one has a monopoly on knowledge. During your lifetime you will learn various topics from a different viewpoint. Hence it is, *"Said another way."* Recall earlier I shared my course load in working on my dual master degree. There was one course, Market Research, where my Columbia University PhD professor required reading twenty-one books. Each of these books provided a different perspective on similar marketing research topics. There are a plethora of books on leadership; each recycling previous concepts, theories, examples. Do you get my drift? Ok, let's get back to goods ideas are teachable.

As deputy CIO for business strategic services for the City of Atlanta, I would conduct lunch-and-learn sessions to teach my quantum ideas around formalizing project management, process management, and change management citywide. The ideas focused on a lean project management methodology, a plan for implementing multiple releases of a software program, and a template to assess the organization change management capability. Figure 15.1 provides an illustration for the lean project management methodology. Table 15.1 illustrates the plan for multiple releases. Table 15.2 illustrates an organizational assessment matrix focused on technology, culture, and political.

Figure 15.1: Lean Project Management Methodology

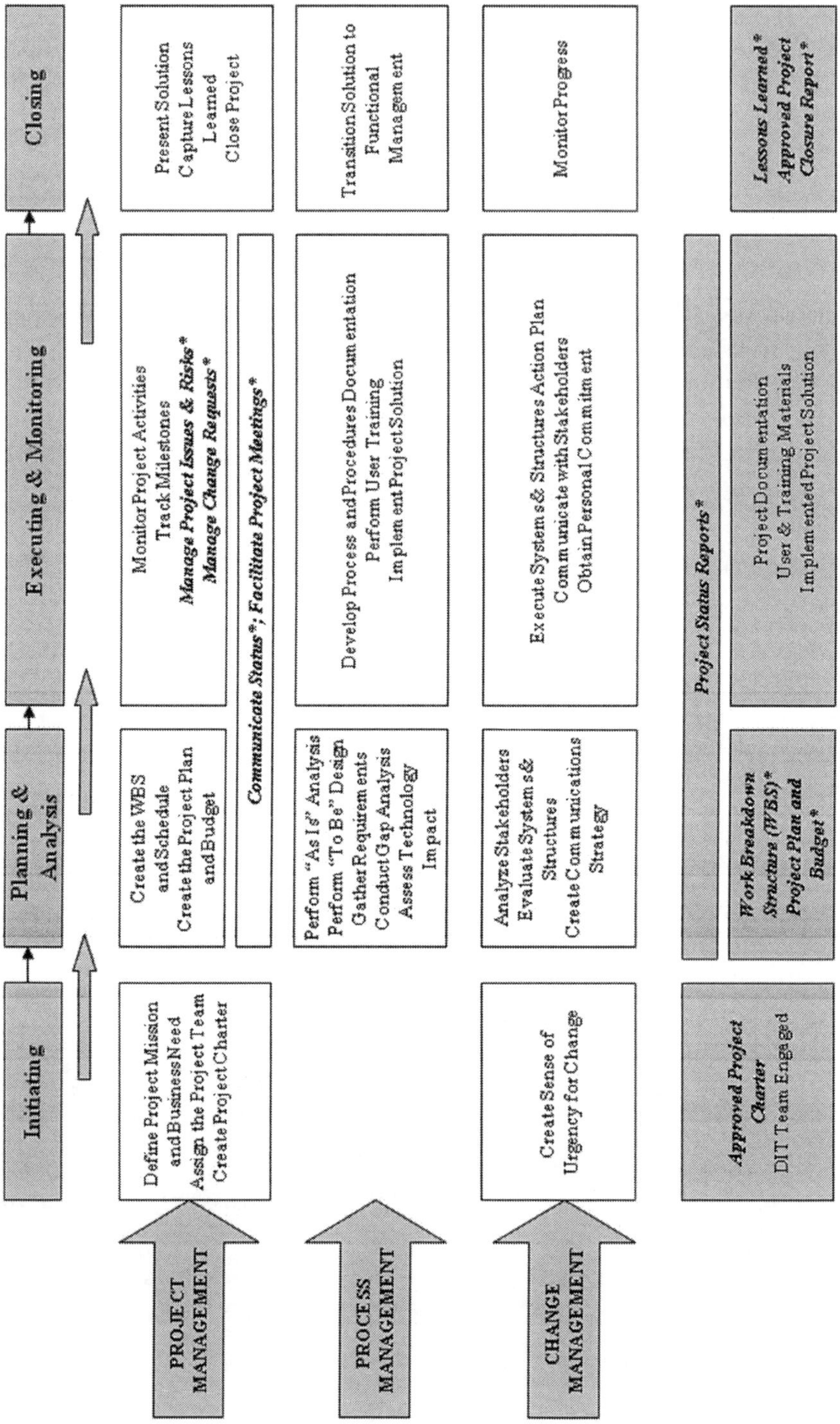

	Initiating	Planning & Analysis	Executing & Monitoring	Closing
PROJECT MANAGEMENT	Define Project Mission and Business Need / Assign the Project Team / Create Project Charter	Create the WBS and Schedule / Create the Project Plan and Budget	Monitor Project Activities / Track Milestones / *Manage Project Issues & Risks** / *Manage Change Requests**	Present Solution / Capture Lessons Learned / Close Project
		Communicate Status*; Facilitate Project Meetings*		
PROCESS MANAGEMENT		Perform "As Is" Analysis / Perform "To Be" Design / Gather Requirements / Conduct Gap Analysis / Assess Technology Impact	Develop Process and Procedures Documentation / Perform User Training / Implement Project Solution	Transition Solution to Functional Management
CHANGE MANAGEMENT	Create Sense of Urgency for Change	Analyze Stakeholders / Evaluate Systems & Structures / Create Communications Strategy	Execute Systems & Structures Action Plan / Communicate with Stakeholders / Obtain Personal Commitment	Monitor Progress
			Project Status Reports*	
	Approved Project Charter / DIT Team Engaged	*Work Breakdown Structure (WBS)** / *Project Plan and Budget**	Project Documentation / User & Training Materials / Implemented Project Solution	*Lessons Learned** / *Approved Project Closure Report**

Source: Intelligent Systems Services, LLC

282

Table 15.1 Multi Generation Systems Plan

	Release # Project Focus Date: TBD	Release # Project Focus Date: TBD	Release # Project Focus Date: TBD
Vision			
Key Functionality			
Technology Requirements			
Target Customers			
Critical Metrics			
Legacy Systems Targeted			
Dependencies			

Table 15.2 Organizational Change Assessment—Technical, Cultural, and Political Analysis

Area	Potential Issue/Barrier	Influencing Strategy
Technical		
Cultural		
Political		

The "quantum" ideas mentioned above were not exotic. Once they were stated, they seemed pretty self-evident. The key was the incremental ideas that brought the quantum ideas to life. When implemented they led to enormous improvement in the appropriate operations areas simply because they aligned the efforts of all workers toward a common goal and a common understanding of how to get there.

Your Quantum and Incremental Ideas

A *Strategic hustler*™ needs ideas to become an effective leader. These ideas can be business or personal. Recall that you need ideas to build your teachable point of view. I've summarized five simple steps to creative thinking and idea generation; they are from James Webb Young's highly recommended book,

A Technique for Producing Ideas. I needed an idea generation process to help my teenage niece, who wanted to enter a poetry-writing contest. This process allowed me to help her become a finalist in the "My South Speaks" contest. She wrote a poem, "All Because Of You," which brought her international acclaim in being awarded the prestigious Editor's Choice Award, Poet Fellow for 2007, and membership in the International Society of Poets. This process has become part of my T-N-T as it has a proven track record of success for creating new ideas across a wide sphere of disciplines, from poetry to painting, engineering to science, from advertising to legal. The aim is to make new connections between existing events or subjects, completing a new picture, analogous to making a jigsaw for the first time. It is essential to understand this as a sequence and not just a list of tasks. Therefore, each step should be completed in the sequence listed. Each individual step is the foundation for success at the next stage.

1. Collect Raw Materials

This step is often skipped or only partly completed but is a key to the overall success of the process. The quality of ideas generated depends on the quality of the preparation and assimilation of the raw materials. Raw materials can include paper and magazine cuttings, photographs, advertisements, original observations.

Two types of raw materials should be collected:

Specific—Those relating directly to the area of interest, customer group, proposed product, etc.

General—Those relating to the broad subject of life events and current affairs. The more widely we spread our net for general materials, the greater our chance of generating creative ideas. We can build each day on this ongoing process.

It is a good idea to assemble these into some kind of order or pattern. Scrapbooks are a great way to collect general materials. Specific materials can be catalogued in some way to make retrieval easier.

Do not short-cut step 1

2. Digest the Materials

This step involves taking each piece of information and studying it from as many angles and in as many different ways as you can. Really try to "get inside" what it is about, what it is saying, how it looks, etc. Continue this process with each piece of specific and general information, looking at the facts and trying to bring them together to see how they fit. A "fit" may be found for some pieces of information without looking too deeply. As bits of ideas come to mind, write these down, no matter how wild or part-formed they are. This process will help cement them in the mind and is a precursor to generation of complete ideas.

It is hard work and at some stage, the mind will become tired, but keep going at this stage, as you will develop a second burst of mental energy. Only when everything becomes a complete jumble with no clear solution anywhere should you stop this process.

3. Drop the Subject

A common trait in the creative process and idea generation is that these ideas come to us when we are least expecting them to, and often when we are doing something totally unrelated to the area in which we have been seeking to generate ideas.

So, this third step is quite simple; get as far away as possible from the thinking process of our chosen area. Do something different, preferably something where you can relax and something you really enjoy. Typically, this will be a topic or activity in which you feel most creative, such as listening to music, reading poetry, playing a sport.

This allows our subconscious to mull over the information we have input in steps one and two.

4. The Idea from Nowhere

At some stage, an idea will "appear as from nowhere," and usually during a pretty mundane activity, such as eating breakfast, having a bath or shave, going for a walk. This is the point, when possible, you must write it down to capture it (having a pencil and notebook in the pocket or somewhere where it is easily assessable, at all times is a very useful exercise) and then test the idea.

5. Test the Idea

Once ideas have been generated, it may be apparent they are not the complete picture or not as great as first thought. However, the best way to test these is to expose them to a trusted judicious few. This may seem a bit of a threat. After all, we may not feel like sharing ideas with others (hence the word "trusted"), and we may be afraid of them being shot down in flames (hence the word "trusted").

What is most interesting is a good seed of an idea will generate more flesh from those who encounter it. So, our idea *(Quantum)* will benefit from the wisdom and experience of others and grow as they add their ideas *(Incremental)* to it. The idea expands into opportunities and possibilities we may have overlooked. What we end up with is a creative solution, shaped and developed from an idea into a practical solution. Why not apply this process to answer the four questions for your business:

Business Ideas

1. What are the key changes in your external environment? (Recall our discussion on systems thinking—strategists must take an outside-in perspective to think outside of the box)
2. How do your core competencies match up to this changing environment? (You must show courage assessing your abilities to meet up with the demands of reality—recall the discussion on integrity)
3. What is the change from the old quantum idea? What is the transformation required? (This requires behavior that is adaptable, goal-oriented, intelligent, learning, and effective.)
4. How are you monitoring the environment constantly to pick up new ideas? (You will need to learn more about **G.R.I.P.** management to answer this question. But give it a try anyway)

Building Systems to Support Your Ideas

Now that you have thought about the quantum ideas shaping your business, you have to consider how to build an organization that is going to operate in the changing environment you are facing. Remember an earlier story I discussed employing a "Retreat, Regroup, and Redeploy" strategy at the City of Atlanta. This strategy should be applied in this situation to rework the fabric of the company at the most basic levels. Note: This strategy can also be applied personally. Keep on reading and learning.

A company consists of technical, political, and cultural systems. The technical system organizes how people, capital, and technology come together to produce goods or services for the marketplace. The political system influences power, career opportunities and reward allocation. And the cultural system creates a shared set of norms, beliefs, and attitudes for people in the company.

Table 15.2 can be applied to both business and personal ideas. For each system, identify potential issues and/or obstacles (barriers). The influencing strategy is developed based on a combination of things you've learned to this point. This is an opportunity to apply what you have learned to a real world problem.

Recall "influencing" is one of the "6 *I*s" of intelligent behavior. It is the art of persuasion. Using the **P.R.O.G.R.E.S.S.** approach, you can begin to identify potential issues or barriers for each system. How? Refer to the idea generation process above along with the four business idea questions. You will eventually use these to develop a high-level, or quantum, influencing strategy. Let me show you how. Earlier in the book, I talked about embracing challenges, giving you examples of the obstacles I had to overcome in seizing opportunities. Here are a couple of them:

Challenge #1 - Professional

As executive consultant/coach/corporate trainer, I was recognized by clients as an "excellent" instructor, mentor, and consultant in helping them overcome technical, political, and cultural barriers to realize success. I am going to use a *"war story"* to summarize a transformation program for a major client. Earlier in the book, I spoke about this project when discussing "the magical number 7±2." The war story addresses the business processes to be managed; the reason why it needed to be managed; the key success factor; the solution; and the payoff:

Organization: ABC Corporation

1. **Business processes to be managed:** Request to understand a customer's purchases across business units.
2. **Why:** No common standards (business-specific limitations within United States/geographical difference outside of United States) to track customers, products, and sales, resulting in inconsistent summary-level sources and unreliable sales and customer data.
3. **Key success factor:** A *lean* realignment of the organization and *mean-information technology solution* implementation to centralize information, enabling executives to implement a strategy to understand each customer and channel partner's business and buying habits.
4. **Solution:** A *lean* organization—fifty disparate business units into seven marketing groups—and *mean-information technology solution,* Eureka Portal/Strategy single point of entry to centralized information in a global enterprise data warehouse.
5. **Payoff:** Common vision. One view of its worldwide activity. On an investment of less than $50 million, a net benefit greater than $100 million within the first five years.

This "war story" is the result of answering the four questions around the business idea using the idea generation questions within the **P.R.O.G.R.E.S.S.** framework. See below.

Business Ideas

1. What are the key changes in your external environment? (Recall our discussion on systems thinking—strategists must take an outside-in perspective to think outside of the box.)

   Answer: Competition is migrating to lean, A.G.I.L.E. organizations— moving from product-centric business model to a customer-centric business model.

2. How do your core competencies match up to this changing environment? (You must show courage assessing your abilities to meet up with the demands of reality—recall the discussion on integrity.)

   Answer: No common standards (business-specific limitations within United States/geographical difference outside of United States), to track customers, products, and sales, resulting in inconsistent summary-level sources and unreliable sales and customer data. To satisfy a request to understand a customer's purchases across business units takes months.

3. What is the change from the old quantum idea? What is the transformation required? (This requires behavior being adaptable, goal-oriented, intelligent, learned, and effective.)

   Answer: A *lean* realignment of the organization and *mean-it* implementation to centralize information, enabling executives to implement a strategy to understand each customer and channel partner's business and buying habits.

   Solution: A *lean* organization—fifty disparate business units into seven marketing groups and *mean-information technology solutions* Eureka Portal/Strategy single point of entry to centralized information in a global enterprise data warehouse.

4. How are you monitoring the environment constantly to pick up new ideas? (You will need to learn more about **G.R.I.P.** management to answer this question. But give it a try anyway.)

   Answer: Common vision. One view of its worldwide activity. On an investment of less than $50 million, a net benefit greater than $100 million within the first five years.

Table 15.3 shows the resulting Technical-Cultural-Political (TCP) Analysis for this professional challenge.

Table 15.3 Technical-Cultural-Political Analysis – Professional

Area	Potential Issue/Barrier	Influencing Strategy
Technical	No common standards (business-specify limitations within United States and geographical difference outside of United States) to track customers, products, and sales, resulting in inconsistent summary - level sources and unreliable sales and customer data. To satisfy a request to understand a customer's purchases across business units takes months.	A *lean* realignment of the organization and *mean* technology implementation to centralize information, enabling executives to implement a strategy to understand each customer and channel partner's business and buying habits.
Cultural	Turf wars—my data, my process mentality.	Implement organizational change management program focused on process redesign, training, and individual **ADKAR**® change model: **A**wareness of the need to change **D**esire to participate and support change **K**nowledge on how to change **A**bility to implement new skills and behaviors **R**einforcement to keep the change in place
Political	Lack of career opportunities, loss of power base.	Develop answers to nine performance variables (will be discussed in the Performance chapter).

Challenge #2 - Personal

Let's do a TCP analysis for the following:

First-generation graduate from high school and college who survived the perils of an inner-city red zone to earn recognition from *Who's Who in High School Athletics*, *Who's Who among High School Students*, and *Who's Who among Students in American Colleges and Universities*.

Business Ideas—Remember I Learned to Brand Myself as a Business

1. What are the key changes in your external environment? (Recall our discussion on systems thinking—strategists must take an outside-in perspective to think outside of the box.)

   Answer: I lived in an inner-city red zone, filled with crime, death, and destruction. Within my household, I had jealous brothers, a mother and sister with mental issues, but a dad who kept me focused on becoming better. Educational opportunities for at-risk kids were becoming available.

2. How do your core competencies match up to this changing environment? (You must show courage assessing your abilities to meet up with the demands of reality—recall the discussion on integrity.)

   Answer: I was a smart, straight-A student with willingness (motivation, confidence, and commitment) to make something of my life.

3. What is the change from the old quantum idea? What is the transformation required? (This requires behavior being adaptable, goal-oriented, intelligent, learning, and effective.)

   Answer: The old quantum idea in this case was to follow my brothers' and sister's footsteps. The transformation required was to change from a "woe is me" attitude to a "just do it" attitude.

   Solution: Attended, applied myself, and excelled at Yale University; elementary, middle, and high school; and college.

4. How are you monitoring the environment constantly to pick up new ideas? (You will need to learn more about **G.R.I.P.** management to answer this question. But give it a try anyway.)

   Answer: My goal was to graduate with honors from every school attended. While in high school, my guidance counselor and coaches took an interest in me in picking out a field where the skills gained in college would always be in demand.

Table 15.3 shows the resulting Technical-Cultural-Political (TCP) Analysis for this personal challenge.

Table 15.4 Technical Cultural Analysis – Personal

Area	Potential Issue/Barrier	Influencing Strategy
Technical	I lived in an inner-city red zone, filled with crime, death, and destruction. Lack of funds.	Educational opportunities for at-risk kids were becoming available. "Get my hustle on!" shine shoes, work in grocery store, cut hair.
Cultural	Within my household, I had jealous brothers, a mother and sister with mental illness issues, but a dad who kept me focus on becoming better. No role model to follow in the household who completed elementary, high school, and college. Generational curse.	Develop a pioneering "I can do it" attitude. Attend, apply myself, and excel at Yale University; elementary, middle, and high schools; and college.
Political	Lack of education, motivation, and inspiration opportunities in the household.	Seek education, motivation, and inspiration from dad and outside community leaders.

So you see, *"It's the same soup but a different bowl."* It doesn't matter where you come from. Always remember, "Leaders are born to be made!" I've just demonstrated to you how a tool used in corporate America can be applied to a noncorporate America environment. This is what my life journey from *Street hustler* to *Strategic hustler*™ has taught me.

The influencing strategy is driven by your teachable point of view. Your ideas are determined by your life experiences, which help mold your values.

Values—Talk the Talk and Walk the Talk

Earlier I discussed how ideas provide people with a common purpose and a clear understanding of their mission, allowing them to work independently toward achieving it. The ideas unify them with a shared vision of what they are trying to accomplish, so they can each develop their own ideas and take the actions necessary to get the job done. Values provide a similar shared understanding, allowing people to act independently by addressing the "how." Values enable people to design their own actions by defining the rules of behavior and establishing the forms of conduct to be rewarded, or not tolerated. Effective leaders reflect on values and work on establishing them just as seriously as they do ideas.

Historically, great leaders have always known morals and values are the cornerstones of society. Moses brought the Ten Commandments down to the Israelites, who had lost their way, not only in the desert, but also in their relationship with Father God and with each other. Jesus, Gandhi, Muhammad—the Prophet of Islam, the Reverend Dr. Martin Luther King Jr., and the authors of the Declaration of Independence all focused on values as much as ideas. They created a sense of community without which we would all be alone, pitted against everyone else in the world. Even commerce would be impossible without shared understandings about the sanctity of an agreement and the delivery of goods and services and remuneration.

As a thirty-plus-year veteran who has served as an individual contributor and a leader delivering consulting/training services to thousands of companies, I have seen that each unique culture reflects its values. It has always intrigued me how a leader could lead thousands. Surely, in the twenty-first century, you cannot control, dictate, or monitor everybody; the only thing you can do is trust. Therefore, leaders have to be sure the people they are trusting have values that are going to elicit the decisions and actions they want.

So whether through inherent wisdom or smart learning, effective leaders recognize the importance of having corporate values supporting the organization's goals, and of making sure everyone in the organization understands and lives by them. In order to do this, I have observed, effective leaders deliberately and consciously do five things:

1. They clearly articulate a set of values for the entire organization or team
2. They continually reflect on the values to make sure they are appropriate to achieving the desired goals
3. They embody the values with their own behavior—I have an exception to the rule that will be discussed below
4. They encourage others to apply the values in their own decisions and actions
5. They aggressively confront and deal with pockets of ignorance and resistance

These five activities allow effective leaders to develop other effective leaders who share their values and who can teach them to other people in their companies, communities, teams, etc. Furthermore, when the values are straight and people who believe in them are in place, effective leaders make sure those values are reflected and reinforced in every decision and action, from compensation and appraisal systems to customer service practices. *Said another way* they not only talk the talk but insure they and others walk the talk.

In chapter 4, "①ntelligent Behavior," we talked briefly about "bigger things" to make a point in understanding; self-centered behavior is unproductive behavior. *Said another way*, a person with a "me, myself or I" attitude will not and cannot "take one for the team" (the team in this case is the "bigger thing"). Within the same chapter, (see "Can You Handle the Truth?"), we also discussed reputation. Let's broaden our discussion on values to include reputation.

You recall when a person invests time and energy with any business entity— i.e. organization, partnership, or any other kind of working association, he or she leaves a reputation behind in these two areas: task and relationship. What did the person accomplish (task), and how did the person deal with people (relationship)? Therefore, we can tell a lot about a person from the nature of his or her reputation. A person's reputation is reflected in his or her ideas (the "what") and values (the "how"). As I proceed, the term "how" means the way a person shows respect for values.

Values form a lot of the architecture of a person's character, his or her shape, and personhood. They do the same thing for an organization or a relationship. What we value is what we esteem or put above all else, including our self-interests, and then guide our behavior from that heading. If a boss or a company values employees and people as well as profits, then he or she or it will bow to the demands of that value, even at the expense of his own self-interest. If a company values the environment, it will behave in ways that are at the expense of just gaining "more profit." If a person values his or her family, then he or she makes choices that cost his or her self-interests, or career interests, in order to serve the greater good that is valued.

But if a person values himself or herself above all else, then when there is conflict, the self always win. If a company values its own interests above all else, then the other things take a backseat. It's problematic when dealing with these timeless universal values; they are like lighthouses. They do not get out of the way, and the person or the company ultimately crashes upon the reality. Universal values such as love, compassion, justice, freedom, honesty, faithfulness, responsibility, and the like are not really "optional" any more than gravity. We can choose to ignore them and not bow to them, but if we do, there are inevitably consequences.

This is what happened in the huge corporate meltdowns of the early twenty-first century. When a few people valued themselves and their own interests as the ultimate interests, the ultimate reality, then everything was there to serve them. This is the egocentric behavior that says, "I am God" and "It all exists to serve me." In the end, they found that there are things bigger than their own interests, and that by getting it wrong they wreaked huge damage. Their reputation was enormous. They left serious damage behind not only for themselves, but also for the very things larger than them as well. As a consequence, they also lost their own interest. As stated in chapter 4, " (I)ntelligent Behavior," the paradox holds true. Give up things for yourself, and you get more. Seek only yourself, and you will lose even what you have. Ask yourself how many people whose attitudes follow this pattern have caused their demise.

You cannot have a conversation about values without integrating it with the topic of integrity. The lack of integrity in these people caused them to forget some big things that transcended them and their interests. Recall my earlier definition of *Street hustlers*; they think short term, burning bridges as they go along. What's being talked about here can best be described as *"It is the same soup but a different bowl."* These corporate *Street hustlers* did not think, or care about how their negative behavior would affect the stockholders, the employees, the investors, the markets, the business partners, values and accepted ethics, longstanding accounting principles, governments, people's retirements, the trust of the nation, and the economy itself. These are the bigger things, the bigger realities. They did not bow to those reality demands, but instead did "off-balance-sheet deals", funny accounting, and lots of other irregularities. They ignored ethics and values. As a result, they brought down many things larger than they were, and all suffered as they learned why those transcendent realities are in fact reality. You cannot ignore the transcendent things and expect all to come out well—you do when you are a *Street hustler*. Gravity and lighthouses have the last say.

By looking out for only themselves, they dealt a devastating blow on the ability of entire markets to function. They destroyed the trust of investors, private or institutional, who did not want to put money in anything because they could no longer trust the numbers. The integrity of long-respected companies was undermined by this lack of transcendence, as well as the integrity of the markets themselves. Legislation had to be passed to make executives more accountable for the reputation their lack of transcendence created. The interesting result is that remedies such as the Sarbanes-Oxley reform end up being debated by business leaders who say it will take up a lot of time and resources needed for other things, and not solve the problem of corporate shenanigans.

The takeaway from this is that anything of value can be brought down by enough individuals who do not bow to the larger things. A spouse who does not bow to the bigger issue of faithfulness can bring down a family, rather than achieving their own immediate gratification in an affair. A business can be brought down by not bowing down to the bigger picture of the customers' needs or the employees', or their values. Always remember companies and individuals that live out their uplifting values will win in the long run. As you learned in chapter 4, "(I)ntelligent Behavior," during the discussion on integrity—character always wins.

A Company's Values

I always make it a point to see the value statements for the companies requesting or receiving my services. As you can see, it tells me a lot about the people and the culture. The following are the value statements for an international pharmaceutical company. They are my favorite.

- We will be an innovation-driven leader in the provision of products and solutions which enhance the health, well-being, and performance of human beings
- We will be the recognized benchmark in providing value to our customers, employees, and shareholders
- Our values:
  - Focusing on the Customer
  - Respecting People
  - Acting with Integrity
  - Promotion of Innovation
  - Fostering Empowerment
  - Supporting Teamwork
  - Committed to Performance

Summary

Effective leaders live their ideas and values privately and publically. Their personal conduct embodies values while their actions reinforce values in others. Personal conduct and actions are demonstrated in ideas. This is the "walk the talk" demonstration that links ideas and values. The individuals included in this book are people whose ideas echo their values. Their ideas are energizers that engage people's minds and open them to new possibilities. Their values focus on the betterment of mankind. I am going to help you put ideas and values into perspective. In the previous sections, we covered the **P.R.O.G.R.E.S.S.** approach, specifically "G," generate alternative solutions. This is an idea generation phase focused on unifying a team by giving people an intellectual understanding that allows them to come up with their own good ideas for reaching a common goal. It is here where one's value can promote or hinder the idea generation process. Changing people's values is even harder than changing their ideas, but in the long run, it is probably more important. *Said another way*, a person convinced against their will is of the same opinion still! Thanks Pastor Stanley G. Wise for this wisdom.

This leads us into our next trait of **A.G.I.L.E. L.E.A.D.E.R.S.H.I.**Ⓟ**.—** Ⓟersistence through Perseverance.

CHAPTER 16

Persistence through Perseverance

Introduction

I touched briefly on perseverance in an earlier discussion on energizing. Allow me to introduce a word that is closely related to it—persistence. Persistence means:

- Finishing what one has started
- Keeping on despite obstacles
- Staying on task

Perseverance is a day-by-day decision not to give up; it is about mustering our will to perform in the face of contrary impulses. What often gets in the way of finishing what we start are boredom, tedium, frustration, difficulty, and the temptation to do something easier and perhaps more pleasurable. My attempt is to not offer the usual feel-good, rah-rah messages. Instead, my focus is on the situations, feelings, and challenges that can, over time, cause us to lose heart or lose our way. When we feel lost, overwhelmed, betrayed, or exhausted, we need to know we have a choice for how we respond. And we have to nurture the rewarding times, when we experience the joy of working together on something hard but worthwhile, when we realize we have made a small difference. I am going to combine both behaviors—persistence through perseverance—and call them *"P-T-P"* for the remainder of this chapter and book. So when you read P-T-P think of persistence through perseverance.

P-T-P happens "in the moment." While we all are different, as human beings we face trials and tribulations and have to make in the moment decisions that take us down unique paths. How did I transcend from a *"Street hustler"* to a *"Strategic hustler™,"* by consciously keeping the good parts and disposing of the bad? As I reflect on P-T-P, there are plenty of stories to share with you to provide education, inspiration, or valuable information you need. The stories will come from a number of my P-T-P sources: my dad, high school administrators, an ex-convict, college football coach, international businessman, a single mother, a pastor, and a former professional football player. As you read each of these stories, meditate on the words of wisdom. Yes, meditate on the words and apply them to your life. If you don't have any comparison, then use the examples in each story and make them yours. You have my permission—*to be great!*

It's Not Where You Start, It's How You Finish

My dad, Frank Lee Harper Sr., a.k.a. "Old Buddy," was a spiritual man who believed God was a *big* God. He encouraged me to put God first in everything I did and he would see me through. My P-T-P comes from my faith in God. I believe Father God uses people to execute his perfect will. His word exists in many sources—the Bible, Quran, and various Buddhist texts. I watched my dad aspire to his level of greatness, within his reality, as a man with a third-grade education. His keen natural ability and street wit enabled him to become an award-winning gun inspector for Olin-Winchester; stay married to my mother for forty-three years; serve as director of the Men's Choir for Immanuel Baptist Church for thirty-five years; be a part-time singer for the Fabulous Ink Spots; serve as a role model to his sisters' kids, one who became a Vietnam hero, being awarded two Purple Hearts and one Silver Star while another went on to become a Grammy-nominated gospel artist and yet another was a pianist for the great gospel artist John P. Kee; keep his kids out of prison and the morgue; and be a pillar in the community. "Big Frank," as he was called, was the nicest man you would ever want to meet, as long as you didn't try to hurt his family. Perseverance was my dad, who instilled it in me as a spiritual blessing with lectures and songs that included such scriptures as:

- *Greater is* he *that is in me than* he *that is in the world (First John 4:4)*
- *I can do all things through Christ, who strengthens me (Philippians 4:13)*
- *No weapon formed against me shall prosper (Isaiah 54:17)*
- *In all that you do,* trust *in the Lord with all thine heart and lean not on thine own understanding (Proverbs 3:5)*
- *In all thy ways acknowledge him and he shall direct your paths (Proverbs 3:6)*
- *All things work for good for them that love God and are called according to his purpose (Romans 8:28)*
- *If God be for us, who can be against us (Romans 8:31)*
- *You are more than conquerors (Romans 8:37)*

- *Beware of false prophets who come to you in sheep's clothing but inwardly are savage wolves (Matthews 7:15)*
- *Humble yourselves therefore under the mighty hand of God, that he may exalt you in due time (First Peter 5:6)*
- *Be sober, be vigilant, because your adversity the devil, as a roaring lion, walketh about, seeking whom he may devour (First Peter 5:8)*
- *Resist him, steadfast in faith, knowing that the same afflictions are accomplished, in your brethren that are in the world (First Peter 5:9)*

My dad always had time for me. I recall being so sick with the measles at the age of five that the doctor wanted to keep me in the hospital. My dad wasn't having it. He took me home, used old Southern remedies, and took care of me throughout the whole night while my mother was asleep. By the next morning my fever was gone, the swelling in my eyes was no more, and the sores causing my underwear to stick to my body had improved to a point allowing my underwear to be removed without me crying. *That's P-T-P*, and the difference between being a father and *being a daddy!* I hurt him once in high school, recall the car accident, and swore to never do it again. Graduating from high school with honors made him and my mom so very proud of me. While I was attending Virginia State College in Petersburg, Virginia, he would write me every week. Along with the letter, he would include a picture of a card my baby sister created along with $5. His lack of mastery in writing was apparent, but he was not afraid to let me see his weaknesses. His effort just made me stronger. What he lacked, he made sure that I didn't. He made numerous round trips from New Haven to bring me home for the holidays and school breaks. I remember one trip from Virginia the car tire needed to be changed. My dad, who was the consummate teacher, allowed me to change the tire. Well, as we were on the side of the road, I proceeded to retrieve the jack from the trunk, place the jack appropriately under the car, lift the car, and remove the tire. My girlfriend, who had made the trip with my dad, was watching. When it came to put the spare on, it would not fit. I tried and tried. Then finally, I said, "Daddy, the tire doesn't fit." He looked at me smiling, which turned into laughter, as he barely was able to say, "Baby, maybe if you turn the tire around on the correct side it will go on!" He and my girlfriend laughed all the way back to New Haven, Connecticut. Needless to say, that was another lesson I learned from him.

During my first semester at VSC, I had a professor who gave the class an assignment to plan their twenty-four-hour day. It was an exercise in time management which was designed to increase our probability of not wasting time, because he felt that was the major reason leading to the demise of many students. I called and told my dad of the assignment and, as usual, he made a joke and gave me what I call a series of "ignorant, stupid, and dumb" speeches. He was not ashamed of his third-grade education because he made up for it with common sense and street smarts. He would say, "A dumb man can't act smart, but a smart man can act dumb!" He would also say, "When you aren't listening, you aren't learning, and you end up being stupid!" However, when I told him about the assignment, he hit me with a different story that I tell everybody who will listen. He said, "Baby, everybody starts off being ignorant about something. A know-it-all will always be stupid and end up dumb. So be nice, study hard, listen, learn, and become smart." His pep talk made me take this exercise very seriously, because I was *not* going to flunk out of school and I didn't want to be dumb! I attacked this exercise with fervor. My day was planned to the minute. I knew how much time would be spent socializing, partying, studying, practicing, etc. This was tough, but I was one of five out of 125 students who completed the assignment on time. Unbeknownst to me, I was learning and applying a very practical skill of project management—time management.

My dad's P-T-P caused me to finish college. When I transferred from VSC, I didn't apply to any other school. My mom suggested getting a job and help around the house. My dad looked at her—I could see the veins about to bust in his head—and in a raised tone told her, "He is *not* working; he is going back to school!" Needless to say, the conversation ended. He told me to go over to my high school to see if they could help me. I will never forget walking into the office of Jack Garrity, my high school guidance counselor, and telling him what was on my mind. He immediately called Mr. Salvatore "Red" Verderame and my football coach, Dan Casey, into his office. Mr. Verderame was beside himself, telling me he would not let "one of the most decorated scholar-athletes in New Haven High School history fall by the wayside." You see, Mr. Verderame, one of the most respected boys' basketball coaches in New England history, went to bat for me when I was overlooked for a state scholar-athlete award. He would always tell me, "You are going to be *big-time!*" They teamed up and got me into the University of New Haven (UNH). Mr. Garrity made the call, gave the presentation, and closed the deal. *This was P-T-P!* Thank God, I listened and did what my dad told me to do when he told me to do it. How many people start college, never finish, and wished they had been persistent and persevered?

Once at UNH, my dad's P-T-P inspired me to succeed. He provided me with a little red and white car to get back and forth to school. As the senior computer operator at UNH's computer center, I was responsible for closing down the operation. My duties were complete around 11:30 p.m.; it was time to come home. Sometimes my car would not start. All it took was a phone call and by 12:30 pm armed with jumper cables my dad would show up smiling; get me going; and follow me to make sure I made it home safely. Every time I made the dean's list, got an award, scored a touchdown, I could see in his eyes the pride and the praise he was giving to Father God. All his life he was teaching me P-T-P. Finally, when I graduated cum laude and the first minority in UNH's history to graduate with a degree in computer technology, my dad could not contain himself. He just simply cried in secrecy and smiled in public.

My dad suffered his share of ailments. He was diabetic when high blood pressure developed along with kidney cancer and arthritis. But with P-T-P and he never complained, winning the battle and surviving them all! I recall him telling me, "What you do when you are young will determine what you have to deal with and how you deal with it when you get old." He was always teaching me something about life. Though I was a college graduate, the lessons kept coming. During one of his lectures, he was singing gospel tunes and making gospel tapes. I was telling him all my plans. He listed attentively and then said, "God is a *big* God." He continued, "Put God first, and don't ever be afraid to be great!" Looking at him, he was no longer physically the six-foot-three, 305-pound specimen of a man, but mentally those words were epic. He taught me how to live like a man and die with integrity.

Before his death, my dad gave me one last lesson in P-T-P. On his deathbed, his body riddled with bedsores from nursing home neglect, I needed my hero to get better. The night before his death, I was sitting at his bedside thinking he was asleep. At midnight, it was time to leave. I leaned over the bed, kissed him on the forehead, and told him he was going to get better. He opened his eyes, pulled himself up, and spoke these inspiring words, *"I got to!"* My dad spoke these last words to me, as he was pronounced dead the next day. Up until his death, my dad was teaching me P-T-P. He started off in the rural setting of Royston, Georgia, but he ended up not in a hospital bed, but on the right side of Father God, providing me with more incentive to work toward earning the ultimate proclamation, "Well done, thy good and faithful servant."

Get Out of Your Feelings and Get into the Game

David White is a former *Street hustler* whom to this day I admire and love like a big brother. We met at his mother's, Mrs. Boomer's, grocery store in New Haven, Connecticut. He had just gotten out of prison and was assisting her at the checkout counter. I would always joke with Mrs. Boomer, and one day we were joking in David's presence she introduced us. One night when I was out our paths crossed again. He was sitting at a table and invited me to join him. We started talking about any and everything. He was older but he was so down to earth. I mentioned my major in college and my position on the football team. He looked at me as if to say—if I've got anything to do with it, you are going to make it! From that point on, we were running buddies. I could talk to David about anything since he was strectwise; in fact, if they were giving out PhDs in "streetology," he would certainly be a strong candidate. I gave him the nickname "Soul Daddy Number One," since he was a womanizer, or lady's man. Soul Daddy Number One was a master chess player who could beat me in less than five moves. On the academic side, David was also trained in transactional analysis (TA). He always knew what to say or do to keep me focused. During my college days, I remember a conversation we had about my dissatisfaction with the amount of football playing time allotted me, and my thoughts went to the question, was I being racially discriminated against? David let me vent and then asked me what I went to college for. We argued, but he was not hearing it. He confirmed with me that my education was for free. He confirmed I was a dean's list student. He had this nickname he gave me, and no, it wasn't "Soul Daddy Number Two." He would call me a "little poop butt turkey" when he was talking "Garbazz" (you recall this describes street trash talk). David, man, could this brother get under my skin, just as a big brother should do to his little brother. But it kept me grounded. You've read my accomplishments; David kept me from being a victim of my success. God sent an ex-convict to keep me from becoming a convict or, even worse, a statistic. When he thought I was talking or acting crazy, he would call me a "little poop butt turkey." "You little poop butt turkey, you need to get out of your feelings and get into the game!" Anytime I would try to rebut him, he would say the same thing. This phrase became part of my repertoire when speaking to anybody. It would amaze them that such phraseology would come out of an educated man's mouth. **Said another way**, it surprised them that I had the courage to keep it real!

Graduation day from UNH was a memorable occasion, but I had a heavy heart. This was because I had learned a few days earlier that a good friend was shot dead in an argument with a family member. I went to talk to David visibly shaken, and he let me grieve and vent, but then uttered those words, "Get out of your feelings and get into the game!" You see, I was about to graduate cum laude, being a first-generation college graduate, and was named to *Who's Who among Students in American Universities and Colleges* and was preparing to start a new job as a programmer analyst in GE's Housewares and Audio Business Division. It was time to be mentally tough (remember edge?) and do what I worked so hard to do. David was determined I would not get caught up in life's circumstances. He needed to say no more, because I knew exactly what he was talking about. I persevered, and you know the rest of the story.

Never Let It Rest

I had the privilege to play football at the middle school, high school, college, and semi professional levels in addition to attending a National Football League (NFL) free-agent tryout camp and coaching (park-recreational and high school) for a combined total of thirty years.

As a player, my ego motivated me to do whatever it took to become the best. Yes, I knew I was good, but I also knew that I would have to get better to eventually be the best! **Said another way** I knew to be the best required me to improve! My desire to be the best allowed me to "See It Through" all the trials and tribulations.

My sports accolades aren't really important. What was more important was the journey that allowed me to develop work habits that have sustained me for a life time. From receiving an "Outstanding Leadership" trophy as a midget football play to being named "Most Improved Player" in high school and college, I learned to always give it my best in everything that I do.

I am proud to say my accomplishments as a coach/mentor overshadow any accomplishment as a player. My blessings provided opportunities to learn, teach, and mentor hundreds of young people and thousands of adults. Playing sports prevented me from being another "at-risk statistic." Yes, I was a great student but I also needed to vent my frustrations and playing sports was my outlet. My coaches and coaching colleagues in park-recreation, high school and college all contributed to my growth. There was Van Spruill, my park-recreational coach, who gave me my first lessons in being a leader. He was also a football official who officiated some of my high school and college games. When I made a play, he had a way of still coaching me during the game. I loved that man!

At James Hillhouse High School, my head coach and position coach were an inspiration in my growth as a person and a player. I improved from being a part-time starter as a sophomore to a full-time starter as a junior on a team with eleven players who received either all-District, all-State and all-America recognition. My performance offensively, defensively and on special teams earned me Most Improved Player. The P-T-P demonstrated helped me during my senior year. We experienced my first losing season in any sport. Though a nagging back injury, which required taking medicine, hindered my performance; I learned to never give up and give the best effort you can. My P-T-P paid off as the honors received confirmed what other people thought about my talent at the district, county, state, and country levels. My coaches did everything to help me get into college. The head coach arranged a one-on-one meeting with Floyd Little—who was the starting halfback for the Denver Broncos. We've talked about my experience with him in chapter 14, "Having a Teachable Point of View." Mr. Little told me to forget the [losing] record: "you got it, so go do it!" My position coach was also my track coach. He gave me my first coaching experience as his assistant with cross-town rival Wilbur Cross High School. I was the only senior given that honor. These inspirational acts proved edifying.

Earlier I spoke of being named Most Improved Player at Virginia State College (now Virginia State University). Because of my versatility the coaches tried me at five positions (cornerback, safety, wide receiver, flanker, and running back). After the annual Blue and Orange spring game my P-T-P earned me a scholarship as a flanker/running back. The teammate who was ahead of me on the depth chart would eventually become a top special teams performer in the NFL, and the Canadian Football League (CFL) where he broke the all time CFL total yardage record, that had stood for 28 years.

Finally, at the University of New Haven, my head coach was Tom Bell, a master motivator who made an impression on me as I watched him take a losing football program and turn it into a league champion. He saw the best in everything and everyone. Always upbeat, he was always in my ear inspiring me. At the time, I didn't agree with some of the things he said or did, but in the end, it contributed to making me who I am today.

Recall St. Jerome's quote:

> *Good, better, best. Never let it rest.*
> *Until your good is better and your better is best.*

The phrase that drives me is, "Never let it rest." Why? Because it speaks to doing whatever it takes to be the best. In the twenty-first century you have to keep plugging away. It matters not where you are in life **excellence requires sweating the small stuff.** People with a passion for what they do sweat the small stuff. They know that it's the small stuff that can make a big difference—possibly the difference between success and failure. *Said another way,* they know turning their dreams into their reality requires a "Get Your Hustle On" mentality. Keep on reading and learning how universal this phrase has become.

Get Your Hustle On

"Press On…

Nothing in the world can take the place of persistence. Talent will not; nothing is more common than unsuccessful men with talent. Genius will not; unrewarded genius is almost a proverb. Education alone will not; the world is full of educated derelicts. Persistence and determination *alone are omnipotent."—Unknown*

These words hang in my home on the wall of my study, and in my heart. For they embody the reasons why I am always "getting my hustle on!" I have met many people who have made the transition from *Street hustler* to *Strategic hustler*™, but I choose to share with you the P-T-P of a gentleman from the United Kingdom by the name of Audley Parara. I sometimes call him "Sir Audley" because he is such a humble English gentleman, committed husband, loving father/brother/son/uncle, community leader, and a great friend. I met Sir Audley during a consultant engagement at ChoicePoint (now Lexus Nexus). In fact, he was largely responsible for getting me hired.

Audley personifies "get your hustle on." He grew up in a tough area in western London where, through P-T-P, he became an honors graduate with a master's in communication from the prestigious University of London. Audley's professional success earned him leadership roles as a program/project management expert for a number of leading companies in the United Kingdom. He decided to try his fate in the United States (US) market, and he has been a resounding success. At LexisNexus (ChoicePoint), he was responsible for program and project management of the two largest, more complex portfolios under Insurance Risk Solutions (Claims Solutions and Motor Vehicle Records). The products and services he was responsible for generated over $125 million in revenue. Watching him give lively presentations to a room of his colleagues was a clinic in self-awareness, confidence, and self-efficacy, all of which we discussed in chapter 12, "Ⓡespect Diversity." He reminded me of a *Street hustler.* As of this writing, he continues to provide expert program/project management consulting services to major US companies like Macy's and MunichRe.

That being said, it is the degree of his P-T-P that makes him a welcomed story I am honored to share in this book. I had the privilege to visit Sir Audley's neighborhood where he grew up. Let me say this, a ghetto is a ghetto, whether it's in the United States, the United Kingdom, or Africa. **Said another way, it is the same soup but a different bowl.** His neighborhood had changed and was now occupied by East African immigrants all "getting their hustle on." I learned Audley is a hometown hero recognized as a promotions genius. He and a childhood friend, Lendon Lumsden, whom I was blessed to be given a tour by, were the orchestrators of some of the largest promotions in the United Kingdom. These promotions, along with community outreach programs, brought him national attention as he was interviewed by TV, radio, and news channels—i.e., BBC News. He hosted "Back to Black" seminars aimed at reinvesting the "black" earned pound back into the black community. He and Lendon set up, and ran an independent school and pioneered a mentorship program in West London. To put it in perspective, Audley was a high-level program/project management consultant who had an outside hustle involving thousands of Great Britain pounds (GBP) and people.

He moved to the United States for better opportunities for himself and his family. Audley defied all reason in making his move the United States. He had no job waiting for him. And he was confined to a wheelchair during his initial months. Furthermore, there was no guarantee his request for US citizenship would be granted. Now this is faith! He attended his job interview at ChoicePoint in a wheelchair and was hired as an enterprise program manager. To quote a ChoicePoint senior executive's opinion of Audley, "*Audley's talent and professionalism as an enterprise program manager were very impactful in building relationships and improving interdepartmental communication. Audley orchestrated the delivery of many challenging assignments that enhanced our strong position in the insurance data market. Audley not only focused on projects, but also people. Audley's leadership of the Men's Championing Diversity affinity group has impacted the lives of many within the company and community for years to come. Special people have a special purpose in life, and Audley is indeed a special person with a special purpose.*"

During a time between consultant engagements, Audley took the initiative to enroll in an entrepreneurship program at Kennesaw State University (KSU), located in Kennesaw, Georgia. KSU was rated alongside Harvard University and Stanford University as one of the top fifty entrepreneurial programs in the country. The program was similar to the Market Smart! program mentioned earlier. The end goal was to teach students to create a business-marketing plan for a business venture that would be graded by a panel of business experts from the metro Atlanta area.

Audley's plan not only received a top grade but also was selected as the top plan in the class! His current strategic hustle was birthed from the plan. It is a company called Informed Associates. The company is a consortium of business professionals who provide specific services to various businesses.

Now how is that for P-T-P?

A Call to Arms

Dr. Yamile Jackson, whom I've talked about earlier, epitomizes a *Strategic hustler*™ extraordinaire. Taking excerpts from her detailed discussion what jumped out at me were the words, "my life has been all about transforming those challenges and obstacles into something positive. At the time I was too focused on what I wanted to do with my life and how to get there." Her next statements are epic because they demonstrate she had a plan, "My thoughts included: emigrate to the United States of America (the land of professional opportunities, especially for a woman in a technical field), become an engineer, finish both master's and doctorate degrees, work for a global and influential company, ultimately to run a company, have a family, and be a world-class mother and wife."

Recall in chapter 3, "Ⓖoal-Oriented Behavior," we discussed having an innopreneur state of mind and the following tenets of Marketing 101, keys to a successful business:

1. Find a need
2. Fulfill the need
3. Provide a service
4. And a Guarantee

As I read Dr. Jackson's teachable point of view, all of these tenets jump out at me. She states, "More than products, we provide comprehensive ergonomic solutions that reduce life-threatening events like apnea/bradycardia* and significantly improve self-regulation and organization, which are important for brain development and ultimately for the long term physical, physiological, psychological, and neurological development of infants. We know the importance of and involve the family warmth to the care and healing of babies. By providing the best possible results, the Zaky and the Kangaroo Zak complement and facilitate the work of doctors, nurses, parents, family, and society at large."

*See definition in chapter 14, "Having a Teachable Point of View"

Her perseverance allowed her to overcome the challenges of being a pioneer. As she continues, "Introducing new products such as Nurtured by Design's suite of neonatal devices into the infant care industry was not easy, especially because we were the first company in the world to apply ergonomic principles and maternal instinct to neonatal developmental care. The medical profession has over time developed miraculously and in the last few decades have made amazing strides into technologies and capabilities that save the lives of babies born at twenty-two weeks of gestation (eighteen weeks prematurely) and weighing just as much as a soda can. Nurtured by Design has focused on complementing the miracles of medicine available today and providing the best possible quality of life for every baby by improving the psychological, physical, physiological, and, most importantly, neurological development of the baby, no matter the size or medical condition, and not only in the hospital but for a lifetime."

As an avid football fan, I am always looking for a player who does something extraordinary to get my attention. While watching ESPN *Sports Center* highlights of a National Football League (NFL) game between the Cincinnati Bengals and Arizona Cardinals, I saw a Bengals receiver catch a pass. He took off running toward the end zone as a would-be tackle approached him at the goal line. Just as the receiver approached the goal line, the tackler stood in his way. Not to be denied, the receiver did a complete flip over the tackler, who stood six foot two, to land into the end zone as if he were mimicking Olympic gold medal winner Mary Lou Retton "sticking" one of her patented landings. I said, "Now that's what I'm talkin' about, *greatness personified.*"

Well, as I read Dr. Jackson's account of her company and what a former colleague says about her, their words have the same effect on me as the Bengals player flipping over the would-be tackler.

First Dr. Jackson states, "Homework, education, evidence-based research, and tenacity are all a 24/7 routine at Nurtured by Design, but it barely seems like a job because we have a 'call to arms' to help babies develop their brain and have as normal lives as possible. By providing holistic solutions and concentrating in evidence-based work, labor of love and passion, maternal instinct, and ergonomic principles, we have been able to rise to the top and deliver results.

The greatest rewards for us are the sincere thanks from people that have experienced firsthand how the Zakys and Kangaroo Zaks decisively helped in the healing of their babies and their smooth inclusion into their families or in many cases helped them cope if the baby didn't make it. Our 'call to arms' become stronger and stronger so we are implementing courses and seminars that allow more and more people all over the world to be able to use and recommend them, making a positive contribution to improve the lives of these special and convalescent babies."

Secondly, Dr. Jackson colleague writes, *"I have known Yamile since 1989, when we were both students at the University of Houston. I remember Yamile standing out as a bright and smart person, and she left a very positive impression on me. Yamile worked as my grading assistant when I was a course instructor for engineering numerical analysis courses. With the fervor and zeal she exhibited to understand course material and perform on her job, I could foresee at that time—twenty years ago—that Yamile would have a bright future ahead of her. After over a decade of being out of touch, Yamile and I only recently reconnected through LinkedIn. Much to my delight, I found out that Yamile had completed her PhD in industrial engineering and has also founded a company, Nurtured by Design (formerly Zakeez), based on her "Zaky" invention to help premature babies.*

As a longtime friend, I am proud of Yamile for her achievements. As a professional, she is a great role model for young women and men to work hard with determination to achieve their dreams.

Going by her success in academics, as an inventor, as a certified engineer, and, not least, as a working mom, it is clear to me that Yamile maintains the same fervor and zeal that I saw when working with her twenty years ago.

Needless to say, if I had the opportunity to work with Yamile on any project again, I would certainly take it. What a pleasure it is to know Yamile!"

Dr. Jackson, my friend, "Now that's what I'm talkin' about, *greatness personified!"*

Brains and Biceps

I met William "Willie" Whitehead Jr., husband, father, entrepreneur, motivational speaker, personal and professional development coach, at our church, Spirit and Truth Sanctuary. I had seen him during church and, from his imposing physique, guessed he was a former athlete. He and his family were introduced to the congregation by Pastor DE. It was then I learned Willie was a former National Football League (NFL) player with the New Orleans Saints. One Sunday, Willie led the congregation in prayer. Having known a few professional athletes, I could see he was a spiritual man who possessed the qualities of being very articulate, sincere, extremely humble, and friendly.

Willie and I have a few things in common: we both graduated from college; we both are members of college fraternities he, Phi Beta Sigma, and I, Omega Psi Phi; we both were college football scholarship walk-ons; we both love the spirit of the Lord; we love helping people; and we both respect and love our pastor, DE. His professional football career and post-NFL career make him a role model for P-T-P.

As I was talking to Willie and reading about him in preparing for his story in this book, an epiphany came over me. During high school, I was featured as a Player of the Week honoree, and the newspaper article had a picture of me sitting on a helmet reading an Algebra book having the appearance of being upside down—boy, was that funny. The caption on the newspaper article read, "Frank Harper Has Brains and Biceps." Willie's P-T-P in achieving his athletic, academic, spiritual, and life goals allows me to confidently say that, "Willie Whitehead Has Brains and Biceps." Let me share his inspiring story with you.

In playing college football as a defensive end with Auburn University of the Southeastern Football Conference, arguably college football's toughest conference, his P-T-P allowed winning a scholarship as a walk on player. He seized the opportunity to not only play big-time college football but to get a world-class education. Willie used his "brains and biceps" to not only excel at football during his senior season, with sixty-five tackles and five sacks, but to graduate with a degree in communications. His performance didn't get him drafted by the NFL, but Willie would not be denied his dream to play professional football. He signed as an undrafted free agent with the San Francisco 49ers for the 1995 season. Though his time with the 49ers was short lived, when they cut him, he continued to P-T-P as he split time between the Canadian Football League's (CFL's) Baltimore Stallions active roster and the 49ers practice squad. Again, his P-T-P allowed him to excel in the CFL the following season as he played with the CFL's Montreal Alouettes and then in 1997 he led the Hamilton Tiger-Cats in sacks and added forty-four tackles. After his strong showing in the CFL, Whitehead spent the 1998 training camp with the Detroit Lions before having a brief stint with the Frankfurt Galaxy of NFL Europe.

In 1999, Whitehead's P-T-P paid off as he finally found his place on a permanent NFL roster, earning a starting position as defensive end with the New Orleans Saints. He and Charles Grant—former *Parade* magazine All-American, first-round draft choice, and eventual Super Bowl champion—gave the Saints imposing players at defensive ends. Willie played eight season of his NFL career with the Saints, and when he was released he had 266 tackles (168 solo), ranked second most in sacks among current Saints players with 24.5 sacks (the other defensive end, Charles Grant led with 33), a pair of forced fumbles, and three fumble recoveries. In 2003, Whitehead earned NFC Defensive Player of the Week honors for his performance at Tampa Bay (November 2) after recording five solo tackles, a career-high three sacks, and a forced fumble. He suffered from dehydration and was admitted to a local hospital after the game.

In 2004, he was voted by his teammates the winner of the Ed Block Courage Award, an honor bestowed on a player who best exemplifies the principles of sportsmanship and courage.

His life after football demonstrates that when you are prepared, you are in position to seize opportunities crossing your path. Through his not-for-profit foundation, the Willie Whitehead Foundation, the former NFL defensive end continues to give back to the community. Many underprivileged children in Atlanta and Union, City Georgia have benefited from his kind heart. Thirty children were invited to dine at Willie Whitehead's Wing Lab in Union City, and they were given gift cards to shop at Wal-Mart. Among his many philanthropic deeds, Willie works with the youth at the Spirit and Truth Sanctuary. I've been blessed to cross paths with many professional athletes, all whom were stellar athletes, but even better people. Willie Whitehead takes a back seat to none of them. He is well on his way to receiving the ultimate proclamation, "Well done, thy good and faithful servant!"

For the Love of Mankind

I have really been blessed to meet some truly great leaders whom helped me formulate the behaviors of **A.G.I.L.E. L.E.A.D.E.R.S.H.I.P.** with a **G.R.I.P.** This next gentleman is from India. He is not only a former colleague and boss but also a friend. His P-T-P is beyond reproach. I took a $70,000 pay cut to work with him because of his very inspiring vision. Earlier in the book, we spoke about Dr. Srinivas Kilambi's integrity. You may recall he is an expert in clean, green innovations and technologies. His passion for sustainable technologies and businesses is infinite and very infectious on all his colleagues and employees.

Dr. Srinivas Kilambi, PhD, CFA, is the founder of Sriya Green Materials Inc. and served as its chairman, chief executive officer, president, and chief financial officer. Dr. Kilambi cofounded Sriya Innovations Inc. in 2003 and served as its chief executive officer, chief technology officer, and chief financial officer. He has over six years of executive-level experience in biorefineries for Fortune 100 companies. He served as senior vice president and managing director of India operations of Chip Engines Inc. Dr. Kilambi is a chemical engineer, serial entrepreneur, and served as chief executive officer at an $85 billion India-based conglomerate, Reliance Industries, and chief technology officer at the $80 billion Tata group. Currently he serves as a board director for Sriya Innovations Inc., which has since been renamed to Rematix, Inc.

In addition to his industry management and technology accomplishments, he has delivered many presentations in conferences and exhibitions spanning seven countries; holds many Indian process patents and six international and US patents; and has over five publications in leading journals. He holds a PhD in chemical and environmental engineering from University of Tennessee. In achieving his CFA/MBA from Institute of Chartered Financial Analyst, India, Dr. Kilambi was ranked second in a field of over five thousand candidates. He has an MS in chemical-environmental engineering from Johns Hopkins and Clarkson Universities with a BS in chemical engineering from Indian Institute of Technology, Madras, India.

Named after his five-year-old daughter, Sriya, the company epitomized his heart and soul in the nascent and blossoming green energy business. The whole essential of Kilambi's ideas is to convert widely available nonfood biomass to sugars, fuels, and chemicals. Dr. Kilambi's ventures also include a startup focused on a novel cement manufacturing technology, which uses 75 percent less energy during production and emits 70 percent fewer greenhouse gases than conventional processes. His third startup addresses the global food problem and focuses on food production through nanofertilizers. His ventures have received millions of dollars the venture capital community, including such companies as Kleiner Perkins Caufield and Byers (KPCB) and Matrix Partners. The combine valuation of the companies exceeds $300 million.

Dr. Kilambi received the "Top Up-and-Coming Entrepreneur" award from the IndUS Entrepreneurs (TiE), a global, not-for-profit organization created for the advancement of entrepreneurship. While receiving the honor, he expressed his big dreams for Sriya. "This is an award for the entire Sriya family and not just mine. Let us all work harder to win many more such awards and become the Chevron of biorefining and the Lafarge of green cement." To date Dr. Kiliambi's ventures have been funded to the tune of well over $60 million.

His love for mankind team with his P-T-P continues to fuel his creative juices.

Perseverance and Uplift = Omega Men

As an esteemed lifetime member of my beloved fraternity Omega Psi Phi Fraternity, Inc. two of our four cardinal principles are perseverance and uplift. Here are some quotes which embrace both cardinal principals from some of our most notable Omega men.

- *"I can accept failure, but I cannot accept not trying"*—*Michael Jordan*
- *"Hold fast to dreams, for if dreams die, life is a broken-winged bird that cannot fly. Hold fast to dreams, for if dreams go, life is a barren file, frozen with snow"*—*Langston Hughes*
- *"Both tears and sweat are salty, but they render a different result. Tears will get you sympathy; sweat will get you change"*—*Jesse Jackson*

- *"It isn't a calamity to die with dreams unfulfilled, but it is a calamity not to dream"—Benjamin Mays*
- *"I'm here because I stand on many, many shoulders, and that's true of every black person I know who has achieved"—Vernon Jordan*
- *"Our challenge is to continue to work and uplift humanity"—Warren G. Lee Jr*

I was blessed to be selected as a United States ambassador, which led to an invitation from the International Biographe Centre (IBC) in Cambridge, England to attend an International Congress of Arts, Communication, and Science in Lisbon, Portugal, and Paris, France. Of all the engineers in the world, I was the only one who decided to seize the opportunity and attended. Still recovering from a personal tragedy, I remembered my archbishop, Earl Paulk, saying, "My field is the world!", so with P-T-P made my first trip to Europe.

Surely, I was stepping out on faith, a brother from the hood trying to do good—who didn't know what to expect. One of the traits inherited from my dad was a magnetic personality. He was a southern gentleman, who never met a stranger he would not befriend; he would step on to an elevator with people he never met and strike up a conversation.

It was an eventful week, meeting dignitaries from all over the world. I even stepped outside of the box by trying out and making the Congressional Glee Club. Unbeknownst to me, my magnetic personality was allowing me to become well-known and respected by the congressional sponsors and my fellow USA Ambassadors. During the week, I attended every plenary session, time permitting, communicating how the arts, science, engineering and technology could contribute to world peace with fellow ambassadors from Japan, China, Nigeria, Ethiopia, Turkey, New Zealand, Canada, Guam, Lithuania, Ireland, and various parts of the United States—all of whom had impressive biographies.

On our last night in Lisbon, Portugal there was an honorary black-tie gala affair held at the Ritz Carlton Hotel. While walking to the dining area, the director general of the IBC approached and informed me that I had been selected to represent and speak on behalf of the United States delegation to greet the other delegates—over 160 attendees from all over the world. I was stunned, humbled, and honored. My dad would always tell me the best speeches were the ones from the heart. I remembered a poem my Omega fraternity brother taught me, "Live Your Creed" written by Langston Hughes. God put on my heart to deliver the greeting, which concluded by reciting this poem. With a heavy heart, remembering my daddy, I delivered my greeting and recited the poem:

"I'd rather see a sermon than to hear one any day.
I'd rather one walk with me than just to show the way.
The eye is a better pupil and more willing than the ear.
Advice may be misleading but examples are always clear.

And the very best of teachers are the ones who live their creed,
For to see good put into action is what everybody needs.
I can soon learn to do it if you let me see it done.
I can watch your hand in motion but your tongue too fast may run.
And the lectures you deliver may be very fine and true,
But I'd rather get my lesson by observing what you do.
For I may misunderstand you and the fine advice you give.
But there's no misunderstanding how you act and how you live."

At the conclusion of the poem, I said, "Thank you and God bless you all, and in the words of my late daddy, who I pay tribute to, 'It's been a plum, pleasing pleasure and a profusely profound privilege to speak to you all.'" Before I left the podium, there was this load roar, a standing ovation—later almost every delegate approached me and told me how much of an inspiration my words were to them. I looked up to the heavens, thanked Father God, and my daddy— because he told me one day I would meet people who have done great things from all over the world. When I got back to my seat, a female PhD who taught at the University of North Carolina came over to me, gave me a hug, and whispered in my ear that my daddy would have been proud. With tears in my eyes, I said to her, "Thank you."

Because of my P-T-P in: my faith, adherence to my Omega cardinal principles, my desire to be **S.U.C.C.E.S.S.F.U.L.**, my association with this International Who's Who organization has proven to be a great career decision.

Summary

Once you have a worthwhile goal, you must go after it with fervor, never quitting until you've achieved your objective. This is P-T-P; the glue required to hold all of the behaviors discussed to this point. *Said another way*, the "**P**" in P-T-P is needed to have **L.E.A.D.E.R.S.H.I.P.** Without it your leadership does not exist.

We've concluded our discussion on the behavior traits required for **A.G.I.L.E. L.E.A.D.E.R.S.H.I.P.** These behavior traits begin with you! The final chapters of this book focus on management. What is management? What do managers do? How should you manage?

Earlier in chapter 6, "Ⓔffective Behavior," we spoke of the book *The Knowing-Doing Gap* (Robert Sutton and Jeffrey Pfeffer, 2008), because one of the themes of the book equated to the goal of "Knowing the Terrain" mentioned in chapter 3, "Ⓖoal-Oriented Behavior." This book provides examples where leaders use various reasons distinguishing leading (knowing) and managing (doing) to avoid the hard work of learning about the people they lead, the technologies their companies use, and the customers they serve.

I talked about hearing of a cell phone company CEO who never visited the stores where his phones were sold because that was a management task that was beneath him, and he kept pushing strategies that reflected a complete misunderstanding of customer experiences. I also dropped a golden nugget stating how often the late Steve Jobs dropped in at Apple stores. That story is typical. "Big picture only" leaders often make decisions without considering the constraints that affect the cost and time required to implement them, and even when evidence begins mounting that it is impossible or unwise to implement their grand ideas, they often choose to push forward anyway. My belief that these unacceptable practices for twenty-first century leadership are what inspired me to write the remaining chapters of this book. *Said another way*, twenty-first century effective leadership requires applying the appropriate amount of hands-on management. Let's swim a little deeper to look at management before learning more about **G.R.I.P.**, the final acts of **A.G.I.L.E. L.E.A.D.E.R.S.H.I.P.** with a **G.R.I.P.**

Most of us in the management profession have been asked these standard questions more than once. They are questions we asked once in our careers too. Here, then, is a basic look at management, a primer, Management 101 from my perspective.

Art and Science

Management is both art and science. It is the art of making people more effective than they would have been without you. The science is in how you do that. *Said another way*, management is an art in terms of its application and a science because it can be learned. There are four basic pillars: plan, organize, direct, and monitor.

Make Them More Effective

Four workers can make six units in an eight-hour shift without a manager. If I hire you to manage them and they still make six units a day, what is the benefit to my business of having hired you? On the other hand, if they now make eight units per day, you, the manager, have value.

The same analogy applies to service, or retail, or teaching, or any other kind of work. Can your group handle more customer calls with you than without? Sell higher value merchandise? Impart knowledge more effectively etc. That is the value of management—making a group of individuals more effective.

The acronym **"G.R.I.P."** implies being in control. *Said another way*, **"G.R.I.P."** implies **G**oal management, **R**esource management, **I**nterface management, and **P**erformance management. Without it there is no effective and efficiently managed business, organization, or personal life. *Bluntly stated,* to be an effective leader you must be flexible, upfront, and in control.

Before starting our discussion, the four basic pillars—plan, organize, direct, and monitor—are applied in each area of **G.R.I.P.** So let's dive into a brief discussion of each.

Basic G.R.I.P. Management Skill #1: Plan

Management starts with planning. Good management starts with good planning. And proper prior planning prevents...well, you know the rest of this one. For those not familiar the saying is *"Proper prior planning prevents poor performance."*

Without a plan, you will never succeed. If you happen to make it to the goal, it will have been by luck or chance and is not repeatable. You may make it as a flash in the pan, an overnight sensation, but you will never have the track record of accomplishments of which success is made.

Figure out what your goal is (or listen when your boss tells you). Then figure out the best way to get there. What resources do you have? What can you get? Compare strengths and weaknesses of individuals and other resources. Will putting four workers on a task needing fourteen hours to complete cost less than renting a machine capable of doing the same task with one worker in six hours? If you change the first shift from an 8 a.m. start to a 10 a.m. start, can they handle the early evening rush so you don't have to hire an extra person for the second shift?

Look at all the probable scenarios and plan for them. Figure out the worst possible scenario and plan for it too. Evaluate your different plans and develop what, in your best judgment, will work the best, and what you will do if it doesn't.

TIP: *One of the most often overlooked management planning tools is the most effective. Ask the people doing the work for their input.* **Said another way**, *get the right people involved.*

Basic G.R.I.P. Management Skill #2: Organize

Now that you have a plan, you have to make it happen. Is everything ready ahead of your group so the right stuff will get to your group at the right time? Is your group prepared to do its part of the plan? Is the downstream organization ready for what your group will deliver and when it will arrive?

Are the workers trained? Are they motivated? Do they have the equipment they need? Are there spare parts available for the equipment? Has purchasing ordered the material? Is it the right stuff? Will it get here on the appropriate schedule?

Do the legwork to make sure everything needed to execute the plan is ready to go, or will be when it is needed. Inspect what you expect by developing the habit of "management by walking around." Check back to make sure everyone understands his or her role and the importance of his or her individual role to the overall success.

Basic G.R.I.P. Management Skill #3: Direct

Now flip the "on" switch. Tell people what they need to do. I like to think of this part as conducting an orchestra. All those in the orchestra have the music in front of them. They know which section is playing which piece and when. They know when to come in, what to play, and when to stop again. The conductor cues each section to make the music happen. That's your job here. You've given all your musicians (workers) the sheet music (the plan). You have the right number of musicians (workers) in each section (department), and you've arranged the sections on stage so the music will sound best (you have organized the work). Now you need only to tap the podium lightly with your baton to get their attention and give the downbeat.

Basic G.R.I.P. Management Skill #4: Monitor

Now that you have everything moving, you have to keep an eye on things. Make sure everything is going according to the plan. When it isn't going according to plan, you need to step in and adjust the plan, just as the orchestra conductor will adjust the tempo.

Problems will come up. Someone will get sick. A part won't be delivered on time. A key customer will go bankrupt. This is why you developed a contingency plan in the first place. You, as the manager, have to be always aware of what's going on so you can make the adjustments required.

This is an iterative process. When something is out of sync, you need to plan a fix, organize the resources to make it work, direct the people who will make it happen, and continue to monitor the effect of the change.

Is It Worth It?

Managing people is not easy. However, it can be done successfully. And it can be a very rewarding experience. Remember management, like leadership, is something you can improve with study and practice.

Now that you have graduated from Management 101, let's begin our discussion on the key to optimum performance, having a "G.R.I.P." *That is*, be in control. It all begins with managing (G)oals.

CHAPTER 17

(G)oal Management

Introduction

Earlier we discussed (I)ntroducing ideas through uplifting values. We also discussed the *Goals to Success*:

Goal 1: Know the terrain
Goal 2: Seize the opportunity
Goal 3: Find a mentor
Goal 4: Radiate zeal
Goal 5: Work with tenacity
Goal 6: Give mind-boggling service
Goal 7: Build the team
Goal 8: Get more from less
Goal 9: Notch it upward and onward
Goal 10: Give something back

To establish goals that energize yourself and others, you first must introduce ideas through uplifting values. **Recall** ideas, or dreams, must be written down as goals before they can be managed to fruition. This discussion on goal management will provide a road map for managing goals starting with setting smart goals.

Setting Smart Management Goals

You can find all kinds of goals in all kinds of organizations. Some goals are short term and specific (*starting next month, we will increase production by two* *units per employee per hour*), and others are long term and nebulous (*within the next five years, we will become a learning organization*). Some goals are easily understood by employees (*line employees will have no more than twenty rejects per month*), but others can be difficult to fathom and subject to much interpretation (*all employees need to show entrepreneurial spirit*). Still others can be accomplished relatively easily (*reception staff will always answer the phone by the third ring*), but others are virtually impossible to attain (*all employees will master the five languages that our customers speak before the end of the fiscal year*).

How do you know what kind of goals to set? The whole point of setting goals, after all, is to *achieve* them. It does you no good to go thru the trouble of calling meetings, hacking through the needs of your organization, and burning up precious time, only to end up with goals that aren't acted on or completed. Unfortunately, this scenario describes what far too many managers do with their time.

The best goals—personal or professional—are smart goals. **SMART** is a handy acronym for the five characteristics of well-designed goals.

- **Specific:** Goals must be clear and unambiguous; unpredictable actions and meaningless statements have no place in goal setting. When goals are specific, they tell employees exactly what is expected, when, and how much. Because the goals are specific, you can easily measure your employees' progress toward their completion

- **Measurable:** What good is a goal you can't measure? If your goals are not measurable, you never know whether you or your employees are making progress toward a successful completion. Not only that, but it's tough for anybody—you or your employees—to stay motivated to complete specific goals when they have no milestones to help monitor progress

- **Attainable:** Goals must be realistic and attainable by average people. The best goals require people to stretch a bit to achieve them, but they aren't extreme. The goals are neither out of reach nor below standard performance. Goals set too high or too low become meaningless, and people naturally come to ignore them. Note: This is critical to being able to Ⓔnergize people with ever-greater challenges

- **Relevant:** Goals must be an important tool in the grand scheme of reaching any type of vision and mission. You may have heard 80 percent of worker productivity comes from only 20 percent of their activities. You can guess where the other 80 percent of work activity ends up! This relationship comes from Italian economist Vilfredo Pareto's 80/20 rule. This rule states, 80 percent of the wealth of most countries is held by only 20 of the population, this rule has been applied to many other fields since its discovery. Relevant goals address the 20 percent of worker activities that have such a great impact on performance and bring your organization closer to its vision (source: Blanchard, Schewe, Nelson, and Hiam, *Exploring the World of Business*)

- **Time-bound:** Goals must have starting points, ending points, and fixed durations. Commitment to deadlines helps people to focus their efforts on completion of the goal on or before the due date. Goals without deadlines or schedules for completion tend to be overtaken by the day-to-day crises that invariably arise in an organization

SMART goals make for smart people, who enable smart organizations. Ecology teaches us that every organism has an inherent interaction with its environment. Applying this important truism to Goal management, remember: Everything in an organization's internal and external "ecosystem" (customers, products and services, reward systems, technology, organization structure, etc.) is connected. To improve organization and individual performance, we need to understand these connections. In my experience, many supervisors and managers neglect to work with their staffs to set goals together. And in the ones that do, goals are often unclear, ambiguous, unrealistic, unrelated to the organization's vision, immeasurable, and uninspiring. By developing SMART goals from a wholistic perspective with your staff, you can avoid these traps while ensuring the improved performance of your organization and its staff. *The key point is* goal management must be a collaborative team effort to be effective.

Earlier we discussed systems thinking as a cornerstone for becoming a learning organization. We are now going to continue to develop this concept. I am going to give you nine *performance variables* as levers enabling you to apply systems thinking to goal management. We will start this discussion by looking at how you can apply systems thinking to an organization.

Systems (Horizontal) View of an Organization

There are two kinds of thinking—systems and siloed. We've talked about systems thinking. Siloed thinking is the extreme opposite. First, think of a silo as a thick, tall, windowless structure supporting vertical thinking. Systems thinking in this type of structure requires the ability to think outside of the box. Products go through a series of internal customer-supplier relationships across functional boundaries in the organization before we see them in their finished state. *In other words,* products are built horizontally in an organization. Understanding these nine performance variables requires thinking systematically and embracing three levels of performance—the organizational level, process level, and job/performer level. This systems (horizontal) view will increase your ability and willingness to engage in systems thinking.

The Organizational Level

This level—the organizational level—emphasizes the organization's relationship with its market and the basic "skeleton" of the major functions comprising the organization. Variables that affect performance include strategies, enterprisewide goals and measures, organization structure, and deployment of resources. As mentioned earlier, this is the organization's internal and external "ecosystem."

The Process Level

The next sets of critical variables affecting an organization's performance are process level. Let's consider the organization a human body. If we were to put our organization's "body" under a special x-ray, we would see both the skeleton on the organizational level and the musculature of the cross-functional process that make up the process level. Looking beyond the functional boundaries that make up an organization chart, we see the customer-supplier relationships where the work gets done. These are the workflows.

Assuming the organization has good people, they will only be as good as the process allows them to be. To manage performance variables at the process level, goal management ensures processes are installed to meet customer needs, those processes work effectively and efficiently, and the process goals and measures are driven by the customers' and the organization's requirement. These goals and measures are called key performance indicators (KPIs).

The Job/Performer Level

A life lesson learned as a Keane Consultant is projects don't fail, people do. Organization outputs are produced through processes. Processes, in turn, are performed and managed by individuals doing various jobs. If we increase the power of our x-ray, we can see the third level of performance, which represents the cells of the body. The performance variables needing to be managed at the job/performer level include hiring and promotion, job responsibilities and standards, feedback, rewards, and training.

Now we have an organization x-ray depicting the three critical, interdependent levels of performance. The overall performance of an organization (how well it meets the expectations of its customers) is the result of goals, structures, and management actions at all three levels of performance. As the director of commerce and information technology/acting CIO for a startup biochemical company, one of my responsibilities include corporate procurement. The nature of our business required ordering machinery equipment, materials, etc., from all over the world. Sometimes we would receive a faulty piece of lab equipment. To determine the cause, let's examine the vendor who sold us the lab equipment. Using our x-ray analogy we know the cause could be in any or all three levels of performance. The performer may have assembled the lab equipment incorrectly and/or let faulty lab equipment be shipped. The processes influencing lab equipment quality (including design, procurement, production, and distribution) may be at fault. The organization—represented by top managers who determine the role of lab equipment in the organization strategy, provide the budgets for staff and equipment, and establish the goals and measures—may also have cause the problem. Let's look at how thinking "horizontally" allows us to address the solution wholistically.

Assembly performers can be trained in quality control techniques, can be grouped into self-managed work teams, and can be empowered to stop the line if they encounter problems. However, those actions will have little effect if the design process has produced lab equipment that is difficult to assemble correctly, or if the purchasing process can't acquire enough subassemblies, or if out-of-sync sales and forecasting processes lead to project changeovers requiring the assembler to follow a different procedure every day. The desire of the assembler to produce high-quality lab equipment will be further compromised if, in this organization, the primary measure and basis of rewards is "the number of units shipped."

The moral to the story is the three levels of performance framework represents an anatomy of performance. The anatomy of the human body includes a skeletal system, a muscular system, and a central nervous system. Since all these systems are critical and interdependent, a failure in one subsystem affects the ability of the body to perform effectively. Just as an understanding of human anatomy is fundamental to a doctor's diagnosis and treatment of ailments in a body, and understanding of the three levels of performance is fundamental to a manager's or analyst diagnosis and treatment of ailments in an organization.

The Nine Performance Variables

Let's continue to extend your ability in systems thinking. The *three levels of performance* combine with the following performance needs to have nine performance variables. The performance levels are horizontal and the performance needs are listed vertically in the graphic. (Rummler-Brache, 1995)

The performance needs determine the effectiveness at each level (and the effectiveness of any system)

1. *Goals:* the organization, process, and job/performer levels each need specific standards reflecting customers' expectations for product and service quality, quantity, timeliness, and cost
2. *Design:* the structure of the organization, process, and job/performer levels need to include the necessary components, configured in a way that enables the goals to be efficiently met
3. *Management:* each of the three levels requires management practices ensuring goals are current and are being achieved

Organization Goals	Organization Design	Organization Management
Process Goals	Process Design	Process Management
Job/Performer Goals	Job/Performer Design	Job/Performer Management

The first column listing the goals and last column listing management are the basis of **G.R.I.P.** management. The variables that appear in the table represent a comprehensive set of improvement levers that can be used by effective leaders at any level.

To illustrate the three levels approach, let's take a brief look at a company called The Millennium Management Group Inc. (TM²G). It is a project management consulting company specializing in organizational change management and process excellence. The company began as a software development and systems engineering firm with 80 percent of its business from custom software development and consulting services. The other 20 percent of revenues were generated delivering training.

TM²G was successful for years but, like all companies, it hit a period where it experienced erosion of its market share. Internal problems include high turnover and sinking morale. Senior management studied the organizational culture and completed programs on total quality, customer focus, and entrepreneurship. The next program was slated to be on reengineering. So far, company performance had not improved.

Recalling our doctor analogy, we realized previous medication (total quality, customer focus, entrepreneurship, reengineering) may or may not have attacked the disease, so let's begin by diagnosing TM²G. We decide to conduct this diagnosis using the nine performance variables that make up the framework of the three levels approach. Thus our focus is on goals and management.

Organizational Goals

It is important that goals at the organizational level are part of the business strategy. All three levels and all of the other performance variables build on the direction established by the organizational goals. In this example, our primary question is whether TM²G has established clear companywide goals that reflect decisions regarding (1) the organization's competitive advantage(s), (2) new services and new markets, (3) the emphasis it will place on its various products or services and markets, and (4) the resources it is prepared to invest in its operations and the return it expects to realize on these investments. Through this line of questioning and applying the SMART approach, we discover TM²G has not established a clear strategy.

Organizational Goal Management

An organization may have appropriate goals and organizational design, enabling it to function as an efficient system. However, to operate effectively and efficiently, the organizational goals must be managed. This involves creating functional subgoals supporting the achievement of the overall organizational goals. Failure to set goals reflecting a function's expected contribution to the entire organization will lead to the silo-based suboptimization discussed earlier. At the University of New Haven, where I was played football, we had season goals, which drove the creating of weekly game goals. At the City of Atlanta, the fifteen departments and agencies had to develop their strategic organizational goals supporting the citywide strategic goals developed by the mayor. As for TM²G, the lack of a clear strategy impacted establishing SMART goals, which made managing goals inefficient. Lacking quantum ideas and incremental ideas, discussed in chapter 15, "Ⓘntroduce Ideas with Uplifting Values," feeds into this inefficiency.

Process Goals

A process is a sequence of goal-directed activities that consume resources and produce a value-added output for specific customers—internal or external. Since processes are the vehicle through which work is produced, we need to set goals for processes. The goals for processes that touch the external customer (for example, sales, service, and billing) should be derived from the organizational goals and customer requirements. The goals for internal processes (for example, planning, budgeting, and recruiting) should be driven by the needs of the internal customers.

Functional goals, which are part of the organizational goals, should not be finalized until we see the contribution each function needs to make to the key processes. Each function exists to serve the needs of one or more internal or external customers. If a function services external customers, it should be measured on the degree to which its products and services meet those customers' needs. If a function serves only internal customers, it should be measured on the way it meets those customers' needs and on the value it ultimately adds to the external customer. In both cases, the key links to the customer are the processes to which the function contributes.

Let's look at an example of having equipment installed by Comcast (cable/TV/Internet) and Stanley Security (closed-circuit TV/security system). The installation process is critical to any company installing equipment in a business or a residence. One function that contributes to the installation process is the sales department. Even though sales may not be part of the installation itself, it is part of the installing process because salespeople usually write orders that include specifications for equipment installations. Because it has a significant impact on the quality and timeliness of an installation, the sales department should be measured on the accuracy, specificity, understandability, and timeliness with which its people provide installation specifications to the department that performs the installation. Installation specification goals are not necessarily part of the sales measurement system. However, when you look at the organization as a set of processes, and at the sales department in terms of the contributions, it makes to all the processes it supports; a richer set of goals emerges.

For our overview of TM²G's performance in terms of process goals, we have two primary questions:

1. Does the company have goals for its processes—particularly those cross-functional processes influencing the strategy?
2. Are the process goals linked to customers' requirements and to the organization goals?

Given TM²G's strategic thrusts and vulnerabilities, its key processes are the product/service development process, the customer support process, and the solutions delivery process (for its consulting and training). There are no goals for these processes. Furthermore, its functional goals do not support the optimal performance of these processes.

Process Goal Management

Aprocess within a logical structure will be ineffective if it is not managed. Process goal management involves establishing subgoals at each critical process step. These goals should drive functional goals and follow the SMART criteria previously discussed. Table 17.1 provides some examples of actual process improvement projects.

Table 17.1 Process Improvement Projects

Motivation	Metric	Baseline	Goal	Units of Measure	Target (%)
Reduce process time	Transaction time	4	2	Hours	50%
Improve quality	Exceptions produced	10	2	Exceptions	80%
Reduce manual processing	Processing time	40	20	Hours	50%
Reduce case investigation time	Investigation elapsed time	40	1	Hours	99.75%
Reduce complexity	People involved in process	5	1	People	80%
Reduce processing time	Cost per request	$840	$420	Dollars	50%
Improve customer service	Response time to client	12	4	Hours	67%
Reduce costs	Cost per document	$50	$10	Dollars	80%
Improve compliance	Fines	$10,000	$1,000	Dollars	90%
Reduce training time	Training modules	7	3	Modules	57%

This is how the information for each column is completed.

1.) Motivation   Define your motivation (why you are motivated to improve this process)—this is a freeform description of the motivation behind improving this process

2.) Metric   Identify what you can measure to best establish a baseline of the current state and then your goal—make sure the metric you use will indicate a process improvement if the value (goal) of that metric is reduced (less than) the baseline

3.) Baseline   Enter your baseline. This is the current value of the metric as a number—the value should come from an actual measurement

4.) Goal   Set your goal—the goal is the new value of the metric that represents what we want it to be after improvement—it sets the scope for what we want to accomplish

5.) Units of Measure   Document the units of measure.—these are the measurement units for the metric being applied to the baseline and goal

6.) Target   Calculate your target—this is the goal as a percentage change (baseline minus goal divided by baseline)

Job/Performer Goals

Just as we need to establish process goals that support organizational goals, we need to establish goals for the people in those jobs that support the processes. In examining TM²G, we ask what job roles contribute to each key business process, and whether the outputs and standards (goals) of these jobs are linked to the requirements of the key business processes (which are in turn linked to customer and organization requirements). Notice the pattern to systems thinking.

One of TM²G's key processes is the solutions delivery process. A variety of jobs in the sales, production, and finance functions contribute to this process. Like most companies, TM²G is not doing a good job of goal setting at the job/performer level. The job goals that have been set have not been tied to process requirements. TM²G needs to establish process-driven goals for each job in the functions just listed. If the company does not take this step, the odds of achieving the strategic (organizational level) goals are low.

Job/Performer Goal Management

The focus here is to engage in line of sight goal setting. Line of sight refers to creating a connection between an employee's (Job/Performer) individual goals and the larger organizational direction; helping the individual to make personal connections with the organization's strategy and their role in it. A key aspect of attaining and sustaining this alignment is for employees to have a line of sight with their operating committee member's overall priorities and goals. In other words think of this as aligning with the organizational and process goals previously discussed

Creating the line of sight to TM²G priorities and the Business/Function priorities is critical to enable employees to set goals that are consistent with the strategic direction, achieve high performance and focus on high priority rather than low priority goals.

Goal Setting: Creating a Line of Sight

A *Strategic hustler*™ creates a line of sight by clarifying:

1. Overall priorities and goals (i.e. TM²G's direction)
   - Where is your Business/Function going?
   - What is required to achieve success?
2. Team contribution to the priorities, goals and behaviors
   - What specific contributions does your team make to accomplish these priorities and goals?
3. Contribution towards the overall priorities and goals at the manager and individual contributor level
   - What are the key deliverables that managers are accountable for to contribute to the accomplishment of these overall priorities and goals?
   - What are the key deliverables that individual contributors are accountable for, to support the accomplishment of these priorities and goals?

Once you've done the above there is one more step before you and your team can "*Get your hustle on!*"

4. Craft and deliver your line of sight message
   - Using the goals cascade you have created, craft your line of sight message both for teams and individual contributors.
   - Ensure that your message is focused and tailored to the audience.

The previous line of reasoning allows you to craft job/performer goals by connecting the dots between overall goals, team goals, manager goals, and individual goals.

The idea of cascading goals isn't new. What's happened is that leaders have latched on to the first part (passing the goal down through the organization) while abandoning the second part (modifying the goal to reflect a unique contribution). The result is an avalanche. The key to creating cascading goals is having a clear understanding of how each successive layer in an organization contributes to the one above it. *Strategic hustlers™* consistently think... *"To achieve this..... We need to do this....."*

Later you will learn how job/performer performance management links human performance management system (HPS) to job/performer goal management.

Summary

A.G.I.L.E. L.E.A.D.E.R.S.H.I.P. is all about achieving optimal performance personally and professionally in the twenty-first century. However, whatever you are leading must be done with control. *This is the essence of* **A.G.I.L.E. L.E.A.D.E.R.S.H.I.P.** with a **G.R.I.P.** It starts with goal setting but it ends with goal realization. In the middle of the alpha (goal setting) and omega (goal realization) is goal management, which drives the three levels of performance. Recall an earlier discuss on the six principles of productivity management.

1. Define the job in detail
2. Get the right people involved
3. Estimate time and costs
4. Deliver tangible deliverables in eighty hours or less (eighty-hour rule)
5. Define a change procedure
6. Agree upon an acceptance criteria

These principles are essential to effective goal management. With a little creativity they can be extended to achieve not only your professional realities but your personal realities also. Here is an acronym to help you remember the purpose of **G.O.A.L.S.**:

G = Get to the defined finish line
O = Obtain short-term and long-term satisfaction
A = Aspire to be part of something *great*, and never give up!
L = Line your goals to connect with the organization's direction
S = Seek a wholistic solution through systems thinking driving goals for organization, process, and job/performer

To realize your goals you'll need resources. Let's take a look at the next area of **G.Ⓡ.I.P.** management—Ⓡesource management.

CHAPTER 18

Ⓡesource Management

Introduction

Ⓘn organizational studies, resource management is the efficient and effective deployment of an organization's resources when they are needed. Such resources may include financial resources, inventory, human skills, production resources, or information technology (IT). Earlier they were referred to as the *five Ms—see* Redeploying in chapter 12, "Ⓡespect Diversity." We will talk more about them later. In the realm of project management, processes, techniques, and philosophies as to the best approach for allocating resources have been developed. These include discussions on functional vs. cross-functional resource allocation as well as processes espoused by organizations like the Project Management Institute (PMI) through its Project Management Body of Knowledge (PMBOK) methodology of project management. Resource management is a key element to activity resource estimating and project human resource management. Both are essential components of a comprehensive project management plan to execute and monitor a project successfully. As is the case with the larger discipline of project management, there are resource management software tools available that automate and assist the process of resource allocation to projects and portfolio resource visibility, including supply and demand of resources.

In extending the three levels of performance and nine performance variables discussed in the last chapter, we are going to discuss organizational resource management, process resource management, and job/performer resource management.

Before discussing each, let me share with you some T-N-T (Tools and Techniques) on managing key project management resources. Many people find resource management the toughest aspect of project management to implement. This is particularly true when many projects and project managers compete for the same resources. Yet there is a simple way to manage the key resources across an organization's project.

Step 1: Identify the key resources in your organization. This means you should know the specifics of the five *M*s discussed earlier. You recall the five *M*s as man (human) power, materials, machinery (equipment), methods, and money

Step 2: **Since projects don't fail, people do**; focus on the man (human) power because they are the *critical* resource. What is a critical resource? The makeup of this group of individuals is probably 5 percent or less of your total resource pool. The critical resources are those people who have more advanced skills, knowledge, or a combination of skills and knowledge that makes them indispensable

Step 3: Create a project in any project management-scheduling tool which contains only the tasks assigned to those resources

Step 4: Subdivide the project into sections for each critical resource; then, in each section, add the tasks for the critical resource only

Step 5: Resource level only these tasks until no critical resources are overloaded

Step 6: Have team leaders manage all other key resources around this critical resource schedule

Note:

- In a very small organization, this technique is likely to be ineffective because everyone is a critical resource
- Once the plan is created, review all tasks assigned to the critical resources with a critical eye to see if any of them could be accomplished by non critical resources
- Avoid having too many critical resources—the more people in the plan, the harder it is to implement
- Avoid doing the schedule too far into the future—use a scheduling window that is meaningful to everyone

Organizational Resource Management

This involves balancing the allocation of man (human) power, materials, machinery, methods, and money across the system. Resource allocation should enable each function to achieve its goals, thereby making its expected contribution to the overall performance of the organization.

TM²G is not doing well in this area. Resources are allocated on a "whoever shouts loudest" basis, and the silos around product development, marketing, and operations are tall and well fortified.

Process Resource Management

This involves supporting each process step with the man (human) power, materials, machinery, methods, and money it needs to achieve its goals and make expected contribution to the overall process goals. The question that should be asked is, "Are sufficient resources allocated to each process?" Have you ever seen an athletic team improve when it gets the resources needed? Let's look at process resource management of sports at any level—high school, college, and professional.

Each team has a playbook consisting of plays, or processes, that, when executed, lead to a desired result—the process goal. In football the play could involve an offensive play requiring running or passing. In basketball the play could be a pick and roll. In baseball it could be a double play or hit and run. In any of these sports, you need equipment, staff, and budget to make the play successful.

This truism applies to everything in life. To make one of my favorite dishes—vegetable lasagna—the following resources would need to be managed.

Human Power (Staff)

- Knowledgeable chef

Machinery/Equipment

- Cooking utensils (cups, spoons, knives, etc.)
- Oven
- Large saucepan
- Large pot
- Sink

Materials (Ingredients)

- 1 (16-ounce) package lasagna noodles
- 2 (26-ounce) jars pasta sauce
- 1 pound fresh mushrooms, sliced
- 1 teaspoon dried basil
- 3/4 cup chopped green bell pepper
- 1 (15-ounce) container part-skim ricotta cheese
- 3/4 cup chopped onion
- 4 cups shredded mozzarella cheese
- 3 cloves garlic, minced
- 2 eggs
- 2 tablespoons vegetable oil
- 1/2 cup grated Parmesan cheese

Methods

1. Cook the lasagna noodles in a large pot of boiling water for 10 minutes, or until al dente—rinse with cold water, and drain
2. In a large saucepan, cook and stir mushrooms, green peppers, onion, and garlic in oil—stir in pasta sauce and basil; bring to a boil—reduce heat, and simmer 15 minutes
3. Mix together ricotta, 2 cups mozzarella cheese, and eggs
4. Preheat oven to 350°F (175°C)—spread 1 cup tomato sauce into the bottom of a greased 9×13-inch baking dish. Layer 1/2 each lasagna noodles with ricotta mix, sauce, and Parmesan cheese; repeat layering, and top with remaining 2 cups mozzarella cheese
5. Bake, uncovered, for 40 minutes—let stand 15 minutes before serving.

Money

- Budget for chef, ingredients, and equipment

Job/Performer Resource Management

Later you will learn more about HPS' components. For now know that providing answers to the following HPS components contributes to managing each job/performer resource:

- *Skills and Knowledge:* Do the performers have the necessary skills and knowledge to achieve the job goals?
- *Individual Capacity: A "yes" answer to* human factors questions regarding *performance specifications, task support, consequences, feedback, skills and knowledge* indicate the performer has the physical, mental, and emotional resources to achieve the job goals. Strategic hustlers™ emotional intelligence, discussed in chapter 12, " (R)espect Diversity," would address these.

For any team, this due diligence is required to evaluate whether the performer has the appropriate skills and knowledge to execute the prescribed processes. This assessment requires both physical and psychological testing and interviewing of candidates. The assessment tools used were discussed in chapter 2, "(A)daptable Behavior," and chapter 12, "(R)espect Diversity." Here are a couple of examples of job/performance resource management:

1. Sports: Draft candidates participating in combines/all-star games along with meeting and communicating with scouts and coaches
2. Business: Job candidates transitioning through an extensive interviewing process

3. College: Student candidates completing the application process which may include an interview with a college official
4. Extracurricular activities: Candidates attending tryout and/or initiation periods to become a member of a band, fraternity, sorority, etc.

These tasks are necessary to build a great team. In chapter 3, "Ⓖoal-Oriented Behavior" we indicated:

1. Not everyone will take the journey
2. Not everyone should take the journey
3. Not everyone can take the journey

Job/Performer Resource Management is largely responsible for determining who is an asset to the team and who is a liability to the team.

Summary

Ⓡesource management is the glue to achieving goals at the three levels of performance. Determining the appropriate resource requirements needs people. Let's revisit the six principles of productivity management from the previous chapter.

1. Define the job in detail
2. Get the right people involved
3. Estimate time and costs
4. Deliver tangible deliverables in eighty hours or less (eighty-hour rule)
5. Define a change procedure
6. Agree upon an acceptance criteria

Principles one and two are critical, because this is where your resource requirements are defined. Here is an acronym to help you remember the purpose of **R.E.S.O.U.R.C.E.**:

R = Realize goal attainment
E = Estimate time, costs, and people
S = Simplify work effort by having appropriate resources
O = Obtain quality work effort and results
U = Understand the hidden details
R = Rework the *second* time the *first* time
C = Check for optimum resource utilization to avoid unnecessary costs
E = Evaluate each resource's contribution to the project

Thus each **R.E.S.O.U.R.C.E.** is needed to realize a goal(s), provide people to participate in estimating the time and cost it will take to realize goal(s), simplify work effort by having the appropriate resources (the man [human] power, materials, machinery [equipment], methods, and money), obtain quality work effort and result, understand the hidden details, minimize rework, avoid unnecessary costs, and thereby make the expected contribution to the overall performance of the organization. Now you understand the need to manage goals and resources. You are almost ready to be "in control." This requires thinking *horizontally*. We discussed this when covering Goal management. Being *horizontal* requires managing the white spaces, or interfaces, within the organization. Let's take a look at the next area of **G.R.(I).P.** management: (I)nterface management.

ⓘnterface Management

Introduction

For an international oil & gas company, a process safety leader visited a plant his company recently acquired to review its procedures. Keen to see how process conditions were communicated between shifts, he positioned himself in the control room during shift change. He watched as the outgoing shift "high-fived" the incoming shift and slumped out the door. The few words that were spoken were mainly of a personal nature. The new shift then took their positions at the console and assumed control of the plant operations.

The process safety leader wondered what the incoming shift could possibly know about the plant's current condition and operations. Was the process running within normal limits? Was maintenance about to take a key back-up pump out of service? Was there any carryover maintenance? Had the outgoing shift been troubled by alarms? Unless the two shifts were communicating telepathically, this critical information was not shared.

People interface problems have existed almost forever, but first came to light in an industrial setting in 1979 following the Three Mile Island nuclear incident. Several people in key positions in the control room made individual assumptions based on perceived observations, and the result was chaos and confusion. Management interface problems were also highlighted in the investigation findings of Piper Alpha, Phillips Pasadena, and the Exxon Valdez disasters.

Today's trend of streamlined organizations and reduced staffing increases the importance of recognizing that organizational changes usually result in interface changes. With this awareness, companies can then make appropriate adjustments in how information is exchanged.

In a January 2002 meeting, representatives of the Center for Chemical Process Safety (CCPS) member companies conducted a workshop to discuss interface management, recognizing communications critical to process safety don't just happen on their own—each interface at the three levels of performance (organization, process, and job/performer) must be managed. Recall systems thinking requires taking a horizontal, or systems, view of an organization. This horizontal view means understanding the white spaces within an organization—the white spaces being the interfaces. The alternative view would be a vertical, or siloed, view of the organization. Hence, you have situations around interface management mentioned above. The horizontal, or systems, view provides a high-level picture enabling us to see how work actually gets done through processes crossing functional boundaries. It also shows the internal customer-supplier relationships we spoke of earlier that produce products and services.

Performance Opportunities Start with Functional Interfaces

The greatest opportunities for performance improvement often lie in the functional interfaces—those points at which the baton (for example, "design specifications") is being passed from one department to another. Examples of key interfaces include the passing of new product ideas from marketing to research to development, the handoff of a new product from research and development to manufacturing, and the transfer of customer billing information from sales to finance. As stated earlier, critical interfaces (which occur in the "white space" on an organization chart) are visible in the horizontal view of an organization.

For those of you who may not be familiar with an organizational chart, it has two purposes:

- It shows which people have been grouped together for operating efficiency and for human resource development
- It shows reporting relationships

As a *Strategic hustler*™ the systems view of an organization is the starting point—the foundation—for designing and managing organizations that respond effectively to the reality of cutthroat competition and changing customer expectations using a Blue Ocean strategy. The *Street hustler,* because of his or her siloed view, succumbs to cutthroat completion, among other things.

For the reasons mentioned earlier, interfaces must be managed at the organizational, process, and job/performer levels.

Organization Interface Management

Interface management at this level involves ensuring the "white space" between functions is managed. In this capacity, managers resolve functional "turf" conflicts and establish infrastructures to support the collaboration necessary for efficient, effective internal customer-supplier relationships.

Process Interface Management

Interface management at this level involves ensuring the "white space" between process steps, especially those that pass between functions, is optimized. As at the organizational level, where the greatest opportunities for improvement lie between functions, the greatest process improvement opportunities often lie between process steps.

Job/Performer Interface Management

Building on the human performance system previously discussed, this level focuses on feedback enabling performers to know whether they are meeting the job goals.

Criteria for Identifying Interfaces to Manage

There is no silver bullet to identifying interfaces to manage. *Said another way*, a one-size-fits-all approach is neither reasonable nor practical. The approach must be risk based and tailored considering the culture, history, and resources of the company and/or facility. This tailored, risk-based approach must meet the primary criteria of recognizing those situations or activities possibly leading to a loss of containment of incident(s) with ensuing unwanted consequences.

As a secondary criterion, the same approach could be used to designate those communication interfaces possibly affecting product quality or volume of production.

Other operating efficiencies might be addressed as a lower level criterion. In many plants, the control room is considered to be the communication hub. But, there are some communications that must take place between different disciplines in the field, and it may not be possible for supervisory personnel to directly oversee these.

Putting Interface Management into Practice

To address these issues, each operating plant or facility should develop an inventory of communication interfaces important to running the operation safely. Figure 19.1 shows many of the functions in a plant possibly needing to communicate with another function.

These should be risk ranked for criticality. Those containing high-risk critical data or information should be documented. Using our plant, one such example might be a shift turnover log. Merely requiring such documentation be completed may not be sufficient; a standard format including the disclosure of critical operating parameters should be considered.

Once the communication list is established, the timing of critical communication interfaces should be considered. If communications are to be standardized, they must be referenced to a common activity or conducted at a specific hour. This will help ensure their rigor and consistency.

On a similar note, interfaces that could introduce error or confusion should be discouraged. For example, persons who are not authorized to approve work orders or to contact public authorities must be made aware of their authority restrictions.

Many large organizations have standard communication protocols that appear to work effectively. These may be entrenched in the culture as a result of experienced workers or reside within the startup procedures and prestart up reviews. When teaching a military project executive managing a $10 billion program portfolio, I learned of such a communication protocol. If your organization has recently undergone change, if you anticipate change, or even if your organization might lose some of its experienced workers, are systems in place to ensure that interface management will continue at a high enough level to control risk? An audit or analysis of your practices based on risk may be in order.

Although we've focused on interface management with regard to plant operations, similar communication processes are also essential to the execution of major projects, particularly those with many parties involved such as project management, contractors and subcontractors, and future operating personnel. This also applies to the project to cook vegetable lasagna. After all, *it's the same soup but a different bowl.*

Earlier we talked about the systems (horizontal) view of an organization. Figure 19.1 illustrates departments in an international oil and gas company. Remember there are two kinds of thinking—systems and siloed. Image the effect the lack of communication siloed thinking brings would have on this company. There would be 25 departments with no sense to strategic purpose. You will learn more about this in chapter 20, "(P)erformance Management."

Figure 19.1 Source of Communication at a Typical Operating Facility

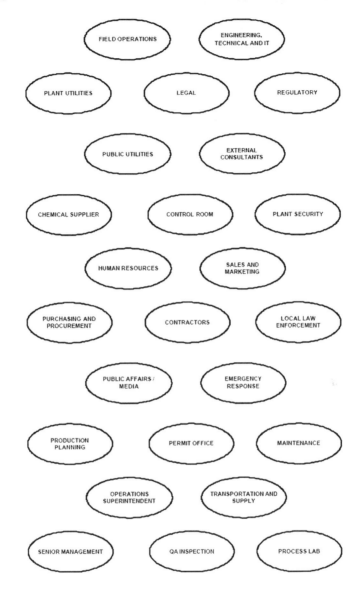

How to Proceed

Regardless of the size of the project, the following steps can be applied:

1. Identify and evaluate interfaces
2. Determine if interface management practices are sufficient
3. Complete action plan to improve interfaces

1. Identify and Evaluate Interfaces

How well established are the interfaces at your facility? Do they control risk to a manageable level? To find out, develop a matrix listing all the sources of information on the left side and all receivers of information across the top. The intersecting boxes on the matrix should be checked if there is an interface requirement. Those interfaces that could result in a significant process safety incident if not conducted properly should be designated as critical and addressed with rigorous standards.

Table 19.1 Example Interface Matrix

Information Receivers	Receiver 1	Receiver 2	Receiver 3	....	Receiver n
Information Sources:					
Source 1					
Source 2					
Source 3					
....					
Source n					

In each cell, identify whether the interface is a critical interface, indicating criticality according to the following key:

P = Process Safety Critical
Q = Quality Critical
E = Environment Critical

2. Determine If Interface Management Practices are Sufficient

The two tables below will help you navigate this process to determine whether interface management practices are sufficiently defined and practiced at your facility. As in any checklist approach, it is important to review all questions to be sure they apply to your situation and you have not omitted any questions important to your company that are not included here.

Table 19.2 Evaluating Interface Management

1. Is a single person designated in charge of your operation or facility on a round-the-clock basis?
2. Are roles and responsibilities regarding communications clearly defined for this individual?
3. Are external communication responsibilities included (e.g., police, fire, medical)?

4. Are formal records and documents passed on to management for their review?
5. Is a system in place that establishes the importance or criticality of communications in the field?
6. Are communication protocols established between key operating positions?
7. Are there any language barriers that might impede effective communications? Are persons identified on shift that can intervene in difficult communications?
8. Is a system in place to communicate the status of equipment between maintenance and operations?
9. Is a system established for procurement of emergency supplies, parts, and chemicals during odd hours?
10. Is a system in place to ensure timely and accurate communications between complementary positions at shift change?
11. Is a system in place to counteract or revoke standing orders and instructions made necessary by changing conditions?
12. Is a system in place to communicate emergency instructions to all personnel, including contractors and subcontractors?
13. Is there a system that allows workers to challenge instructions that may be unclear or inappropriate?

Table 19. 3 Interface Management Considerations

1. What information is required? What is the critical content?
2. Why is this information important, and how will it be used?
3. Who will use this information, and who is authorized to provide it?
4. What is the mode and style of communication? One way or two way?
5. When is this communication required? Regularly scheduled or event triggered?
6. How is it documented? Is there a record of occurrence?

3. Complete Action Plan to Improve Interfaces

Develop your action plan using table 4.

Table 19.4 Action Plan for Implementing an Interface Management Plan

Interface Identified	Criticality	Gap	Action	Resources	Due Date	Responsibility	Comments

Interface Identified	From table 19.1
Criticality:	From table 19.1
Gap:	Results per evaluation per checklist in table 19.2
Action:	Actions to be taken using table 19.3 as a guide
Resources:	What other help—books, courses, experts—is available
Due Date	The date the action plan will be completed
Responsibility	The person responsible for developing the action plan
Comments	Special concerns regarding the any of the above

Summary

By thinking and managing *horizontally*, you will uncover key barriers to and opportunities for organizational goal achievement residing in the "white space" between functions. At the process level these interfaces often represent the greatest opportunities for improvement. Effective interface management requires closely monitoring interfaces and removing any barriers to effectiveness and efficiency. Here's an acronym to help you remember the purpose of **I.N.T.E.R.F.A.C.E.** management:

I =Identify and evaluate "white space" (interfaces) between functions
N =Notice the customer-supplier relationships
T =Tailor a risk-based approach
E =Examine risks and rank them by criticality
R =Remove any barriers to effectiveness and efficiency
F =Find reasonable criteria to identify interfaces to manage
A =Attend to establishing and monitoring measures that indicate quality
C =Create an action plan to improve interfaces
E =Execute interface management action plan

In closing, each **I.N.T.E.R.F.A.C.E.** needs to be identified and evaluated. There are points, called customer-supplier relationships, at which one function provides a project or service to another function. Give special attention to these. There is no one-size-fits-all approach to developing an interface plan. It must be tailored using a risk-based approach. Have you ever tried to eat a whole turkey, chicken, or fish in a single swallow? Probably not; thus, you have to use a divide-and-conquer approach. Apply this same truism to interfaces; examine the risks and prioritize, ranking them by criticality. Interface management removes barriers to effectiveness and efficiency. Remember an effective leader focuses on excellence not perfection. Thus, find reasonable criteria to identify interfaces to manage. Establish key performance indicators (KPIs) to measure the quality of these interfaces. Once the upfront planning is completed, create and *execute* an action plan. Think and manage *horizontally* the white spaces, or interfaces, and you will be on your way to being in control.

Now it's time to put the finishing touches on applying **A.G.I.L.E. L.E.A.D.E.R.S.H.I.P.** with a **G.R.I.Ⓟ**. It's Ⓟ time. As stated earlier, this book was written to educate, inspire, and provide valuable information to help springboard your dreams into your reality. ***The ultimate*** goal of this book is to help you achieve optimum *performance*. The next few chapters will provide golden nuggets of information to improve performance at the organizational, process, and job performer levels.

CHAPTER 20

(P)erformance Management

Introduction

The wealthy owner of a football franchise will often recruit the most highly skilled (and highly priced) talent and wonder why his team doesn't win the Super Bowl. A championship team often pales in position-to-position match-ups; it wins because somehow the "stupendous whole" is greater than the sum of its parts. The distinction is that the winning team as a whole, not just each individual player and function (tackling, blocking, running, offense, defense), is being managed.

Let's apply this truism to a different type of organization—one not involved in the sports business. An organization can be greater than the sum of its parts only if the whole organization is managed. It may have people with outstanding experiential and academic credentials. Its functions, such as service, accounting, and marketing, may look good when benchmarked against those departments in other organizations. However, the results may be less than stellar because the focus is on managing functions and people without placing them in a larger organizational context. There is no control over the management of goals, resources, interfaces, and performance. They have no "**G.R.I.P.**" on the ship, allowing it to steer out of control.

Journey without a Picture—I Don't Think So!

The purpose of applying **A.G.I.L.E. L.E.A.D.E.R.S.H.I.P.** with a **G.R.I.P.** is to increase your ability to realize personal and/or business strategic goals. It is all about performance. You are only as good as your last successful performance. We have all heard the saying, "What have you done for me lately?" This last chapter affords me the opportunity to display my artistic skills to drive home key points and lessons in performance management. Just kidding; I am actually going to use graphics, because as a consultant working for McDonald's World Headquarters in Oakbrook, Illinois, there was a senior director to whom I would report the status of my work. He would emphatically tell me, "Don't take me on a journey without a picture!" Good point; after all a picture is worth a thousand words. So the pictures you are about to be exposed to will illustrate and reinforce key points enabling you to measure, monitor, and manipulate goals, resources, and interfaces at the organizational, process, and job/performer levels. As Aristotle pointed out, "The soul never thinks without an image."

Organization Performance Management

Earlier we spoke of three levels of performance. To understand what a person is thinking, you should walk in his or her shoes. Recall that people of integrity demonstrate six qualities; one being able to connect with people and build trust. Thus our first step in managing organization performance is to acknowledge the viewpoints that often characterize an underperforming situation from the customers, suppliers, employees, and shareholders.

The *customer's view of the organization* could be, "What is going on with these people? Why can't they give me a product that does what I need it to do the first time? Where is the customer service I was told I'd be getting? Why do I feel more knowledgeable about the product than they do? Why can't there be a single point of contact each time I contact them? Why can't these people get their act together?"

The *supplier's view of the organization* could be, "Why don't these people ever know what parts they need more than three days ahead of time? Do they realize that when last minute orders have to be expedited it costs more? Why do they keep changing the specifications? Why do they discontinue at least one product every four months, which results in a large number of part returns? Why don't they ever accept our offer to visit their plant, at our expense, so we can learn what's happening in their business? Why can't these people get their act together?"

The *employees' view of the organization* could be, "Why can't we match our competitor's quality using more cost effective quality assurance and quality control? Who told sales that we have the capacity to offer that service and meet that deadline? Where do the product development people come up with these ideas? So, what are our priorities this week? Why don't department managers cooperate with each other? Don't these people realize that if we don't change the way we do business, we won't survive? How does top management expect us to believe that quality comes first when, at the end of every month, they say 'I don't care; ship it! Why are these people, who are paid above the industry average, still not motivated? Why can't we get our act together?"

The *shareholders' view of the organization* could be, "Why do I continuously see reorganizations, executive shuffles, product launches, and improvement campaigns, but no money in my pocket or increase in the value of my stock? Why can't these people get their act together?"

Linking Performance to Strategy

Before we can effectively address the bleak but all-too-common situation just depicted, we have to understand it. It is my viewpoint that any project or program must be linked to a strategy objective to justify allocation of the five Ms. The essence of the behaviors associated with **A.G.I.L.E. L.E.A.D.E.R.S.H.I.P.** is to promote a big picture, or strategic, view of the organization. Without it, it is impossible to achieve and demand excellence because you don't know the extent of the contribution that your effort contributes to the whole.

Organizational strategy, structuralist or reconstructionist, is made up of three parts: strategy assessment, strategy formulation, and strategy execution. There are many questions to crafting a winning strategy they include but are not limited to: what are the industry/environment conditions and where do we stand as an organization in relation to our competitors (assessment); what are we going to do about it to gain a competitive advantage (formulation) and how are we going achieve the desired strategic results (execution).

We are going to cover some questions that require you to think *strategically*. These questions need to be answered if an organization's strategy is going to guide the three levels of performance. Later, I will discuss an approach used for measuring, managing and communicating strategy called a Balanced Scorecard. For now, at the core of strategy formulation are five strategic elements. They begin with Marketing 101:

1. Finding a need
2. Fulfilling the need
3. Providing a service
4. And a guarantee

Earlier during our Market Smart! discussion we learned *marketing drives the business*. Thus Marketing 101 drives the following five strategic elements:

1. Products and services you will offer
2. Customers and markets you will serve

3. Competitive advantage
4. Product and market priorities
5. Systems and structures

Regardless of the business size each element of Marketing 101 mandates answering five fundamental business strategy questions. Table 20.1 shows the relationship.

Table 20.1 Strategic Relationships

Marketing Strategy Element	Business Strategy Element	Strategy Formulation Question
Finding a need Providing a service	Products and services we will offer	1.) What we are going to do?
Finding a need	Customers and markets we will serve	2.) Whom will we do it for?
Finding a need Fulfilling the need Providing a service And a guarantee	Competitive advantages	3.) Why will the customers buy from us?
Fulfilling the need	Product and market priorities	4.) Where will we place our emphasis?
Fulfilling the need	Systems and structures	5.) How are we going to deliver our: product and/or service, business identity, business values, and to our customer's locations?

The key point is that marketing strategy is business strategy. Remember Marketing 101 and you will have a good foundation for understanding business strategy. With that being said, the five strategic elements are not all there is to strategy. All other strategic analysis, decisions, and actions are either:

- Inputs to the first four elements (market research, industry analysis, competitive analysis, environmental monitoring, portfolio planning)
- Ways of measuring the effectiveness of the first four elements (financial results, market share, nonfinancial critical success factors)
- Philosophical guides to all five elements (values, culture)

- Subparts of the fifth element (budgets, marketing plans, human resource plans, technology plans)
- Problem solving and action planning to remove barriers to the fifth element

What questions need to be answered before improving organization performance? The absence of answers to these questions creates an organizational ship with no rudder. I am going to refer to these questions as "the five elements of a strategic rudder."

Questions that focus on fulfilling the need (element five):

1. What values are going to guide our business?
2. How far down the road, are we going to look?
3. What assumptions about the external environment (regulation, the economy, resource availability, technology, competition, the market) stabilize the foundation of our strategy?

Questions that address finding the need and providing a service (element one):

4. What existing and new products and services will we be offering (and not offering)?
5. What criteria will we use to evaluate a new product or service opportunities?

Questions that address finding a need (element two):

6. What existing and new customer groups will we be serving (and not serving)?
7. What criteria will we use to evaluate a new market opportunity?

Questions that address Marketing 101 (element three):

8. What factors (price and/or the various dimensions of quality) are meaningful to our customers?
9. Which of these factors will represent our competitive advantages?

Questions that address fulfilling the need (element four):

10. In which of our current product or market areas will we be placing the greatest emphasis (resources and attention)?
11. In what new product or market areas will we be placing the greatest emphasis?

Figure 20.1 illustrates "The five elements of a strategic rudder" applied to a "super system map" which shows an organization is a processing system. By answering the above questions it helps to effectively define each part of the systems view of performance discussed earlier.

Figure 20.1: The Impact of Strategy on the Components of an Organization System

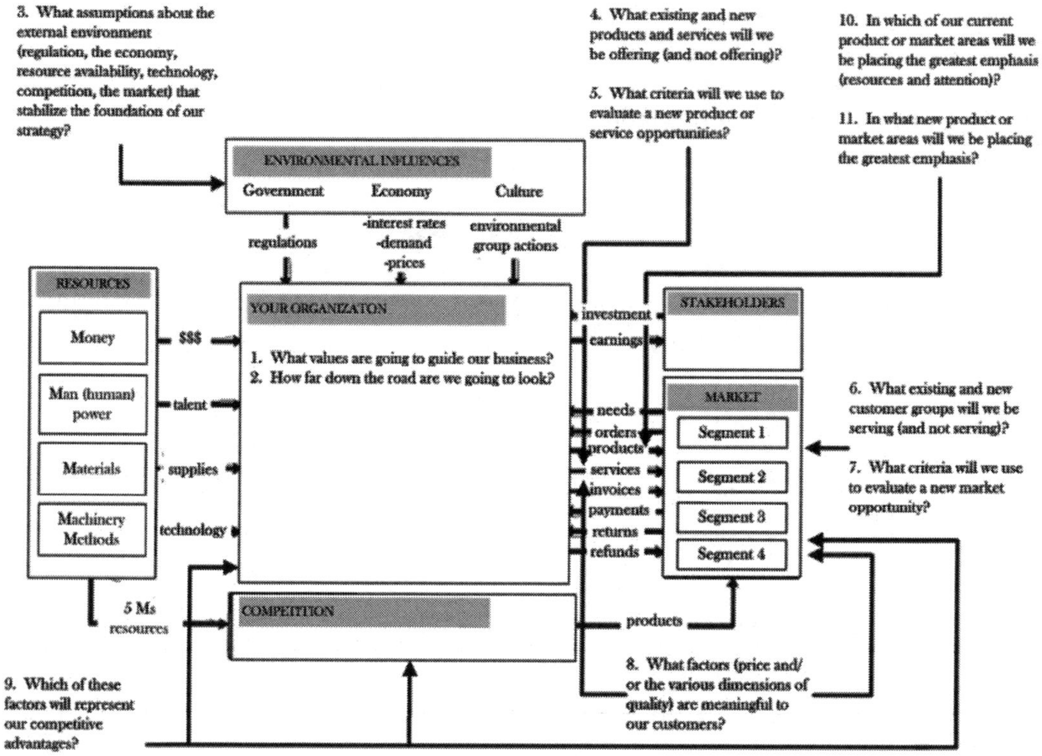

Source: Intelligent Systems Services, LLC

Without a strategy, performance management becomes at best a guessing game. Recall from our earlier discussion on leaders and managers that "managers do things right; leaders do the right things." The right things are those activities that are in alignment with a well-articulated strategy.

Managing the Organizational Level

Operational excellence begins with managing performance at the organizational level. Star performers seek answers to the above questions as a starting point to achieve optimum performance. Without this, all efforts at other levels will be unsuccessful. In fact, a transformation program whose goal is performance improvement is a high-risk endeavor with a failure rate estimated to be in the range of 65 percent to 85 percent, according to the Working Council of Chief Financial Officers (CFOs). Business transformation gains aren't more dramatic because:

- The various business transformation efforts are not driven by a clear statement of organization strategy. The strategy should define the role of process improvement in the business, the kinds of process improvement that represents the competitive advantage, and the organization-wide, customer-driven measures of process improvement.
- The organization has not been designed in a way that supports optimum transformation. The impact of the noble efforts in training, tools, systems, and procedures is limited by the organization structure, and relationships among departments.
- The organization is not managed with transformation as the driver. Transformation has not been built into tactical goals, performance tracking, feedback, problem solving, or resource allocation. Transformation typically has a focus on technology instead of people and process. The tremendous threats and opportunities within the white space, or interfaces, on the organization chart are ignored.

Each of these shortcomings represents a failure to manage one of the three performance variables at the organizational level. To "get their act together" (the plea of the customers, suppliers, shareholders, and employees quoted at the beginning of this chapter), effective leaders must understand and pull the levers of organizational goals, organizational design, and organizational management. The answers to the above questions help focus strategic management.

The Performance Variables at the Organizational Level

Though I will mention organizational design, the focus of this book is on organizational goals and organizational management. Organizational goals are strategic goals. I am going to introduce you to a best-in-class approach for strategic performance management. It is called a Balanced Scorecard. Introduced in 1992 by Robert Kaplan and David Norton, the Balanced Scorecard is the most commonly used framework for ensuring that agencies execute their strategies. Today, about 70 percent of the Fortune 1,000 companies utilize the Balanced Scorecard to help manage performance. Balanced Scorecard is a strategic performance management framework that allows organizations to manage and measure the delivery of their strategy.

Why use a Balanced Scorecard?

- It allows the organization to become more "strategically focused"
- People at all levels have relied heavily on tactical performance measurements, such as a number of maps
- It provides a more balanced approach to looking at performance, both tactical and strategic
- It helps the workforce understand their company's strategy
- Executive teams can have productive meetings discussing strategy

There are some basic principles you need to understand about this strategic performance management tool. The Balanced Scorecard:

- Quantifies the organizational strategy in measurable terms. Remember, if you don't measure it, then you can't manage it–you are going to learn more about the basics of good performance measures later
- Strategy is summarized on a Strategy Map over four views of performance (perspectives)—we will look at these four views of performance in detail
- A cause-effect relationship must be captured between strategic objectives over the four perspectives on the strategy map—this is critical for driving the execution throughout the organization, as you will learn
- Critical components include measurements, targets, and initiatives
- Everything must be linked: goals to objectives, objectives to measurements, and measurements to targets

Balanced Scorecard Perspectives

Like most good ideas, the concept of the Balanced Scorecard is very simple. Kaplan and Norton identified four generic perspectives that cover the main strategic focus areas of a company. The idea was to use this model as a template for designing objectives and measures in each of the following perspectives.

- The **Financial Perspective** covers the financial objectives of an organization and allows managers to track financial success and shareholder value
- The **Customer Perspective** covers the customer objectives, such as customer satisfaction, market share goals, as well as product and service attributes
- The **Internal Process Perspective** covers internal operational goals and outlines the key processes necessary to deliver the customer objectives
- The **Learning and Growth Perspective** covers the intangible drivers of future success such as human capital, organizational capital, and information capital, including skills, training, organizational culture, leadership, systems, and databases

Understanding Cause-Effect Relationships

This is a book for the ages, so I am going to assume that some readers may be unfamiliar with the term "cause-effect." For every problem or quality characteristic, there is a possible reason, or cause, for its existence. The concept of cause-effect applies to everyday life, not just strategic performance management. Here are some basic examples.

Tim forgot his math book, so he was unable to complete his homework.
Cause: Tim forgot his math book.
Effect: He was unable to complete his homework.

Keegan was hungry because he skipped lunch.
Cause: Keegan skipped lunch.
Effect: He was hungry.

Erin's car had a flat tire, so she called a tow truck.
Cause: Erin's car had a flat tire.
Effect: She called a tow truck

Erica studied her spelling words and she got an A on the test.
Cause: Erica studied her spelling words.
Effect: She got an A on her test.

Cause-and-Effect Logic

A strategy map highlights that delivering the right performance in one perspective (e.g., financial success) can only be achieved by delivering the objectives in the other perspectives (e.g., delivering what customers want). You basically create a map of interlinked objectives. For example:

- The objectives in the Learning and Growth Perspective (e.g., developing the right competencies) underpin the objectives in the Internal Process Perspective (e.g., delivering high-quality business processes)
- The objectives in the Internal Process Perspective (e.g., delivering high-quality business processes) underpin the objectives in the Customer Perspective (e.g., gaining market share and repeat business)
- Delivering the customer objectives should then lead to the achievement of the financial objectives in the Financial Perspective

Strategy maps, therefore, outline what an organization(s) wants to accomplish (financial and customer objectives) and how it plans to accomplish it (internal process and learning and growth objectives). This cause-and-effect logic is one of the most important elements of best-practice Balanced Scorecards. It allows companies to create a truly integrated set of strategic objectives. The danger with the initial four-box model was that companies can easily create a number of objectives and measures for each perspective without ever linking them. This can lead to silo activities as well as a strategy that is not cohesive or integrated.

The following diagram illustrates four views of strategic performance. Note: This is from a previous Balanced Scorecard presentation delivered to a government client. I interchanged "Customer" with "Stakeholder" and "Financial" with "Organization Investment."

Four Views of Strategic Performance Management

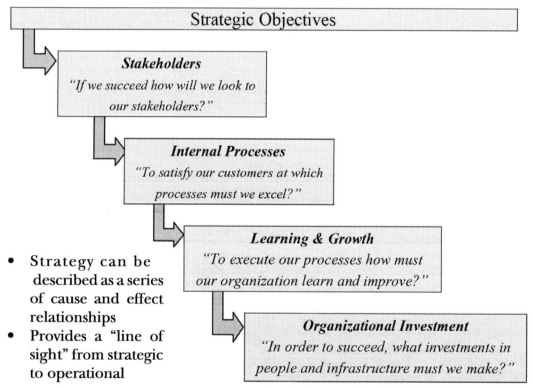

A stakeholder is a person who has the most to gain/lose by achieving specific strategic objectives. As you can see, the diagram depicts a series of cause-and-effect relationships, from strategic objectives, which flow to internal processes view, which flows to learning and growth view, which flows to organization investments view. Figure 20.2 illustrates the "line of sight" goal setting created by this alignment.

Figure 20.2 "Line of Sight" for a government client

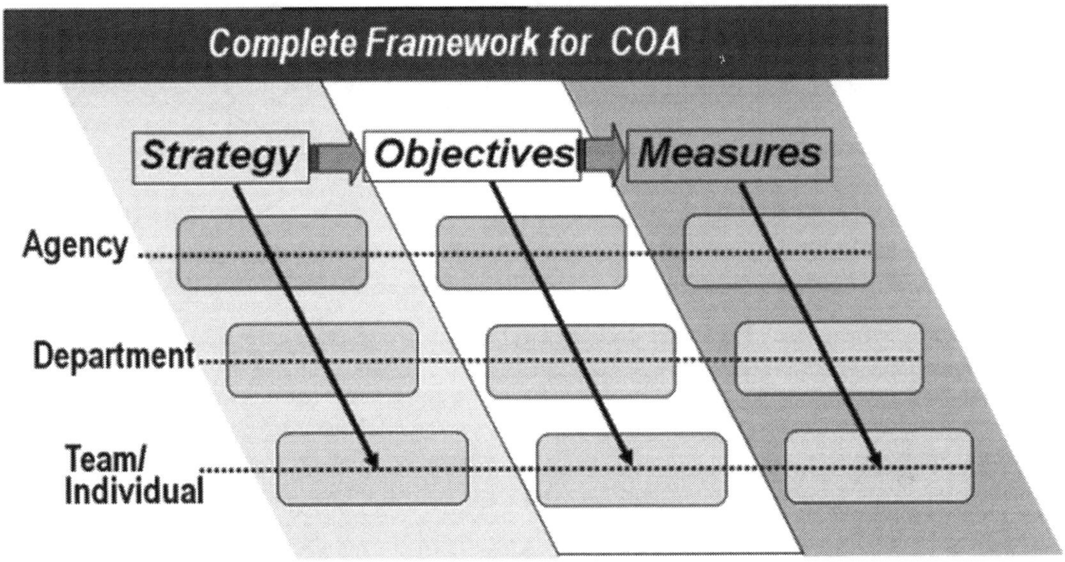

Source: Intelligent Systems Services, LLC

Developing a strategy using a balanced scorecard approach begins with developing strategy maps. Before you can map a strategy, we have to get down to a set of quantifiable strategic objectives. In chapter 17, "Ⓖoal Management," we discussed the **S.M.A.R.T.** criteria for setting smart goals. An objective such as "improve customer service" is too vague. A more precise objective would be to reduce average wait times by 30 percent by year end. Remember to make sure your objectives have a direct relationship to your goals and your goals have a direct relationship to your mission and values. We will talk more about basic guidelines for good performance measures later.

Creating a Strategy Map

When it was first introduced, the Balanced Scorecard perspectives were presented in a four-box model. Early adopters created Balanced Scorecards that were primarily used as improved performance measurement systems, and many organizations produced management dashboards to provide a more comprehensive at a glance view of key performance indicators in these four perspectives.

However, this four-box model has now been superseded by a strategy map (see below), which is the heart of modern Balanced Scorecards. A strategy map places the four perspectives in relation to each other to show that the objectives support each other. Figure 20.3 illustrates an example of a strategy map developed for a biopharmaceutical client.

Figure 20.3: Strategy Map for Biopharmaceutical Company

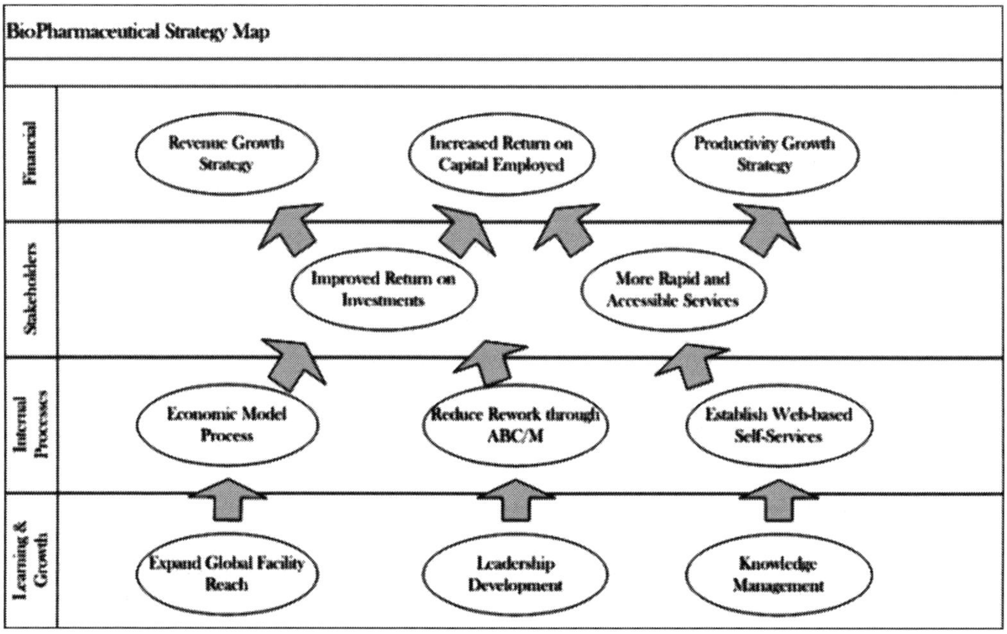

Source: Intelligent Systems Services, LLC

Balanced Scorecards tell you the knowledge, skills, and systems that your employees will need (learning and growth) to innovate and build the right strategic capabilities and efficiencies (internal processes) that deliver specific value to the market (stakeholder, customer), which will eventually lead to higher shareholder value (financial). Note: organizational capacity and learning and growth will be used interchangeably in this book.

Key Benefits of Strategy Maps

Recall a picture is worth a thousand words. Through a picture, your organization will:

1. Articulate how the organization creates value for its stakeholders.
2. Display key priorities and relationships between outcomes (the "what") and performance enablers or drivers (the "how).
3. Provide a clear view of "how I fit in" for suborganizations, teams, and individuals.

4. Cascade the scorecard throughout the organization and clearly map the various units and functions back to the organization or agency-wide map, which is critical to leveraging and ensuring alignment.

Cascading the scorecard throughout the organization is done once you have completed your strategy map to make sure it aligns with agencies or divisions you report up to. This overall alignment of scorecards throughout the entire organization forms the strategic management system for our client, XYZ Company.

Figure 20.4: Strategy Map for XYZ Company

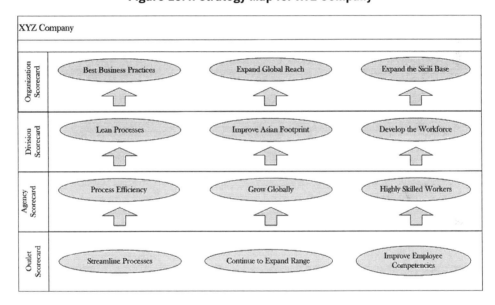

Source: Intelligent Systems Services, LLC

From Strategic Theme to Strategy Map

Strategic Themes

A discussion on organization performance management would not be complete without talking about strategic themes. Strategic themes are essential strategic elements that form the foundation for a balanced scorecard. However, once the scorecard is built, the fundamental role they play is not always clear to the naked eye.

Think of a strategic theme as a "load-bearing wall." Look around your office or house. Can you readily point out the load-bearing walls? If you have ever embarked on a remodel of your home or office, you quickly learn that load-bearing walls not only play a critical role in supporting the entire structure of your building, but their placement and design may actually dictate what you can and cannot do in terms of redesigning the layout and function of your space.

The same is true of strategic themes. They provide structure, support, and often boundaries for your strategic balanced scorecard. More importantly, they define your business strategies and business model.

This section will address how strategic themes are developed and used in a strategic balanced scorecards system.

Developing Strategic Themes

Strategic themes are the main, high-level business strategies that form the basis for the organization's business model. They are part of the strategic planning work of building a balanced scorecard. The vision, a picture of the future or designed future state, is agreed upon then systematically decomposed into three or four strategic themes. I sometimes refer to themes as "pillars of excellence". The strategic themes (pillars of excellence) are very broad in scope. They apply to every part of the organization and define what major strategic thrusts the organization will pursue to achieve its vision. Themes affect all four of the balanced scorecard perspectives (financial, customer, internal process, learning and growth). Understand, a strategic theme is an area in which your organization must excel in order to achieve your vision.

Developing strategic themes requires considerations of other strategic elements, such as the challenges, enablers, customer value proposition, and other components of the strategic assessment work. Themes also represent deliberate strategic directional decisions made by the leadership team. Taken together, one can look at the proposed set of strategic themes and ask this question: "If we excel in these three or four areas, will we achieve our vision?" and receive a resounding answer of "Yes!" This is similar to an engineer looking at an architecture design and answering this question, "If we put these walls of this thickness in these locations, will the building stand solid?"

Strategic Themes and Strategic Result(s)

Each theme has a "strategic result" associated with it. This is a statement of a desired end state. *Said another way*, how will you know when you have achieved success? Recalling one of the six productivity management principles discussed earlier, the result is stated in such a way that you will clearly recognize success when you see it. Strategic results are measurable and explicitly defined using language that describes the impact on the business/client (outcome language).

For example, in addition to stating that employment and training services were provided to fifty clients, outcome language would state that of those fifty clients receiving employment and training services:

- Ten obtained full-time jobs above minimum wage, including benefits, and are employed ninety days after placement
- Twenty obtained permanent full-time jobs at minimum wage without benefits
- Ten obtained part-time temporary jobs
- Five are participating in on-the-job training programs
- Five remain unemployed after ninety days in the program

Strategic themes are often similar from organization to organization. Some of the examples I've come across include business growth, operational excellence, customer service excellence, innovation, and sustainability. However, *what makes strategy different, or a strategic differentiator, lies in the strategic results.* The uniqueness of the result guides the organizational transformation. For example, for a biopharmaceutical client, the result of business growth might be, "We supply biopharmaceutical products and services our customers need when they need them, now and in the future," and might be measured by a "build the business composite indicator" (made up of market share, biopharmaceutical availability ratio, and a new services customer acceptance ratio). For a financial services client, this same theme might have a completely different strategic result, such as "Our customers choose us over other lenders in all the financial markets we serve, now and in the future" and be measured by a compound measure of current and future-looking indicators. We will look at more concrete examples later.

Figure 20.5 illustrates the strategic elements that form the structure of the balanced scorecard "house." The roof represents the mission (what is our purpose) and vision (what are we trying to achieve). The balanced scorecard perspectives represent the floors of the house. These are the lenses, the dimensions of performance through which the organization is viewed. The foundation of the house represents the human dimensions of the system—without fully engaged leadership and proactive communications and change management; your house is built on shaky ground. The strategic themes/results are the load-bearing walls which support the missions and vision of the organization and provide stability by linking all the way from the foundation, through each perspective level, to the roof.

Figure 20.5: Strategic Themes are the Pillars that Support the Mission and Vision

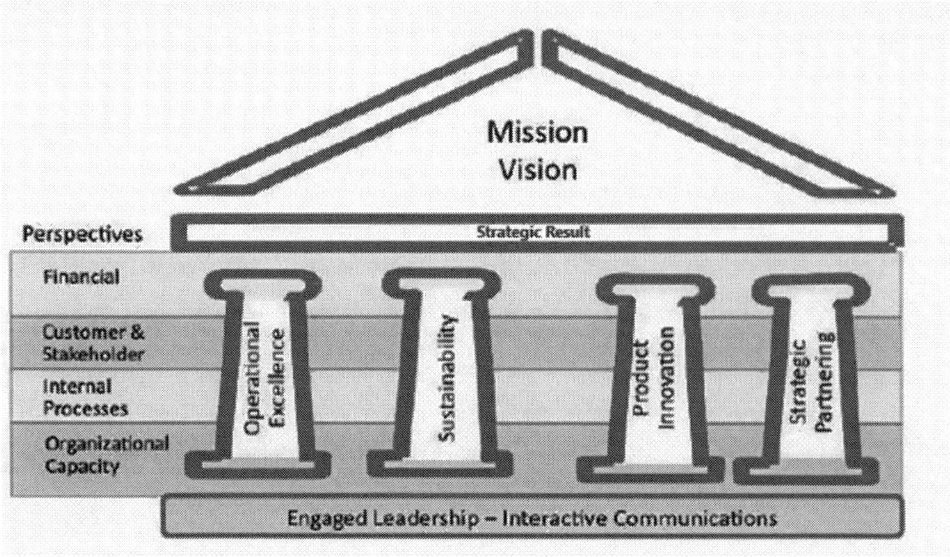

Source: Intelligent Systems Services, LLC / Terry L. Harper Jr., Artist

Translation Themes into Strategy Maps

We spoke earlier on creating strategy maps. Now I want to show you the relationship between themes and strategy maps. Remember effective leaders have a teachable point of view that is based on their ability to tell life stories see chapter 14, "(H)ave a Teachable Point of View." A strategy-based Balanced Scorecard system involves a collaborative effort in which the team creates the story of the strategy, which identifies the connection between capacity, processes, customer value, and financial outcomes. This is their teachable point of view.

To map this "story of the strategy," assemble a team of subject matter experts for the theme and use their expertise to methodically decompose each theme into a set of strategic objectives, mapped in a story of value creation, to achieve the desired strategic results. Figure 20.6 illustrates how themes are translated into strategy maps. In chapter 4, "(I)ntelligent Behavior," during our discussion of innovation and creativity, we uncovered seven habits found in highly innovative and creative people, summarized from *The Myths of Innovation* (Berkun, 2007). Each is critical when engaging in this mapping exercise. As a member of the leadership team, setting the themes and results, deliberately defines certain strategic boundaries or parameters to give guidance to the theme teams. The aim is to develop a Blue Ocean strategy. Look to change/challenge the status quo, go where the profits and growth are—and where the competition isn't. Winning habits include persistence, removing self-limiting inhibitions, taking risks and making mistakes, escaping, writing things down, finding patterns and creating combinations, and curiosity. The leadership team's guidance, coupled with these habits, provides some creative latitude to develop the "how" of the strategy—to consider many options for achieving the desired strategic result. So, to continue our load-bearing wall analogy, selecting where to put the wall will, by design, open up or limit options for the footprint and function of potential rooms within the building.

Figure 20.6: Well-Executed Strategy Leads to Desired Strategic Results

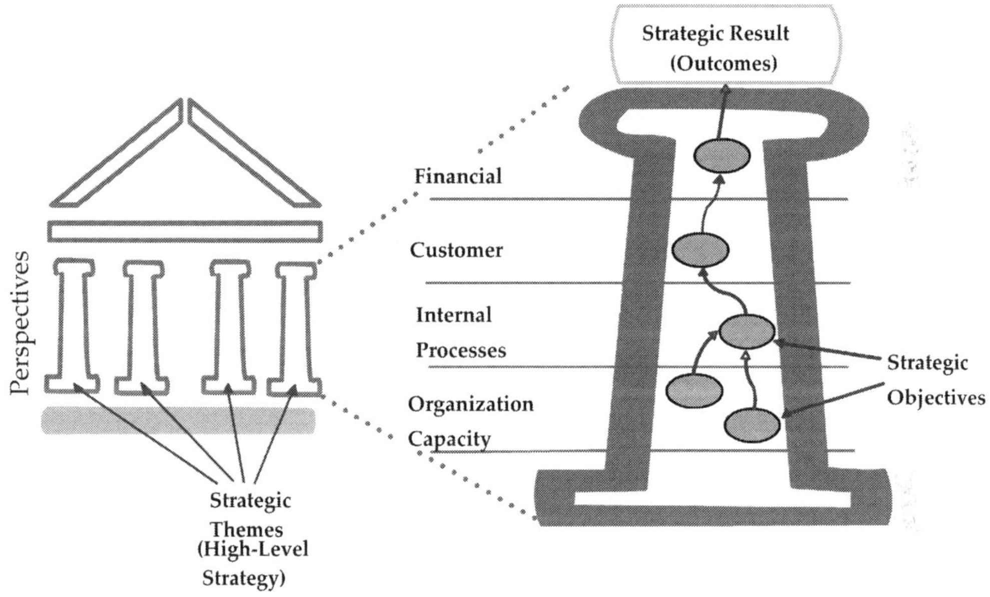

Source: Intelligent Systems Services, LLC / Terry L. Harper Jr., Graphics Artist

The Final Steps

Once all the theme maps are developed, they should be combined to create a compelling, mutually beneficial business strategy. Figure 20.7 illustrates how the theme maps are combined. I advocate building the theme maps to minimize the risk of missing major objectives that will be critical to achieve a strategic result. As an effective leader mandating or an individual contributor building, theme maps for each department or agency and combining them proved valuable to ensure that major objectives for each department and agency reinforced the business strategy. This cascading is necessary to allow people to contribute to the effective execution of the business strategy. Recall that one of the characteristics of a person with integrity is to connect, collaborate, communicate, and coordinate. It's all related. Themes ensure the structural integrity of your system.

Figure 20.7: Theme Maps Combined into a Single Tier 1 Map.

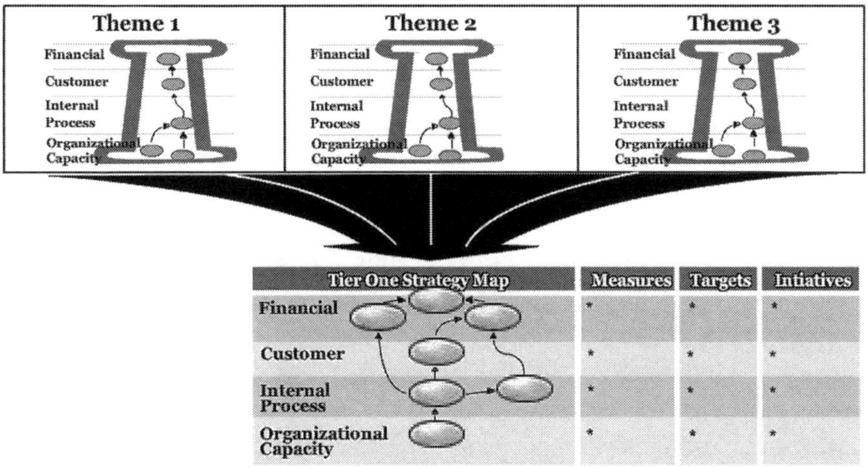

Source: Intelligent Systems Services, LLC / Terry L. Harper Jr., Graphics Artist

There are additional benefits to strategic themes that can be traced back to our discussion on team building in chapter 3, "(G)oal-Oriented Behavior," and emotional awareness in chapter 12, "(R)espect Diversity." Creating strategic themes is the opportunity to involve more people (their voices, their experiences, and their knowledge) in developing strategy through their inclusion on themes teams. This not only results in a better solution, product, or service, but, as stated in chapter 2, "(A)daptable Behavior," chapter 9, "(A)cknowledge the Burning Platform," and chapter 10, "(D)eliver Results through Effective Delegation," it contributes greatly to buy-in, understanding, empowerment, and accountability. Furthermore buy-in and transparency are key components of changing hearts and minds, which are critical to transforming an organization into a higher-performing entity.

Building strategy maps requires consensus, clarity, and commitment to strategy at the executive level:

- Clarifying the desired state of evolution for the organization: desired state, mission, vision, and value drivers
- Specifying objectives in the scorecard areas necessary to realize the organizational strategy. One of the overriding contributions of the Balanced Scorecard development rests in the clarification and expression of the links between performance drivers and their impact on progress toward strategic success, conveyed through the strategy-mapping process

Simply, a strategy map charts the impacts of activities. Once maps have been constructed, linking actions and their impact operations can be managed to achieve desired outcomes. Figure 20.8 illustrates a strategy map developed for a financial services company.

Figure 20.8: A Strategy Map for a Financial Services Company

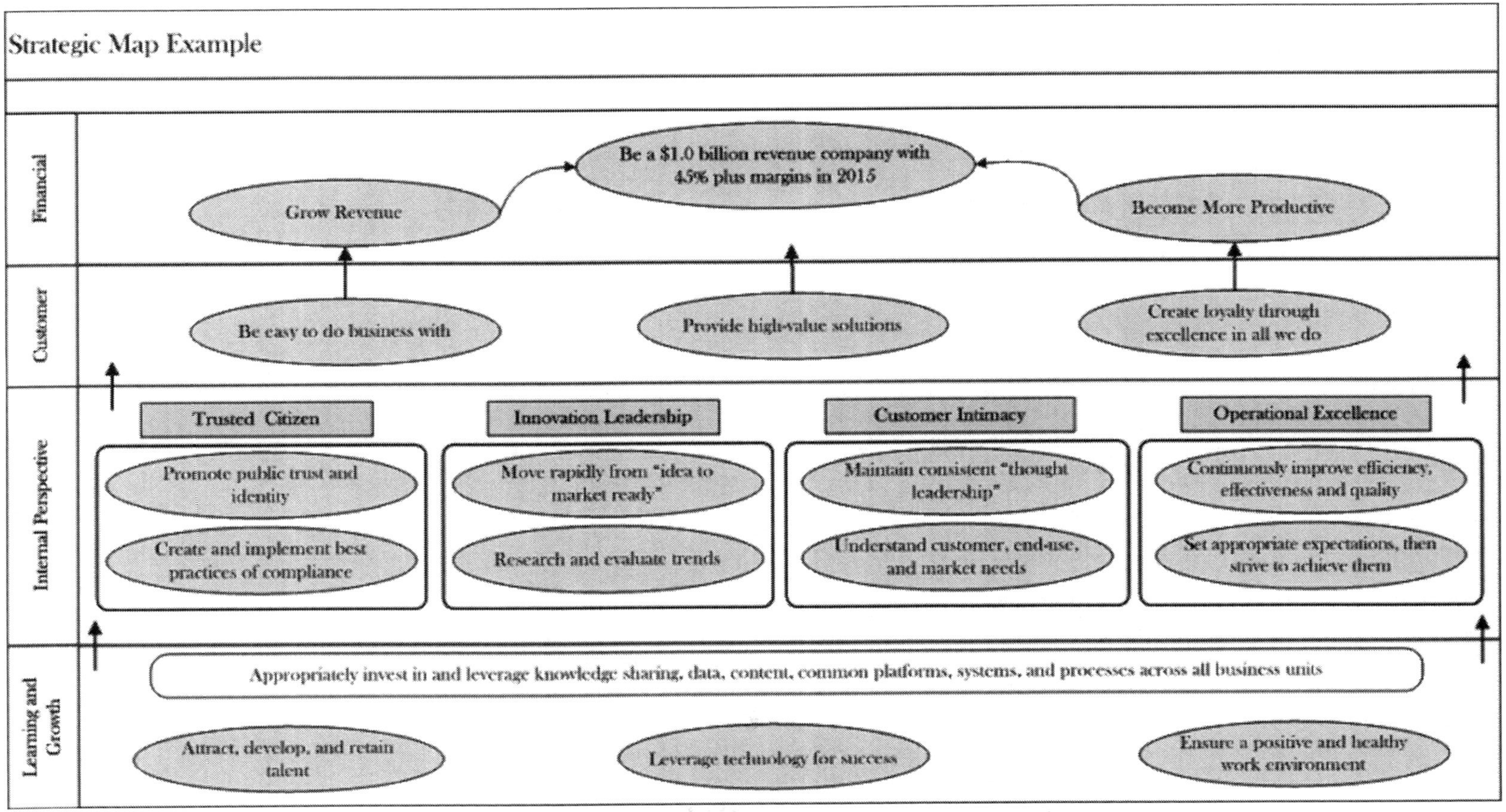

Strategic Map Example

Financial
- Become More Productive
- Be a $1.0 billion revenue company with 4.5% plus margins in 2015
- Grow Revenue

Customer
- Create loyalty through excellence in all we do
- Provide high-value solutions
- Be easy to do business with

Internal Perspective

Operational Excellence
- Continuously improve efficiency, effectiveness and quality
- Set appropriate expectations, then strive to achieve them

Customer Intimacy
- Maintain consistent "thought leadership"
- Understand customer, end-user, and market needs

Innovation Leadership
- Move rapidly from "idea to market ready"
- Research and evaluate trends

Trusted Citizen
- Promote public trust and identity
- Create and implement best practices of compliance

Learning and Growth
- Ensure a positive and healthy work environment
- Appropriately invest in and leverage knowledge sharing, data, content, common platforms, systems, and processes across all business units
- Leverage technology for success
- Attract, develop, and retain talent

Source: Intelligent Systems Services, LLC

Extending Strategy Map into Measurements, Targets, and Initiatives

Once the strategy map is completed, you extend each into measurements, targets, and initiatives for execution. Because every company has a different strategy, strategy maps may also differ. In our example below, the strategy map identifies from an internal process perspective that the overall strategy must include process value map analysis, lean processes, and self-service applications. Each component of the strategy map extending to measurements, targets, and initiatives requires:

- Objective description—creating a detailed statement of what is critical to successfully achieving the strategy
- Measure—answering how success in achieving the strategy will be measured and tracked
- Target—the level of performance or rate of improvement needed
- Initiative—key action programs required to achieve objectives

Figure 20.9 illustrates what is critical to successfully achieving the strategy for lean processes. The objective description details eliminating waste, reworks, and other errors in our processes. Measuring the number of reworks will allow measuring and tracking of the success of the strategy (measure); the level of performance or rate of improvement needed to call the strategy a success is two per setup per month each outlet office (target), and the key programs required to achieve objectives is lean/Six Sigma (initiative).

Figure 20.9: Linking Measurements, Targets, and Initiatives to Strategy Map

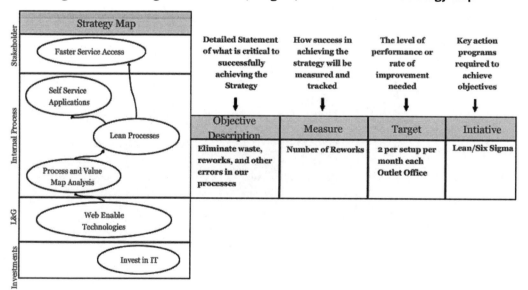

Source: Intelligent Systems Services, LLC / Terry L. Harper, Jr. – Graphic Artist

Creating a Tight Model

Make sure the components of your scorecard fit together. We want to create a tight model for driving execution of your strategy. Here is a basic example of how everything should connect and link up from goal to objective, objective to measurement, measurement to target, and, finally, close the loop with an initiative to drive strategic execution upstream. We want a good, solid, tight model where everything is aligned together. Let me share this quote with you:

Jack Welch, the former chairman and CEO of General Electric, once quipped:

"Simplicity applies to measurement...too often we measure everything and understand nothing."

The measurement, target, and initiative are the foundations for process performance management. For those of you who aren't familiar with activity-based costing/management and Lean/Six Sigma, both are quality management tools. There are a number of good books and courses available for those of you who want to learn more about these approaches. Table 20.2 shows the strategic relationship beginning with goal and ending with an initiative.

Table 20.2 Relating Goals To Initiatives

Goal	Objective	Measurement	Target	Initiative
Achieve agency operational efficiencies with best practices in the private sector	Reduce operational service costs by 50% over the next 5 years	Cost per outlet office, Cost per region, Cost per full time equivalent	5% - Year 1 10% - Year 2 15% - Year 3	Activity Based Costing / Management
	Reduce identified reactivities within primary processes by 80% over the next 3 years	Waste volume charts, rework tracking, cycle time end to end in 5 to 7 regions	Waste stream reductions of 5% each year, reworks cut in half for next 3 years, cycle time cut by 75%	Lean / Six Sigma

Good Performance Measures

Let's continue our discussion on basic guidelines for good performance measure. This starts with understanding the relationship between performance measurement and performance management. Performance measurement is a process to objectively assess and evaluate the extent to which a specific objective, goal, or mission is being achieved. For it to be effective performance management is needed to provide a systemic link between strategy, investments, and processes. It is a comprehensive management process. To manage something it must be measured. For, without measurement, management has no basis for:

- Knowing what is going on in their enterprise or reality
- Effectively making and supporting decisions regarding initiatives
- Specifically communicating performance expectations to followers
- Identifying performance gaps that should be analyzed and eliminated
- Providing feedback that compares performance to a standard
- Identifying performance that should be rewarded

Table 20.3 provides examples of various types of performance measurements.

Table 20.3 Performance Measurement Types

Measure Type	Definition	Example
Leading	Intermediate outcomes that predict or drive bottom-line performance results	Employee turnover rate
Lagging	Bottom-line performance results resulting from actions taken	Employee satisfaction rating
Input	Amount of investments, assets, equipment, labor hours, or budget dollars used	Number of cashiers
Output	Units of a product or service rendered—a measure of yield	Number of Value Meal orders fulfilled
Outcome	Resulting effect (benefit) of the use or application of an output	Customer satisfaction rating
Objective/ Quantitative	Empirical indicators of performance	Wait time
Subjective/ Qualitative	Perceptions and evaluations of major customers and suppliers	Customer complaints received as a percentage of total customers served

Recall the Balanced Scorecard quantifies the organizational strategy in measurable terms. As mentioned performance measures are of different types. Table 20.4 lists examples of various measures for each Balance Scorecard perspective.

Table 20.4 Performance Measurement by Balance Scorecard Perspective

Stakeholder/Customer	Internal Processes
• Current customer satisfaction level • Improvement in customer satisfaction • Customer retention rate • Frequency of customer contact by customer service • Average time to resolve a customer inquiry • Number of customer complaints	• Number of unscheduled maintenance calls • Production time lost because of maintenance problems • Percentage of equipment maintained on schedule • Average number of monthly unscheduled outages • Mean time between failures
Learning and Growth	**Investments**
• Percentage of employee absenteeism • Job posting response rate • Personnel turnover rate • Ratio of acceptance to offers • Time to fill vacancy	• Percentage of facility assets fully funded for upgrading • Percentage of IT infrastructure investments approved • Number of new hire positions authorized for filling • Percentage of required contracts awarded and in place

Finally, some guidelines for good performance measures are:

1. You should have at least one measurement for each objective.
2. Measurements define or explain objectives in quantifiable terms:
   a. Vague: We will improve customer service.
   b. Precise: We will improve customer service by reducing response times by 30 percent by year end.
3. They should drive change and encourage the right behavior along with being able to influence the outcome.

Here are the selection criteria for performance measures that have proven to be very useful:

1. Relevant
   – Addresses an operational or strategic performance issue
   – Are results or outcome focused
   – Provides useful information to enable decision making

2. Measurable
    – Quantifiable and objective
    – Facilitates analysis
    – Can be done in a timely manner with high accuracy
    – Data is available and collectable
3. Actionable
    – Can be tracked to an appropriate person or team responsible for the activity measured
    – Measure relates to process inputs that can be controlled/adjusted to address concerns

Final Balanced Scorecard Components

How to Set Targets and Prioritize Initiatives

A Balanced Scorecard is three things: measurement system, strategic management system, and communication tool. The section provides the final pieces to create your Balanced Scorecard measurement systems and communications tool: setting targets and prioritizing initiatives. Let's set the stage.

You're the operations manager in a local biorefinery and your organization produced ten thousand tons of cellulosic sugar from biomass (wood, energy crop) this week. Should I congratulate you or ask you what happened with production? *It's simply impossible to know without a target.*

A target allows putting actual performance into context. **Said another way** having a comparator or target to compare actual results allows transforming raw data into actionable information. The actual-to-target comparison allows you to assess performance; evaluate strategic progress; make better decisions for action; and learn, improve, and grow.

You can conclude that without a comparator or target, actual performance results are useless. In chapter 3, "Goal-Oriented Behavior," the aim was to prepare you for the management task of setting targets or goals. Why? There is a very important relationship between target attainment and job performer motivation for goal realization that makes the job of setting good performance targets much more than a mechanical exercise. In chapter 17, "Goal Management," we covered the **S.M.A.R.T.** criteria for setting smart management goals. Though goals and targets are different; setting targets should adhere to the same criteria. Most importantly, like goals, targets must be realistic and attainable by average people. The best targets require people to stretch a bit to achieve them, but they aren't extreme. They are neither out of reach nor below standard performance. **Said another way,** targets set too high or too low become meaningless, and people naturally come to ignore them. In the ideal situation, the job performer feel confident that they can produce the desired business performance results but with some element of hard work, uncertainty, and risk involved.

We are almost ready to discuss setting targets you need to know a little bit more information. Keep on reading and learning.

Different Types of Targets

Before discussing setting targets you should understand targets can be categorized within a different time frame: Long-Term, Midrange, and Short Term. The following paragraphs will discuss each. We will then talk about setting targets.

Long-Term Targets: Big Bold Audacious Goals (BBAGS) are outrageous goals designed to stimulate progress over a long period of time. Companies such as Microsoft, BET, and Rocawear are where they are because of BBAGS. BBAGS can also be personal. For example, my earning a doctoral degree was a BBAG. Most BBAGS take at least ten years to accomplish. The long time frame serves two purposes. First, a worthy BBAG is unlikely to be met in a year or two. The extreme challenge it represents will take many years to conquer. Second, an extended time horizon ensures that leaders do not sacrifice long-term results for the sake of achieving a short-term goal. ***Said another way***, leaders in dealing with day-to-day challenges to meet short-term goals they must keep their eyes on the prize—the BBAGS.

Midrange Targets (Stretch Goals): Stretch targets are set three to five years in the future. Although they are not quite as dramatic or outrageous as BBAGS, they do represent discontinuous operations. Moving customer loyalty from 40 percent to 80 percent over a three-year period would constitute a stretch target, as would doubling stock price or inventory turnover. A good piece of self-help advice is St. Jerome's quote:

> *Good, better, best. Never let it rest.*
> *Until your good is better and your better is best.*

This required laser-like focus to become more, or to grow. Think about that for a moment, recalling times in your life when you had a single-minded determination to achieve something. Better yet, start living it today, focusing intently and sending positive energy toward what you want in life. ***It's the same soup but a different bowl*** when it comes to organizations. The goals we set reflect our energy and our focus. Recalling my dad telling me to, "Reach for the universe so that if you miss, you will be among the stars." The twenty-first century is about excelling in a global economy. You must "Get Your Hustle On!" to prevent being steamrolled by your competitors.

Short Term (Incremental Targets): My journey from *Street hustler* to *Strategic hustler*™ covered thousands, maybe even millions of miles. Regardless of how far the journey is, ten miles or thousand miles or million miles, it begins with a single step. So it is with the incremental performance target. For each of the measures on the Balanced Scorecard, these goals are normally established on an annual basis. They provide the measuring stick to allow us to gauge our progress toward stretch goals and ultimately BBAGS. Incremental targets act as an early warning system, providing timely feedback relating to the achievement of our desired future state as represented in stretch targets and BBAGS. The increments should be not more than one year. Greater benefits can be derived by aligning targets with the reporting frequency of performance measures. Many companies like quarterly measurements; this allows staying ahead of the curve to be proactive. Having targets for each of the quarters endows actual results with more meaning for decision making since you can now make valid comparisons between actual and targeted results.

Like the three performance levels, the three classes of targets can work together in shaping the organization's, or your personal, future. Having a long-term vision which is then decomposed into stretch goals which are driven by short term goals is critical to being **S.U.C.C.E.S.S.F.U.L.** Recall our discussion about this earlier.

Setting Targets

Here are suggested instructions for setting targets. Always remember to be (A)daptable no business target is set in stone. If you find your target was too conservative or aggressive, make changes mid-stream. It's more important to have a visible target than it is for that target to be 100 percent reasonable and accurate.

1) Pick one aspect of your business where you want growth. It's best to set business targets one at a time rather than trying to set them all together. Do not try to boil the ocean. This allows you to give each target the focus and attention it deserves.

2) Pick the metrics you want to use when you measure progress towards your business target. Income could be measured by gross sales, net income or growth percentage. Personnel targets could be measured by employee turnover, reduced sick days or an abstract measure of employee morale.

3) Assess where your company or department stands in regards to the metric you chose. It's important to be honest with this assessment, even if the result tells you something you'd be happier not knowing. Remember the discussion on integrity in chapter 4, "(I)ntelligent Behavior," having the courage to meet the demands of reality.

4) Assess your company's status for that metric one month ago, and for the following month in the past year. Get these records, and information for the current month, for the past three years. If setting goals in February 2011, for example, you would want records for January and February 2011, 2010 and 2009; plus records for March of 2008 through 2010. If you don't have records for those periods, do what you can with what you have.

5) Use the information you gathered earlier to determine what your average growth has been in recent years. Analyze the data to see if seasonal fluctuations in the metric will have any effect. For example, retail sales often experience a sharp rise in late November and December.

6) Pick a realistic improvement rate based on past performance and any new information or initiatives. A realistic rate of growth will depend on many factors, including the economy, your particular industry and competition in your area.

7) Select a set time by which you want to meet the business target you have set.

8) Establish benchmarks by subdividing the goal and timeline. For example, if you wanted to increase sales 30 percent in 6 months, you could set benchmarks of 5 percent every month. Benchmarks give you opportunities to assess progress mid-mission, so you can make changes you need in order to meet your targets successfully.

The following is a checklist for setting targets along with an [**A.G.I.L.E. L.E.A.D.E.R.S.H.I.P.**] behavior they relate to:

- Targets match up with measurements, one to one [Ⓖoal-Oriented Behavior]
- Targets require improving current levels of performance [Ⓖoal-Oriented Behavior]
- Targets are a stretch, but achievable: they may require improvements to existing processes [Ⓔnergize People with Ever-Greater Challenges, Ⓛearning Behavior]
- Targets are quantifiable so that the target communicates if the expected performance was met [Ⓖoal-Oriented Behavior and Ⓘntelligent Behavior]
- Long-term targets are established before short-term targets [Ⓘntroduce Ideas with Uplifting Values]
- Financial/budget related targets are established before nonfinancial targets [Ⓖoal-Oriented Behavior]

Once you have the targets, it is time to identify and set up the initiatives to achieve them. *Said another way,* plan the work and work the plan.

Identifying and Setting Up Initiatives

Identifying and setting up initiatives is an important step of the Balanced Scorecard implementation process. Initiatives are the engine that put the strategy into action, and address the identified gaps between the stretched targets set for scorecard measures and the current performance of those measures (Kaplan and Norton, 1996). In their seminal book, The Balanced Scorecard, Kaplan and Norton (1996) identified four important steps for using the scorecard in an integrated, long-range strategic plan and operational budgeting process:

- Set stretch targets
- Identify and rationalize strategic initiatives
- Identify cross-business initiatives
- Link to annual resource allocation and budgets

Table 20.5 illustrates how initiatives should link to strategic goals or objectives. Using the program management and project management disciplines provides the tools and techniques (T-N-T) to drive the initiatives putting the organizational strategy into action.

Table 20.5 Strategic Initiatives Linked to Goals or Objectives

Initiatives	Goals or Objectives
Value Mapping Project	Improve identification and delivery of all agency services across the full stakeholder spectrum
Employee Rotation Program	Improve the employee turnover and satisfaction scores
Web Self-Service Portal	Reduce agency costs and streamline our services for more direct service delivery
Common Knowledge Center	Expand the overall knowledge base so that inter-functions can learn from one another
Customer Survey and Analysis Tool Program	Develop a more systematic process across the entire agency to better connect to our customers
Shared Service Center Tracking System	Reduce rework and overlaps between our seven shared service centers

Importance of Defining Initiatives

At any given time, organizations have dozens of initiatives or projects running. However not all of them are aligned to the organizational strategy. In fact, most of the time, only those people who are working on the project, or those who are close to it, know what the project is all about. Subsequently, it becomes hard to create any synergies between different initiatives. In this context, Balanced Scorecard provides an organized framework in which initiatives can be evaluated in the context of strategic significance.

When the Balanced Scorecard is used as the strategic management tool of a company's management system, the portfolio of initiatives or projects are focused on achieving organizational objectives, measures, and targets.

As mentioned earlier, at any given time, an organization has a myriad of initiatives under way. Many of them, however, are not linked to target improvement. Setting a Balanced Scorecard helps to assess the current portfolio of initiatives and prioritize among them.

Working with Initiatives

When evaluating the portfolio of initiatives, two situations usually appear: there are too many or too few initiatives. Here is my practical advice on dealing with these two extremes. When too many initiatives are under way, usually with different sponsors and competing against each other for scarce resources [these are the 5Ms], the ones most significant for achieving the scorecard [strategic] objectives and targets must be prioritized. If necessary, they should also be reviewed for a better strategic alignment. When too few initiatives are underway, new initiatives must be established.

From the Balanced Scorecard implementation experiences of close colleagues and myself, we have discovered that for approximately 20 percent of the measures in the newly built scorecards, data was not available. Therefore, a new project or initiative—i.e. Lean Process / Six Sigma, Activity Based Costing / Management, Employee Competency Models, etc.—needed to be established to allow data collection and to validate the strategic objectives for which initial measures and targets were set.

With every strategic mandate for new initiatives to fill the void space created by new performance objectives or measures, one must assure they are built on solid strategic program/project management foundations. This means that a new executive willing to sponsor the initiative must be found and an accurate and realistic program/project plan must be set in place, supported by a legitimate budget and necessary resource commitment.

Effective initiatives close the gap between current and desired performance, which in turn drives the desired outcomes aimed for, as long as a few conditions are followed.

- Each initiative should clearly document which strategic business objective it supports— *manage* goals
- Any initiative, no matter how extensive or narrowly it is defined, needs to have the necessary resources allocated—*manage* resources
- Dependencies with other initiatives must be clearly established and all key milestones identified—*manage* interfaces
- All initiatives must be updated on a constant basis and reflected in the budgeting process—*manage* performance

When you first launch your initiative, you probably want to use an output measurement. Once the initiatives are up and running, change your measurement to an outcome to see if the initiative is really having strategic impact. Here is the distinction between the output and outcome.

The output is to produce, deliver, broadcast or supply something. It is the "*what*" that a process, project, or project provides. Here are some examples of outputs:

1. Electricity produced by a power plant
2. Producing 1,000 cases of a product
3. Deliver information on a disk or tape

The outcome is the final result of something, or the way things end up. It is the "*why*" of the process, project, or program. When thinking of example(s) to illustrate outcomes, a statement made by current ESPN Football Analyst and former National Football League Coach and Player, Herman Edwards, when he was head coach of the New York Jets comes to mind. During an interview after a very disappointing loss he responded to a question from a reporter with, "You play to win the game!" Mr. Edwards is one of my favorite personalities because he exhibits emotional energy and edge. This is an example of outcome—the "why" of the initiative—i.e. project, program, process, movement, etc.

Table 20.6 shows the relationship between the initiative, the output (what) measurement and the outcome "why" measurement.

Table 20.6 Initiative Relationship To Output and Outcome

Initiative ⟹	Output Measurement ⟹	Outcome Measurement
Lean Process / Six Sigma	Number of Projects Defined by Region	Overall reduction in errors, reworks, and cycle times
Activity Based Costing / Management (ABC/M)	Percentage of Service Center Outlets with ABC Models in place for Allocation Costs	Reductions in identified reactivities per process study
Employee Competency Models	Percentage of Employees who have a Competency Model in place	Higher skill levels of employees using the models

Summary

You are on your way to becoming a twenty-first century *Strategic hustler*™. The five elements of a strategic rudder, Blue Ocean strategy, and Balanced Scorecard are tools and techniques (T-N-T) applied at the organizational level to set the performance expectations at the process and job/performer levels of an organization. Without it, there is no context for or driver of efficient and effective human and system performance. In this environment, well-intentioned activities are carried out in a vacuum and are frequently off the mark. Understanding the big picture [ecosystem] related to the organizational level is important to any organization unit, from an entire company or agency to smallest department. These organizational level T-N-T can be used by:

- *Executives*, to understand how the business' internal and external ecosystem operates, to refine the organization strategy and measures from an outside-in perspective, to use their wisdom to establish appropriate departmental relationships, to create a efficient and effective organization structure, and to effectively manage the interfaces among departments.
- *Managers*, to understand how their businesses operate and how they fit into the big picture [ecosystem], to establish department goals that align to organization goals, to strengthen relationships with other departments improving collaboration, to create a efficient and effective organization structure, and to effectively manage the interfaces among subunits within their departments.
- *Analysts*, to understand how their client organizations currently operate and how they measure results, to identify areas where their process improvement efforts will have the greatest payoffs, to determine the impact of system changes and other proposed improvements on the organization as a whole, and to recommend enhancements that will have a positive effect on organization-wide performance.

By answering the five elements for a strategic rudder and by using tools such as the super systems map and Balanced Scorecard for each of the three performance variables at the organizational level, one can guide or contribute to organizational performance and bring it under control—**G.R.I.P.** We began with a bleak scenario involving customers, suppliers, employees, and shareholders. Effective management, teamed with effect leadership, at the organizational level goes a long way toward converting those viewpoints.

The *customers' view of the organization* becomes positive because the company is responsive to their needs, product- and service-wise, leaving the customer with a memorable customer experience.

The *suppliers' view of the organization* becomes positive because they have the perception the company treats them as business partners.

The *employees' view of the organization* becomes positive because they know and see what is in it for them and take responsibility for doing the job right the first time.

The *shareholders' view of the organization* becomes positive because the company is making them money.

The performance variables and tools at the organizational level help identify what needs to get done (goals), the resources need to get it done (resources), the relationships necessary to get it done (interfaces/design), and the practices that remove the obstacles to getting it done (management/performance). With an effective organizational level as a foundation, we can begin to understand, analyze, and manage performance at the process and job/performer levels which are covered in the next two sections.

Process Performance Management

Introduction

Processes are the glue that makes an organization work. A company may have great people, but if the process is broken, then the people and organization suffer. The only way to understand how work truly gets done is to view an organization horizontally (as a system) rather than vertically (as a hierarchy of functions). Viewing an organization horizontally allows seeing the business processes.

A process is a sequence of goal-directed activities that consume resources, are subjected to specific rules, and produce a measurable output (product or service) that adds value. Some processes (such as programming) may be contained wholly within a function. However, most processes (such as order fulfillment) are cross functional, spanning the "white space" between the boxes on the organizational chart.

Processes are part of a value chain—a chain of activities that a firm operating in a specific industry performs in order to deliver a valuable product or service. Each step in a process should add value to preceding steps in contributing to the creation or delivery of a product or service. As stated in my definition of a process, processes are also consumer of resources. They need to be assessed not only in terms of the value they add, but also in terms of the amount of people, machinery (equipment), materials, time, and capital needed to produce that value. They are also subject to constraints in terms of regulation, legal, and services levels.

At the organizational level, we "peel the onion" to increase our understanding of the customer-supplier relationships among functions. At the process level, we peel the onion by breaking processes into subprocesses. A manufacturing process may be comprised of subprocessors such as scheduling, tooling, fabrication, assembly, and testing.

Figure 20.1.1 illustrates a tool I've used called a Question Model to formulate critical questions about each anatomy (part) of a business process.

Figure 20.1.1 Question Model

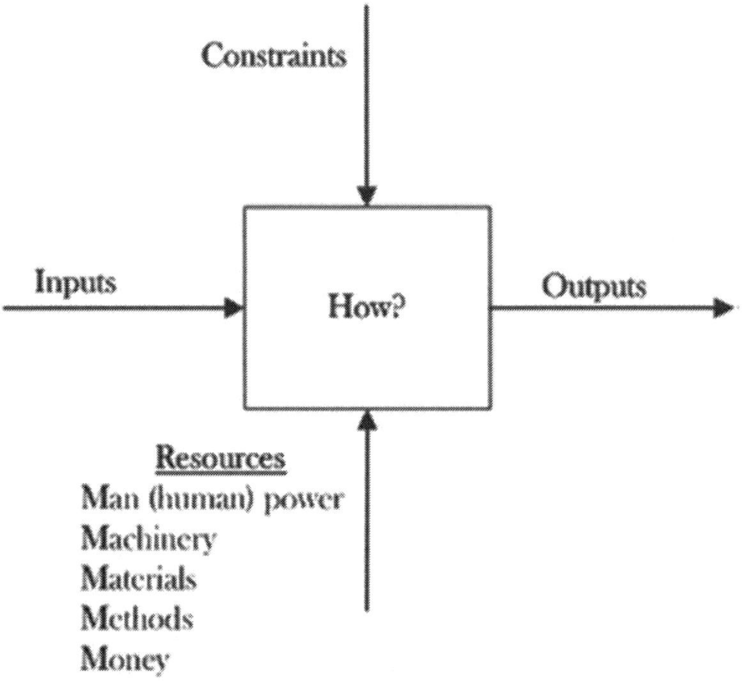

Constraints

Inputs   How?   Outputs

<u>Resources</u>
Man (human) power
Machinery
Materials
Methods
Money

Courtesy: Professional Development Services, LLC / Intelligent Systems Services, LLC

The above diagram illustrates a useful tool for understanding the inner workings of any organization, process, and job/performer. Recall the three levels of performance comprising the nine variables of performance. Earlier, when discussing the nine variables of performance, I stated that discussions on the variables relating to organizational design, process design, and job/performer design would be address in a later discussion. Well, now is later. This tool has allowed me to recommend and implement solutions saving companies millions of dollars. Regardless of the performance improvement effort, you are going to have to find the answers to questions regarding inputs, processes, outputs, resources, and constraints.

Remember that an organization functions as an adaptive system. The Question Model allows uncovering details of the high-level processes documented in the "supersystem map" presented earlier. This tool allows a drill-down inquiry into the anatomy of a business process, which converts inputs (such as resources and customer orders) into outputs (products and services) that it provides to its customers while meeting constraints (regulatory and legal). The organization continuously adapts in order to maintain equilibrium with its environment, or ecosystem, which includes its markets, its competition, its resource pool, and the socioeconomic context in which it functions. As we discuss in chapter 2, (A)daptable Behavior," an organization that adapts nimbly is likely to succeed; an organization that adapts lethargically is likely to fail. Using a football analogy and elusive player will likely avoid injuries; a clumsy player is likely to get injured. ***It's the same soup, but a different bowl!*** Every process has a trigger, which initiates the process. The process itself consists of suppliers, input, process, output, and customers. These can be diagrammed in a document called a SIPOC diagram. Figure 20.1.2 illustrates each component and its contribution.

Figure 20.1.2 SIPOC Diagram

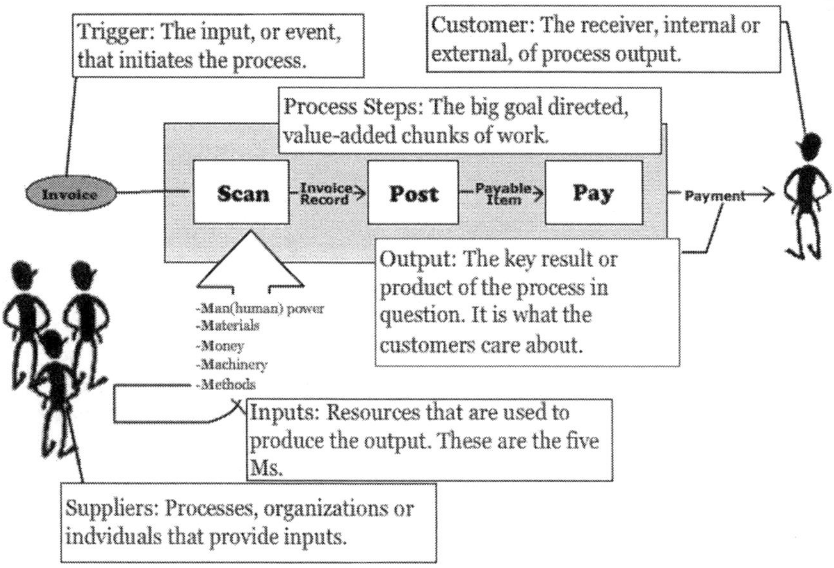

Trigger: The input, or event, that initiates the process.

Customer: The receiver, internal or external, of process output.

Process Steps: The big goal directed, value-added chunks of work.

Invoice

Scan — Invoice Record → **Post** — Payable Item → **Pay** — Payment →

-Man(human) power
-Materials
-Money
-Machinery
-Methods

Output: The key result or product of the process in question. It is what the customers care about.

Inputs: Resources that are used to produce the output. These are the five Ms.

Suppliers: Processes, organizations or indviduals that provide inputs.

Courtesy: Intelligent Systems Services, LLC

The SIPOC diagrams, along with a profile of the process, are excellent tools for process performance management.

When to Use

Use a process profile to:

1. Establish process boundaries
2. Communicate the essence of the process to others
3. Reveal logical locations to place a performance metric
4. Compare one process model to another
5. Help distinguish between process and function

How to Use

1. Identify the process *output*. This output should be expressed as a physical product, an information product, a completed task, or some other tangible/predictable result of process action. Don't confuse the *output* process with the desired *outcome* (e.g., satisfied customers, increased market share, profitability, etc.). The output is the "what" of the process, not the "why"

2. Identify the *customer(s)*. This is the person or organization receiving the process output. They will be the primary source of requirements for the process output

3. Identify the *trigger* for the process. The trigger is the input, event, or condition that sets the process in motion. There are two basic types of trigger:
    Event: A predefined occurrence or condition triggers the process
    Examples:
    – An order triggers a fulfillment process
    – A threshold level of expenditure triggers an approval process
    – A certain probability of hurricane landfall triggers an evacuation
    Time: The process is always set in motion at a specific time
    Example: A payroll process may be executed biweekly

4. Identify the process *inputs* and their *suppliers*. Inputs are materials, information, or other resources required *in addition* to the trigger in order for the process to function correctly. Suppliers can be internal or external, and may be expressed as either a process or an organization

5. Now that you have the beginning (trigger) and the end (output), it's time to define the middle. Identify the three to eight process "macro" steps and their key outputs. The macro steps are also referred to as subprocesses or phases. Write each subprocess on a Post-It and place them in order. Connect the Post-Its with arrows and label the arrow with the output(s) produced by that subprocess

6. Check to see that the profile is logical and intuitive. Make adjustments as needed (the Post-Its really help here)

HINT: Defining the macro steps should not be complicated. If you're stuck, try asking the following:
> – *Has something been converted from one form to another*

Example: An order taker converts information gathered from a customer phone call into a record in a database.
> – *Has something been added, assembled, or altered*
> – *Has something been formally reviewed and approved*
> – *Has something been stored or delivered*

As a final sanity check, ask yourself the following:
- Does this subprocess add significant value to the transaction, *or*
- Does this subprocess expend significant resources, *or*
- Does this represent an intuitive segment of the work to anyone familiar with the process

If the answer is yes to one or more of these questions, then you've probably got a viable subprocess

For an international banking client based in South Africa, as a lead business process strategist, I led a team of executives and managers improving core operations. Using an approach called **P.R.O.G.R.E.S.S.** and an **A.G.I.L.E.** project management approach, we covered the following:

1. **P**icking issues and/or problem identification in the various bank operations
   a. Designate a process owner to oversee the entire process—this should be an executive responsible for the integrity and efficiency of the cross-functional process
   b. Identify a permanent process team, which would meet monthly to review and improve process performance
2. **R**esearching current situations involving people, process, information, and technology
   c. Engage in a discovery process to understand the current process and/or operation
   d. Identify potential problems, or opportunities for solution(s)
   e. Document current process flows, procedures, policies, timings, employee count, regulations, etc. [This is where tools such as Question Model, SIPOC, etc. will prove extremely valuable] [See references mentioned in step 3 below]
3. **O**btaining the root cause. I have used techniques called business process modeling (see previous steps on process profiling), activity-based costing, and the five whys to get to the real cause of the issue or problem— Note: Discussing the details of these approaches is beyond the scope of this book—here are excellent references: *Lean Six-Sigma Green Belt/Black Belt Training*, Rummler-Brache *Process Improvement*, Gary Cokin's *Activity Based Costing/Management*, and Kepner-Tregoe *The New Rational Manager*
4. **G**enerating alternative solutions fusing people, strategy, process, information, and enabling technology to resolve the issue or problem
   a. Engage the team to shift from analytical thinking to creative thinking
   b. Facilitate brainstorming
   c. Document the new process flows, procedures, policies, timings, employee head count, etc.

5. **R**unning a pilot before investing in any technical solution, I conduct a sanity check consisting of a walk-through, talk-through, and run-through. There are a number of simulation products that can help expedite this process

6. **E**xamining the results—remember the delegation axiom mentioned in chapter 10, "(D)eliver Results through Effective Delegation," people respect what you inspect. Therefore you should inspect what you expect.

   a. Rating the performance of the process, giving it a grade in such areas as customer satisfaction, cost, clarity, and thoroughness of documentation, and quality and quantity of measures—each function's contribution to the process could also be rated—see the section called "The Metrics Chain" later in this chapter

2. **S**etting up for transfer from test to production, develop an organization rollout plan that focuses on implementing the solution in phases. Remember you are not trying to boil the ocean. Implement the solution is logical phases to ensure the rollout is effective and efficient

   a. Engage organization change management (OCM) team
   b. Process excellence team collaborates with OCM to define rollout plan

8. **S**eeking continuous improvement. According to PMI's Organizational Project Maturity Model® (OPM3®), a process matures to where it is: standard, measure, control, and continuously improve. Rummler-Brache, or Lean process improvement, improves a bad process to a good one; Six Sigma improves a good process to an excellent one—it focuses on continuously monitoring the process to ensure any variability is remove or kept to minimal so as to not impact the desired output and outcomes of the process

   i. Hold monthly operations reviews, in which process performance would be reviewed first and function performance would be reviewed second
   j. Reward people within a function only if process goals were met and if the function's contribution goals were met

The Metrics Chain

In order to manage anything you need measurements. Logically, if you can't measure it, then you can't track performance. Earlier we discussed how to use the SIPOC diagram. One of the topics covered process "macro" steps and their key outputs. The macro steps were also referred to as subprocesses or phases. We started by identifying the process *output*. This output would be expressed as a physical product, an information product, a completed task, or some other tangible/predictable result of process action. Remember not to confuse the process *output* with the desired *outcome* (e.g., satisfied customers, increased market share, profitability, etc.). The output is the "what" of the process, not the "why."

Figure 20.1.3 illustrates the relationship of the work process and improvement process. It shows work process is focused on transforming inputs into outputs. The improvement process focuses on the output to determine the improvements necessary on the process and inputs.

Figure 20.1.3 Work and Improvement Process Flow

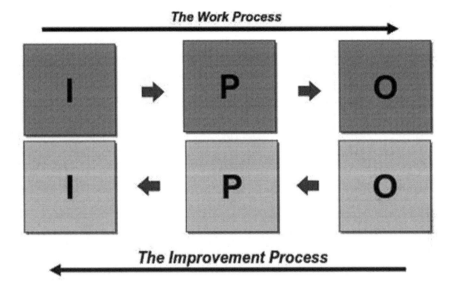

Courtesy: Intelligent Systems Services, LLC

Moving forward, we're ready to talk about measurements using a tool called a metrics chain. The types of measurements that need to be captured include subprocess metrics (M2) that are linked to results metrics (M1). Each process has at minimum critical dimensions (quality, time, financial, and capacity). Using a metrics chain ensures you've adequately covered these critical dimensions of the process. It also shows where within your process a particular metric is measured.

There are two primary categories of measurements to determine process performance. They are process effectiveness and process efficiency. *Adaptability* is a process objective involving effectiveness and efficiency over time. *Note: You see it not only applies to behavior but also to process.* Here are formal definitions and examples for each process measurement category:

Process Effectiveness The extent to which customer requirements are met	– Defect Rate – Accuracy – Actual Plan	– Service Level(s) – Timeliness – Response Time

Process Efficiency
The internal allocation of resources
	– Cost Per Transaction
	– Time Per Activity
	  (Cycle Time)
		– Output Per
		  Unit (Space,
		  FTE, Time)

Adaptability The ability to quickly adapt to changing requirements	– Setup Time for New Customer Needs – Cycle Time for Special Customer Requests – Percentage of Special Requests Not Met	

Process adaptability is an objective that a project team should aim for after effectiveness and efficiency goals have been achieved. A "robust" process is adaptable to changing customer needs, and has the ability to remain capable in spite of variations that may exist within ones customer group's needs. Table 20.1.1 lists examples of M1 and M2 measurements from past projects.

Remember if performance is not being measured, it is not being managed. Performance—that is output—needs to be measured at all three levels—Organization, Process, Job/Performer. Keep on reading and learning on how to establish measurements for M1 and M2.

Table 20.1.1 M1 and M2 Measurements

Input Measures (M2)	Process Measures (M2)	Output Measures (M1)
Measures that are placed on suppliers to ensure quality inputs are received.	Measures that are placed on internal processes. These are the measures for internal customers (i.e., departments) or those that influence output measures.	Measures used to determine how well customer needs and requirements are met.
Examples: • Number of customer inquiries • Type of customer inquiries • Number of orders • Number of positions open • Accuracy of the credit analysis • Timeliness of the contract submitted for review	Examples: • Availability of service personnel • Time required to perform credit review • Percent of nonstandard approvals required • Number of qualified applicants • Total cost of service delivery • Total overtime hours	Examples: • Number of calls/hour taken by each service rep • Second-year customer retention • Total number of meals delivered • Number of positions open • Percentage customer complaints

Figure 20.1.4 illustrates a metrics chain. Notice the M2 for the subprocesses and M1 for the outputs. This is a valuable tool for establishing the various process—output—measurements.

Using a sports analogy, in order for any athletic organization to be effective a measurement system must be created so that the Organization, Process, and Job/Performer levels are all heading in the same direction. For example, any sports owner or executive needs a measurement system that is common knowledge to the team—i.e. GM, VP, Coaches, Players] enabling them to assess whether they are making the appropriate contribution to achieving their *strategic* [Division, League Champion, etc.], *tactical* [Weight Training, Skull Sessions, Practices, etc.] and *operational* [Number of passing yards per game, Number of rushing yards per game, Turnovers per game, etc.] goals. A measurement network is needed that ties the three levels together in a system. This seamless system allows cause and effect thinking, discussed earlier, making it possible:

1. To monitor performance at all levels and proactively "troubleshoot" failure. For example, a deficient Organization Level output (M1) can be traced back to a faulty process and process step (M2) and a missing or fault job output (M1), where corrective action can be taken
2. For all performers along the chain to see and measure their impact on the critical organization output

Let's dive deeper into using the metric chain.

Figure 20.1.4 Metric Chain

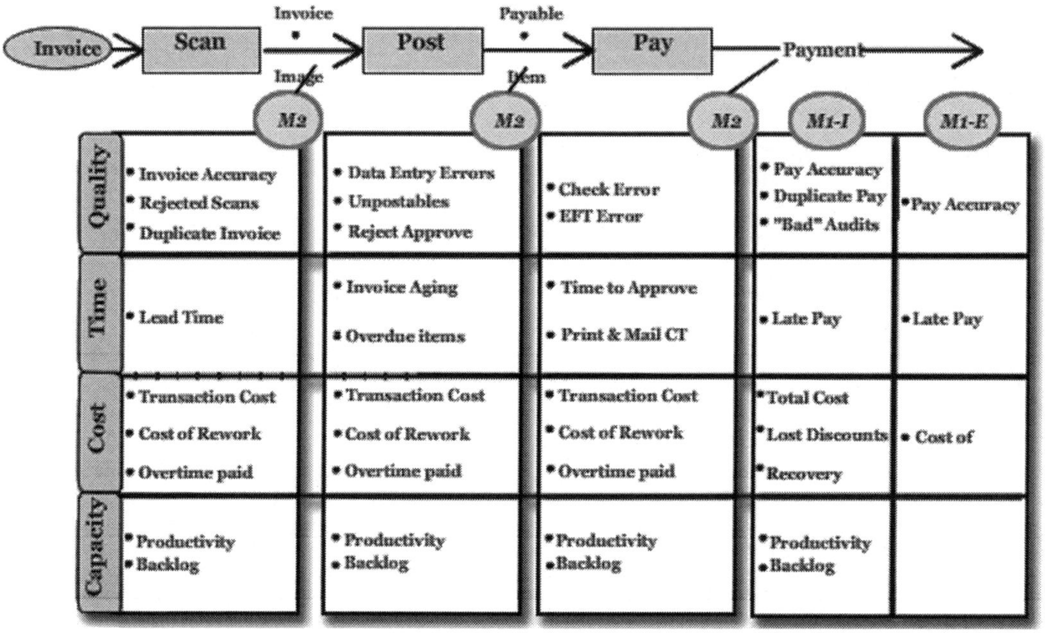

	Scan (M2)	Post (M2)	Pay (M2)	M1-I	M1-E
Quality	• Invoice Accuracy • Rejected Scans • Duplicate Invoice	• Data Entry Errors • Unpostables • Reject Approve	• Check Error • EFT Error	• Pay Accuracy • Duplicate Pay • "Bad" Audits	• Pay Accuracy
Time	• Lead Time	• Invoice Aging • Overdue items	• Time to Approve • Print & Mail CT	• Late Pay	• Late Pay
Cost	• Transaction Cost • Cost of Rework • Overtime paid	• Transaction Cost • Cost of Rework • Overtime paid	• Transaction Cost • Cost of Rework • Overtime paid	• Total Cost • Lost Discounts • Recovery	• Cost of
Capacity	• Productivity • Backlog	• Productivity • Backlog	• Productivity • Backlog	• Productivity • Backlog	

Source: Intelligent Systems Services, LLC / Terry L. Harper Jr., Graphics Artist

How to Use

1. Begin with a process profile, discussed earlier, that includes subprocess outputs
2. Place two columns underneath the final process output
3. Place a column underneath each subprocess
4. Add a row for each of four basic critical dimensions: quality, timeliness, financial, and volume

Note: Not all of these categories may be relevant, or you may wish to include *additional* critical dimensions depending on the situation. Some groups also find that subdividing the categories helps their initial brainstorming.

If you have more than one end-of-process output, you might want to build a separate worksheet and chain for that output.

Beginning with the final process outputs, brainstorm a list of potential metrics for each output and write them on a Post-It note. Be sure to consider both the customer (M1—External) [M1-E]and shareholder (M1—Internal) [M1-I] perspectives. Place the Post-It into the row corresponding to the critical dimension that metric is measuring.

HINT: *Don't* worry about defining the metric with absolute precision during this exercise. The precise calculation, frequency of collection, and performance targets can be determined later. *Do* specify enough so that the meaning is clear to the rest of the team. If this requires specifying units and calculation, then do so.

For each M1-I established, begin building an M2 metrics chain, moving from right to left. M2s are subprocess metrics. Not every subprocess needs to have an M2 in every critical dimension.

In summary, the procedure for determining the M2s is to start with an M1-I and work backwards (left) up the chain identifying relevant M2s for that particular M1-I. Then select the next M1-I and do the same thing until all M1-Is have been considered.

Summary

Process improvement projects systematically improve the process level of performance, which serves as the link between the strategic goals of the organization level and the job/performer level at which the goals will ultimately be carried out. This is why effective leaders with this skill are high in demand. Effective leaders have come to realize that no other tool has the deep and long-lasting impact of process improvement management. The next section addresses performance management where the rubber meets the road, the job/performer level.

Job/PerformerⓅerformance Management

Introduction

The branding label for my company, Intelligent Systems Services, LLC, is *"Delivering Intelligent Solutions through Strategy, People, Process, and Technology."* There was a strategic reason for putting *People* directly next to *Strategy*: because organization and process goals, or strategy, can only be achieved through performance at the job/performer level. I believe most people want to do a good job. However, if you put a star performer in a bad system, the system will introduce inefficiencies into the star performer's work habits rendering them ineffective.

For you Doubting Thomases, I am going to use a sports analogy to prove my point. Every athletic team has a human performance system (HPS). The HPS is a model that describes the variables influencing the behavior of a person in a work system, and, contrary to popular opinion, sports is work. Performance analysts and others have used the HPS for some forty years to diagnose and even predict the likely behavior of human beings in given performance situations. Human performance pioneers Drs. Geary Rummler and Dale Brethower created the earliest version of this model in the 1960s. Today, there are any number of versions of this model, but the original, shown in figure 20.2.1, is still powerful and relevant to anyone interested in understanding or improving performance. The model is based on several important tenets:

- Every organization is a complex system designed to transform inputs into valued outputs for customers
- Every performer, from CEO to line worker, inside any organization is also part of a unique personal performance system

- When an individual fails to produce a desired outcome in an organization, it is due to the failure of one or more components of that person's HPS

Figure 20.2.1: Human Performance System

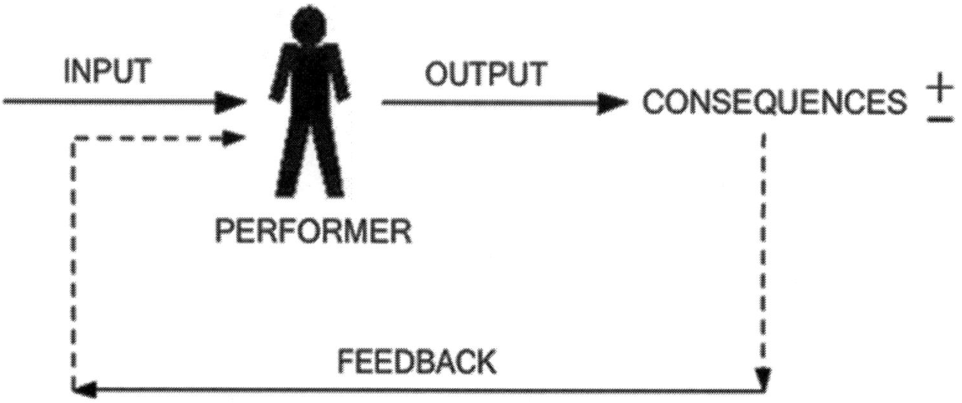

Source: Intelligent Systems Services, LLC/Terry L. Harper, Jr. Graphic Artist

The Components of the HPS

The components of any HPS are as follows: The performer (1) is expected to produce some set of outputs (2). For each output, there is a set of inputs (3). For every output produced (as well as for the action it took to make the output), there is a resulting set of consequences (4)—something that happens to the performer, which in turn is interpreted by the performer as either positive or negative. This interpretation is the key to understanding the performer's future behavior, because the HPS is governed by the behavioral law that people's behavior is affected by consequences, meaning they are likely to repeat behaviors that bring them positive consequences and also likely to avoid behaviors whose payoff is negative. The final element of the HPS is feedback (5) to the performer about the output.

This template of human performance can be used to diagnose any performance problem, and, perhaps even more important, it can be used to design better jobs. In figure 20.2.2 is the ideal HPS, with descriptions of each component in its ideal state.

In its usage over the past years, some patterns of performance have become apparent. For example, 90 percent of the time, performance deficiencies that might appear to be caused by a human performer or a class of performers all doing a given job are actually the result of other things being wrong in their HPS:

- Missing materials
- No clear direction or expected output
- Interference while trying to do their work
- Lack of any meaningful feedback
- Strong negative consequences for trying to do the job
- No positive consequences for succeeding
- Broken, unavailable, obsolete equipment
- Lack of training or other preparation

It is sometimes stunning to find out the circumstances in which average performers keep on grinding away in their duties in spite of a dreadful lack of support. Figure 20.2.2 shows how HPS analysis can help bring this kind of situation dramatically to light.

Figure 20.2.2: The Ideal HPS

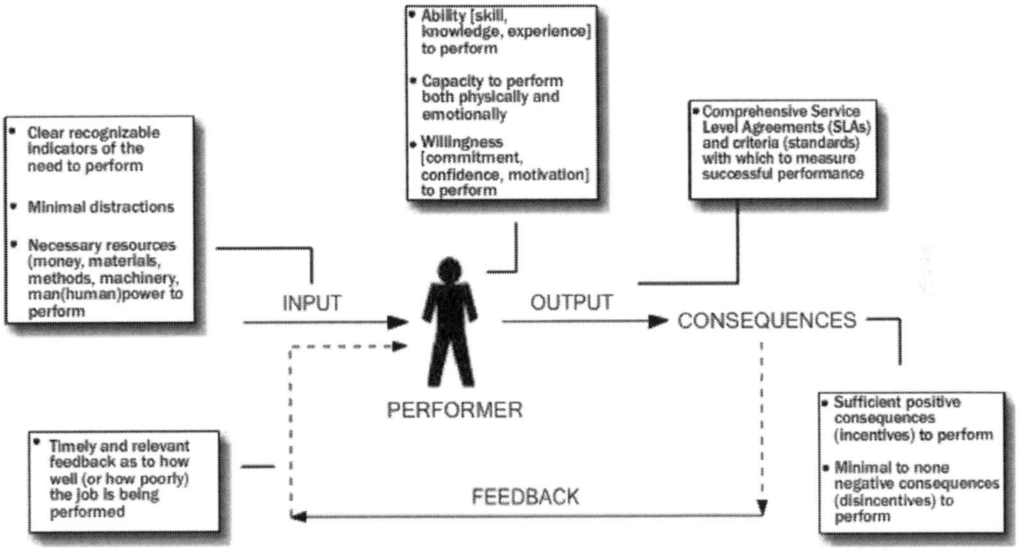

Source: Intelligent Systems Services, LLC / Terry L. Harper, Jr. Graphic Artist

The ideal HPS presented above can be achieved by understanding factors affecting the HPS and then identifying a cure for the deficiency.

Going back to our sports analogy, when an athlete goes from high school to college and from college to the pros (if he's lucky), he is becoming the performer in that HPS. How many times have you heard of an athlete transferring from one college to another, or a great high school player not being able to cope with college and deciding to drop out altogether? If we take a closer look at professional sports—players, coaches, administrators—they either flourish or perish in a specific human performance system. Continuing with our sports analogy, let's examine each component of the HPS.

Managing Performance at the Job/Performer Level

Managing the job/performer level is managing the seven components of the HPS depicted in figure 20.2.2. The end states shown in the diagram are the answers to questions to each HPS component:

1. Performance Specifications
   a. Do performance standards exist
   b. Do performers know the desired output and performance standards
   c. Do performers consider the standards attainable
2. Task Support
   a. Can the performer easily recognize the input requiring action
   b. Can the task be done without interference from other tasks
   c. Are the job procedures and work flow logical
   d. Are adequate resources available for performance (time, tools, staff, and information)
3. Consequences
   a. Are consequences aligned to support desired performance
   b. Are consequences meaningful from performer's viewpoint
   c. Are consequences timely
4. Feedback
   a. Do performers receive information about their performance that is:
   – Relevant
   – Accurate
   – Timely
   – Specific
   – Easy to understand
5. Ability
   a. Do the performers have the necessary skills and knowledge to perform
   b. Do the performers have the experience to perform
   c. Do the performers know why desired performance is important
6. Willingness
   a. Do the performers have the confidence to perform
   b. Do the performers have the commitment to perform
   c. Do the performers have the motivation to perform
7. Individual Capacity
   a. Are the performers physically, mentally, and emotionally able to perform

The purpose of job management is to put capable people in an environment that supports their accomplishment of job goals.

1. *Performance specifications* are the outputs and standards that comprise the job goals. A running backs coach who is participative in establishing

process-driven job goals is taking steps to ensure that the questions behind this factor are answered positively. By contrast, the answers are *no* for running backs who are not clear on their mix of duties in the passing and running game. They have a performance specification deficiency

2. *Task support* is about providing the appropriate resources for the performer to meet the job goals. You'll recall the five *Ms*, man (human) power, materials, machinery, methods, and money. Let's see how each of these applies to a salesperson:

   a. Man (Human) Power—To meet sales quotas, support needed from a team of professionals performing detailed tasks as defined by methods

   b. Materials—To perform contact management, need pens, pencils, paper, erasers, etc

   c. Machinery—This is equipment such as computers, cell phones, etc

   d. Methods—This involves well-documented and clear procedures to get the job done. This could include sales manuals, product brochures, etc

   e. Money—This involves having a sales budget

3. *Consequences* must support attaining job goals. Building upon the sales quota example, because of a strategic initiative, one of a salesperson's job goals may be to sell a certain volume of new product, *Widget New*. If the payment plan doesn't support this goal, then salesperson's consequences are not aligned to support desired performance. The consequence must motivate the salesperson to achieve the desired performance. A promotion to a high level may not be inspiring to a salesperson. Lastly, consequences must occur quickly enough to provide an ongoing incentive. If the salesperson has to wait years for a promotion to be delivered, though it may be aligned to the desired performance, it does not come quickly enough to serve as the sole incentive

4. *Feedback* reinforces the performer's current performance or indicates a change in performance is needed. Recall in our discussion in chapter 2, "Ⓐdaptable Behavior," we spoke of Situational Leadership® and individual change management. The purpose of the ADKAR® Individual Change Model is to open up the communication with an individual to allow him or her to make the appropriate changes in behavior to achieved desired results. If feedback is delivered only to the sales force as a whole, individual salespeople may not perceive it as relevant or be able to use it to guide their performance. Remember, feedback must be specific, relevant, accurate, easy to understand, and timely. Imagine being a performer and getting negative feedback on your performance two weeks before your performance review. There is no time to change for the better

5. *Ability* discussed earlier in Situational Leadership® is the knowledge, experience, and skill that an individual or group brings to a particular task or activity

    When considering the ability level of others, one must be task-specific. If either of the above is missing, job performance may be impaired and training may be required. The experience enables some to be star performers

6. *Willingness* discussed earlier in Situational Leadership® is the extent to which an individual or group has the confidence, commitment, and motivation to accomplish a specific task

    Willingness is only one word that describes the issue. Sometimes, it isn't so much that people are unwilling; it's just that they've never done a specific task before. Perhaps they don't have any experience with it, so they're insecure or afraid. In general, if it is an issue of never having done something, the problem is insecurity. The term *unwilling* might be most appropriate when, for some reason, the individuals have slipped, or loss their commitment and motivation. It might imply that they are regressing

    A salesperson that is capable, well-trained, and placed in a setting with clear expectations, task support, reinforcing consequences, and appropriate feedback may be motivated to achieve the desired performance if they have the appropriate confidence and commitment

7. *Individual capacity* involves a performer's emotional awareness. We spoke of this in chapter 12, "Ⓡespect Diversity," under the topic of "Emotional Awareness." People with this competence:

   * Recognize which emotions they are feeling and understand why
   * Understand the connection between their feelings and behavior
   * Identify how their performance is impacted by their feelings
   * Knows what to say and do (behavior) in a specific social setting
   * Recognize that each of the above has a direct impact on their existence in a diverse society

   A salesperson who cannot take rejection may have an emotional awareness deficiency

Diagnosing and Overcoming Deficiencies

As the examples illustrate, one powerful use of the questions of the HPS is as a trouble-shooting checklist. Each *no* answer to any question represents an opportunity for performance improvement.

My experience is consistent with that of Deming (1982), who maintains that only 15 percent of performance problems are worker problems and 85 percent are management problems—not leadership. Since the odds are against the performer being the broken component of the HPS, the typical management responses to performance problems—such as *train them, transfer them, coach and counsel them, threaten them, or replace them*—are not likely to address the need.

By applying process improvement disciplines—i.e., streamlining, process redesign, or process reengineering, ADKAR® individual change model, along with Situational Leadership® theory—effective leaders can diagnose HPS problems. There is bad news and good news. The bad news is that diagnosing a situation does not in itself bring about performance improvement. The good news is that each diagnosed deficiency within the seven factors (each no answer) suggests an action. Let's look at some deficiency scenarios.

Table 20.2.1 Deficiency Scenario By Type

Deficiency Type	Deficiency Scenario
Process Specification	Loans are submitted to closing with defects with significant risks that cause the loan to be in violation of credit policy or investor eligibility guidelines
Task support is missing	Assessing and specifying the defect severity of a loan is unclear and difficult; unclear on what is to be done with a loan that has errors
Consequences	Desired behavior, or responses, are not consistently rewarded
Feedback	Once errors have been identified the source of the error is not made aware to allow them to improve
Ability and willingness are lacking	Job Performer does not know how to use a feature in the advanced supply chain computer system
Individual capacity	The Job Performer is unable to produce the desired output according to specification

Table 20.2.2 Deficiency Solutions

Deficiency Type	Solution
Performance specification is unclear	Create a job model, which specifies the outputs and standards that are linked to process requirements. You can start with the question model of the SIPOC diagram.
Task support is missing	Restructure the job so that it has clear inputs, a logical sequence of activities, minimal interference among tasks, and sufficient resources—remember the five Ms.
Consequences	Add positive consequences and remove negative consequences for desired responses. This is very easy; just ask performers what they find punishing and what incentives work for them. Remember my story at Sikorsky Aircraft.
Feedback	Develop an efficient means of regularly and frequently providing specific performance information to people. There are 1,001 ways to reward employees (Nelson, 1994).
Ability and willingness are lacking	Provide classroom training, on-the-job training, and/or a job aid.
Individual capacity	Either change the job to fit the person, develop the fit the job, or remove the person from the job.

Effective Leaders of the Twenty-First Century

In many of today's organizations, technology has become so pervasive that it functions as a frequent enabler of human performance as well as, in many cases, functioning as a performer itself. Can the HPS model be useful here as well?

Absolutely. Technology can fail to support a process or its human performance because the circumstances in which it exists don't support its effective utilization. I am going to call it the Technology Performance System (TPS). It can suffer from missing or poor inputs (bad data, bad data entry); unclear goals or outputs (meaning the technology may be designed to produce outputs different from what is actually desired), or a bad surrounding performance environment (interface problems, software issues).

Even consequences play a role in the effective performance of a TPS, in that a system, database, or application can be misused or abused so that it does not do the job it was designed to do. Witness the jerry-rigging of legacy systems to perform tasks they were not originally made for, eventually leading to a crash and burn. Even machines don't necessarily just suffer silently.

For process designers, improvers, and managers, the HPS and TPS are essential conceptual tools for their arsenal.

Summary

Performance is delivering the most efficient and effective product and service that fulfills the need. It starts at the organizational level with strategic decision-making processes that include assessment, formulation, and execution. Strategic themes are the main, high-level business strategies that form the basis for the organization's business model. They are part of the strategic planning work of building a balanced scorecard. Once the vision, a picture of the future or designed future state, is agreed upon, it is systematically decomposed into three or four strategic themes. These themes are a company's "pillars of excellence." The strategic themes are very broad in scope. They apply to every part of the organization and define what major strategic thrusts the organization will pursue to achieve its vision. Themes affect all four of the Balanced Scorecard perspectives (financial, customer, internal process, learning and growth). A strategic theme is an area in which your organization must excel in order to achieve your vision. Each theme has a strategic result associated with it.

Strategy themes translate into strategy maps. Strategy maps outline what an organization wants to accomplish (financial and customer objectives) and how it plans to accomplish it (internal process and learning and growth objectives). They use cause-and-effect logic, which shows for every problem or quality characteristic that there is a possible reason, or cause, for its existence. It is one of the most important elements of best-practice Balanced Scorecards. It allows companies to create a truly integrated set of strategic objectives.

These strategy maps are extended into measurements, targets, and initiatives. The processes need to bring these initiatives into existence is done at the process level. At the organization level, we "peel the onion" to increase our understanding of the customer-supplier relationships among functions. At the process level, we peel the onion by breaking processes into subprocesses. A manufacturing process may be comprised of subprocessors: scheduling, tooling, fabrication, assembly, and testing.

At the process level, we can use the question model, process profile, process maps, and metric chains to understand, measure, control, and continuously improve processes.

And, finally, organization and process goals can be achieved only through performance at the job/performer level. Rather than hiring good people and hoping for efficient, high-quality performance, effective leaders use the human performance system (HPS) to manage the factors that enable those good people to perform at a star performer level. Effective leaders apply leadership with a **G.R.I.P.** to influence the effectiveness of that system.

CHAPTER 21

You Reap What You Sow

So now, you have it. It has taken me years to figure out the behaviors that have allowed me to transition from a *Street hustler* to a *Strategic hustler*™. I learned to adapt, set goals, be intelligent (with innovation, insight, initiative, influence, and interpersonal skills with integrity), learn, and be effective. **Said another way**, I learned to be [**A.G.I.L.E.**]. With this *flexibility*, I developed the ability and willingness to look to challenge the status quo; energize myself and others with ever-greater challenges; acknowledge the burning platform; deliver results through effective delegation; make tough, hard decisions with emotion and edge; respect diversity; sustain success by achieving excellence; have a teachable point of view, introduce ideas with uplifting values; and be persistent with perseverance. **Said another way**, I learned [**L.E.A.D.E.R.S.H.I.P.**]. In the twenty-first century being *upfront* is not good enough. You learned that leaders use various reasons distinguishing leading (knowing) and managing (doing) to avoid the hard work of learning about the people they lead; the technologies their companies use; and the customers they serve; making them ineffective. The *Strategic hustler*™ can minimize this knowing-doing gap with

[**G.R.I.P.**] management—focused on managing goals, resources, interfaces, and performance. ***Said another way***, good enough requires being *in control.*

A devoted Christian, I am a spiritual man—*not religious.* There is a difference, in which a discussion is beyond the scope of this book. God can be worshipped through many avenues—Christianity (God), Hinduism (Brahman), Islam (Allah), Jewish (Jehovah/Yahweh), and Taoism (The Tao)—all of which I respect because it proves the Almighty cannot be put in a box. HE loves EVERYBODY! My spirituality will be shared with you in this chapter.

In the twenty-first-century, highly downsizing, dynamic, fast-paced, and competitive world, there exists an abundance of opportunities for one to be successful. *Don't wait for your ship to come in…swim out to meet it!* The Bible says *Ask, Seek,* and *Knock* (Matthew 7:7). Start with putting *God* first! The ability to *ASK* and recognize these opportunities is essential to one's success. However, proper preparation with the skills and tools enhances ones readiness to exploit opportunities when they present themselves. Your intellectual and emotional investments provide the confidence to seize the opportunity and exploit it. *You draw nothing out of the bank of life except what you deposit in it.* ***Said another way,*** faith without work is dead.

To be an effective twenty-first-century leader you have to be an effective [**M.A.N.A.G.E.R.**]. Learn to finish what you start—this will require self-management skills. Successful people from all walks of life work [**S.M.A.R.T.**], show [**P.R.I.D.E.**], work with [**P.A.S.S.I.O.N.**], and value [**T.E.A.M.W.O.R.K.**] to turn their dreams into reality. These acronyms embody behavioral qualities allowing all of us to seek higher levels of satisfaction and rewards in everything we do.

The following paragraphs complete the journey of this book. They uncover these practical, applicable, and simple behavior qualities you can develop through training and practice to be highly successful in achieving your reality. As with all things in life you have to crawl, walk, run, and sprint in stages. ***Said another way it's the same soup but a different bowl.***

STAGE 1 (Years One to Five) During this period you work **S.M.A.R.T.**

S – Self Confidence
M – Motivation
A – Ambition
R – Responsibility
T – Training

During the early stages of your career, the first five years, develop ***self-confidence.*** Take the ***responsibility*** to get the ***training*** and acquire the skills to turn your dreams into reality. This *ambition* will allow you to hurdle any obstacles that prevent you from achieving your professional/personal goals. Early in your career requires building the foundation to springboard your dreams into reality. Always *motivate* yourself in creative ways to enjoy all tasks. *Remember the only place where success comes before work is in the dictionary.* Effective leaders pay their dues—so prepare to join the ranks. Learn to crawl, then walk, and then run. Paying our dues gives a testimony to overcoming obstacles to achieving our ultimate goal (John 16:33). Getting the *training* enables the learning that brings knowledge, power, and confidence to turn your dreams into reality. Allow your rise to the top to be a spirit-filled, adventurous journey. For example, many successful and respected corporate executives or entrepreneurs have grown from the ranks. They started at the lowest level, had the *ambition*, took the *responsibility*, sought the *training*, develop *self-confidence*, and, best of all, stayed *motivated* to complete the process.

STAGE II (Years Five to Ten) Continue to work **S.M.A.R.T.** and with **P.R.I.D.E.**

P – Performance
R – Responsibility / Ownership
I – Initiative / Integrity
D – Dependability
E – Excellence / Innopreneur

Actions speak louder than words. Let your *performance* do your talking. The Bible speaks of longsuffering (Galatians 5:22). Longsuffering is patience. Everyone has a due season (Galatians 6:9). Your turn will eventually come. Being [**S.M.A.R.T.**] will allow you to seize the opportunity when it does. *Integrity* is having the courage to face the demands of reality—when it comes demonstrate intelligent behavior. This means take the *initiative* to show that you are a valued team member—remember you are not at the top yet! Finding a vendor, employee or partner who will consistently play their part is one of the great challenges in business. Want to win in this world? I've found that the most simple and effective tactic is to be the most dependable. Even your enemies cannot refute *dependability*. Take *responsibility* of *ownership* to ensure your assigned task(s) are completed with *excellence* as if you were the business owner (*innopreneur*). You develop [**P.R.I.D.E.**] as you apply your [**S.M.A.R.T.**] s resulting in others labeling your *performance* top notched; aggressively take the *responsibility* and *ownership* for your actions and results; show the kind of *initiative* that demonstrates your *integrity*; exhibit a *dependability* that even your enemies admire; and develop an *innopreneur* state of mind focused on *excellence*.

AT EVERY STAGE work with P.A.S.S.I.O.N.

People who have a [**P.A.S.S.I.O.N.**] for what they do always sweat the small stuff. Why? They know that it's the small stuff that can make a big difference—possibly the difference between success and failure. *Said another way*, the little things turn into big things. Let's look at what having [**P.A.S.S.I.O.N.**] really means.

P –	Purpose
A –	Attitude
S –	Sacrifice
S –	Self-Motivation/Determination
I –	Inner strength
O –	Optimism
N –	Never Give Up

Purpose—know your life goal(s)—*said another way* know your 'why?' for turning your dream(s) into reality; purpose is the foundation of your passion; without it your passion will fizzle away. *Attitude*—determines your altitude. Remember integrity is having the courage to face the demands of reality. This is all about having the right attitude always seeing the positive side of everything—you are not a failure you just discovered something that doesn't work! *Sacrifice*—give up short-term gratification for long-term gratification. *Self-motivation/determination*—have a mind-set that "if it is to be, it is up to me." *Inner strength*—having a spiritual connection with a High Power fuels your will power to keep you from feeling down or drained; remember you are on a journey! *Optimism*—be positive and see the good in everything. *Never give up*—you're only a loser if you give up persevering to turn your dreams into reality. "Keep on, keeping on!"

> *Good, better, best. Never let it rest.*
> *Until your good is better and your better is best.*

Know, your [**P.A.S.S.I.O.N.**] is your burning desire to achieve and succeed.

Become an effective leader by managing your success. Let me say this; before you can lead anything, you must first manage something—starting with yourself. This requires having integrity. Remember integrity is having the courage to face the demands of reality. Here is a formula to learning self-management skills. As a self-[**M.A.N.A.G.E.R.**] you should learn to do the following:

M –	Motivate and Inspire
A –	Appraise and Counsel
N –	Nurture and Develop
A –	Act Rather than React
G –	Guide and Set Goals
E –	Educate and Train
R –	Recognize, Reward, and Reprimand

*The following stories on motivation (**motivate**) and inspiration (**inspire**) were reprinted from a blog post with permission from Suzie Price, www.pricelessprofessonal.com.*

Motivate and Inspire - Let's consider the following 'cry' I often hear from frustrated leaders who want and need more from their team:

*"How do you define motivation and inspiration? What is motivation and why does it seem to be so elusive on my team and in my life? I want more motivation, results, energy and commitment from my team. **I want everyone to be self-motivated NOW!"***

Before addressing the above let's look at the difference between motivation and inspiration.

To **motivate** is to provide with an incentive; to move to action; impel. This is what you do when you want people to take action—quick, fast, and in a hurry. Motivation is good.

To **inspire** is to stimulate to action; to affect or guide; to stimulate energies, ideas or reverence. How does this definition grab you? Can you see the subtle, but big difference between how we define motivation and inspiration?

Motivation IS better than being apathetic, but it requires a lot of pushing and prodding from you the leader. **Inspiration on the other hand involves more of a person's inner drive.** When you're focused on inspiration you're **activating a follower's desire** to act, which is less labor intensive and longer-lasting.

Motivation is the pedal car.

It goes. You DO get movement, but it requires more work on your part. You've got to push, pedal and be there for it to work. The pedal car, like motivation, can be labor intensive.

Inspiration is the race car.

Less work on your part because the engine is strong and self-powered. The race car, like inspiration, is much more powerful and can cover greater distance, faster.

Dwight D. Eisenhower, the 34th president of the United States said, *"Motivation is the art of getting people to do what you want them to do because they want to do it."* You cannot motivate anyone who is not inspired to want to be the best they possibly can be. As mentioned earlier, "they gotta wanna or they ain't a gonna."

When people truly want to do something, as a result of their interactions with you, you have now **stepped into the realm of inspiration. In inspiration you're guiding NOT forcing and prodding, NOW you're leading!** As we define motivation and inspiration I include this slight play on words and focus on inspiration, but the difference between motivation and inspiration means a **big performance difference.**

Let's change the focus from the team to individual.

Motivation

You decided to run the 5k to lose weight, stay in shape, raise money for cancer; maybe to prove something. It's on your bucket list. You made a bet. Only ten pounds to go. Achievement is thrilling. All fine reasons.

Inspiration

The runner's high. *My body simply has to run. When I run, I feel closer to life.*

Motivation

You write the book, the blog, the brochure to raise your profile so you can sell more stuff, serve more people. You compose and package your thoughts. A 1000 words a day until you've crossed the finish line. All fine reasons.

Inspiration

I have something to say that needs to be heard. When I write I feel bigger, freer, like God is using me well.

We seem to need motivation to get stuff done. Typically there's a lot of "measuring" that happens in the realm of motivation. Check lists and goal posts and markers and such. There is often a fear of loss involved. We are on duty. All are perfectly natural.

But beyond finish lines and well done, is a different call–Inspiration. It is magnetic and progressive. Its reasoning cannot always be reasoned — *I just gotta do it.* It busts you outta shouldsville into the unfenced field of freedom and possibility. Inspiration is a completely different force of creativity.

What is motivating you?
What is inspiring you?
What is pushing you?
What is pulling you?

Follow the pull. It's the first step toward flying as I remember my dad's shoot for the universe saying.

Appraise and Counsel - These are competencies that show you are:

- Aware of your strengths and weaknesses
- Reflective, learning from experience
- Open to candid feedback, new perspectives, continuous learning, and self-development
- Able to show a sense of humor and perspective about themselves
- Seek counseling to improve on the all the above if necessary

Nurture and Develop - This is all about educating and developing yourself—mind, body, and spirit—to be able to make a difference in your community. Earlier we covered taking the *responsibility* to get the training and acquire the skills to turn your dreams into reality. Nurture your personal development to achieve professional/personal goals.

You should have a strategic plan on maintaining balance around work, family, and yourself.

Act Rather than React - Be proactive! Expect the unexpected. ***Said another way***, control your destiny or someone else will. Take it from a *Strategic hustler*™, it pays to act rather than react in the following five situations.

1. Relationships
   In an ongoing relationship, it's easy to get into the habit of anticipating and reacting, rather than observing and acting. While this approach certainly takes the work out of relationships, it's also true that a relationship you don't work on soon ceases to be a relationship at all, and becomes simply two people orbiting a common center.

Train yourself to observe the other person's behavior and weigh your options against your own values, wants and needs. Then choose how you wish to act, instead of letting their behavior choose for you. It might not always be easy, but it beats winding up in a relationship all by yourself.

2. Work
Like being in a relationship, work can become a predictable dance of expected reactions to expected events. But opting to work like this is a bad decision. You'll be bored, the quality of your work is unlikely to rise above merely adequate and higher-ups will find nothing noteworthy in either your performance or your personality.

Instead, decide what you want out of your position (besides a paycheck) and consciously plan and act to achieve those goals. You may not get everything you want, but you'll certainly get more of it than you would otherwise.

3. Important decisions
This would seem to be an obvious point, but it's surprising how many people let habit, expectations and reactions make even the most important life decisions for them. Every day people get married, embark on careers and even start families by simply "going with the flow," which is just another way of describing passive reaction.

Anytime you are faced with an important decision, stop and take the time to evaluate what you really want or need, versus what you or others think you should want or need. This is true even, or perhaps especially, if the choice seems obvious. It's unfortunate, but not unusual, for people to spend their entire lives going with the flow only to discover in the end that the flow never took them anywhere they wanted or needed to go. Don't let your life flow through your fingers. Learn to paddle your own boat and there's no limit to where you can go.

4. Finding your place in the world
You only get one chance to be who you want to be. Why spend it letting others or your environment make those choices for you? Take some time to really think about what's important to you and how you want to express those values in your life.

Figure out what you need and want out of life, instead of accepting or reacting to whatever comes your way. Actively choosing your path in life based on your own values and goals isn't always the easiest way to live. But it is by far the most rewarding.

5. Your future

Planning for the future isn't something that should be left up to chance. But too many people simply bounce from one reaction to the next throughout their lives with no real goal or plan in mind.

Know what you want, why you want it and how you plan on getting it. Then create a plan for reaching your goals, rather than simply reacting to events as they happen. A thoughtful strategy combined with intentional action is a far better strategy for success than playing pinball with your life and hoping you get lucky.

Guide and set goals - It is not a bad thing to dream, it's great to be a dreamer. Earlier we mentioned how dreams are ideas. However you have to take the next step to turn your dreams into reality. This starts by writing them down as goals. By applying the [**S.M.A.R.T.**] criteria you can begin to put legs on your goals. Become good at turning awe-inspiring ideas into [**S.M.A.R.T.**] goals and you will be well on your way to turning your dreams into your reality.

Educate and Train – Put on your armor to prepare to do battle in the real world. ***Said another way***, become a self-directed learner ready to compete in a global society. Get advanced degrees, industry specific training, and on-the-job training. Along the way you will be developing teachable point of views. Having this skill will allow you to add value and meet the demand for excellence in any organization, movement, or cause needing your services. Remember the trilogy of success.

Recognize, Reward, and Reprimand – First of all no one is perfect except Father God. But everyone can be excellence provided they have the courage to face the demands of reality (integrity). You have to recognize you strengths and weakness; reward yourself for a job well-done; and reprimand yourself when you know haven't done your best—this is why having integrity is so important. Beware of the blind spots that will lead you into the arrogance of ignorance. Always seek the "Last Ten Percent." Work to become a star performer because only then will you have teachable point of views that will make you an effective leader.

Ok now you've sharpened your self-[**M.A.N.A.G.E.R.**] skills. And because you practice what you preach you're ready to demand from others what you demand from yourself….excellence. Remember that you are only a leader when you have followers. Thus, you must know the essence of [**T.E.A.M.W.O.R.K.**]! This acronym summarizes the essence of being able to apply [**A.G.I.L.E. L.E.A.D.E.R.S.H.I.P. with a G.R.I.P.**].

T	– Trustworthiness
E	– Emotional Awareness
A	– Adaptability
M	– Motivation and Inspiration
W	– Work Together
O	– Optimize toward Excellence
R	– Respect Diversity
K	– Keep Your Eye on the Prize

Remember, "As you sow, so you reap" (Galatians 6:7-8), so learn to be a [**M.A.N.A.G.E.R.**] with [**P.A.S.S.I.O.N.**], work [**S.M.A.R.T.**], take [**P.R.I.D.E.**], and believe in [**T.E.A.M.W.O.R.K.**]!

After all, *it is not how you start but how you finish.*

HOW TO HELP THIS BOOK: A REQUEST FROM THE AUTHOR

Thank you for buying this book. If somehow it exceeded your expectations or left you feeling like "wow, people and/or organizations could really be blessed if they read this book," this page is for you.

As you know by now, I'm a mature independent author. I don't have a huge marketing machine behind me, nor a gang of billionaire friends, or even a magic genie offering me three wishes. But that's OK. Because as my daddy used to tell me, "Ain't Nothin' Like Family!" You all are members of my spiritual family. So if you're willing to chip in a few minutes of your time, you can seriously help this book finds its way in the cold tough world, where many good books never reach all the people they should.

Please consider any of the following:

- Write a review on Amazon.com
- Post about this book to your blog, Facebook, or Twitter
- Recommend the book to coworkers, your friends, and your friends' friends, or even to your friends who blog, or your coworkers' friends who blog, or even your friends of friends who blog about their friends' blogs. The possibilities are endless
- If you know people who write for newspapers or magazines, drop them a line—or perhaps Oprah or Steve Harvey or Tom Joyner or Yolanda Adams or Rickey Smiley or Ellen—owes you a favor; if so, now is a good time to cash it in
- If you like to pretend you're a secret agent, secretly leave a copy of this book on the desk of someone important or influential
- Go to www.intelligentsystemsservices.com or www.facebook.com/Strategichustler and discover all the great things I write about daily. If you like what you find, run through this list again with that in mind

These little things make a huge difference. As the author, my opinion of the book does not carry the same weight as you—the reader. Succinctly stated, you my dear reader have all the power in the world.

Not only can you help this book find its way, but you'd also make the many risks of writing the next book easier to overcome, increasing the odds I'll do an even better job the next time around.

As always, thanks for your help and support.

REFERENCES

Bass, B. M. 1960. "Leadership, Psychology, and Organizational Behavior." In B. Bass, *Leadership, Psychology, and Organizational Behavior* (pp. 88-89). New York: Harper & Brothers.

Berkun, S. 2007. *The Myths of Innovation*. California: O'Reilly Media, Inc.

Carvell, F. J. 1970. "Human Relations in Business." In F. J. Carvell, *Human Relations in Business* (p. 182). Toronto: Macmillan.

Certo, A. Appelbaum, S. 1998. *Principles of Modern Management: A Canadian Perspective*. Boston: Allyn and Bacon.

Cloud, H. 2006, *Integrity*. New York: HarperCollins Publishers.

Cohen, A. R. 1993. *The Portable MBA in Management*. 22-24. New York: John Wiley & Sons

Covey, S. 1989. *Seven Habits of Highly Effective People*. United Kingdom: Simon & Schuster.

Darwin, C. 1990. *Origin of Species*. New York: Gramery Boos and Random House.

Drucker, P. F. 1973. "Management: Tasks, Responsibilities, Practices." In P. F. Drucker, *Management: Tasks, Responsibilities, Practices* (p. 45). New York: Harper & Row.

Edwards, B. 1987. *Drawing on the Artist Within*. New York: Simon & Schuster.

Edwards, B. 2012. *Drawing on the Right Side of the Brain*. New York: Penguin Group.

Glauser, M. 1998. *Glorious Accidents—How Everyday Americans Create Thriving Companies*. Utah: Shadow Mountain

Goleman, D. 1998. *Working with Emotional Intelligence.* New York: Bantam Dell.——. 2006. *Social Intelligence.* New York: Bantam Dell.

Harper, F. 2004. *Effective Leadership for Enterprise Commerce Management.* Atlanta: Millennium Management Group, LLC.

Kanter, R. M. 2009. *SuperCorp.* New York: Crown Publishing Group.

Luthans, F. 1988. "Successful versus Effective Real Managers." *Academy of Management Executive, 11, no.2,* pp. 88-89.

Morris, Betsey. 1986. "Roberto C. Goizuetta, Remarks to the American Bankers Association, The Wealth Builders", p. 80 *FORTUNE.*

Nelson, Bob. 1994. *1001 Way to Reward Employees.* New York: Workman Publishing.

Parkinson, C. N. 1957. *Parkinson's Law.* Boston: Houghton Mifflin.

Senge, P. M.1990. *The Fifth Discipline: The Art and Practice of the Learning Organization.* Doubleday/Curreny.

Sheehy, G. 1995. *New Passages: Mapping Your Life Across Time.* New York: Random House.

Sutton, Robert, and Jeffrey Pfeffer. 2008. *The Knowing-Doing Gap.* Boston: Harvard Business School Press.

Tichy, N. M. 2007. *The Leadership Engine—How Winning Companies Build Leaders at Every Level.* New York: HarperCollins Publishers.

Towers, M. 1993. *Dynamic Delegation: A Manager's Guide for Active Empowerment.* Mission, KS: Sill Path Publications.

Verma, V. K. 1995. *Organizing Projects for Success.* Project Management Institute Publishing Division.

Webb, J. 2003. *A Technique for Producing Ideas.* Columbus: The McGraw-Hill Companies.

Wess, David J. 2013. *Don't Stay Stuck! Unlock the Success Within! Now Is Your Time.* Lexington, KY: CreateSpace Independent Publishing

Made in the USA
Lexington, KY
04 August 2016